❧ AWAKE THE COURTEOUS ECHO

Awake
the Courteous Echo

The Themes and
Prosody of *Comus*, *Lycidas*, and
Paradise Regained
in World Literature with
Translations of
the Major Analogues

WATSON KIRKCONNELL

University of Toronto Press

© University of Toronto Press 1973
Toronto and Buffalo
Printed in Canada
ISBN 0-8020-5266-5
LC 78-185721

cc.

❧ CONTENTS

*Analogues marked with an asterisk are quoted in whole or in part.

PART TWO: Analogues of *A Monody* (*Lycidas*, 1638)

PART THREE: Analogues of *Paradise Regained* (1671)

APPENDIXES

❧ PREFACE

In the early 1930s, the late Arthur Woodhouse persuaded me to collaborate with him in a work on the analogues of Milton's *Paradise Lost*. He was to supply a brief critical introduction to the prospective volume and I was to translate and edit analogues by Grotius, Andreini, Salandra, and Vondel. By 1942, when his introduction had grown to book dimensions in itself and when my primary analogues, swollen by scores of others, were nearing one thousand manuscript pages, we agreed on separate publication, while keeping closely in touch with each other's labours. In 1950, I suggested the inclusion, in my almost finished volume, of analogues of *Comus, Lycidas, Samson Agonistes*, and *Paradise Regained*, many of which had turned up in my research nets while I fished for analogues of *Paradise Lost*. Woodhouse, however, urged that these be reserved for later publication, since the original project was already one of inordinate size. The wisdom of this counsel was confirmed by the dimension of my *Celestial Cycle* (University of Toronto Press, 1952, pp. xxvii, 701). This volume included complete or partial translations of 24 analogues and a descriptive catalogue of 329. The next instalment, dealing with analogues of *Samson Agonistes*, was *That Invincible Samson* (University of Toronto Press, 1964, pp. x, 218). Retirement from administrative duties in 1964 and from the university classroom in 1968 has permitted the completion of the task that I began nearly four decades ago. *Awake the Courteous Echo* combines the analogues of *Comus, Lycidas*, and *Paradise Regained*.

I should like to record my gratitude, for counsel and encouragement, to Douglas Bush, Lane Cooper, Roy Daniells, James Holly Hanford, Thomas P. Harrison, Jr., Merritt Y. Hughes, Barbara K. Lewalski, Kenneth Muir, J. Max Patrick, F.T. Prince, Malcolm Ross, and R.M. Wiles; also to Miss Nancy K. Sandars of Little Tew, Oxfordshire, who has permitted me to lean on her prose draft of the Sumerian-Assyrian *Epic of Gilgamesh* for my heroic-quatrain versions of the Forest-episode and the Ishtar-episode. I had originally intended, as in the two earlier volumes, to carry my analogues down to the present; but I have been glad to accept the advice of Kenneth Muir and Douglas Bush to omit everything later than Milton. The chief losses are Shelley's *Adonais* and Arnold's *Thyrsis*, but these are readily available elsewhere. Also on grounds of availability and lack of space, I have omitted extracts from Spenser, Drayton, Jonson, Beaumont, and Milton himself.

The headnotes of the individual analogues give, except for the commonest items, the sources from which I secured the originals. My quotations from Milton's three poems under consideration are based on the Scolar Press Facsimiles of the 1645 text of *Comus* and *Lycidas* (founded on a Bodleian copy of the *Poems*, Shelf-mark 8°. s. 8. Art BS) and of the 1671 text of *Paradise Regained* (drawn, for legibility, from three British Museum copies, 684.d.33, G.11559, and C.14.a.12).

For the sake of the general and the undergraduate reader, I have inserted descriptive sub-titles for most of the analogues in the Contents. The precise scholarly titles will be found in the separate listings, but vague and often recondite nomenclature in unfamiliar languages is usually neither helpful nor self-identifying, except for scholars. As a reminder that verse analogues are verse in the original, I have supplied my own metrical translations of all quoted passages (except those by Chapman, Cowper, Hobbes, Pope, and Morris in Co-4 and by Aurelian Townshend in Co-17), but have either added my own prose translations (as in Ly-1 and Ly-3) or have stated where prose versions may be found (if known to exist). A further discussion of metrical problems may be read in Appendix A, "On Metre," and in the notes on Co-4 (pp. 12–16), Ly-1 (pp. 79–90), Ly-3 (pp. 97–104), and Ly-74 (pp. 219–25). Since Milton is England's greatest master of prosody, some knowledge of metrics is essential to any complete appreciation of his poetry, even as some knowledge of musical structure is needed for any ultimate comprehension of a Mozart or a Beethoven sonata. In our age, when contemporary verse has become almost completely formless, there is a danger lest even scholars should assume that the metrical architectonics of past generations (which were intensely metre-conscious) may be safely left uncomprehended.

As in the two earlier volumes, my initial concern was not with sources but with analogues as analogues, in this case the Jonsonian masque, the pastoral elegy, and the brief epic. As the book took shape, however, it seemed desirable to include a number of items whose kinship with Milton's poems was less one of genre than of subject-matter.

Warm thanks are due to Harry W. Ganong, Acadia's chief librarian, and his staff, for long years of kindness in securing books for me on microfilm, in Xerox, and on interlibrary loan. Back of these services lies the co-operation of the Bodleian Library, the Cambridge University Library, the British Museum Library, the Bibliothèque Nationale (Paris), the National Library (Ottawa), the National Central Library (London), ASLIB (for tracking down rare editions), the Harvard Library, the Yale Library, the New York Public Library, and (for interlibrary loans) the libraries at such universities as Alberta, Dalhousie, King's (Halifax), Queen's (Kingston), Mount Allison, Mount Saint Vincent, Pennsylvania (Philadelphia), and Toronto, as well as the Nova Scotia Provincial Library.

This book has been published with the help of grants from the Humanities Research Council of Canada, using funds provided by the Canada Council, and from the Publications Fund of the University of Toronto Press, to whom I wish to express my thanks.

Wolfville, Nova Scotia   W.K.

❧ INTRODUCTION

The potentialities of the masque as an artistic form go back as far as ancient Egypt, if we may accept the testimony of the Greek author, Lucian.[1] The Greeks in their turn, and later the Romans, developed pantomime as an artistic"ballet of action."This was apparent not only in the public performance of the mythological ballet, set to florid music, but likewise in the activities of the mummer (*mimus*) who walked in a funeral procession, imitating the gestures of the deceased and followed by"a train of men wearing the *imagines* or portrait-masks of his ancestors."[2] There was also a good deal of spontaneous masquerading as part of the public licence practised at the time of the Saturnalia; and the mumming that prevailed through long centuries in England and elsewhere is sometimes considered "a survival of the Roman custom."[3] Stephen Orgel[4] has described occasions in 1377, 1430, and 1501 in which a group of masquers performed in the presence of English royalty, but feels that the origin of the court masque came on an historic occasion in 1512 when masquers, including Henry VIII, took their dancing partners from among the ladies of the court. The significant quotation is from the Tudor historian, Edward Hall: "On the daie of the Epiphanie at night, the king with xi. other were disguised, after the maner of Italie, called a maske, a thyng not seen afore in Englande ... these maskers came in ... and desired the ladies to daunce ..."[5] As the reference to Italy makes clear, this form of entertainment had developed in that country, where the *balletto*, or figured dance, at

---

1 Cf. Lucian, "Of Pantomime," in *The Works of Lucian*, tr. H.W. and F.G. Fowler (1905), II, 245
2 John Edwin Sandys, *Companion to Latin Studies* (1910), pp. 181, 512
3 Cf. *Encyclopaedia Britannica*, 1943 ed., XV, 954a
4 Stephen Orgel, *The Jonsonian Masque* (1965), pp. 19–22
5 *Hall's Chronicle*, 3rd yr., ed. Henry Ellis (1809), p. 40

carnival time, had merged with masked balls and triumphs into an elaborate"grand ballet"at a state marriage at Tortona as early as 1489. In Tudor and Elizabethan England, the "revels" or masked dances involving lords and ladies of the court became the productions of a Revels Office under the department of the lord chamberlain; and the evolution of the court masque took place under its management down to, and including, Stuart times. Influential throughout Europe in its day was Beaujoyeulx's *Balet Comique de la Royne* (Co-19) in 1581, expressly designed at the French court as a harmonious unifying of the arts of music, choreography, and stagesetting under the control of Neoplatonic philosophy. Structurally, it included a musical overture, a spoken prologue, a main masque action and spectacle, *a deus ex machina* solution, concluding main masque figured dances, and, of course, the final"revels"in which the whole court danced.

It was Ben Jonson who contributed a final element of pattern to the Stuart masque by devising a grotesque dance group or "antimasque"(of evil characters) formally balanced against the main masque (of good characters) and their final figured dance. This structure becomes clear as early as 1606 in his *Hymenaei* (Co-25) and is basic in seventeen of his twenty remaining masques. He also stressed a"hinge"of plot and a greater place for poetry in the libretto. Milton's *Comus* coincides almost exactly with the Jonsonian pattern in its prologue by the Attendant Spirit, its antimasque by the crew of Comus (who dance their"Measure"between lines 144 and 145), its *deus ex machina* release by Sabrina, and the main masque dances and the revels at the close. There had also been vocal solos by the Lady, the Attendant Spirit, and Sabrina. Only its hinge of main masque action and spectacle are closer to drama than to Jonson's masques. The influence here may have stemmed from the pastoral dramas of Tasso (*Aminta*, Co-18) and Guarini (*Pastor fido*, Co-20), mediated also through the pastoral comedies of Shakespeare (*Two Gentlemen of Verona*, *Love's Labour's Lost*, *A Midsummer Night's Dream*, and *As You Like It*) and Fletcher (*The Faithful Shepherdess*, Co-27).[6] It is in part a matter of romantic setting and atmosphere and in part an inner "landscape of the mind" in which the Neoplatonic idealism of Ficino and his school becomes the natural idiom of the dialogue.

If mumming goes back to Egypt and the allegorizing of ethics to

6 See Richard Cody, *The Landscape of the Mind: Pastoralism and Platonic Theory in Tasso's "Aminta" and Shakespeare's Early Comedies* (Oxford, 1969)

Plato and the Greek mysteries, the "argument" of Milton's *Comus* is also venerable in its ancestry. The story of a seductive deity who turns human beings into animals roves back at least as far as the Ishtar-episode in the *Epic of Gilgamesh* (Co-2) as found on Tablet VI of the Assyrian recension of the seventh century B.C. Similar themes are found in the almost contemporary Circe-episode in Homer (Co-4) and later in Ovid (Co-9). Plato, especially in the *Republic* (Co-6), spiritualizes the epic situation as the moral embrutishment of those who surrender to evil thoughts. In the long prose dream, *Comus* (Co-26), by Puteanus, temptation of the Circe sort is transferred to the youthful god Comus, the hermaphrodite son of Hermes and Aphrodite. In the meantime, Dante's *Vita Nuova* (Co-13) and Petrarch's *Trionfo della Castità* (Co-14) had exalted sexual purity to a height found opprobrious by many critics in the twentieth century when echoed by the Lady and her brothers in Milton's *Comus*. Milton had paid special tribute to the two Italian poets (cf. Co-39). The universally popular *Balet Comique de la Royne* made the enchantress Circe its dominant evil character, and this cast and setting were transposed into English in 1631 by Aurelian Townshend in his *Tempe Restored* (Co-36). Spenser's Acrasia (Co-22) and Busirane (Co-23) also presented formidable powers of evil enchantment, and harmonized, like the masques, with the pastoral theology of the Platonic academies. Milton, in his choice of a plot, was fishing in the main stream of Renaissance pastoralism.

Far back of the PASTORAL ELEGY lie the nature myths of Daphnis, Adonis or Linus, by which ancient Mediterranean religions shadowed forth the death of springtime's floral beauty in the withering heat of summer. The Hellenic imagination was presently to humanize this as the death of a youthful shepherd-poet, dearly loved by men and gods, streams and mountains, wild beasts and herds. For such a one, the blighting passion of love could sometimes take the place of the fatal heat of summer. In a later variation, any untimely death could be mourned, especially in some youthful genius.

The prime inventor of the pastoral elegy was Theocritus (*fl* 270 B.C.), a native of Syracuse in Sicily, who spent some years in the huge city of Alexandria and on the pleasant Aegean island of Cos. His first and seventh idylls yield precedents for most subsequent developments in the genre. Idyll I (*Daphnis*, see pp. 79–90, Ly-1) provides a framework of dialogue, destined some centuries later to share in the rise of the pastoral drama and the masque.

Technical details include an elaborate description of a gift for the shepherd-singer, an apostrophe to the nymphs who had failed to save Daphnis, the use of a cyclic refrain, the visits of various deities to the dying man, and a prayer that nature might reverse her course in sympathy with the shepherd's fate. Idyll vii (*The Harvest Home*, see pp. 91–6, Ly-2), however, involves the personal participation of the poet in the narrative framework, disguised as a shepherd, and even includes his comments on his contemporaries and their art. By this path came the later use of allegory to communicate the poet's views on a personal situation or experience.

Bion's *Lament for Adonis* (see pp. 97–104, Ly-3), sung by one person only, has neither dramatic nor narrative framework, and its almost Asiatic richness of music and emotion, reinforced by a cyclic refrain and the pathetic fallacy, is in keeping with the tradition that it was written for the annual Festival of Adonis. The flower motif is vivid, as when the blood-drops of Adonis spring up as roses and the tear-drops of Aphrodite beget anemones. In the *Lament for Bion* (see pp. 104–10, Ly-4) by Moschus, we have the personal grief of the latter for a fellow-poet, represented as a cowherd. The pathetic fallacy is pushed to the limit and the refrain comes in with melancholy iteration. The most notable contribution of Moschus is his contrast between the annual return of life in nature and the finality of death for the individual man.

Vergil, a consummate scholar as well as a great poet, sought like Milton in a later day to recreate certain genres of Greek poetry in his native tongue. From the pastoral models of Theocritus, he reproduced both the dialogue-framework type (Eclogue v, *Daphnis*, Ly-5) and the personal-participation type (Eclogue x, *Gallus*, Ly-6), the latter beginning with a few lines that state the theme and ending with a few lines of valedictory conclusion, a pattern found in the later *Lycidas*. Upon both eclogues, however, Vergil imposed an unprecedented amount of allegory. That the Daphnis of Eclogue v is to be taken as C. Julius Caesar, recently murdered, and the Gallus of Eclogue x as C. Cornelius Gallus, a boyhood friend and fellow-poet, does not go far beyond the identifying of "Simichidas" as Theocritus and "Lycidas" as Astacides in Theocritus' Idyll vii; but Vergil then proceeds to ascribe to his Daphnis a deification that led in later pastorals (such as *Lycidas*) to the consolation of transferral after death to a Christian heaven, while to Gallus he awkwardly ascribes not only his actual status as a soldier on active service but also the romantic melancholy of an unhappy love affair in the experience of a young shepherd.

A third-century eclogue (*Meliboeus*, Ly-11) by M. Aurelius Nemesianus paid memorial tribute to an old man instead of to a youth who had suffered an untimely death. With the ninth-century Paschasius Radbertus (see Ly-12), two monasteries, allegorized as two nuns, praise the life and character of the old Benedictine abbot, Adalhard, who has died recently. The second part of the elegy expands the consolation of a Christian hereafter.

The fourteenth-century Latin eclogues of Petrarch (1304–1374) purify the Latinity of the style but thicken the allegory to the point where comprehension is difficult without elaborate decoding. In his Eclogue vi (Ly-15), Saint Peter comes back to earth to denounce the corruption of the Church with ten times the detail and the vehemence of Milton's brief rebuke (cf. *Lycidas*, 113–131). The same poetic denunciation of the clergy had already been placed on Saint Peter's lips by Dante in his *Paradiso*, canto xxvii, 10–66 (see p. 138, below), and was presently to be given vigorous expression by the General of the Carmelite Order, Mantuan, in his Eclogue ix, *Falco* (see p. 163, Ly-28). All these, and still earlier utterances by Ezekiel and Saint Gregory, stand in the background of Milton's so-called "digression." Petrarch's friend, Boccaccio (1313–1375), in his Eclogue xiv, *Olympia* (Ly-19), widens the range of the pastoral elegy with a dream-allegory of his little daughter, Violante, who had died at the age of five. Much of the imagery is drawn from Dante's *Purgatorio*, as when Violante (see p. 158) describes the Paradise that is now her home.

A new era begins with Giovanni Pontano (1424–1503) and Jacopo Sannazaro (1458–1530), whose pastorals cease to be so root-bound in allegory. Part of the cause for the change lay in the rediscovery of the unallegorized pastorals of Theocritus, Bion, and Moschus in the original Greek as models for imitation. Part lay also in Sannazaro's literary creation of a Golden Age in a remote pastoral Arcady as a form of escape from the wars and horrors of Renaissance Europe. His prose *Arcadia* was spangled with poems, including such pastoral elegies as laments for the poet's father as "Androgeo" and for his mother as "Mamillia" (see Ly-31 and pp. 169–74). Sannazaro also broke fresh ground by naturalizing the pastoral in his native Italian. From his phenomenal popularity, both in Latin and in the vernacular, there followed two great streams of imitative successors during the next two centuries.

Italians who wrote pastoral elegies in Latin included such men as Anisio (Ly-29), Castiglione (Ly-32 and see pp. 174–80), Vida (Ly-36), Berni (Ly-37), Navagero (Ly-39), Giraldi (Ly-44), Pasquale

(Ly-48), Zanchi (Ly-46, 47), Vinta (Ly-57), Angelio (Ly-61), Arcucci (Ly-62, 63), Arnolfino (Ly-65), Fontana (Ly-69), and Barberini (Ly-78). The cult of the Neo-Latin pastoral spread also to the northern and western parts of Europe: (a) in France we find specimens by J.C. Scaliger (Ly-41), Sepin (Ly-50), Dorat (Ly-53), Fumaeus (Ly-67), and Tillier (Ly-66); (b) in the Netherlands there were Sluperius (Ly-55), Dousa (Ly-75), Aetsema (Ly-96), and Heinsius (Ly-87); (c) in Germany one may list Eobanus (Ly-33), Lotich (Ly-56), Fabricius (Ly-52), and Pretorius (Ly-79); Englishmen who wrote worthy pastoral elegies in Latin were Giles Fletcher the Elder (Ly-64, 68), Thomas Watson (Ly-71), William Gager (Ly-73, 74, see pp. 219–225), and John Milton (Ly-102); (e) Scotland can boast of Latin elegies by George Buchanan (Ly-49, 60), David Hume (Ly-86), John Barclay (Ly-88), John Leech (Ly-97), and Arthur Johnston (Ly-98). The stream of pastoral elegy in the vernaculars includes Alamanni (Ly-34, 35) and Tasso (Ly-72) in Italian; Marot (Ly-40), Baïf (Ly-51), and Ronsard (Ly-54, see pp. 203–206 above) in French; Garcilaso de la Vega (Ly-42), and Sá de Miranda (Ly-43) in Spanish; Camoens (Ly-58, 59) in Portuguese; Spee (Ly-99) in German; and Drayton (Ly-80), Spenser (Ly-77, 81), the Countess of Pembroke (Ly-82), Bryskett (Ly-83, 84), Roydon (Ly-85), Browne (Ly-95), and Drummond (Ly-94, 100) in English. These represent only a small sample from the total crop; for example, the elegies written by poets and poetasters on the deaths of Sir Philip Sidney in 1586 and of Henry, Prince of Wales, in 1612, were almost as numerous as those begotten in a later age by the assassination of President John F. Kennedy. For Sidney alone, some two hundred elegies were published, and 462 for Prince Henry. A significant example of the collective tribute of elegies to a dead friend is *Justa Edouardo King naufrago* (Ly-101), in which thirty-three poems in Greek, Latin, and English were issued as a single volume in memory of Edward King (1612–1637), of Christ's College, Cambridge. Milton's *Lycidas* was the last poem in the book and its only genuine pastoral elegy.

The European vogue of Latin pastorals did not end with the *Epitaphium Damonis*. They flourished, indeed, until well into the eighteenth century, so that the admirable Jesuit poet, Niccolò Giannettasio of Naples (1648–1715), was so successful that he was able to build a church to the Virgin Mary with the proceeds of his many volumes. Among other late pastoral elegists in Latin were Pierre de Vallongnes, Pierre Hallé, René Rapin, Peter Francius, Robert d'Esnaval, and Peter Lotich ii.

Among later pastoral elegies in English we may cite John Dryden's *On the Death of Amyntas* (1692), Ambrose Philips' *Pastorals* (1709), Alexander Pope's *Pastorals* (1709), John Gay's *The Shepherd's Week* (1714), Percy Bysshe Shelley's *Adonais* (1821), and Matthew Arnold's *Thyrsis* (1866). The neo-classical heroic couplet laid its metrical restraints upon the first four of these, but there is a range of skilled variation in vowel, consonant, and pause within its twenty syllables rarely realized or properly admired in the twentieth century. To Alexander Pope's *Pastorals,* written at the age of sixteen, Edith Sitwell ascribes "an astonishing perfection," yet she also concedes that Pope's shepherds are less shepherds than wits from the coffee-houses. When John Gay sought to satirize Philips by deliberate rusticity in his *Shepherd's Week*, he actually came closer to the rural realism in Theocritus than had any intervening poet. With Shelley's lament over Keats, we have a carefully wrought work of art, based primarily on Bion and Moschus but framed in the Spenserian stanza and sharing in Spenser's Neoplatonism and pastoral themes.

Arnold himself has stated that the diction of his *Thyrsis* was modelled on that of Theocritus, whom he was reading continually during the two years that his pastoral elegy on Clough was distilling itself in slow sincerity. Its realistic description of nature reveals his close sympathy with Wordsworth; but in its allegory of college life and its remembered fellowship with a college friend (especially in the *Epitaphium Damonis*), *Thyrsis* is deeply linked with Milton. What is less often realized is that the printer's varied indentations of the line-margins conceal the fact that Arnold is using the identical metre of *Lycidas* but has regularized it into exact stanzas, each consisting of nine iambic pentameter lines and one iambic trimeter, all woven together in the rhyme-pattern *abcbcadeed.* Arnold's thought, moreover, is built up stanza by stanza (24 of them), whereas Milton organizes his theme in eleven leisurely paragraphs.

With *Paradise Regained,* as with *Comus,* we need to distinguish between its subject (the Temptation of Christ) and the genre of the brief epic.

The former is notably paralleled in the conflict between a spiritual hero and a satanic adversary in the *Book of Job* (PR-1) and in Aeschylus' *Prometheus Bound* (PR-2). Epic treatments of the scriptural account of Christ's Temptation may be found as incidental episodes in the more extensive verse treatments of biblical narrative in the

Anglo-Saxon *Christ and Satan* (PR-4), the Old Saxon *Heliand* (PR-5), the *Cursor Mundi* (PR-6), its French counterpart by Macés de la Charité (PR-7), the *Stanzaic Life of Christ* (PR-9), Vida's Latin *Christiad* (PR-13), Folengo's *Della Humanità del Figliuolo di Dio* (PR-14), Ramsey's *Poemata Sacra* (PR-21), and Alexander Ross's *Vergilius evangelisans* (PR-22). Mystery play versions occur in the York (PR-10), Chester (PR-11), and Coventry (PR-12) cycles and in Jordan's *Cornish Drama* (PR-19). John Bale's *Temptacyon of Our Lorde* (PR-15) is not far beyond their rude simplicity. A notable narrative treatment is found in the Mammon episode in Spenser's *Faerie Queene*, Book II, canto vii (PR-17). A lush baroque version appears in *Christs Victorie and Triumph*, Book II (PR-18), by Giles Fletcher the Younger. The only single epic (other than *Paradise Regained*) concentrating on the Temptation is the Latin poem, *Christi victoris et Satanae Pugna in Deserto* (PR-16) by Jacobus Strasburgus of the University of Leipzig.

The matter of genre is something else again. Milton's catalogue of poetic types in *The Reason of Church Government* speaks of "that Epick form whereof ... the book of *Job* [is] a brief model."[7] Very little evidence of such a "brief epic," particularly of the length and pattern of *Paradise Regained*, may be found among the surviving examples of classical (pre-Christian) epic in Greek or Latin. Six lesser epics, listed by Gilbert Murray along with the full-length *Iliad* and *Odyssey* as making up the "Trojan Cycle,[8]" are the *Cypria*, the *Aethiopis* (5 books), the *Little Iliad* (4 books), the *Sack of Ilion* (2 books), the *Nostoi* or *Homecomings* (5 books), and the *Telegonia* (2 books); and apart from that cycle there were other epics, such as the *Thebais*, the *Herakleia*, the *Naupactia*, the *Battle of Gods and Titans*, and an early *Argonautica*; but all these have gone with the wind. Some have suggested that Aristotle (with all this literature before him) made a structural distinction between diffuse and one-plot epics; but a careful reading of the passage in question, *Poetics*, XXVI (5–6), will discover that he is not comparing the *Iliad* (or the *Odyssey*) with a shorter, one-action type of epic but with Sophocles' *Oedipus Tyrannos*, which as a drama had an essential unity of action.[9]

The problem is no clearer when we come down to the Alexandrian

7 *The Works of John Milton*, ed. Frank E. Patterson *et al*. (Columbia Ed., 1931–8), III, Part I, 237–8

8 Gilbert Murray, *The Rise of the Greek Epic*, 3rd ed. (1924), pp. 340–1

9 *Aristotle's Theory of Poetry and Fine Art, with a Critical Text*, etc., ed. S.H. Butcher (1920), p. 110, sect. 1462b

period. Apollonius Rhodius did write a long *Argonautica*, stifled at birth with its own erudition, but the honours of the time went to Theocritus' epic idylls, *Hylas* (76 lines) and *The Infant Herakles* (140 lines) and to Callimachus' epyllion[10] *Hecale*. In Latin, the best example of an epyllion is the *Epithalamion of Peleus and Thetis* (374 lines) by Catullus, a *doctus poeta* who also translated Callimachus' *Lock of Berenice* (94 lines). Ovid's *Metamorphoses* represent an attempt to fabricate an epic-length work out of scores of erotica or sensational epyllia; but the success of Vergil's *Aeneid*, in a learned and powerful reshaping of the Homeric tradition, determined the form of such subsequent epics as Lucan's *Pharsalia*, Statius' *Thebaid*, Claudian's *Rape of Proserpine*, Tasso's *Gerusalemme Liberata*, Camoens' *Lusiads*, and Milton's *Paradise Lost*. We have not yet found any extant classical precedent[11] for *Paradise Regained*; and it is significant that Milton, who in his list of poetic patterns in *The Reason of Church Government* cited Homer, Vergil, and Tasso as models for the long epic and Sophocles and Euripides for the drama, has to fall back on the non-classical *Book of Job* as his exemplar.

The probable basis for that choice has been summarized by Barbara Kiefer Lewalski,[12] citing Jerome as a dubious authority for *Job's* "hexameters" – an opinion reaffirmed at second hand by a host of successors – and naming such authors as Drepanius Florus, the Venerable Bede, Suidas, Mantuan, Guillaume Du Bartas, Victorinus Strigelius, Gasparus Sanctius, Christianus Chemnitius, and Steuchius as witnesses that "some fifteen Christian centuries viewed the Book of Job as epiclike ..." The tentative list of biblical epics in Appendix B (pp. 315–22 below) shows that apart from the Genesis tradition, already surveyed in my volume, *The Celestial Cycle* (Toronto, 1952, pp. xxvii, 701), there had been some 156 "epics" on biblical subjects prior to *Paradise Regained* and that eleven of these, *all brief epics on Job*, had been published in Latin (5), English (4), and French (2) between 1615 and 1668. Most of the 156 poems represented devout piety more than poetic art, but Vida's *Christiad* (1535, 6 books, some 6000 lines) (PR-13), was a model of strict Vergilian form and

10 M. Marjorie Crump, *The Epyllion from Theocritus to Ovid* (1931): "The epyllion is a short narrative poem ... never more than a single book." (pp. 22–3)

11 Disregarding such unlikely didactic poems as Hesiod's *Works and Days* (828 lines) and Vergil's *Georgics* (4 books, 2188 lines)

12 Barbara Kiefer Lewalski, *Milton's Brief Epic: The Genre, Meaning and Art of "Paradise Regained"* (Providence and London, 1966), chap. ii, "Job as Epic: The Exegetical and Literary Tradition"

won high fame for the Scriptural epic. While Milton quietly repudiates the Renaissance insistence on a military hero and the avoidance of typology, his choice of a peaceful subject is in keeping with the widely held estimate of *Job* as a model epic, and he challenges comparison with the neo-classical epic by portraying the contest between Christ and Satan in military terms, in the infinitely subtle thrust and parry of debate. The unities of time, place, and action are approximately observed. The action begins *in medias res;* soliloquies by Christ and Mary recapitulate the hero's earlier life; and the weaving into the dialogue of references to types of Christ from the Old Testament and classical history presents him in the perspective of all human heroism.

Succeeding ages found other uses for biblical subject-matter. Thus, when John Dryden attempted the theme of *Paradise Lost,* he turned it into an opera (*The State of Innocence and Fall of Man*); and in his hands an episode from the reign of David became a political satire (*Absalom and Achitophel*). When Coleridge took a subject from *Genesis,* it became a romantic fantasy, *The Wanderings of Cain.* When Robert Browning chose situations from New Testament times, he recast them in dramatic monologues as *An Epistle of Karshish, Cleon,* and *A Death in the Desert,* and manipulated them as replies to rationalistic critics of traditional Christianity.

A closing word of disclaimer is in order. The long echelons of analogues marshalled in this volume and in its two forerunners (*The Celestial Cycle* and *That Invincible Samson*) are not meant to imply that Milton's achievement in each of his major poems was a pedantic emulation of some genre from Greece, Rome, or Renaissance Europe. While he certainly sought to fulfil the traditions of his great precursors, he regarded these poets not as patterns to be aped but as rivals to be outsoared. His sense of genre and of poetic decorum was intense, but his expertise subsumed and outdid the artistry of his models. For example, *Lycidas,* in its general outline, is modelled after Vergil (especially Eclogue x), Theocritus, and Moschus; but its texture is woven and embroidered after the *canzone-* measure as expounded by Dante in his *De vulgari eloquentia* and later by Tasso in *La Cavalletta.* Even this statement is inadequate, for Milton handles this measure with the profound freedom of an independent master. The metre seems made for this poet and not the poet for the metre. In short, a study of the three volumes of analogues ought only to enhance our awareness of the subtlety, complexity, and powerful originality of Milton's art.

PART I: Analogues of *A Mask* (*Comus*, 1634)

ABBREVIATIONS

AJP *American Journal of Philology*
Co an analogue of *A Mask* ("Comus")
ELH *Journal of English Literary History*
HLQ *Huntington Library Quarterly*
JEGP *Journal of English and Germanic Philology*
JHI *Journal of the History of Ideas*
Ly an analogue of *A Monody* ("Lycidas")
Mi microfilm copy
MLN *Modern Language Notes*
MLQ *Modern Language Quarterly*
MP *Modern Philology*
N&Q *Notes and Queries*
Ph photostat
PL an analogue of *Paradise Lost*
PMLA *Publications of the Modern Language Association of America*
PR an analogue of *Paradise Regained*
SA an analogue of *Samson Agonistes*
SP *Studies in Philology*
TRSL *Transactions of the Royal Society of Literature*
UTQ *University of Toronto Quarterly*
Xe xerox copy

Co-1 (Sumerian, Assyrian)

ANONYMOUS. *The Epic of Gilgamesh*: Gilgamesh and the Forest. 2000–
700 B.C.

Begins: O Gilgamesh, lord of Kullab, great is thy praise ...
  Ends: O Gilgamesh, lord of Kullab, great is thy praise.

The earliest versions of this epic were composed in Sumerian, as separate narrative poems, in the third millennium B.C. and were first
written down on clay tablets in the cuneiform as an integrated epic
about 2000 B.C. Thereafter, it was mediated, with creative incre-
ments, through Babylonian (Akkadian) to Hurrian (fourteenth century B.C.) and Assyrian (under Assurbanipal, seventh century B.C.)
and from the former to Hittite, Ugaritic, and Phoenician. Some forty
more or less fragmentary cuneiform tablets survive in most of the
foregoing languages. Among the chief translators have been Samuel
Noah Kramer (for Sumerian), E.A. Speiser (for Akkadian), and Alexander Heidel (for Assyrian). The standard reference work for speci-
alists is *Ancient Near Eastern Texts*, edited by James B. Pritchard,
2nd edition (Princeton, 1955). This has been the main source for the
popular prose version by N.K. Sandars (Penguin, 1960, 1964); and
it is on Miss Sandars' text that my extracts in heroic quatrains, given
hereunder, have been based. There have been two English verse
renderings of the epic, into hexameters (1928, 1930) by Campbell
Thompson and into free rhythms (*Galgamesh*, 1934) by William
Ellery Leonard.

  Two motifs in the Gilgamesh epic are relevant to a study of
Comus, namely the theme of the gloomy forest (inhabited by supernatural powers of evil) and the theme of a goddess who changes men
into animals. The first of these, given here as Co-1, is based largely
on the early Sumerian poem, "Gilgamesh and the Land of the Living," supplemented in part by Assyrian Tablet IV (almost entirely
missing) and Tablet V. The theme is very widespread, both in literature and in folklore. It commonly presents a heroine (or a hero, or a
group) lost in a magic wood or wood of error. It characterizes
Homer's island of Aeaea (Co-3). It is the figure that opens the first
canto of Dante's *Divine Comedy* (see Co-12). The dark wood
emerges again in *Syr Gawayne and the Grene Knight* (see Co-15).
In the *Mabinogion*, Peredur (Percival, Parsifal) goes through this
experience no fewer than five times (Everyman edition, pp. 178, 184,

186–7, 198, 218). In Spenser, it is the Wood of Error (see Co-21); it casts its shadows over George Peele's *Old Wives' Tale* (Co-24), John Fletcher's *Faithful Shepherdess* (Co-27), William Drury's *Aluredus* (Co-30), and Tronsarelli's *La Catena d'Adone* (Co-33). The whole setting of Puteanus's *Comus* (Co-26) is in the gloom of a forest at night. In the folklore tales of the Brothers Grimm it appears as the wood where Hansel and Gretel wander (and find a witch's magic house), where Rapunzel strays and is imprisoned by a witch, and where the fugitive Snow-White is pursued by the wicked step-mother. The mysterious supernatural person in the wilderness is "writ large" in Rider Haggard's *She* (1887) and Pierre Benoît's *L'Atlantide* (1919). So widespread is the theme that it may be possible to think of it, not as a widening literary ripple from a single source but rather as a Jungian archetype (cf. C.G. Jung, *The Archetypes and the Collective Unconscious*, tr. by R.F.C. Hull, London, 1959, pp. 222, 285–6, etc.), preserving primordial man's fears in confronting the forest, together with the subconscious projection of the anima or the animus.

Readers seeking additional background reading for the Gilgamesh poetry may be referred to C. Leonard Woolley (*The Sumerians*, 1929, and *Excavations at Ur*, 1954), Vere Gordon Childe (*New Light on the Ancient East*, 4th ed., 1953), Alexander Heidel (*The Gilgamesh Epic and Old Testament Parallels*, 2nd ed., 1949), James B. Pritchard (*Archaeology and the Old Testament*, 1958), *The Cambridge Ancient History* (rev. ed., 1962, espec. I, vi, 23–69, M.B. Rowton on "The Chronology of Ancient Western Asia," and I, xiii, 1–60, Cyril J. Gadd on "The Cities of Babylonia"), and Samuel Noah Kramer (*Sumerian Mythology*, 1961, and *The Sumerians*, 1963). In the last-named work (pp. 170, 184–5) Dr Kramer emphasizes that Sumerian verse employs almost all poetic devices except metre and rhyme. Parallelism and repetition are basic, with skilful variations in the patterns of repetition. Simile and metaphor, standard epic epithets, recurrent formulas, chorus and refrain, all are handled with high art. Description is important and much space is given to speeches. See also PL-1, PL-2, and PL-3 (Kirkconnell, *The Celestial Cycle*, pp. 483–5).

Gilgamesh and the Forest

Then Gílgamesh made answer to his friend:
"Because great evil lingers in the land,

We to the cedar forest will ascend
And slay this fatal thing, with dauntless hand.

For in the gloomy wood Humbába[1] dwells,
A giant fierce, whose very name means 'Vast.'"
But bitter harm Enkidu then foretells:
"Once with the beasts I ranged, in years long past;

The forest then my fearful steps explored;
It spreads ten thousand leagues from side to side.
There Enlil[2] set Humbaba as its lord
And sev'nfold terrors to his hand supplied.

His roars are like the torrent of the storm,
His breath is like an all-consuming fire,
His jaws are death, in horror multiform,
He guards the cedars as the gods require.

When the wild heifer murmurs in unrest,
He hears her though full twenty leagues away.
What man would willingly those woods molest,
Or walk their gloomy deeps without dismay? ..."

Shamash[3] accepted then his humble tears;
He showed him mercy and provided aid,
Gave Gilgamesh defenders for his fears,
Strong brothers in the mountain-caves arrayed.

The great winds he appointed for defence:
The north wind, and the whirlwind, and the gale,
The icy wind, the tempest fierce and tense,
The scorching wind whose power cannot fail ...

They strode for twenty leagues, and broke their fast;
They strode for thirty more, and night came on.
Thus in one day through fifty leagues they passed;
In three short days a journey they had gone

1 The Assyrian form, Sumerian "Hawawa"
2 The Sumerian god of earth, wind, and air
3 The Assyrian god of the sun and of wisdom, Sumerian "Utu"

Where other men six weary weeks would need.
By seven mountain-summits, dark and great,
They crossed until deep woods their path impede;
They stare in wonder at a mighty gate ...

Together from the gate they then went down.
To the green mount they came and stood stark still.
They saw the trees that towered on its crown,
They marked the cedars' height with fearful thrill.

They saw the path that through the shadows led,
The track by which Humbaba used to walk;
His road stretched broad and pleasantly ahead;
The cedar-mountain's mass subdued their talk ...

From his strong cedar house Humbaba came.
He tossed his head, he shook it to and fro;
He fixed on Gilgamesh his eye of flame;
His eye of death looked fiercely on his foe ...

Co-2 (Assyrian)

ANONYMOUS. "Gilgamesh and Ishtar," from *The Epic of Gilgamesh*,
Assyrian recension. See Co-1 for general background

The episode of Gilgamesh and Ishtar is the opening part of Tablet
VI from the library of Assurbanipal (seventh century B.C.). There
had been an earlier Sumerian original, "Gilgamesh and the Bull of
Heaven," written down a thousand years earlier, but according to
Samuel N. Kramer (*The Sumerians: Their History, Culture and
Character*, 1963) its remains are quite fragmentary. We can there-
fore only conjecture as to its contents, although we know that Tablet
XII is a direct translation from a Sumerian original that has survived
in large part. In the Assyrian version in Tablet VI, the Sumerian
goddess of love, Inanna, has been reidentified as the Assyrian Ishtar.
In this passage, Ishtar solicits the intercourse of the hero Gilgamesh,
but is repulsed on the ground that she has weakened all her lovers

and turned some of them into animals. The Assyrian version has many anticipations of the Odysseus-Circe episode in Homer's *Odyssey*: (a) its hero is a wanderer on the face of the earth and the ocean and even visits the underworld, (b) the goddess has her abode in a forest, (c) the hero, after washing up, becomes gloriously beautiful, and (d) he fears that she will unman him or turn him into an animal. Incidentally, Ishtar is the daughter of Anu, the firmament of heaven, while Circe is the daughter of the sun. A comparable minor Sumerian figure is Siduri, the female wine-maker, also a daughter of the sun, who urges Gilgamesh to "eat, drink, and be merry"(as in the gospel according to Comus) but later gives him instructions on how to cross the ocean of death, even as Circe tells Odysseus how to sail to Hades, across"the river of Ocean."

The question of possible influences of Sumerian-cum-Assyrian poetry on the Homeric poems is still a matter of bitter debate. In T.B.L. Webster's *From Mycenae to Homer* (London, 1958), Greek ceramic art from 1400 B.C. to 700 B.C. is analysed for insights into complex oral epic poems, alleged to have been sung long before in Mycenean palaces, as forerunners of the Homeric epos. Other scholars have objected violently. Thus G.S. Kirk (*The Songs of Homer*, 1962, p. 107) declares that"the only motif in Gilgamesh that I am inclined to accept as a faintly possible model for Homer" is "the underworld visit." Dr Kirk is also sceptical as to the extent of any influence of Mycenean poetry on Homer. Some critics have even pointed out that the Assyrian Gilgamesh-Ishtar story, imprinted (on clay) in the seventh century B.C., might be later than the eighth-century date sometimes proposed for Homer. Kirk, himself, however (*The Songs of Homer*, p. 287), is inclined to place the composition of the *Odyssey* early in the seventh century, and points out (p. 284) that there are no identifiable epic scenes on Greek pottery before *ca.* 700 B.C. He considers the composition of the epic to be the work of a supreme poet named Homer, who took the short lays of whole generations of oral poets and unified, expanded, and transmuted them into a vast masterpiece. Later stages in stabilizing his text were the Pisistratean recension at Athens in 550 B.C. and the Aristarchan recension in Alexandria about 150 B.C. For further background see H.L. Lorimer, *Homer and the Monuments* (Oxford, 1950); D.L. Page, *The Homeric Odyssey* (Oxford, 1955); M.I. Finley, *The World of Odysseus* (London, 1956); and C.H. Whitman, *Homer and the Homeric Tradition* (Cambridge, Mass., 1958).

Gilgamesh and Ishtar[4]

Then Gilgamesh washed out the blood and dust
From his long locks; he cleaned his dripping sword;
Back from his shoulders then his hair he thrust,
Threw off his blood-stained clothes in filth abhorred

And changed them all for new. In stately style,
He donned his royal robes and made them fast,
And put his crown on. With seductive smile,
Her eyes the glorious Ishtar on him cast.

She saw the hero's beauty, and she said:
"Come to me, Gilgamesh, and be my mate.
Grant me your body's seed upon my bed.
Let us as bride and bridegroom celebrate.

"I will prepare for you a chariot
In which bejewelled gold the gazers feeds;
With wheels of gold, with horns of copper hot;
And demons of the storms shall be your steeds.

"When in soft cedar's fragrance, passing sweet,
Into our royal house you enter now,
Threshold and throne will gladly kiss your feet,
Rulers and princes of the earth will bow.

"They will bring tribute from both hill and plain.
Your she-goats shall bear triplets and your ewes
Drop twins at every birth. Your pack-ass train
Shall outrun mules in spite of all their thews.

"No rivals shall your sturdy oxen know;
Your horses' speed far off will live in fame."
But Gilgamesh to Ishtar answered slow;
His mouth he opened, and his words brought blame:

4 A verse paraphrase by Watson Kirkconnell from the prose version of
   the epic by N.K. Sandars. The passage given here covers lines 1–78, out
   of 194, of Tablet VI as edited by Pritchard

"If as your husband I should enter in,
   What kind of wedding gifts could I present?
   What clothing and what ointment for your skin?
   What sort of bread to give you nourishment?

"What dinner can I give a deity?
   How can I offer drink to Heaven's Queen?
   What fate, moreover, will there be for me,
   When, as your husband, I grow old and mean?

"Your lovers in the past have found you false:
   A luke-warm brazier, smouldering in the cold,
   A door that keeps out neither storms nor squalls,
   A castle crushing all within its hold,

"Soft pitch that leaves the bearer black as jet,
   A leaky wine-skin that on carriers drips,
   A stone that tumbles from the parapet,
   A broken shoe on which the wearer trips,

"A siege-machine set up among the foe.
   Which of your lovers found you always true?
   What swain's embraces did you not outgrow?
   Listen: your record I shall now review.

"Tammuz, the lover that your youth preferred,
   You cursed with bitter wailing down the years;
   You loved the many-coloured roller-bird
   But struck and broke his wing, with cruel jeers.

"Now in the grove he sits and sadly wails:
   'Oh, kappi, kappi! How my wing is sore!'
   You loved the lion, who in strength prevails:
   You dug him seven pits, and seven more.

"You loved the stallion, glorious in fight;
   For him you have decreed whip, spur and reins,
   To gallop seven leagues with bridle tight,
   And hear his old dam weep as he complains.

"You loved the gentle shepherd of the flock;
  He made you meal-cakes gladly, day by day;
  He killed his kids for you; your laughing-stock
  He found himself when smitten in dismay.

"You turned him to a he-wolf for his pains;
  His faithful herd-boys chase him down the banks;
  Baying and snarling as they course the plains,
  The man's own hounds are worrying his flanks.

"And did you not once court Ishúllanu,
  Who in your father's palm-grove plied his task?
  Baskets of dates he daily filled for you,
  He brought your board such food as you could ask.

"Then on the man you turned your burning eyes.
  'Dearest Ishullanu,' you softly said,
  'Let me enjoy the manhood that you prize.
  Seize me, and take me, in my fragrant bed.'

"Ishullanu made answer to your plea:
  'Why are you asking for my truest good?
  My mother's baking is enough for me.
  Why should I come to such as you for food?

"Tainted and rotten is the love you give.
  When was a screen of rushes, rudely tossed,
  Enough to shield a man that he might live?
  Sufficient to preserve a man from frost?'

"But when you heard his answer, with a screech
  You changed him to a blind mole, deep in earth,
  One whose desire is always past his reach;
  A sightless wretch he is, of little worth.

"Should I, then, if I loved you, be unnerved,
  And by a change of form your falseness prove?
  Why may not I in such a way be served
  As all these others who have known your love?" ...

Co-3 (Greek)

HOMER. *Odyssey* ("Odysseus and the Forest"). For provenance, see Co-2. Extracts quoted in Co-3 and Co-4 have been checked with *Homeri Opera et Reliquiae*, ed. D.B. Munro (Oxford, 1901)

Begins: Ἄνδρα μοι ἔννεπε Μοῦσα, πολύτροπον, ὃς μάλα πολλὰ
πλάγχθη, ἐπεὶ Τροίης ἱερὸν πτολίεθρον ἔπερσε ...
Ends: Παλλὰς Ἀθηναίη, κούρη Διὸς αἰγιόχοιο,
Μέντορι εἰδομένη ἠμὲν δέμας ἠδὲ καὶ αὐδήν.

"Odysseus and the Forest" is a makeshift title by which we may link Book x, lines 187–97, to the long tradition of persons confronting a forest and its supernatural dangers (cf. Co-2).

The theory and practice of translating Homer have been objects of vehement debate ever since 1861–2, when Matthew Arnold, as professor of poetry at Oxford, crossed swords with Francis W. Newman, professor of Latin in University College, London. So far as the *Odyssey* was concerned, he weighed the merits of George Chapman's enjambed couplets (1614–16), Alexander Pope's closed couplets (1725–6), William Cowper's blank verse (1791), and Francis W. Newman's hexameters, and finds them all false to Homer's basic qualities of rapidity, plainness, simplicity, and nobility. In theory, he gives his vote to the epic hexameter as the ideal measure for this task in English, but his own brief performance in this kind (as Newman was quick to point out) was far from happy. Incidentally, and contrary to his own theories, he gives high praise to Philip Stanhope Worseley's translation into Spenserians (1861). Still other poetic versions, published since Arnold's lectures, are William Morris's rhymed fourteeners in couplets (1887), J.W. Mackail's Omar-Khayyam stanzas (1903), H.B. Cotterill's hexameters (1911), and Sir William Marris's blank verse (1935). Prose translations of the *Odyssey*, each with its own flavour, are those of S.H. Butcher and A. Lang (1879), Samuel Butler (1900), T.E. Lawrence (1932), and E.V. Rieu (1945). In view of this long and varied tradition of *Odyssey*-translation, several different specimens are given hereunder to illustrate Co-3 and Co-4.

Odysseus and the Forest

(x, 187–97, tr. by Alexander Pope (closed couplets)

But when the rosy morning warm'd the east,
My men I summon'd, and these words address'd:
"Followers and friends, attend what I propose:
Ye sad companions of Ulysses' woes!
We know not here what land before us lies,
Or to what quarter now we turn our eyes,
Or where the sun shall set, or where shall rise.
Here let us think (if thinking be not vain)
If any counsel, any hope remain.
Alas! from yonder promontory's brow
I view'd the coast, a region flat and low;
An isle encircled with the boundless flood;
A length of thicket and entangled wood.
Some smoke I saw amid the forest rise,
And all around it only seas and skies."

Co-4 (Greek)

HOMER. *Odyssey* ("Odysseus and Circe"). See also Co-3

A passage in Book x, lines 135–574, is apparently the chief classical source of legends regarding enchantments that can change men into animals. Milton makes his Comus the son of Homer's Circe, but the spells of Comus alter only the heads and faces of his victims. The herb that renders one proof against such magic is called *haemony*, rather than the Homeric *moly*. Milton's ritual of disenchantment follows Ovid (Co-8) rather than Homer. The episode of Gryll or Gryllus is first found in Plutarch's *Moralia* (Co-10) rather than in either Homer or Ovid.

Odysseus and Circe

(i) x, 203–18, tr. by William Cowper (blank verse)
Then numb'ring man by man, I parted them
In equal portions, and assign'd a Chief

To either band, myself to these, to those
Godlike Eurylochus. This done, we cast
The lots into a helmet, and at once
Forth sprang the lot of bold Eurylochus.
He went, and with him of my people march'd
Twenty and two, all weeping; nor ourselves
Wept less, at separation from our friends.
Low in a vale, but on an open spot,
They found the splendid house of Circe, built
With hewn and polish'd stones; compass'd she dwelt
By lions on all sides and mountain-wolves
Tamed by herself with drugs of noxious pow'rs.
Nor were they mischievous, but as my friends
Approach'd, arising on their hinder feet,
Paw'd them in blandishment, and wagg'd the tail,
As, when from feast he rises, dogs around
Their master fawn, accustom'd to receive
The sop conciliatory from his hand,
Around my people, so, those talon'd wolves
And lions fawn'd.

(ii) x, 219–28, tr. by William Morris (rhymed fourteeners)
    And they feared them when they beheld them, the creatures
        fierce and great.
    But there was the house of the Goddess, and there they
        stood in the gate,
    And Circe heard they singing in a lovely voice within,
    As she wove on the web undying, such works as the
        Godfolk win,
    Such works as are all-glorious, and delicate and fair.
    Then the chief of men, Polîtês, bespake his fellows there,
    A man who to me was dearest and heedfullest of all:
    "O friends, there is some wight weaving a great web there
        in the hall,
    And singing so fair that the pavement is echoing all about.
    A goddess or a woman? but to her let us haste to cry out."

(iii) x, 230–51, tr. by Thomas Hobbes (heroic quatrains)
    This said, they call, and she sets ope the gate,
    Bids them come in; fools as they were, they enter,
    All but Eurylochus; without he sat,

Suspecting somewhat, therefore durst not venture.
She places them, and sets before them food,
Cheesecakes of cheese, and honey, flour and wine;
But had mix'd something with it not so good,
Of wond'rous virtue, with an ill design.
For with a wand, as soon as they had din'd,
She drove them to the sties, and there them pent:
For body, head, hair, voice, all but the mind,
Right swine they were, and grunted as they went;
There to them threw she acorns, crabs and bran,
The things wherewith swine commonly are fed.
Eurylochus stay'd long, but not a man
Came out to let him know how they had sped.
Then back he comes: at first he could not speak,
Though he endeavoured; he grieved so,
The sighs and sobs his words did often break,
Till urg'd by us that long'd the truth to know;
At last he said, Renown'd Ulysses, we
Passing the woods as we commanded were, ...

(iv) x, 274–83, tr. by George Chapman (enjambed pentameter
      couplets)
      This said, I left both ship and seas, and on
      Along the sacred vallies all alone
      Went in discovery, till at last I came
      Where of the manie-medcine-making Dame
      I saw the great house, where encountered me
      The golden-rod-sustaining Mercurie,
      Even entring Circe's doores. He met me in
      A young man's likeness, of the first-flowr'd chin,
      Whose forme hath all the grace of one so yong.
      He first cald to me, then my hand he wrung,
      And said: "Thou no-place-finding-for-repose,
      Whither, alone, by these hill-confines goes
      Thy erring foote? Th' art entring Circe's house,
      Where (by her medcines blacke and sorcerous)
      Thy souldiers all are shut in well-armd sties,
      And turned to swine ...

(v) x, 284–92, 302–22, tr. by Watson Kirkconnell (epic
     hexameters)

Here will you hope to release them? Nay, rather, you too
    will be taken –
Doomed, O man, with the rest. Come then, I plan to
    redeem you,
Bring you salvation. Lo, take now this plant of rare virtue,
Guarding your life from its fate, when you come to the
    dwelling of Circe.
Now I will tell you the wiles in the heart of the subtle
    enchantress.
Goblets of wine she will mix for you, blended with magic
    of poison,
Yet will she fail to enchant you, such is my talisman's
    power. ...
    Then did the slayer of Argos pluck up from the ground
    for my safety
Flower and stem of the plant, and he showed me the way
    of its growing:
Black was its root but its blossom was milky. The gods call
    it *moly*.
Men look in vain, in seeking to dig it, but gods can do
    all things.
    Hermes departed forthwith from the island to lofty
    Olympus,
I, for my part, sought sadly the dangerous dwelling of Circe,
Darkly troubled in heart; and I stood at the goddess's portals;
Loudly I called, and the golden-tressed goddess was instant
    to hear me,
Opened the shining doors, and invited me in; heavy-hearted
With her I went. So she led me and set me a chair
    silver-studded,
Carven in a notable fashion. Beneath, for my feet, was a
    footstool.
Deep in a goblet of gold she prepared for my throat a
    dark potion,
Setting a charm therein, with guile in her treacherous counsel.
This did she give me; I drank it, and felt none the worse
    for its magic.
Touching my head with her wand, she spoke and in
    insolence hailed me:
    "Go to the sty forthwith, and lie with the rest of your
    fellows!"

Such were her words; but I flashed forth my sharp-edged
sword from its scabbard,
Leaping at Circe, as one who was eager in purpose to slay her.

Co-5 (Greek)

PLATO. *Phaedo* (after 399 B.C.)

Begins: ECHECRATES

Αὐτός, ὦ Φαίδων, παρεγένου Σωκράτει ἐκείνῃ τῇ ἡμέρᾳ
τὸ φάρμακον ἔπιεν ἐν τῷ δεσμωτηρίῳ ...
Ends: ... ἀνδρός, ὡς ἡμεῖς φαῖμεν ἄν, τῶν τότε ὧν ἐπειράθημεν
ἀρίστου καὶ ἄλλως φρονιμωτάτου καὶ δικαιωτάτου.

The dialogue between the two Brothers (*Comus*, lines 453–75) is a
close paraphrase of passages from Plato's *Phaedo*, where Socrates,
shortly before his death, expounds the relations between the body
and the soul in the case of the virtuous and the vicious respectively.
Relevant passages run as follows: "the soul which is pure at depart-
ing ... herself invisible, departs to the invisible world – to the divine
and immortal and rational ... But the soul which has been polluted
and is impure at the time of her departure and is the companion and
servant of the body always ... is engrossed by the corporeal, which
the continual association and constant care of the body have made
natural to her ... And this, my friend, may be conceived to be that
heavy, weighty, earthy element of sight by which such a soul is
depressed and dragged down again into the visible world, because
she is afraid of the invisible and of the world below – prowling about
tombs and sepulchres, in the neighborhood of which, as they tell us,
are seen certain ghostly apparitions of souls which have not departed pure, but are cloyed with sight and therefore visible" (translated by Benjamin Jowett).

From an age earlier than Plato came strands of mystical faith associated with Orphism, the mysteries, and Pythagoreanism. In *The
Republic*, Adeimantus (ii. 364E) refers to "a throng of books by
Musaeus and Orpheus, the descendants of Selene [the Moon] and
the Muses," and in the *Phaedo* the chief interlocutors (along with
Socrates) are Cebes and Simmias, disciples of Philolaus the Pytha-
gorean. Plato goes on, of course, to argue from the existence of

eternal ideas to the immortality of the soul in whose comprehension they inhere. Plutarch (ca. A.D. 46–120) is alleged to have been initiated into the mysteries of Dionysus, which also affirmed the immortality of the soul. He was primarily a philosopher, trained in Athens, and later lectured on philosophy in Rome, where he is alleged to have been the teacher of Hadrian. His *Gryllus* (Co-10) shows kinship with Plato's analysis of morality. Plotinus (A.D. 204–270) is regarded as the chief founder of "Neoplatonism," in which most earlier schools of philosophy were absorbed into a system of everlasting values and in which the vision of the divine One is granted only to a rare few after a lifelong quest. St Augustine (354–430), who in youth was stirred by the Plotinian philosophy (cf. his *Confessions*, VII, ix), helped in the almost complete incorporation of Neoplatonism into Christianity. Boethius (480–524), who had been steeped in Neoplatonism and stoicism at Rome, expounded in his *De Consolatione Philosophiae* (IV, ii, prose and metre) a moral allegory of Circe.[5] The old wells of Platonic mysticism began to flow freely in the fifteenth century with the founding of the Platonic Academy in Florence by Cosimo dei Medici the Elder about 1442, with which were associated such men as Marsilio Ficino (the first translator, from Greek into Latin, of the *Enneads* of Plotinus), Pico della Mirandola (who not only studied Plato, Plotinus, and Proclus but the Hebrew Kabbalah as well), and Poliziano (author of *La favola d' Orfeo*, Ly-22). For a detailed exposition of this Renaissance wave of neo-classical allegory, covering all classical myths and fables (like that of Circe) deep in the waters of figurative significance, see Edgar Wind's *Pagan Mysteries in the Renaissance* (London, 1958, 1967). For a Renaissance writer who deals specifically with the allegory of myths, one may turn to Natale Conti,[6] whose doctrines were used by Beaujoyeulx for the Circe-story in his *Balet Comique de la Royne* (Co-19). An English treatise on the subject is that of George Sandys (Co-29), dealing with the allegorical sense of Ovid's *Metamorphoses*. A culminating analysis of this sort of significance, as applied to Milton's *Comus*, is to be found in Rosemond Tuve's "Image, Form and Theme in a mask,"[7] and should be carefully read before reaching any critical judgment on the poem. She

---

5 His prose explanation of the Circe-story is that "he who, forsaking virtue, ceases to be a man ... is turned into a beast"

6 *Mythologiae, sive explicationis fabularum libri decem* (Venice, 1568)

7 *Images & Themes in Five Poems by Milton* (Cambridge, Mass., 1957), pp. 112–61

affirms that "Milton's whole invention moves" on "the great hinge of the Circe-Comus myth," and stresses the idiom of the masque, in which the participants present abstract truth while never ceasing to be themselves. The era was one when "genre was a factor governing all manner of small and large points of decorum," and she exposes the critical folly of a host of scholars who have stumbled badly through plain ignorance.

Co-6 (Greek)

PLATO. *The Republic*, Book VIII, 560 d, to the end. After 399 B.C.

Begins: 'Αρ' οὖν οὐ πάλιν τε εἰς ἐκείνους τοὺς Λωτοφάγους ἐλθὼν
          φανερῶς κατοικεῖ ...
Ends: ... ἀσωτίαν δὲ μεγαλοπρέπειαν, ἀναίδειαν δὲ ἀνδρείαν.

Unlike the enchanted victims of Circe, who assume animal forms but retain their human minds and memories, the animal-headed victims of her son Comus (in Milton's masque) lose their memories and their essential humanity:

> And they, so perfect is their misery,
> Not once perceive their foul disfigurement,
> But boast themselves more comely than before
> And all their friends and native home forget
> To roule with pleasure in a sensual stie ...

Here Milton, hand in hand with Plato, goes beyond Homer's account of Circe's isle and portrays the mental enslavement of those who submit to the power of evil thoughts. There is the same repudiation of home and tradition that overcame those sailors of Odysseus who ate the Lotos (*Odyssey*, II, 82–104), but there is also a complete failure to recognize their own moral degradation. Plato's interpretation reads: "Calling reverence silliness, they thrust it out dishonourably as an exile, calling temperance cowardice, they cast it out, pelted with mud ... insolent pride they call good breeding, anarchy they call freedom, profligacy they call magnificence, shamelessness they call manliness."

Co-7 (Latin)

PUBLIUS VERGILIUS MARO. *Georgicon Liber Quartus*. About 30 B.C.
From *P. Vergili Maronis Opera*, ed. Fredericus Arturus Hirtzel, Oxford,
1900

Begins: Protinus aerii mellis caelestia dona
   Exsequar. Hanc etiam, Maecenas, aspice partem ...
   Ends: Carmina qui lusi pastorum audaxque iuventa,
   Tityre, te patulae cecini sub tegmine fagi.

In shaping the not unimportant theme of Sabrina in the latter part
of his *Comus*, Milton seems to have drawn in part upon Vergil's 4th
Georgic. While setting out to be a versified treatise on beekeeping,
this Book, from line 315 on, becames an epyllion – a genre which,
as standardized by Callimachus of Alexandria, consists of a short
narrative poem, usually containing a second story by way of digression. Here the main story for Vergil is that of Aristaeus, son of
Apollo and the nymph Cyrene, who implores his mother's explanation as to why all his bees have died. She directs him to the sea-god
Proteus, and the second story is one by which Proteus solves Aristaeus' unhappy mystery. It is the tale of Eurydice, stung to death
by a viper while fleeing from Aristaeus, and of Orpheus' ill-fated
attempt to bring her back from the Underworld. Aristaeus' call to
his mother for help resembles the Attendant Spirit's incantation to
call up Sabrina. The river-goddess Sabrina, like Cyrene, has her
bevy of nymph-attendants, one of whom, in both cases, is Ligea.
She is described by Milton as"Sleeking her soft alluring locks,"
while Vergil's phrase for her and her sisters is *Caesariem effusae
nitidam per candida colla* ("with sleek locks cascading down their
white necks"). The Attendant Spirit's invocation includes a reference
to Proteus as"the Carpathian wizard,"i.e., as the marine magician
who haunted the sea near Carpathos, Rhodes, and Crete, in which
Paetus was drowned (Ly-9). The importance of this analogue has
been discussed by John Arthos,[8] who also sees in Sabrina and her
Neoplatonic significance an echo of Homer's *Odyssey*, xiii, 102–4,
as explained in Porphyry's Neoplatonic allegorizing in his *De antro
nympharum*. As originally phrased by Homer, these lines had no
recondite sense:

8 *Anglia*, lxxix (1961), 204–13

An olive, by the haven's head, expands
Her branches wide, near to a pleasant cave
Umbrageous, to the nymphs devoted named
The Naiades.   (Cowper's translation, 1791)

Vergil's version of the Orpheus-story is the chief source of Poliziano's *Orfeo* (Ly-22), where the prologue by Mercury begins not with Orpheus but with Aristaeus:"Silence! Listen! There was once a son of Apollo, a shepherd called Aristaeus."

R. Blenner-Hassett[9] has analysed Milton's"deft rewriting"of the original Sabrina-story as recorded by Geoffrey of Monmouth and in Milton's own *History of Britain*. Sabrina had been the issue of adultery by Locrine and had been murdered by his lawful wife, Guendolen, who drowned her in the Severn River. Milton, seeking to exploit local geography at the inauguration of the highest judicial officer of Wales, therefore stresses Sabrina's innocence and purity, refers to Guendolen as her"step-dame,"emphasizes the respectability of Locrine's ancestry, and represents Sabrina as voluntarily seeking death in the river as she flies from"the mad pursuit"of Guendolen.

T. Jones-Davies[10] invokes the anonymous tragedy, *Locrine* (1591), as a work in which the maiden Sabrina, harried by Guendolen, drowns herself.

Co-8 (Latin)

PUBLIUS OVIDIUS NASO. *Metamorphoses*, x, 519–739

Begins: Labitur occulte fallitque volatilis aetas,
            et nihil est annis velocius: ille sorore ...
  Ends: namque male haerentem et nimia levitate caducum
            excutiunt idem qui praestant nomina, venti.

This tale of the ardent goddess (Venus) and the unwilling youth (Adonis) is a later variant of the wooing of Gilgamesh by Ishtar (cf. Co-2). The one sample will suffice. It finds its place here for cross-reference to Ly-3, the *Lament for Adonis*, by Bion.

9 *MLN* (1949), 315–18
10 *Etudes Anglaises*, xx, 418

Co-9 (Latin)

P U B L I U S O V I D I U S N A S O . *Metamorphoses*, XIV, 248–307. The Circe
Episode

Begins: nos quoque Circaeo religata in litore pinu,
              Antiphatae memores immansuetique Cyclopis ...
 Ends: haeremusque ducis collo nec verba locuti
              ulla priora sumus quam nos testantia gratos.

Here told to Aeneas by Macareus, a former member of the crew of
Ulysses (Odysseus), is a concise narrative of their experience in
Aeaea, the island of Circe. It is substantially a condensation of the
same episode in Book x of the *Odyssey*. Most germane to our present
interest is Ulysses' use of *moly*, a magical white flower with a black
root, and the actions by which Circe restores the imbruted Greeks
to human form:

   spargimur ignotae sucis melioribus herbae
   percutimurque caput conversae verbere virgae,
   verbaque dicuntur dictis contraria verbis.[11]

This goes beyond the version of Homer, in which Circe simply
anointed each one with "another drug" (προσάλειφεν ἑκάστῳ φάρμακον
ἄλλο, *Odyssey*, x, 392). Milton's *Comus* (lines 815–17) apparently
echoes Ovid rather than Homer.

Macareus' Tale to Aeneas

   Then, having beached our ship on Circe's shore,
   We vowed that on the sea we'd go no more;
   Antiphates and the Cyclops had appalled us.
   Next, to explore the isle Ulysses called us.
   Trusty Polites there by lot was sent,
   Eurylochus and I together went,
   The too-much-given-to-wine Elpenor too,
   And twice nine other members of our crew,

11 Tr. "We were sprinkled with the more wholesome juices of an unknown
   plant and tapped on the head with her rod held upside down and words
   were uttered over us backwards to undo the original spells."

To spy out Circe's walls. When there we came
And stood upon the threshold of the dame,
A thousand wolves and, mingled with their throng,
She-wolves rushed up and lionesses strong.
We quaked with terror, but our fears were vain;
No scratch upon our skin did we sustain.
They even wagged their tails, all-courteous,
And fawned upon us as they followed us,
Till gracious handmaids took us all in charge
And led us through the marble palace large
To meet their lady. In a fair retreat,
She sat enthroned upon a lofty seat;
A purple robe she wore, of matchless grace,
A golden veil enveloped her fair face.
Her, nymphs and Nereids attend with dread;
They card no fleece, they spin no woollen thread;
Rather their task it is to sort out grass
And flowers mingled in a motley mass,
And place in separate sacks for her to use
The flowers and herbs that bear related hues.
Circe herself must supervise their work,
In every leaf she knows what powers lurk,
What juices mix; and she directs their tasks,
Weighing each extract as her science asks.
When she beheld us, with a welcome warm
She smiled on us, as if she would perform
The friendly acts for which we made appeal.
At once she bade her maidens spread a meal
Of toasted bread, and honey, and strong wine,
And curds of milk. To these her dark design
Added by stealth sly drugs of baleful power.
We took the cup she offered in that hour
And drained it thirstily with long-parched lip.
Alas, the cruel goddess, with the tip
Of wizard-wand then touched us on the head.
I shame to tell you, but it must be said,
How rough with bristles I began to grow;
Speech failed me; from my throat would only flow
Harsh grunting noises; I began to stoop
And face the earth; I felt my soft lips droop

And harden to a snout; my throaty glands
Were swollen into folds; and with my hands,
That just before had raised the cup with mirth,
I printed swinish tracks upon the earth.
Then in a sty with others I was penned,
My comrades who endured the same harsh end;
Such was the power of her unholy drugs.
Only Eurylochus, with hostile shrugs,
And thinking that some guile he might escape,
Had drunk not, and retained his human shape.
If he had not refused the treacherous drink,
There, in the bristly herd, I still would stink;
Ulysses would have failed to know our plight
Nor come to Circe to defeat her sleight.
To him peace-bearing Hermes gave a holy
And snow-white flower that the gods call moly.
Up from a coal-black root that blossom grows;
Made safe by this, and warned of hidden woes,
He entered Circe's palace, brave of soul,
And when she offered him the fatal bowl,
He stoutly thrust aside her wand abhorred
And threatened the enchantress with his sword.
Then faith was pledged; exchanged were marriage vows;
And since he was accepted as her spouse,
He wished his friends to be his wedding-gift.
Upon us sprinkled then, our nostrils whiffed
More wholesome juices from mysterious plants;
She stroked with wand reversed, and uttered chants
That counteracted all the former spell;
We stood erect; to earth our bristles fell;
We lost our hooves, we gained our shoulders back;
Of arms and hands we felt no more a lack.
And weeping, we embraced our weeping chief,
And thanked him loudly for this glad relief.

Co-10 (Greek)

PLUTARCH. *Gryllus*. About A.D. 100. From the *Moralia*, ed. by G.N.
Bernardakis, Leipzig, 1895, vol. vi, 82–100. There are prose translations

by "Sir A.J." in the Wm. A. Goodwin edition, Boston, 1889, vol. v, 218–33, and (in a more spirited style) by William C. Helmbold, Loeb Classics, *Moralia*, XII, 493–533

Begins: ODYSSEUS

Ταῦτα μέν, ὦ Κίρκη, μεμαθηκέναι δοκῶ
καὶ διαμνημονεύσιν ...

Ends: GRYLLUS

Εἶτά σε μὴ φῶμεν, ὦ Ὀδυσσεῦ, σοφὸν οὔπως
ὄντα κὰι περιττὸν Σισύφου γεγονέναι;

This witty and light-hearted prose dialogue is a discussion on whether"brute beasts are rational."The disputants are Odysseus, Circe, and a Greek-turned-pig, whose original name Circe refuses to divulge, introducing him only as Gryllus (i.e.,"Grunter"or"Mr Pig"). Circe is willing to restore to human form any of her"beasts" whom Odysseus can persuade to accept the transformation. If, on the other hand, they win the argument, Odysseus must acknowledge his discomfiture. The pig is easily victorious. He proves to an unwilling Odysseus that animals have more genuine courage, temperance, continence, and rationality than men. Odysseus angrily tries to demolish all these arguments by denying reason to "creatures who have no inherent knowledge of God." How can it be then, says the pig triumphantly, that a famously wise man like you is the descendant of such a notorious atheist as Sisyphus?

Co-11 (Greek)

FLAVIUS PHILOSTRATUS. *Comus*, No. 2, in *Eikones*, about A.D. 240, ed. Antonius Westermann, Paris, 1849. National Library, Ottawa

Begins: Ὁ δαίμων ὁ Κῶμος, παρ' οὖ τὸ κωμάζειν τοῖς ἀνθρώποις,
ἐφέστηκεν ἐν θαλάμου θύραις χρυσαῖς ...

Ends: ἵν' ὦσιν αἱ χεῖρες ξύμφωνοι πληττόμεναι τρόπῳ κυμβάλων.

Four Greek authors surnamed Philostratus appear to have been born in the island of Lemnos and to have flourished in the third century A.D. The most notable member of the group is commonly referred to as"the Athenian."He was a member of the *salon* of the bluestocking Empress, Julia Domna, and is credited with most of the works assigned to the family name. His *Eikones* (*Imagines* or "Paintings") purports to be a critical description of some sixty-four paintings in a colonnade in Naples, and is addressed to a group of young men who follow the author from picture to picture. First printed in Venice in 1502–3 by Aldus Manutius, the work was introduced to scholarly Western Europe in 1608, in an edition in Paris by F. Morel. Its immediate offspring, published at Louvain in the same year, was *Comus: Sive Phagesiposia Cimmeria, Somnium* (see Co-26), by Puteanus, whose description of the deity owes almost everything to Philostratus. The portrayal by Philostratus appears to be the first instance in recorded literature, although Aristophanes (*Plutus*, 1040) refers to a wreath and a torch as appropriate for a reveller.

In the twenty-fourth picture described in the *Eikones*, the artist deals with a legendary river of wine that flows in the Greek island of Andros. To the harbour of this island Bacchus and his rout are coming by ship and Silenus "is bringing thither Laughter and Comus, the gayest and most liquorous of gods, in order that they may enjoy the river most delightfully."

Goethe published a partial translation and critique of the *Eikones*, under the title *Philostrats Gemälde*, but did not include Comus from either No. 2 or No. 24. Portions of one of the *Letters* (No. 33) of Philostratus were translated almost literally by Ben Jonson in his *Song to Celia*, "Drink to me only with thine eyes."

E.M.W. Tillyard, in *Studies in Milton* (1951), pp. 171–2, in a note on "Milton and Philostratus," suggests in the case of the bridge through Chaos built (*P.L.*, x, 289–324) by Sin and Death that Milton was influenced, perhaps unconsciously, by a remembered tale in Philostratus' *Life of Apollonius* (1,25) of a tunnel of stone and bitumen built by a Babylonian queen. He does not touch on the possible influence of Philostratus' *Imagines* in the case of Milton's *Comus*.

COMUS

The divinity Comus, by whose influence men join in revelry,
is standing, I believe, at the golden door of a bedroom; of
this it is difficult to be sure, because it is represented as
shrouded with night. Night, however, is not painted in her
own person, but is only indicated by nocturnal shadows. The
porchway signifies, moreover, that fairly wealthy spouses
are lying in bed. But Comus comes to youths, himself a tender
and still immature lad, flushed with wine and asleep on his

feet because of intoxication. He is sleeping, moreover, with his face bent down upon his breast, so that nothing of his neck is visible. He supports his left arm on a hunting-spear but the hand that seemed to have grasped it is relaxed and slack, as usually happens during the onset of sleep, when, at the touch of slumber upon us, the mind is drawn into forgetfulness of the things that we grasp; therefore also the torch that is in his right hand seems to be slipping away from it, for slumber appears to be producing drowsiness in him.

Comus, however, fearing the flame that is approaching his left shin, transfers the torch to his left hand, so that the torch sends its flame downwards[12] and his hand leans on the protruding knee. The face, moreover, of those who are in the flower of youth, ought to be a matter of great care to painters, for if this is not considered, the paintings will lack their proper illumination: but the face is not so important in the case of Comus, since he is bending forward and his face is shadowed by his head. It is fitting, moreover, in my opinion, that those of that age ought not to go a-revelling except with their faces covered. As for the other parts of the body, they are accurately expressed, since the torch illuminates them and brings them into the light.

His crown of roses is also to be praised, not because of its beauty (for it is no great matter to represent the likenesses of flowers with yellow and blue colours, if that is the case), but because the softness and delicacy of the wreath is worthy of commendation. I also praise the dewy appearance of the roses and I might even say that they have been painted with their very fragrance. What else is appropriate to Comus? What else but the revellers? Do not the shrill uproar and confused clamour of the castanets strike your ears? The torches shine downwards, so that the revellers may see what is before their feet and they themselves may not be seen by us.

12 Edgar Wind, in his *Pagan Mysteries in the Renaissance* (1958, 1960, 1967), chap. x, "Amor as a god of death," points out that the reversed torch of Comus in the portrait described by Philostratus is actually a sign of funerary mourning and an attitude in which Love is often sculptured on ancient sarcophagi. Wind goes on to cite Ficino, Poliziano, Lorenzo dei Medici, and others on the Love-Death, bitter-sweet mysteries of Orphism.

Moreover, a great throng of men is proceeding along with him and young women are borne along with the men, shod promiscuously and girt up beyond what is customary. Doubtless Comus permits a man to act like a woman, to put on female dress, and to walk in a woman's style. Their wreaths are not very fresh, but, bound loosely to their heads through their disorderly running about, they have lost their gaiety. For the freedom of flowers intercedes with the force that withers them before their time. The picture imitates a sort of clapping, which revelry needs very much, and the right hand, with the fingers drawn together, beats on the hollow of the left hand placed beneath it, so that the hands resound together, smitten like cymbals.

Co-12 (Italian)

DANTE ALIGHIERI. *La Divina Commedia* (for "Dante and the Dark Forest," I, 1–33). From *Le Opere di Dante Alighieri*, ed. E. Moore and Paget Toynbee, 4th ed., Oxford, 1924

Begins: Nel mezzo del cammin di nostra vita
         Mi ritrovai per una selva oscura ...
Ends: Sì come rota ch' egualmente è mossa,
         L'amor che move il sole e l' altre stelle.

The gloomy forest motif opens Canto I of the *Divine Comedy*. Dante finds himself lost in the dark woods and presently is confronted by three supernatural enemies – a leopard, a lion, and a she-wolf. As they force him back towards the sunless region of the lowermost forest, he is rescued, not with *moly* but with the supernatural guidance of the ghost of Vergil, who later (for Paradise) gives place to Beatrice and she in turn to St Bernard. The epic as a whole is a vast allegory of the experiences of the souls of men. The metre (*terza rima*) is largely Dante's own invention, although based on a Provençal prototype. The architecture of the work is built on 100 cantos (one introductory and 33 each for symbolic presentations of Hell, Purgatory, and Paradise).

This greatest of Italian poems was begun, or at least conceived, in the year 1300 (as is made clear in line 1 of the *Inferno*, where the point of reference is the mid-point of a life of "threescore and ten years," dating from Dante's birth in 1265) and cannot have been completed later than 1321, the year of the poet's death. The oldest surviving manuscripts date from 1335 or 1336, and the first printed edition from 1472. Paget Toynbee, writing in 1910 (*Dante Alighieri: His Life and Works*, 4th, rev. ed., pp. 219–20) records that up to that time there had been 44 English translations of the *Inferno*, 29 of the *Purgatorio*, and 24 of the *Paradiso*. See Ly-14 (p. 138) for a brief passage from the *Paradiso* (xxvii, 19–66) that is an analogue of *Lycidas*. For further reading, see the bibliography appended to the *Britannica* article on "Dante," 1969 edition, vol. vii, pp. 63–4.

Lost in the Dark Forest

When half the journey of my life was spent,
   I found me in a gloomy forest lost,
   Where vanished was the road by which I went.
How hard it were in language to have glossed
   That forest's harshness so unparalleled
   That on my soul its fear congeals like frost.
The bitter scent of death its air expelled;
   But to make clear the good that there I found,
   I shall recount what else I there beheld.
How thus I came, I cannot quite expound,
   So full of slumber was I when I left
   The path of truth and trod unholy ground.
But when in wandering, of my way bereft,
   I reached a slope that blocked the valley's end
   That with a panic fear my spirit cleft,
I looked aloft and saw the peaks ascend
   Lit by that planet's ever-blessèd rays
   That leads men straight, wherever they may wend.
Somewhat more quiet grew the wild dismays
   That in my heart's deep pool had lashed the blood
   During the darkness and my piteous daze,
And as a man, whose pulses faintly thud,
   Out of the sea permitted to survive,
   Turns back and gazes at the perilous flood,
So did my soul, which yet its terrors drive,

Turn back to view again the narrow strait
That not a soul has passed and stayed alive.
When by due rest I mend my body's state,
I start again along the lonely steep
So that my lower foot supports my weight;
And lo, just where the slope begins its sweep,
A leopard came, nimble and swift of foot,
Its fur was spotted as I saw it creep ...

Co-13 (Italian)

DANTE ALIGHIERI. *La Vita Nuova*: "Sonetto Vigesimoquinto."
Written about 1292, in Florence, Italy

Begins: Oltre la spera, che più larga gira
       Passa il sospiro ch' esce del mio core ...
  Ends: Perocchè spesso ricorda Beatrice,
      Sicch' io lo intendo ben, donne mie care.

Dante's first work was a little volume of narrative prose begemmed
with 25 sonnets, 5 canzoni, and one ballata, somewhat after the
mixed style of Boethius' *De Consolatione Philosophiae* and the
mediaeval French"chantefable," *Aucassin et Nicolete*. Here is set
forth the moving tale of his boyhood love for Beatrice Portinari
(who before 1288 had married Simone de' Bardi) and here is finally
recorded, after her death in 1290, his elevation of her soul to a place
in heaven towards which his spirit must ever aspire. This is the
apotheosis of womanly purity that he was later to spell out large
in the *Commedia*, as indeed he had resolved, in the closing prose
sentences of *La Vita Nuova* to write concerning her what had never
before been written of any woman. According to Boccaccio, in his
Vita di Dante, the poet in maturer years was"much ashamed of
having written this little book."Certainly he presently, in 1292,
married Gemma Donati, who bore him four children and faithfully
saved his manuscripts from pillage in 1302–7; Beatrice (in *Purgatorio*, xxi, 59) seems to accuse him of misbehaviour with a"dainty
maid"(*pargoletta*); and after an interval of philosophical study he
apparently learned to think of Beatrice in Paradise as something
approaching the embodiment of Divine Wisdom.

Co-14 (Italian)

FRANCESCO PETRARCA. *Trionfo della Castità*. About 1350

Begins: Quando ad un giogo ed in un tempo quivi
          domita l'alterezza degli Dei ...
  Ends: ch' avean fatto ad Amor chiaro disdetto;
          fra gli altri vidi Ippolito e Joseppe.

After the death of Laura in the Great Plague of 1348, Petrarch sought in many poetic ways to give immortality to her fame, even as Dante had done for Beatrice. Along with a host of other poems that he composed in her honour, a set of six "Triumphs" (of Love, Chastity, Death, Fame, Time, and Eternity), written in the *terza rima* of Dante's *Commedia*, was organized about her person. Love, at the outset, had seemed omnipotent; but Laura's chastity is triumphant over Love; Death presently triumphs over her chastity; her Fame outlives her Death; Time will outlive her Fame; but everything will at last find its consummation in the Eternity of God. The genre of the *Trionfi*, like that of the *Commedia*, is a vision, in which his own love is progressively changed from its first sensual and terrestrial species into ever higher and more mystical forms.

The statue of chastity, carved out of white poetic marble by John Milton's spiritual mentors – Dante and Petrarch – stands austerely in the background of his *Comus*. Milton, in his *Apology for Smectymnuus* (see Co-39), testifies to the pure influence of these two Italian poets on his youth. We should remember, of course, that Laura, like Beatrice, was another man's wife; that while Petrarch was writing odes and sonnets to her chaste honour he was also begetting at least two illegitimate children, Giovanni and Francesca, by another woman; and that Dante likewise (see Co-13) may not have been always continent.

Co-15 (Middle English)

ANONYMOUS. *Sir Gawain and the Green Knight*. Fourteenth century. Edited by J.R.R. Tolkien and E.V. Gordon, 2nd. ed., revised by Norman Davis, Oxford, 1967

Begins: Siþen þe sege and þe assaut watz sesed at Troye,
    þe borgh brittened and brent to brondez and askez ...
Ends: Now þat bere þe croun of þorne,
    He bryng vus to his blysse! AMEN.

One of the most remarkable products of the Alliterative Revival in the fourteenth century is this verse romance in the dialect of the northwest midlands, spiced with an eclectic vocabulary from various sources. While the beheading theme goes back to one of the old Ulster tales of Cuchulainn, and while there are many ingredients from mediaeval romance, the sheer originality of the author dominates the whole work. It may be suspected that this tale, with its daring journey through a fearful forest to meet a supernatural opponent is one of the foundation-stones on which one of its eminent editors, J.R.R. Tolkien, built the lofty structure of his *Lord of the Rings* (1954–5), with its perils in Mirkwood and the Mountains of Shadow in Mordor. The prosody of *Sir Gawain* uses the old four-stressed alliterative lines, gathered in strophes, each with a brief rhymed"bob."A specimen of his description (lines 740–7) may be modernized as follows:

> By a mountain that morning he marched on handsomely
> Into a forest unfathomed, that was fearful and wild,
> Between hills that were high, and holts underneath
> Of grey oaks gigantic, in groups of a hundred;
> The hazel and hawthorn were herded together,
> With rough moss and ragged arrayed everywhere,
> With birds all unblithe on the bare spreading twigs,
> That piped most piteously, being pained by the cold ...

Co-16 (Italian)

LODOVICO ARIOSTO. *L'Orlando Furioso*. First complete edition, Ferrara, 1532

Begins: Le donne, i cavalier, l'arme, gli amori,
    Le cortesie, l'audaci imprese io canto ...
Ends: Bestemmiando fuggi l'alma sdegnosa,
    Che fu si altiera al mondo e si orgogliosa.

This immense and lively romantic epic, whose length (15,328 lines in ottava rima) is comparable to that of the *Iliad,* turned out to be a model and a source-book for whole generations of European poets. Spenser's *Faerie Queene* was avowedly written to surpass Ariosto in his own style. That there are borrowings from Ariosto in *Comus,* either coming directly (since Milton was deeply versed in Ariosto) or mediated through Spenser, is the argument of Ainsworth,[13] who cites such instances as the following:

(a) The only partial deformation of Comus's rout of monsters (cf. *O.F.* vi, 60–6) is very different from Homer's physical change along with no change of mind. Says Ariosto: Alcun dal collo in giù d'uomini han forma,/Col viso altri di simie, altri di gatti.[14]

(b) The encounter of Comus and the Lady may suggest the meeting of Angelica and "the lusty hermit" (*O.F.,* viii, 28 ff.)

(c) The ending of Comus's enchantments resembles the wiping out of Atlante's maze (*O.F.,* xxii, 13 ff.)

(d) The comment on courtesy among humble folk (*Comus,* 321 ff.) closely resembles *O.F.,* xiv, 62–9.

Co-17 (Italian)

GIOVANNI BATTISTA GELLI. *La Circe.* Florence, 1549. First translated into English by Henry Iden in 1557, but now readily accessible in *The Circe of Signior Giovanni Battista Gelli,* tr. Thomas Brown, ed. Robert Adams (Ithaca, 1963)

Begins: ULISSE
    Ancora che l'amore che tu mi porti, famosissima Circe, e le infinite cortesie che io a tutte le ore ricevo da te, ...

Ends: ULISSE
    ... di assimigliarsi a loro, ne porgono nuovi venti, molto atti e prosperi a la navicazion nostra.

The author of this spirited series of dialogues was a Florentine shoemaker, who was also an erudite public lecturer on Dante and one of the founders of the *Accademia degli Umidi* ("Academy of the Wet

13 Edward G. Ainsworth, "Reminiscences of the *Orlando Furioso* in *Comus,*" MLN, 46, 1931, 91–2

14 Tr. "Some have human forms from the neck down, with the faces of apes or cats."

Ones") in 1540, an organization kicked upstairs three months later by the Grand Duke Cosimo dei Medici as "The Academy of Florence." Gelli (1498–1563) survived through a difficult period by combining political humility with a keen appetite for literature. The most assured forerunner of his *Circe* is Plutarch's dialogue (Co-10) between Circe, Odysseus, and Gryllus (a man-turned-swine); but Gelli's work was expanded with borrowings from Plutarch's other moral essays, from Pliny's *Natural History*, Oppian's *Halieutica* II, Aelian's *De natura animalium*, and Aristotle's *De Anima* and *Nicomachean Ethics*, and from the Renaissance Neoplatonism of Ficino, Pico della Mirandola, and Pietro Pomponazzi. Circe promises, as in Plutarch, to restore to human form any animal whom Ulysses can persuade to accept this reverse metamorphosis; but instead of an argument with only one animal, as in Plutarch, Gelli's Ulysses argues at great length with an oyster, a mole, a snake, a hare, a goat, a deer, a lion, a horse, a dog, a bullock, and an elephant. Only the elephant, formerly a philosopher named Aglaphemus, is willing to accept a human lot again; and one has an uneasy feeling that what he opts for is not a three-dimensional human existence, complete with dirt and suffering, but only the contemplative delights of abstract thinking. Aglaphemus' hymn in honour of God in His universe, spread eloquently across the antepenultimate page, is in essence a tribute to the human intellect in its ability to survey that universe and its First Cause. With Gelli's other ten beasts, the wry conclusion of the dialogues is that the human lot is not a happy one. In the case of the deer – who had once been a woman – Gelli cuts deep into the selfishness and inconsiderateness of a man-made society. Her plea that women should be companions, not servants, to their husbands, has a modern ring.

Co-18 (Italian)

TORQUATO TASSO. *Aminta. Favola Boschereccia.* Vinegia, 1581

Begins: PROLOGO, AMORE IN HABITO PASTORALE
Chi crederia, che sotto humane forme,
E sotto queste pastorali spoglie ...
Ends: CHORO
Risse, e guerre, a cue segua
Reintegrando i cori, ò pace, ò tregua.

This "pastoral comedy" has been vouched for by Mario Praz as the original model on which Milton based his *Comus* (*Seventeenth Century Studies Presented to Sir Herbert Grierson*, pp. 202–3); but resemblance in plot or form is hard to find. To begin with, it is not a masque, but a regular five-act play. There is a prologue by Cupid, disguised as a shepherd, who announces that he will overcome the stony maiden heart of the heroine; but thereafter he merges indistinguishably with the shepherd chorus. There is no main masque or antimasque ballet, but only a speaking chorus that is gently in favour of wedded love. There is no Attendant Spirit, and no *deus ex machina*. There is no darkness and no one gets lost in a forest. There are no songs and no brothers who can recite Plato. We find no magician, no wand or julep, and no magic spells. All significant action takes place off stage and is reported by messengers. The heroine, Sylvia, has no coherent philosophy of virginity but only a stubborn devotion to Diana. It is not her chastity that saves her naked body from violation, when the Satyr has tied her to a tree with her own hair, but rather the armed intervention of her lover, Aminta. Everybody in the play is in favour of love except Sylvia; and Cupid's prologue denounces her from the outset as "stony-hearted" and "most cruel." The real confrontation in the play is not between Sylvia and the violent Satyr but between Sylvia and the hero-shepherd Aminta, an honest lover who seeks an honourable marriage (on the last page the consent of her father, Montanus, is being sought). Sylvia is a hard case. Her rescue by Aminta, in Act III, scene i, does not touch her heart, and in no time at all she is back in the forest hunting again. It is only when she has heard of his love-suicide by jumping over a precipice that she finally melts. The finding of his body, bruised but saved from death by landing in a thicket, completes her capitulation. The only passage in the whole play that seems like a formal anticipation of *Comus* is the speech (quoted below in translation) in which Sylvia's close friend Dafne rebukes her maiden frigidity by recounting the natural place of love in the whole of nature. The resemblance to a famous speech by Comus is general, however, rather than specific, for not a single phrase or image in Tasso is repeated in Milton.

Tasso is as full of classical borrowings as Sannazaro: from Tibullus, Ovid, Vergil, Catullus, and the rest. Even his prologue is based on the "runaway Eros" in the 1st Idyll of Moschus.

And yet the influence of this play was all-pervasive in the Europe of its time and in the long run contributed some pastoral elements to *Comus*. A very full discussion of its significance is given throughout almost the whole of Richard Cody's *The Landscape of the Mind: Pastoralism and Platonic Theory in Tasso's 'Aminta' and Shakespeare's Early Comedies* (Oxford, 1969). Thus he explains (p. 23) that"To see that the *Aminta* ... is a footnote to Plato, one should come to it by way of the *Phaedrus* and Poliziano's *Orfeo*" [see Ly-22], and further, that the *Aminta* is (p. 82) "a Neo-Platonic landscape of the mind, mythopoeically conceived."The Platonic elements in Milton's *Comus* thus come not only directly from Milton's reading of Plato but indirectly through the whole tradition of Platonic pastoralism that took shape in Renaissance Italy, from Poliziano and Ficino down to Tasso. Both the Attendant Spirit and Comus assume the guise of shepherds; the setting is a countryside; and the whole rationale of the masque is a mixture of Platonism and Christian doctrine. Cody's volume could well serve as a Renaissance supplement to C.S. Lewis's *The Discarded Image* (1964), so completely has the worldview of Marsilio Ficino and his disciples faded from the consciousness of a technological generation – whether humanist, scientific, or Marx-Leninist.

(Act. i, scene i, Dafne to Sylvia)
Would you consider that the ardent ram
Is the ewe's enemy? That as her foe
The heifer sees the bull? Deem you the dove
An enemy beside his faithful mate?
Do you imagine this, the pleasant Spring,
A season filled with enmity and wrath?
Which now with smiles and laughter reconciles
The entire world to love, as well brute beasts
As men and women: do you not perceive
How everything on earth is stirred at heart
With gentle joy and salutary love?
Behold that dove, with cooing flattery,
Who kisses his companion: lend your ear
To yonder nightingale along the boughs
Who sings, *I love, I love*. Even the snake
(Perhaps you know not) lays his venom by
And slides in amorous passion to his mate.
Tigers rush into love; the lion, too,
Proud but impulsive yields his heart to love.
Shall you alone, more savage than all beasts,
Deny sweet love a lodging in your breast?

But why of snakes and tigers is my speech
And lions, all endowed with consciousness?
Even the trees know love. You may observe
With what affection and embracings oft
The vine entwines herself about her spouse,
Fir-tree loves fir-tree, pine feels love for pine,
The willow loves the willow, elm seeks elm,
One beech-tree for another sighs and burns.
That very oak, that seems so rough and harsh,
Feels in its centre a consuming fire.

Co-19 (French)

BALTASAR DE BEAUJOYEULX. *Circe, ou Balet Comique de la Royne.*
Paris, 1582. Mi: New York Public Library (this is Ben Jonson's own
marked copy)

Begins: GENTILHOMME FUGITIF (au Roy)
    Tousiours quelque malheur fatalement s'oppose
    Contre ce que le Ciel, favorable, dispose ...
  Ends: CIRCE
    C'est ce Roy des Francois, et faut que tu luy cedes,
    Ainsi qui ie luy fais, le ciel que tu possedes.
(This is followed by several prose pages, describing the subsequent action
and the ethical significance of the performance.)

An epoch-making performance in Paris in 1581 was a ballet prepared at the request of the Queen Mother, Catherine dei Medici, in
honour of the marriage of Mademoiselle De Vaudemont and the Duc
de Joyeuse. The task was entrusted to an Italian courtier, Baltazarini
de Belgiojoso (Frenchified as "Baltasar de Beaujoyeulx"), who associated with him the King's almoner as librettist and the King's two
music masters as composers, and the four of them, as a sort of
"Revels Office," created the *Balet Comique de la Royne*, the most
famous spectacle in the Europe of its time and one destined ultimately
to beget two artistic offspring – the Florentine *dramma per musica*
(the forerunner of the opera) and when blended with the Tudor masque, the English court masque of the Stuarts.

    The details of the genre are expounded by John G. Demaray in
Milton and the Masque Tradition (Harvard University Press, 1968),

where the influence of Beaujoyeulx's work is made clear, especially in chapter I. Ben Jonson's own marked copy of the *Balet Comique* is still in existence (and was indeed examined for the present note); Inigo Jones copied some of his most fantastic décor from it; and Aurelian Townshend paraphrased its dialogue in English as the libretto for *Tempe Restored* (Co-36). In Beaujoyeulx's ballet, all of the arts of glorified spectacle, baroque music (vocal and instrumental), figured dances, elaborate costumery, neo-classical poetry and Platonic didacticism were woven together into an artistic harmony. Its fundamental tenet was an ordered moral cosmos, organized about the king and queen, from which all elements of evil and violence are exorcised, leaving the aristocratic spectators and participants comfortably assured of the virtue of their world (actually dominated by the vicious and corrupt Henry III and the murderous queen-mother, Catherine).

Ben Jonson added a "hinge" of plot and a greater sense of poetry to most of his masques and therefore contributed to the significant evolution of the form; but Inigo Jones, the infatuated spectacle-master, dispensed with Jonson's services and destroyed the masque by an excess of fantasy over meaning. Two years after Jonson had been shouldered out and the masque was on its way to disintegration (and to its death in 1640), Milton and Lawes returned in *Comus* to the Jonsonian model of entertainment. As Mr Demaray has explained in the minutest analytical detail, all of the machinery and structural elements of the Jonsonian masque are represented in *Comus*, even to the inevitable *deus ex machina* solution at the end, and are tailored into a personal entertainment for the Egerton family in a very special situation. Only an almost complete ignorance of the nature of Milton's genre has given rise, from Samuel Johnson down to our own day, to nearly two centuries of irrelevant judgments on his performance. The inner poetic tension between the form and his creative drive is something else again.

CIRCE, or THE QUEEN'S MASQUE

(Translated and adapted from Beaujoyeulx by Aurelian Townshend, for the verse, and Inigo Jones, for the argument, allegory, and descriptions. This abridged version is listed later as *Tempe Restored* (Co-36). The selections given here will serve both to illustrate Beaujoyeulx and to describe a Stuart masque performed just thirty months before the staging of *Comus* and with the participation of two of the Egerton daughters, one of whom, Alice, became "the Lady" in Milton's masque. The quotations below are taken from a 1631/1632 copy of *Tempe Restored* in the British Museum. The chief innovations made by Jones and Townshend are (a) the elimination of a long series of warlike episodes like those between Circe and the Olympians and (b) the addition of a long sequence of antimasque dances to amuse Circe. These are typically intended by Jones to display his showmanship, at the expense of the hinge. The antimasque dances in Milton's *Comus*, on the contrary, come very naturally in the development of his plot and reinforce its sense of action.)

The Argument

Circe by her alurements inamored a young Gent. on her person, who a while lived with her in all sensuall delights until upon some jealosie conceived, shee gave him to drink of an inchanted Cup, and touching him with her golden wand transformd him into a *Lyon*. After some time shee remembring her former love, retransformed him into his former shape. Which he reasuming tooke the first occasion by flight to quitt the place and coming into the presence of his Majestie, whose sight frees him from all feare he relates the story of his fortune.

   When *Circe* had notice of her Lovers escape, it put her into a furious anger and then into a lamentation or love passion. But being consolated by her Nymphes; shee commands that all such delights be prepared as may sweeten her sorrow: and presently all the voluntary beasts under her subjection are introduced to make her sport. After which the way being first prepared by *Harmony*, and the Influences; divine *Beautie*[15] accompanied with fourteene stars of a happy constellation, descends to the Musicke of the *Spheares* and joyneth with heroicke *vertue*,[16] where in presence of *Jove* & *Cupid*, *Circe* knowing the designe of the destinies on this glorious Enterview, voluntarily delivers her golden rod to *Minerva*. So all the inchantments being dissolved, *Tempe* which for a time had

15 The Queen and fourteen of her ladies, dancing the main masque
16 The King

been possest by the voluntary beasts of *Circes* Court; is restored to the true followers of the *Muses*.

The description of the Sceane

In the upper part of the border serving for ornament to the
Scene, was painted a faire compartment of scrowles and qua-
dratures, in which was written *Tempe Restauratum*. On each
side of this, lay a figure bigger then the life, the one a woman
with wings on her head like *Mercurie* and a pen in her hand:
the other a man looking downe in a booke lying open before
him, and a torch lighted in his hand: that figur'd Invention;
this Knowledge. Neere to these were children holding oughly
Maskes before their faces in action as if they would afright
them; others riding on tame beasts and some blowing such
wrethen Trumps as make confused noyse, in the corners sat
other Children hardning of darts in Lamps. But Invention and
Knowledge seem not to be diverted from their study by these
childish bugbears. In the midst of the two sides of this border
in short neeces sat two oughly figures, the one a woman with
a forked tongue, and snaky lockes, and the under part of a
Satyre, this Hagge held in her hand a smiling vizard crown'd
with Roses, and was figured for Envie, under the Maske of
friendship. On the other side was sitting as horrid a man
Satyre with a wreath of poppy on his head, and a Frog sitting
on the fore part thereof; and above a Batt flying, this represented curious *Ignorance*. The rest of the Border was fild up
with several fancies, which lest I should be too long in the description of the frame, I will goe to the picture it selfe, and
indeed these showes are nothing else but pictures with Light
and Motion.[17]

A Curtaine being drawne up, the Lightsome *Scene* appear'd,
shewing a delicious place by nature and art; where in a Valley
inviron'd with Hils a farre off was seated, a prospect of curious
Arbours of various formes. The first order of marble Pillasters.
Betweene which were neeces[18] of rocke worke and Statues:
some spurting water received into vazes beneath them, and
others standing on Pedestals. On the returnes of these Pill-

17 A very famous statement of Inigo Jones's ideals in the masque
18 Niches

asters run slender Cornishments.[19] From which was raised a
second order of gratious termes[20] with women's faces which
beare up the ornaments. Under this to a leaning height was a
Ballestrata inricht. All this second story seem'd of silver worke
mixt with fresh Verdures which on the tops of these arbours
covered some of the returnes, in the forme of tipes with
slender branches dangling downe: others were cover'd flatt
and had flower pots of gold for finishing: behind these appear'd the tops of slender trees, whose leaves seem'de to
move with a gentle breath comming from the farre off Hills.

Out of this pleasant place comes in hast, a yong Gentleman,
looking often backe, as if he feared a pursuit; and beeing come
into the midst of the roome, looking still distractedly about
him, hee wipes his face with an handkercher, and then advances towards the State,[21] and speakes.

THE FUGITIVE FAVOURITE

Was I a Lyon! that am now afraid!
I feare no danger; nor I feare no Death;
But to be Retransform'd, into a Beast:
Which while I was, although I must confesse,
I was the Bravest: What could shee doe lesse,
That saw me Subject, to no base desire:
Yet was there in me, a Promethean fire,
That made me covet to be man againe,
Govern'd by Reason, and not rul'd by Sense.

Therefore I shunne this place of Residence,
And flye to Vertue: in whose awfull sight,
She dares not come, but in a Maske, and crouch,
As low as I did, for my liberty.

Her Bowre is pleasant, and her Palace Rich;
Her Fare Delicious, and her Language fine;
But shall the Soule, the Minion of the Gods,
Stoope to her Vassalls? Or stand by and sterve,
While they sit swelling, in her Chayre of State?

T'is not her Rod, her Philters, nor her Herbes,
(Though strong in Magicke) that can bound mens minds;

19 Cornices
20 Busts on pedestals
21 The King's canopied chair of state, probably on a dais

And make them Prisoners, where there is no wall.
It is consent that makes a perfect Slave:
And Sloth that binds us to Lusts easie Trades,
Wherein we serve out our youths Prentiship,
Thinking at last, Love should enfranchize us,
Whom we have never either serv'd or knowne:
"He finds no helpe, that uses not his owne."

The further part of the Sceane opening, there appears seated
on the side of a fruitfull hill, a sumptuous Palace, with an open
Tarras before it, and a great staire of returne, descending into
the lower grounds; the upper part environ'd with walles of
Marble, alongst which were planted *Cypresse* trees. From the
foot of the hill, Circe attended by the *Nayades* and *Dryades*
comes foorth in fury, for the escape of the young Gentleman,
her Lover; and having traverst the stage with an angry looke,
sings to her Lute:

CIRCE

Dissembling Traytor, now I see the cause,
Of all thy fawning, was but to be free:
T'was not for nothing, thou hadst teeth and clawes,
For thou hast made a cruell prey of me ...

Her song ended, she sits, and before her are presented all
the Antimasques, consisting of Indians, and Barbarians, who
naturally are bestiall, and others which are voluntaries, and
but halfe transformed into beastes.

Here come forth all the Antimasques: 7 Indians adoring
their Pagole, 1 Idoll, 1 Hare, 2 Hounds, 4 Lyons, 3 Apes, An
Asse like a Pedante teaching them Prick-song, 6 Barbarians,
5 Hogges. The Last Anti-Masque: 2 Indians, 2 Hounds, 2
Apes, 1 Asse, 2 Lyons, 2 Barbarians, 2 Hogges.

The Anti-Masques being past: *Circe* and her Nymphes re-
tire towards the palace from whence she came, and the Sceane
returning into the vale of Tempe.

Harmony comes foorth attended by a *Chorus* of Musique,
and under her conducts fourteene Influences of the stars,
which are to come. She with the *Chorus* goes up to the State
and sings

Not as my selfe, but as the brightest Starre,
That shines in Heaven, come to Reigne this day.
And these the Beames and Influences are
Of Constellations, whose Planeticke sway,
*   Though some foresee, all must alike obey.*

CHORUS

Such a Conjunction of auspicious lights,
Meete but in Honor, of some Regall rights ...

The Queene and the Ladies dance their Entry, after which
Harmony, and the highest Spheare sing, assisted by all the
Chorus together.

How rich is earth? and poore the skies?
Depriv'd of heavenly Beauties eyes?
*   Whose image men adore ...*

CHORUS

But we most happy, that behold,
Two that have turn'd this Age to Gold,
*   Making old Saturns Reigne*
*   In theirs, come backe againe ...*

The *Maskers* dance their maine Dance, which done, and the
Queene seated under the State by his Majestie, the *Scene* is
againe changed into a shady wood, and a new Heaven ap-
peares differing in shape and colour from the other. In the
midst of which *Jove* sitting on an Eagle is seene hovering in
the ayre with a glory beyond him. And at that Instant *Cupid*
from another part of the Heaven comes flying forth, and
having past the *Scene,* turnes soaring about like a bird, and at
the same time *Pallas, Circe* and her foure *Nymphes* appeare on
the Stage: the great *Chorus* consisting of five and thirty
Musitions standing below to assist them.

(There next is sung a highly operatic confrontation scene between
Circe, Pallas, Cupid, and Jupiter, which ends with Circe meekly sur-
rendering her magic wand to Pallas and then making her heirs the
presiding monarchs, originally King Henry III of France and his wife,

Queen Louise, but in the abridged translation King Charles I of England and his young French wife, Queen Henrietta Maria. This action takes the place of a much longer series of scenes in the *Balet Comique de la Royne*, but in both cases it is clearly "The Queen's Masque.")

When this was past, the *Eagle* with *Jove* flew up, and *Cupid* tooke his flight through the Ayre, after which the Heavens close. *Pallas* and *Circe* returnes into the Scene with the *Nymphes*, and *Chorus*; and so concluded the last *Intermedium*. After which the Queene and her Ladies began the Revels, with the King and his Lords, which continued all the night.

The Allegory

In the young Gentleman, who *Circe* had first enamored on her Person, and after, through Jealousie conceived, Transformed into a *Lyon*. And againe remembring her former Love, retransform'd into his former shape, is figured an incontinent man, that striving with his affections, is at last by the power of reason perswaded to flye from those Sensuall desires, which had formerly corrupted his Judgement ...

That divine *Beauty* accompan'ed with a troope of Stars of a happy Constellation joyning with Heiroicke vertue should dissolve the inchantments, and *Circe* voluntarily deliver her golden rod to *Minerva*, is meant that a divine Beame comming from above, with a good inclination, and a perfect habit of vertue made, by the *Harmony* of the Irascible and concupiscible parts obedient to the rationall and highest part of the soule. Making man onely a mind using the body and affections as instruments; which being his true perfection, brings him to all the happinesse which can bee injoyed heere below.

In Heiroicke vertue is figured the Kings Majestie, who therein transcends as farre common men, as they are above Beasts, he being truly the prototipe to all the Kingdomes under his Monarchie, of Religion, Justice, and all the *Vertues* joyned together.

So that Corporeall *Beauty*, consisting in simetry, colour, and certaine unexpressable Graces, shining in the Queenes Majestie, may draw us to the contemplation of the *Beauty* of the soule, unto which it hath Analogy...

Co-20 (Italian)

GIAMBATTISTA GUARINI. *Il pastor fido*. Ferrara, 1590. Queen's University (edited by Gioachino Brognoligo, Bari, 1914)

Begins: ALFEO
>Fiume d'Arcadia
>Se per antica, e forse
>da voi negletta e non creduta fama ...

Ends: CORO DI PASTORI
>Quello è vero gioire,
>che nasce de virtú dopo il soffrire.

Giambattista Guarini (1537–1612) was born in Ferrara, studied at the universities of Pisa and Padua, and before the age of twenty was professor of moral philosophy in his native city. His one verse tragicomedy, *The faithful shepherd*, is commonly regarded as the glittering culmination of the pastoral tradition in sixteenth-century Italy. In some respects it is the poetic twin of the *Aminta* of his friend, Torquato Tasso. All characters are typically Arcadian and the prologue is spoken by the river-god Alpheus (invoked by Milton in *Lycidas*). The plot is comparatively simple. The people of Arcadia sacrifice one young woman to Diana each year, to expiate the ancient infidelity of an Arcadian bride. The curse will be lifted only when Love unites two demigods and when the devotion of "a faithful shepherd" cancels the far-off fault. The nymph Amarilli, descended from the god Pan, is betrothed to Silvio, son of the priest Montano, himself descended through Hercules from Jove. Silvio, however, like Adonis of old, is interested only in hunting, while Amarilli loves, and is loved by, Mirtillo, believed to be the son of Carino. The nymph Corisca, wanting Mirtillo for herself, "frames" Amarilli and Mirtillo in compromising circumstances, so that Amarilli may be put to death. Mirtillo insists that he must die in her stead; he is shown to be actually the son of Montano (and hence the descendant of a god); and a blind prophet, Tirenio, reveals that a "faithful shepherd's" offer of vicarious death (together with the love of these two "demigods") has cancelled out the old curse in Arcadia. Silvio, meanwhile, while hunting, accidentally wounds Dorinda, who has shadowed him out of pure love; he promptly falls in love with her; and Amarilli is set free to marry Mirtillo. So far as *Comus* is concerned, the play is even less of an analogue than *Aminta*; and its basic theme of three melting maidens – Amarilli, Corisca, and Dorinda – is far removed from the rigidity of Milton's Lady. Its chief value in the *Comus*-context is to underline the sharp insistence on virtue in the court masques of the Stuart kings. The speeches by which Linco, in Act i, scene i, tries to persuade his bride-shy friend Silvio that love is a universal and delightful power, are not unrelated to the speeches of Comus to the Lady, and to the arguments of Dafne to the groom-shy Sylvia in Act i, scene i, of *Aminta* (see above, pp. 33–6).

For Guarini's place in the evolution of the pastoral play, see the note on Fletcher's *Faithful Shepherdess* (Co-27).

Co-21 (English)

EDMUND SPENSER. *The Faerie Queene*. London, 1590, etc. The text is readily accessible in the Oxford *Spenser*, ed. J.C. Smith and E. de Selincourt (1912), or in the Cambridge *Spenser*, ed. R. E. Neil Dodge (1908, 1936)

Book i, Canto i
Begins: A gentle knight was pricking on the plaine,
     Ycladd in mightie armes and silver shielde ...
  Ends: But when he saw his labour all was vaine,
     With that misformed spright he backe returned againe.

The dark forest motif (see Co-1) stands in the forefront of Spenser's epic. The Redcross Knight, Una, and her page are quickly lost in the labyrinth of "the wandring wood," where the ugly monster, Error, has its den. A more subtle spiritual danger lurks behind, in the enchanter Archimago, ready to invoke "Great Gorgon, prince of darkness and dead night." The forest setting recurs later in the woods where Orgoglio overcomes St George (i, vii); in the "gloomy glade" where Mammon has his retreat (ii, vii); in the forest where Florimell finds the witch's cottage (iii, vii); and in the woods to which Lust carries off Amoret (iv, vii).

Co-22 (English)

EDMUND SPENSER. *The Faerie Queene*. London, 1590 etc. See headnote to Co-21

Book ii, Canto xii

Begins: Now ginnes this goodly frame of Temperaunce
        Fayrely to rise, and her adorned hed
        To pricke of highest prayse forth to advaunce ...
Ends:"... Let Gryll be Gryll, and have his hoggish minde;
        But let us hence depart, whilest wether serves and winde."

Unlike the brothers in Milton's *Comus*, who fail to bind the magician, Spenser's Guyon and the Palmer hold Acrasia fast and later bind her "in chaines of adamant." The rabble of her former lovers, turned by her spells into "wild-beasts that rag'd with furie mad," are restored to human shape by the "vertuous staffe" of the Palmer.

Temperance, the alleged virtue of Guyon, can be rendered in Greek by either σωφροσύνη ("chastity," "sobriety," Latin "temperantia," cf. Aristotle's *Ethics*, III, 10–12) or ἐγκράτεια ("continence," Latin "continentia," cf. *Ethics*, VII, 1–10), while their respective opposites in Aristotle are ἀκολασία ("intemperance") and ἀκρασία ("incontinence"); and it is significant that Spenser uses the latter, transliterated precisely as "Acrasia," as the name of Guyon's arch-enemy. This surely gives us a clue to the intended meaning of the moral allegory in Book II.

A. Kent Hiett has recently pointed out (*UTQ*, XXXVII, 313–18) a resemblance between Milton's Comus and Spenser's False Genius, Porter of the Bower of Bliss, with his bowl of wizard wine and his conjuring rod (stanzas 46–9).

Co-23 (English)

E D M U N D   S P E N S E R .   *The Faerie Queene*. London, 1590 etc. See headnote to Co-21

Book III, Canto xii
Begins: Tho, when as chearelesse night ycovered had
        Fayre heaven with an universall clowd ...
  Ends: Thence to depart for further aide t' enquire:
        Where let them wend at will, whilest here I do respire.

In the first part of this canto, "the maske of Cupid" presents a parade of allegorical figures, some as a masque ("a jolly company ... enrangèd orderly ... in trim aray") and some as an antimasque ("a rude confusèd rout"), all produced by the "false charmes" of the enchanter, Busirane.

There follows, in cantos 30–45, the defeat of the wizard by the virgin warrior, Britomart, in the midst of his attempts to subdue the "woefull lady," Amoret, to his will by black magic. He is then compelled to free his enchanted victim with "backward mutters of dissevering power." This is the cure that Milton's young Brothers should have imposed on Comus, had they not "let the false enchanter scape."

Co-24 (English)

GEORGE PEELE. *The Old Wives' Tale*. London, 1595

Begins: ANTIC

How now, fellow Frolic! What, all amort? Doth this sadness become thy madness? What though we have lost our way in the woods? ...

Ends: MADGE

Yes, faith: when this was done, I took a piece of bread and cheese, and came my way; and so shall you have, too, before you go, to your breakfast.

Three countrymen, benighted in a dark forest, are found and lodged by Clunch, the local blacksmith. Two of them, Fantastic and Frolic, sit up to hear an "old wives' tale," told by the smith's wife. The characters in that tale wander on and off the stage and present it as a drama.

An enchanter, Sacrapant, son of the witch Meroe, has power to turn human beings into animals. He has turned Erestus, the betrothed of Venelia, into a bear by night and an old man by day. He has also stolen away Delia, daughter of the King of Thessaly, and blotted out her memory. Her two brothers are wandering in the forest to seek for her, but are powerless against the enchanter's magic. Her lover, Eumenides, having generously paid for the overdue burial of a dead man named Jack, is befriended by the Ghost of Jack. The latter kills Sacrapant; and Venelia, who is "neither maid, wife nor widow," blows out the bottled light on which his power has depended. Thomas Warton, writing in 1791, in a search for parallels to Milton's *Comus*, points out that in Peele's play the *brothers*"call on the Lady's name and Echo replies."In *Comus*, it is the *Lady* who asks Echo (in a song, where no names are called on or even mentioned) where her brothers are, and it is not Echo who replies but the evil enchanter. Peele's brothers, moreover, have no share in the rescue of their sister and there is no rabble of semi-beasts as in Milton. The debt to Peele, largely in terms of feeling and atmosphere, has recently been sketched by John Arthos.[22] H.J. Todd[23] has pointed out that the names of some of the characters in Peele (e.g., Sacrapant and Chorebus) are taken from Ariosto's *Orlando Furioso*, while Meroe the witch (mother of Sacrapant) is taken from Apuleius' *Golden Ass* (1, 9), where she transforms three men into a beaver, a frog, and a ram. The magician is disarmed and killed by the ghost of Jack, but the Sister (like the Lady in *Comus*) is still under his spell. The ghost (or spirit) blows a magical horn and thus calls up Venelia (like Sabrina), who proceeds to cancel the evil enchantment. Kenneth Muir[24] surmises that for the Ludlow Castle masque a longer entertainment was needed than the genre usually provided and that Milton"ingeniously blended the masque form with that of the pastoral play,"borrowing elements of plot and setting from *The Old Wives' Tale* and *The Faithful Shepherdess*.

Co-25 (English)

BEN JONSON. *Hymenaei*. London, 1606

Begins: SONG
    Bid all profane away;
    None here may stay
    To view our *mysteries* ...
Ends: TRUTH
    Lastly, this *heart*, with which all hearts be true:
    and TRUTH in him make treason ever rue.

This early masque by Jonson has been cited by John G. Demaray (*Milton and the Masque Tradition*, 1968, p. 24) as first embodying those elements of structure and treatment that were later embodied

22 *A Mask Presented at Ludlow-Castle* (Ann Arbor, 1954), espec. pp.
    1–2, 5, 9, 12, 26
23 *The Poetical Works of John Milton*, ed. H.J. Todd (London, 1801), V, 233
24 *John Milton* (London, 1955), p. 33

by Milton in *Comus*. On the first night of a two-night celebration, Hymen, the god of marriage, has scarcely declared his office before his holy altar, when, "with a kind of contentious musique," a masque of eight men appears, "gloriously attired," to represent the four Humors and four Affections. After a violent dance, they draw their swords and threaten to disturb the marriage ceremony. Hymen protests:

> Saue, saue the *virgins*; keepe your hallow'd lights
> Vntouch'd; and with their flame defend our *Rites*.
> The foure vntemp'red *Humors* are broke out,
> And, with their wild *affections,* goe about
> To rauish all Religion ...

Reason brings the intruders under control, Juno is discovered in the Upper Scene, and eight beautifully garbed ladies, representing her properties in marriage, descend "in two great cloudes," and dance another masque-dance, first by themselves and then paired with the men. The climax of this first night was the "Epithalamion."

The second night began with a heated argument between two similarly garbed ladies, "the one representing *Truth,* the other *Opinion.*" The latter declares that only virgins retain their charm for mankind, while Truth maintains that a chaste wife has a richer, fuller life. A mock tournament was then held on stage with sixteen armed champions on either side. Their warfare is terminated by "an angell or messenger of glory," who imposes the authority of Truth and asserts the superiority of marriage to virginity.

This masque, one of Jonson's greatest and one that helped to establish his form of the genre, was written for the marriage in 1606 of 15-year-old Robert Devereux, 3rd Earl of Essex (whose father had been executed for treason in 1601 and whose mother had been the widow of Sir Philip Sidney) and 13-year-old Frances Howard, daughter of Lord Thomas Howard (former admiral, created Earl of Suffolk in 1603, chiefly for his share in suppressing the father of the groom). The malodorous sequel is told in detail in Edward Le Comte's *The Notorious Lady Essex* (New York, 1969). The teen-age wife proceeded to have affairs with Henry, Prince of Wales (see Ly-89) and Robert Carr, the handsome Scottish favourite of James I, who had come with him from Scotland as a penniless page in 1603. In order to clear the way for Carr, the king helped to arrange for the annulment of Frances's marriage to Essex and created his favourite

Earl of Somerset. John Donne, who was cultivating Somerset in the hope of political or financial help, wrote an elaborate *Epithalamion* for the wedding. Within two years, the sky fell in. Husband and wife were accused, and convicted, of procuring the murder, in the Tower of London, three months before their marriage, of Sir Thomas Overbury, an outspoken opponent of this union of the young paramours. Four humbly-born accomplices were hanged, but the principals, apparently by royal arrangement, got off with short terms of imprisonment. The elaborate tributes to virtue in the Stuart masques bore no necessary resemblance to life at court.

Co-26 (Latin)

ERYCIUS PUTEANUS. *Comus, sive phagesiposia Cimmeria. Somnium.* Louvain, 1608, 1610, 1613, and 1615; Strassburg, 1628; and Oxford, 1634. Xerox of 1610 edition, British Museum

Begins: Quae nec facta, nec futura sunt, dicam; stili, aut ingenii causa.
Non offendetur, quisquis ludum aut amoenitatem amat ...
Ends: Ego ex umbra, silentio et ipso Somno emergens, ad novam lucis usuram reversus sum.

This curious neo-Latin work is neither a play nor a poem but a fantastic 182-page prose "dream," spattered with some incidental scraps of verse (totalling 12 pages), the only noteworthy specimen of which is a 95-line ode to sensuality sung by Comus himself (see below, pp. 59–60). Its author, Erycius Puteanus (Eric or Henrik van der Putten, or Henri du Puy, 1575–1646), was born at Venloo, in Gelderland. He became professor of eloquence, first at Milan and later at Louvain, historiographer to the king of Spain, and governor of the Castle of Louvain. He was a very prolific author.

His description of Comus owes much to the Greek portrayal of that deity by Philostratus (cf. Co-11, above), which had been introduced to scholarly Western Europe in an edition by F. Morel in Paris in 1608, only a few months before Puteanus adopted and adapted the character for his own purposes. He also owes some debt to Cicero's *Somnium Scipionis* and to the *Symposium* and *Vera Historia* of Lucian (some of whose actual phrases are echoed in the first quotation above) and quotes extensively from Homer, Seneca, and Plutarch.

Ralph H. Singleton[25] has analysed in some detail the respects in which Puteanus has altered the picture of Comus that he found in Philostratus: Comus, instead of being asleep on his feet, is wakeful and talkative; his hair is curled and scented; his spear and torch have become torch and intoxicating cup; he is attended by wanton personifications, such as Luxus and Lascivia; most of his crew are wild beasts wearing human masks; his haunts are both dark woods and a stately palace; he is not only a reveller but a seducer, who sings a long ode of invitation to dancing and drinking, feasting and debauchery, addressed particularly to young men and young women. As over against his licentious hedonism, Puteanus and Tabuthius insist on the protective power of philosophy, since "all the Sirens have no power over a mind that is made strong by philosophy" (*nihil in robustam Sapientia mentem Sirenes omnes posse*).

From this summary, the resemblances between the *Comus* and Milton's masque are obvious. Even the former's song of incitation (translated below), not only resembles in its Anacreontic metre the prosody used by Milton in his song by the magician, lines 93–144 (iambic tetrameter, occasionally modulated with trochaic tetrameter catalectic), but also in actual phraseology again and again reproduced in Milton, as in the translation below, at lines 4–8 (*Condiscat ille ... terram gradu pavire*), 12–13 (*Nil turpe, nilque factu foedum putet ...*), 23–8 (*Delere fas severae naevos notasque mentis ...*), 28–30 (*Et tu veni Dione ...*), 53–6 (*Licebit et venusto rorantium impedire serto caput rosarum ...*). As Puteanus picked up the torch from Philostratus in the very year of the publication of the Greek *Eikones* in Paris in 1608, so Milton in turn would appear to have picked it up from Puteanus in 1634, the very year in which the Latin *Comus* was republished in Oxford.

But there are marked changes as we shift from the "dream" to the "mask." Comus, as described by Puteanus, is a completely hermaphrodite deity, with the anatomies of both his parents, Hermes and Aphrodite, while Milton's Comus is an immortal magician and male only, the son of Bacchus and Circe. While the Flemish scholar's Comus is the instigator of all manner of vices, he does not transform men to beasts; although wolves are present at his banquet masked as human beings. Neither is there any conflict of wills between this Comus and a virgin antagonist, such as constitutes the major framework of Milton's masque. The chief human participants

25"Milton's *Comus* and the *Comus* of Erycius Puteanus," *PMLA*, 1943, 949–57

are Puteanus and his friends, Aderba and Tabutius, all of whom are
men of letters and proof against the allurements of evil. The three
are differentiated in character: Puteanus himself is strongly moral
by nature but is curious as to the strange region to which he has
been brought;"amicus Aderba"is an *homme moyen sensuel*, who is
keen to share in the banquet of Comus, just for a little excitement;
while"amicissimus Tabutius"is a clear-eyed old philosopher, hot-
blooded in his distant youth, who has long since seen through all the
wiles of Comus and is ready to preach interminably against them.

The"Cimmerian banquet"is broken up, not through any intervention by aggressive rescuers but through the self-generated quarrels
of the crowd of guests, who proceed to disregard and scorn their host.
The very numbers of the banqueters have brought this about:"The
banquet hall becomes a forum, nay, a sea, in which the voices are
like waves stirred up by the tide, an uproarious likeness πολυφλοίσβοιο
θαλάσσης."

In a letter of dedication to Christopher van Etten, Puteanus explains his work:"It is a satire, a dream, a jest, a labour of night and
darkness, not displeasing, however, if you find pleasure in the ima-
ginary representation of things ... Since I deal with the morals of our
own time, I transfer the setting of my theatre to the Cimmerians and
the unknown regions of the night."

COMUS, OR THE CIMMERIAN BANQUET:
A DREAM

(The partial English translation given below is from the 2nd
(revised) edition of 1610, pp. 13, 15–17, 19–27, 29–31, 34–5,
45–9, 54–9, 193–4.)

I am going to tell of things that never happened and will never
happen; all this to show off my style or my wit. He will not
be offended, whosoever loves a jest or the delight that was
once a sister to Letters and the Muses. It is a DREAM, and
it is permissible for me to tell it, but also to ward off an in-
terpreter who wants to identify things that have actually happened or are destined to happen. Depart, and seek your sheaf
of grain somewhere else, a reward for your mendacity. Onei-
ros, the god of dreams, who shall have told a dream, he is a
god indeed. Why do you torment my words with a file and
adulterate innocent discourse with a fictitious meaning? ... If

there is any Cimmerian land, I was there; if there was any banquet, I shared in it. Whatever things you read are the labours
of a half-buried mind and the ghosts of black silence ...

It was the gloom of night and of sleep advanced in sweetness and at the same time wrapped in a dream. I was wandering through suburban hills along the shadowy highway of
the mind. A certain varied and vernal pleasantness had
enveloped the earth, having driven off the harshness of the
winter season, and when in the very leafy approach to a grove
I was thinking on the Dryads and was racking my brains as
I sought to write a poem to Silvanus, I almost walked into
a very deep cave, whose entrance a natural row of trees had
made, while venerable branches shadowed the threshold.
Next it, on the edge of a crystal spring, tables made of rods
and sods had been set, sprinkled with wreaths and the other
perquisites of dessert. The ground still damp with milk and
wine indicated that there had been a banquet. From the very
depths of the cave a sort of nuptial murmur and light were
issuing, so that it was quite evident that one of the nymphs
had been led into the marriage chamber to her new husband.
I was marvelling at this most chaste recess, perhaps filled with
the divinities of Venus and Cupid as Homer fabled in Ithaca,
when there seemed to emerge upon me from the confines of
light and darkness a form more august than human, itself
surely the image of all the Graces and Loves. The dress and
the countenance bespoke a hermaphrodite, for the sex was
from both Mercury and Venus: the rest of the adornments
could feminize a man and enhance the soft beauty of a woman.
Its head was adorned with roses and gems and a sort of halo
of light; its hair was arranged in neat curls; saturated with
perfumes, it had filled the air. But frequent sour burps and
symptoms of a stuffed stomach disfigured these attractions.
I easily conjectured this to be the Genius of banquets, for his
face was ruddy, with a sanguine temperament, and he seemed
to have put on gaiety over his whole body. Soft in bearing,
he was a youth in age, not yet mature, rosy with wine; traces
of banquets clung to his mouth, and he was picking his teeth
with a silver toothpick. Presently, grasping a torch with his
left hand and with his right hand a golden goblet filled with
the grace of dews and wine, he kept making libations again
and again. You would have said that the cave was being

violated by light and the fountain with a conflagration ... I began to be uncertain whether the mind of a philosopher dwelt in so adorned a body: Wisdom was once dressed in purple, but many among the philosophers not only despised elegant garments but rejected them. There followed behind him a boy with a ruddy face and proud adornments who represented Revelry. A maiden also, representing Wantonness, not to assign sex less to the servant but soft beyond the ultimate for her sex, enhanced the procession, carrying a castanet, variegated with gold, and a rattle and whatever an old-fashioned Muse would have found appropriate to her role. These attended the nod and step of their master and presently circling around him on the receipt of a signal they began to sing softly as if at a monument of Midas. The whole unaccustomed and almost divine melody had captivated me; and vanquished by its sweetness I was already nodding off to sleep, when lo, the Hermaphrodite presented his shaken torch to my eyes and drove away all the mist of sleep. Then indeed, holding motionless and stern the beams of his eyes which surpassed flame, gazing upon me, he said: "Do you not know that wakefulness is necessary at my rites? The sun has not yet set, and are you preparing to sleep? If you do not recognize my divinity, I am an immortal among mortals, of the breed of night, the Genius of Love and Happiness. I am the god Comus, for whom mortals make merry. I have extended my empire far and wide; and from the time when the Sybarites began to live in the whole earth, the traces of my people are everywhere And now my sacred rites, called *Phagesia* or *Phagesiposia* by scholars, are being undertaken by Revelry and Wantonness. In brief, the whole kingdom of pleasure is mine, nor is anyone happy except my worshipper. Do you see my costume? This befits me, and I have acquired the fruitfulness of both sexes, so that you may judge me to be able both to give and to receive sexual pleasure from both. Me, one and the same Spirit, men worship as a god and women as a goddess. Nor is this irrational for a divinity. I bear the sign of Venus (keeping silent about other matters of anatomy), born in Cyprus long ago with a bearded body and a woman's dress but with a man's sceptre and stature, so that I seemed both male and female. For that reason, Aristophanes called me *Aphroditos*. Though I was born of her, I cannot represent

my mother unless I am able to avail with both sexes. What
need of words? I shall represent both Aphrodite and Hermes
also, if he is my father. Therefore both boys and girls attend
me, men and women attend me, so that each sex may make
itself fertile by the one deity and delight its age. What is the
life of mortals without pleasure? It is a punishment. This
flee, if you have decided to be wise; or lay hold on it and
consider to what end a kindly nature bore you: Not to torture
your poor soul with harsh virtue or to drive it away from
fellowship with happiness: but that you may bless it with
comfort and water it and nourish it with all sweet affections
as the most tender flame of a brief life. Therefore, O mortal
man, let the year and the hour that carries off the gracious
day warn you not to hope for immortality!" As I endured
the boldness of so profane a speech with no patience, I was
detesting the unfavourable deity as an evil portent. Flight
was in my mind, and I prayed for wings; when suddenly,
surrounded and lifted up by a very dense cloud, I was carried
off by the breath and driving force of some wind or other –
a Zephyr or a Dream? You might think of Psyche being
carried to the very palace of Cupid. Even so, swathed in a
dense mist of air, in a moment of time I came to an unknown
realm and region of the night. Here were the people and the
shadowy walls of the Cimmerians, whom a dense smoke of
foul air oppresses in eternal darkness; from whose world the
Sun is an exile ... Scarcely had I touched the moist earth with
my feet, and suddenly the cloud that had been poured around
me split, and on one side a river, as if wearied in its course,
lay stretched out on the leafy edge of the neighborhood; on
the other side, the sky, besieged with darkness, made it dense
with a new poultice of night. I began to cast my eyes about
and in a withdrawn valley I perceived a certain marvel of a
structure – a vast, august roof, not notable for a hundred
columns only but for as many as could support the gods and
the sky if Atlas were dismissed. The threshold was distinguished by laurels and lamps, and it was declared by an
almost mad inscription that this was the palace of Comus.
Now my steps were drawing close to the entrance, when
someone or other came close behind me. I looked back at the
sound and lo, I saw present my dear friend Aderba, as if
drawn here by the same divinity. I hailed him and said: "Do

the manners of youth bring you also here, and are you not afraid of the magistrates and the police? Joking aside, a magic staff of the night and the place has joined us here. I had been hoping for a witness and partner of my fortune; you especially, whom I have made a friend in spirit and studies." He, having embraced me most closely, said: "Yours I shall be, my dear Puteanus, even when I shall not be here. But, by Hercules, I don't know whether I am here, or have been, altogether separated from the company of the living ..." I was already advancing my foot when from the nearest hollow and what was clearly the house of Diogenes a black dog ran out and attacked us. He pricked up his ears; he gaped with his nostrils; he threatened us with his mouth. His barking indeed, rendered with the most false semblance of a threefold shape, filled us with a new terror. It was clearly to be suspected that he was Cerberus. So, turning to Aderba, I said: "Now you may say that we are dead and that this is that famous hall of Orcus and is guarded by three-headed frenzy ..." A golden collar, studded with steel nails, surrounded his neck and on its edge was this inscription: "The dog Lycus, the brother of Cerberus, the darling of Comus, the guardian of his palace ..."

Meanwhile Comus enters, thronged by Revelry and Wantonness; and what pertains to describing the procession? The Hours were scattering the sweetest odours of Spring and all purple flowers. The Graces followed Love, as did Delights, Charms, and the other allurements of Gaiety. Laughter and Jests followed Pleasure. With Satiety was her sister Temperance, with flowing hair and the face of the rosy Dawn. In brief, the parade expressed the whole of Bacchus, for next came Madness, Frenzy, Quarrels, Insults, Fights; then Vomiting, Indigestion, Idleness, Sudden Death and intestate Old Age. But among these disgraceful figures, some were eminent in dignity: the priests of the banquet, the tribunes of pleasures. At the end of the parade were gluttons, guzzlers, bellygods and prodigals, and a crowd of epicures. There were some who played the role of Sardanapalus, Lucullus and Heliogabalus, and, lest a philosopher be lacking, one who represented Epicurus ... Aderba was following me and when he saw some faces stiff with impudence and many wearing masks, "What is this?" he whispered in my ear, "Does wantonness now lack limbs? And are mortals beginning to cover their faces, with

a loss of shame? For here there are more masks than men."
I raised my eyes, and disturbed by the strangeness of the
matter, I tugged at the lapel of an old man who stood by.
"Tell me, father," said I, "Is one's face unpropitious to these
rites? Ought it to be covered?" He laughing said, "You see
mountain creatures, and savageness is restrained by these
bonds of face and teeth. Those whom you think are men are
really wolves, monsters from Daunia or Gaetulia, with dangerous bite. Shall I speak further? It is fine to live under a
mask, to have a false forehead so that the soul may be hidden, to put on a false pretence, so that your character may be
commended. Yet Comus has marked out his priests with dis-
guises of this sort and has wished to have perpetual festivals
in his palace." Listening to this courteous discourse, we proceed to the opening of the threshold facing us ...

   With a great shout, the boys announced that Comus had
taken his place at table and that the guests were expected.
Without delay, all that crowd of walkers and talkers slipped
away, and soon the place was so deserted that the porch
seemed drained not only of men but also of letters themselves. Therefore Aderba, seizing my hand, said: "Why do we
stand here? So great a crowd has gone in without peril. At
least, if your stomach is queasy, we shall again have sport for
our eyes and form our judgement of the very festival that I
hear is being celebrated." "I don't refuse," said I. "Go ahead,
and I follow." And with a password, like the rest of the
crowd, we too were admitted to the huge banquet. Comus
had taken his place, apart from the rest, surrounded by more
than Asiatic luxury. His array showed that he was some sort
of divinity. Then every rank, age and sex had crowded the
rest of the tables in a long seating order. Ceres herself, with
loins girt up, and Bacchus toiled to supply their wants. What
is the use of describing the proudest delicacies with inadequate words? The banquet was quite in keeping with the
lordliness of the house. For although the mosaic pavement
displayed various emblems, and although the glittering
panelled ceiling shone with pictures wrought with gold, yet
the banquet surpassed all this in art, cost and aspiration. But
how great was the uproar, and how everything was like
madness! ...

   Behold, I saw an old man with a still ruddy face, gazing at

whom I said: "Do I see you, my most excellent and most dear
friend, Tabutius? Or do my eyes deceive me in this shadow-
show of things?" He, speaking without constraint, said: "You
indeed see me, beset with years, brought hither from North
Italy itself." I replied in my turn: "And at such an age as
yours, does sleep bring you here on his wings?" "Yes," said
Tabutius, "And now as if I had changed my place, not my
age, I seize by strict thought the likeness of my first youth."
Meanwhile, Aderba had drawn near; and clasping his arms
around his neck as he spoke, with a very tender embrace he
gave him a kiss of greeting. Then indeed Tabutius, leading us
beneath the last arch of the vaulted banquet-room, began to
speak thus:

"This Cimmerian Comus is no stranger to me. In my body
also the blood used to be hot. I have given something to the
sport of a good age and of desire. We have had Spring, not
without flowers. Nor is it granted to every hour to grow flowers. And so, having given up trivialities, I have composed
myself for serious things, for quiet and for wisdom; and the
years have confirmed my resolution. I gaze on this type of
dissolute and corrupt living, that I may condemn it and laugh
at it. Think of me as a sort of Ulysses; all the Sirens cannot
avail against a mind that is stalwart in philosophy. Nay more,
think of me as Democritus, denouncing the most degraded
morals of the times by at least the silent censure of a smile.
It is fitting for you to be strangers to these rites, and especially
to these regions, and not to frequent them even in thought.
Comus himself is the instigator of vices; he captures souls
with delights in order to weaken them. Those whom you see
as Revelry and Wantonness are ruin itself; and whatever is
honourable in any man, they extinguish. And what of the
rest of the crowd, melting away in weakness? They are crimes
and a raging Autumn wind that you cannot inhale without
disease or the risk of a disease. Let not their allurements deceive you; they are frauds and corruptions; there is no love
here, but the rouge of deceit; they are not friends but tyrants.
Do you see those faces, charming with smile and allurement?
They hide spite and malice. Here you are living in another
world and outside the world of men. A forged humanity
deceives the incautious. What more shall I say? Here you
may not accept a benefit without loss. Comus has decided to

exile Honour and Honesty; he has bestowed his citizenship
on Deceit and Fraud ..."

Comus, in order that with new enticements he might spur
on a crowd already verging on frenzy, heaped rugs into a
pile, sat upright upon them, and spread out his gesticulating
fingers, intending to sing to the lyre. Then, with the skilled
genius of fingers he began to pluck the strings; nay more, he
aroused the melody of chords along with matched and mellifluous song:

He who beats with heart aflame
Upon our doors will give the name
Phagesia to our noble rites;
Let his throat now know delights
5   Of honey, let his breast now arm
Itself with Bacchus' gentle charm.
Let him learn to beat the ground,
Dancing with a gleeful bound.
Watchman of the yellow lamp,
10   Worshipper whose breath is damp,
Priest of night and priest of wine,
Let him no stain of wrong assign
To aught beneath Night's shadowy cowl.
What can be evil there, or foul?
15   Why are we slow in Bacchus' court?
Why does not Pleasure rage in sport,
Sister of Venus, Bacchus too?
Come, Bacchus, Comus waits for you.
His vigorous mates are all aroused.
20   Come, it is pleasant to be soused.
Come, comrades, let it be your task
To gulp Falernian by the cask,
For it is right to wipe away
The moles and wrinkles that betray
25   The sour mind, the brow severe,
With ladles full of liquid cheer,
With goblet, flagon, flask and cup.
And thou, O Venus, come to sup,
Inciting laughter, smile and jest,
30   These wanton leaders of the rest

In bringing on the rage of lust
That ends the lover's heady gust.
Come, pressing from thy bosom bright
The milky dew of love's delight.

35   Begone, sad cares! For here ye see
The rites of soft Tranquillity.
Here pretty Graces come to prove,
All the allurements of our love,
Of wantonings and longing blisses,

40   Of struggles that are eased by kisses,
Tender embracings, eager rites
Made keen by tender little bites.
Now boys to youths respond again
And girls are gentle to young men.

45   Fervour is here and here is youth,
And all the joys of love, forsooth.
I, Comus, father of all joy,
Am here my chorus to deploy.
Great arbiter of elegance,

50   I softly sway your joyous dance.
To perish softly is your fate
By alcoholic opiate.
Who is not glad to shade his brow
With ivies that the gods endow

55   And wear a circlet on his head
Of buds and dewy roses spread?
So crowned, he will with joy be able
To snore at last beneath the table,
After a night of lustful mirth

60   And dancing on the blossom'd earth
With those whose eyes are filled with fire
And drunken arteries with desire.
Thus every rank with wine is laden,
Every youth and every maiden,

65   Breathing love with tipsy breath
To die in a delicious death.

The whole banquet seemed to sway with the motion and the
theme of the harp-player, and to follow the harmony that fled
into the air with wandering sense: tables, platters, cups and
the very busts and statues around us seemed to live and act

like men; while the torches and lamps, beaten on by the air-waves, swayed lasciviously with trembling flames ...

Angers had flared up and were threatening some final ruin. The god, therefore, since he saw himself neglected and even scorned, disappeared, along with Revelry and Wantonness. Therefore everything was mixed and confused all the more; and as if arms were lacking to their frenzy, they turned to their torches and lamps as weapons, and whatever light there had been was put out in the fighting. Then Night, the Shades, and the whole black throng that had remained in the vestibule of the palace, rushed in; and whatever there had been among the Cimmerians, ceased to exist. I, emerging from shade, silence and sleep itself, returned to a new usufruct of light.

Co-27 (English)

JOHN FLETCHER. *The Faithful Shepherdess*. London, 1609

Begins: CLORIN
    Hail, holy earth, whose cold arms do embrace
    The truest man that ever fed his flocks ...
Ends: CLORIN
                And to thee
    All my master's love be free.

There is a superficial resemblance between Milton's *Comus* and Fletcher's *Faithful Shepherdess,* in that both present lust running loose in a gloomy forest by night; but in the latter play, most of the would-be seducers are women. Fletcher's nearest female equivalent of Milton's male Comus is the nymphomaniac Cloe, who tries in vain to seduce first Thenot and then Daphnis, but finally meets answering passion in Alexis. Only slightly less loose-moralled than Cloe is Amarillis, who is willing to go to any lengths in order to seduce Perigot. Next milder in the scale of free love is Clorin, the allegedly constant mourner of her dead lover; but she scares Thenot out of his sentimental love-fit by making advances to him. Of the four women, only Amoret, the "faithful shepherdess," remains normal and constant throughout the vicissitudes of night and evil enchantment.

Fletcher's pastoral drama had been revived for presentation at

the court of Charles I on Twelfth Night in 1633–4 and also for
Black Friars Theatre in the same year; and was reprinted in its third
quarto. It could hardly have helped being in Milton's consciousness
while he was writing *Comus*.

See also W.E. Axon, "Milton's 'Comus' and Fletcher's 'Faithful
Shepherdess' compared," *Manchester Quarterly*, VIII (1882), 285–95.

The significance of Fletcher in the development of English pastoralism is suggested by John Arthos: "In adapting Guarini, who has
much of the wit and passion and obscenity that made the strength
of plays written after *Aminta*, he [i.e. Fletcher] is diverging from
the kind of pastoral for which Spenser set the tone in England"(*A
Masque Presented at Ludlow-Castle*, 1954, p. 11). One should go on
to read Arthos's exposition (pp. 12–15) of the way in which Milton's
Comus turns aside to a new type of innocence, as known to the
sophisticated philosophers of the court. There is a direct line of
descent from Plato, Vergil, Poliziano, and Tasso, mediated also in
atmosphere through Guarini's *Pastor Fido* and Fletcher's *Faithful
Shepherdess* (the pure "pastoral" type of play in Polonius' enumera-
tion in *Hamlet*, II, ii, 417) and Shakespeare's *A Midsummer Night's
Dream* and *As You Like It* (the "pastoral-comical" in the same list).

Co-28 (English)

BEN JONSON. *Pleasure Reconciled to Vertue. A Masque*. Played before
James I, 1619. First printed, London, 1640

Begins: SONG. THE CREW OF COMUS
            Roome, roome, make roome for the bouncing belly,
            first father of Sauce & deviser of gelly ...
Ends: SONG. MERCURY AND CHORUS
            There, there is vertues seat.
            Strive to keepe hir your owne,
            'tis only she, can make you great,
            though place, here, make you knowne.

The theme of this masque is a reconciliation of the personified ab-
stractions, Pleasure and Virtue, celebrated by dances at the foot of
Mount Atlas by twelve male maskers and twelve ladies (the daughters of Hesperus). Before this can happen, however, the grosser
pleasures represented by drunken Comus and his crew are driven
away by Hercules; and a second "antimasque," composed of pyg-

mies, does not wait long to endure his stern displeasure. Mercury on behalf of his grandfather, Atlas, crowns Hercules with a garland of poplar leaves. To entertain him, and to celebrate her reconciliation with Pleasure, Virtue "brings forth twelve princes [who] have byn bred in this rough *Mountaine*, and neere *Atlas* head, the *hill* of *knowledge*," while Hesperides are brought from "faire Beuties garden" to dance with them. Daedalus leads them in three songs about the labyrinths of love and beauty; and a closing song by Mercury warns them all that Virtue has her right of birth in heaven. In conclusion, "They daunce their last Daunce and returne into the Scene: which closeth, and is a Mountaine againe, as before."

The Comus of this masque has his abode at the foot of Atlas in a grove of ivy "out of which, to a wild music of cymbals, flutes and tabors, is brought forth Comus, the god of cheer, or the belly, riding in triumph, his head crowned with roses and other flowers; his hair curled: They that wait upon him crowned with Ivy, their Javelins done about with it." His kinship with the seductive magician of Milton's *Comus* is very remote. Jonson's Comus is a mute glutton, not a lecherous and talkative wizard, and his role is negligible. Those who criticize Milton for lack of plot will find that Jonson's masque has far less. If Jonson's work is a standard type of this genre, Milton will be found to have woven a much subtler and more complicated web of action. With Jonson, for example, the disposal of Comus and his revellers is a summary matter. A stern speech by Hercules, denouncing their gluttony, ends:

> But here must be no shelter, nor no shroud
> for such: Sinck Grove, or vanish into clowd.

And the stage directions then read: "After this, the whole Grove vanisheth." Hercules does not even have to wave his omnipotent club.

While E.M.W. Tillyard, in *Studies in Milton* (1951), refers (p. 95) to this masque as the one "to which Milton owed most," John G. Demaray, in *Milton and the Masque Tradition* (1968), p. 166, points out that, while Jonson's masque is similar to Milton's in abstract theme, *Pleasure Reconciled to Vertue* was utterly different in character and treatment, was performed twelve years before Henry Lawes entered the King's Music, and was not published until 1640, six years after the writing and staging of *Comus*. G.W. Whiting, in *Milton and This Pendant World* (1958), pp. 3–4, also dismisses any influences as "quite negligible."

Co-29 (English)

WILLIAM BROWNE. *The Inner-Temple Masque*. Produced 1620. First published in *Works*, London, 1772. Mi: Harvard

Begins: SIREN
    Steere hither, steere, your wingèd pines,
    All beaten mariners ...
  Ends: SONG
    But since he calles away, and time will soon repent,
    He staid no longer here, but ran to be more idly spent.

A masque portraying the arrival of Ulysses in Aeaea and his amorously flattering reception by Circe and her sirens. When Circe first appears, she is followed by "two with harts' heads and bodies ... two like wolves ... two like baboons, and Grillus (of whom Plutarch writes ...) in the shape of a hog." The antimasque is presented by these grossly metamorphosed Greeks, transformed by the power of Circe's potions. The masque ends with Circe restoring Ulysses' "knights," who dance graceful measures severally or with Circe's "ladies" as partners. Songs are interwoven with the choral dances and close the performance. A detailed analysis of this masque may be found in John G. Demaray,[26] who points out that Circe is here a sympathetic character, whose alleged good intentions are meekly accepted by a simple-minded Ulysses. In the whole Epicurean work, there is no real conflict between virtue and vice; in fact, the moral atmosphere is that into which Milton's *Comus* would dissolve if the Lady were as sexually accommodating as some of Milton's twentieth-century critics appear to wish.

Co-30 (Latin)

WILLIAM DRURY. *Aluredus, sive Alfredus*. Douai, 1620. Xe: British Museum

Begins: ST CUTHBERTUS (prologuizes)
    Quod cura superos generis humani pio

26 *Milton and the Masque Tradition* (Cambridge, Mass., 1968), pp. 85–7

Solicitet affectu, et ministrantes Deo ...
Ends: ST CUTHBERTUS (epiloguizes)
Aderit triumphans contra Avernales minas.
Audete. Sero veniet, at certo salus.

Written at Douai by an English Jesuit for presentation by students
at the English college there, this long Latin drama bears some very
superficial resemblance to *Comus*. The analogy was first pointed out
by Edward A. Hall,[27] who itemized some of the similarities: (a) The
spirit of St Cuthbert (like Milton's "attendant Spirit") descends to
announce by way of prologue that he has been sent from Heaven to
watch over the English, especially King Alfred the Great and his
family; (b) Prince Edward, Alfred's son, searching in a forest for his
lost sister Elfreda, learns of her whereabouts and plight by question-
ing an echo; (c) Elfreda is captured in the woods by Danish soldiers,
two of whose officers, Gormo and Osbern, fight each other for the
privilege of raping her; (d) the brother Edward enters with drawn
sword and rescues her. It must be objected, however, that Elfreda
plays a small and totally unessential part in a drama with five acts
and seventy-three scenes, in all of which we find no magic transfor-
mations, no magic antidotes, no music, and no Platonic philosophiz-
ing. The main plots are utterly dissimilar.

Co-31 (English)

GEORGE SANDYS. "Upon the Fourteenth Book of Ovids Metamorphosis." In *Ovids Metamorphosis Englished, Mythologized, and Represented
in Figures*. London, 1640 (second edition)

Begins: Glaucus, rejected by Scylla, sollicits the arts of Circe ...
Ends: ... that they never might be thought to have been mortall.

The moral allegory read into the Circe story by Milton's whole generation was spelled out by George Sandys (1578–1644), Oxford
graduate and treasurer of the Virginia Company, in an extensive
moralistic commentary, printed along with his translation of Ovid
published in 1621–6. Significant extracts are given below:

27"*Comus, Old Wives' Tale* and Drury's *Aluredus*," pp. 140–44 in *The
Manly Anniversary Studies in Language and Literature* (Chicago, 1928)

THE ALLEGORY OF CIRCE AND SCYLLA

Glaucus, rejected by Scylla, sollicits the arts of Circe; daughter to the Sun and Persis, sister to Aeta, and Aunt to Medea; who having poysoned her husband Scythus king of Sarmatia, assumed that government: but shortly after expelled for her tyranny; she fled with a few of her women into Italy; seating her selfe on a little Iland in the Tyrrhen sea, now joyned to the continent, and called at this day by her name. A famous inchantresse; and skilfull in all magicall simples; who lustfull by nature, or the revenge of Venus, for her fathers detecting her adultery, endeavours to divert the affections of Glaucus to her selfe from Scylla. But failing, and full of indignation, infects the bay, by the Nymph frequented, with her charmed poysons; wherein Scylla bathing contracts that monstrous deformity; her loynes invironed with howling Wolves and barking dogs, now a part of her body; destroying all that came neere her. Scylla represents a Virgin; who as long as chast in thought, and in body unspotted, appears of an excellent beauty, attracting all eyes upon her, and wounding the Gods themselves with affection. But once polluted with the sorceries of Circe; that is, having rendred her maiden honour to be deflowred with bewitching pleasure, she is transformed to an horrid monster. And not so onely, but endeavours to shipwrack others (such is the envy of infamous women) upon those ruining rocks, and make them share in the same calamities. That the upper part of her body, is feigned to retaine a humane figure, and the lower to be bestiall; intimates how man, a divine creature, endued with wisdome and intelligence, in whose superiour parts, as in a high tower, that immortall spirit resideth, who onely of all that hath life erects his lookes unto heaven, can never so degenerate into a beast, as when he giveth himselfe over to the low delights of those baser parts of the body, Dogs and Wolves, the blinde and salvage fury of concupiscence ... How Circe is said to be the daughter of Sol and Persis, in that lust proceeds from heat and moisture, which naturally incites to luxury; and getting the dominion, deformes our souls with all bestiall vices; alluring some to inordinate Venus; others to anger, crueltie, and every excess of passion; the Swine, the Lions, and the Wolves, produced by her sensual charmes; which are not to be resisted, but by

the divine assistance, Moly, the gift of Mercury, which signifies temperance.

Co-32 (Italian)

GIOVANNI BATTISTA MARINO. *L'Adone*. Paris, 1623. Reprinted unchanged, ed. by Gustavo Balsamo-Crivelli, Torino and elsewhere, 1922

Begins: Io chiamo te, per cui si volge e move
            La piu benigna e mansueta sfera ...
  Ends: Tornaro a Stige le tartaree genti,
            L'altre a le stelle, e l'altre a gli elementi.

This huge work, dedicated on the title-page to Louis XIII of France
and in a long prefatory letter to his Italian mother, Marie dei Medici,
consists of 40,984 saccharine lines. Each of its twenty cantos is pre-
faced with an elaborate explanation of its allegory, together with a
four-line verse "argument." Both in style and in architecture, Marino
is a master of far-fetched artificiality. The deities of the Graeco-
Roman world are equated with the personages and virtues (or vices)
of Christian theology, and these are often further explained in terms
of an amorous psychology or a fluent astrology. With this diffuse
allegorical infrastructure, all things are possible – even the visit of
the living Adonis to heaven: "That Adonis soars to heaven under the
escort of Mercury and Venus means that with the favorable 'constellation' of these two planets the human intellect can rise to the loftiest
speculations, even of celestial things."

In launching his plot, Marino goes far beyond the purely accidental arrow-wound in Ovid (*Metamorphoses*, x, 525). Thus his
small boy-god, Cupid (Amore), having been spanked by his mother,
Venus, determines on revenge. From Vulcan he secures an arrow that
can pierce even Venus; from Neptune he obtains a storm that drives
Adonis from Arabia to Cyprus. Cupid, simulating an accident, then
pierces Venus with his arrow, and she is overwhelmed with love for
Adonis.

The poem is padded out with many subordinate narratives, e.g., in
Canto II the shepherd Clizio tells Adonis the story of the judgment
of Paris; in Canto III, Cupid tells Adonis the story of Cupid and
Psyche; and in Canto XIX, 2448 lines are devoted to the stories of
unfortunate lovers.

Co-33 (Italian)

OTTAVIO TRONSARELLI. *La Catena d' Adone. Favola Boschereccia.*
Rome, 1626. Xe: British Museum

Begins: APOLLO
De' puri campi Regnator lucente
Abbandono del Ciel la via serena ...
Ends: TUTTI
Giunge Adone à goder la Dea d'Amore,
Ch' arde di lieto zelo,
Chi dopo i falli fa ritorno al Cielo.

In the same tradition as the plays *Aminta* (see Co-18) and *Pastor Fido* (see Co-20) is the early baroque opera, *The Chain of Adonis*. A summary of the plot will make this clear. The youth Adonis, fleeing from the jealous anger of Vulcan, enters a rough tract of forest that is the abode of the sorceress, Falsirena. Seeking to seduce him, she turns the forest into a beautiful garden, with a golden palace; assails him with ardent advances; and makes him her prisoner with an invisible magic chain of gold. He is proof against all her charms, however, and she finds by divination that her successful rival is Venus. With her enchantments, she then assumes the form of Venus, and Adonis is ready to fall into the arms of what he assumes to be his true love. Venus herself then appears, exposes the fraud, and ties Falsirena to a crag with the magic chain. Music for the opera was supplied by the composer, Domenico Mazzocchi. There are two choruses, one of nymphs and one of shepherds, and a troupe of ballet-dancers. Adonis, when lost in the woods and uncertain of his fate, sings a long solo in which the answers that he desires are sung in reply by Echo. There are five acts and sixteen scenes, each preceded by a prose "argument," while a final "Allegory" explains (for our edification) that Adonis exemplifies Man, who falls into error when he is remote from God but is finally restored by divine aid and shares in the delights of heaven.

Co-34 (English)

BEN JONSON. *Chloridia: Rites to Chloris and her Nymphs.* London,
1630

Begins: ZEPHYRUS

  Come forth, come forth, the gentle Spring,

  And carry the glad newes, I bring ...

Ends: CHORUS

  The ornament of Bowres;

  The top of Par-amours!

The parts of Chloris and her nymphs are taken by the Queen of England, Henrietta Maria, and her ladies, in a masque at court to entertain her husband, King Charles I. Out of a cloud descends "a plumpe Boy," Zephyrus, who sets the scene for the goddess of flowers. Antimasque dancers intrude: a "Dwarfe-Post from Hell" (who announces that Cupid, to spite his mother Venus, has mobilized hell so as to make life miserable, especially for Chloris, queen of the flowers), then Cupid and evil affections, the Queen's dwarf and six devils, the nymph Tempest, winds, lightnings, thunder, rain, and snow. Juno intervenes to drive them out, and Chloris and her nymphs dance the entry of the grand-masque. Cupid sues for peace, Fame proclaims the glory of Chloris, and the evening ends with the masquer-nymphs dancing with "the Lords." Lady Penelope Egerton, elder sister to the children in *Comus*, was one of the nymphs on this occasion. The lament of the shepherd, Aeglamour, over his drowned sweetheart, Earine, in Jonson's uncompleted pastoral play, *The Sad Shepherd* (printed 1641), is too much broken up amongst the several scenes, and too incoherent in its frenzy, to count as an elegy in itself.

Co-35 (English)

BEN JONSON. *Loues Triumph through Callipolis.* London, 1630

Begins: EUPHEMUS descends singing

  Joy, ioy to mortals, the reioycing fires

  Of gladnes, smile in your dilated hearts! ...

Ends: VENUS

  Need onely speake their names: Those them will glorify.

  MARY, and CHARLES, CHARLES, with his MARY, named are,

  And all the rest of Loues, or Princes famed are.

A disorderly pantomime begins this entertainment with an anti-masque of depraved lovers in "a distracted *comoedy of Loue*, express-

ing their confus'd affections in the Scenicall persons, and habits, of
the foure prime *European* nations." The theme of the masque is then
stated by a messenger from heaven, Euphemus, who, like the attendant in Comus,"descends," singing. A chorus, with censers, next
walks about to make lustration of the place after the departure of
the foul intruders. The main masque presents a triumphant procession, consisting of fifteen true lovers, with his Majesty, Charles I, in
the centre. Finally, Venus herself descends from heaven in a cloud
and "is seene sitting on a throane."

Co-36 (English)

AURELIAN TOWNSHEND. *Tempe Restored. A Masque.* London, 1631.
Xe: British Museum

Begins: THE FUGITIVE FAVORITE
          Was I a Lyon, that am now afraid!
          I fear no danger; nor I feare no Death ...
Ends: VALEDICTION
          Should you, these Loanes of Loue forsake
          The Gods themselves, such Sommes would take
          And pay us, use.

This masque, like Jonson's *Pleasure Reconciled to Vertue* (Co-28),
and Milton's *Comus,* seeks edifyingly (though spectacularly) to em-
phasize the transcendent importance of virtue. In its slender plot, a
young gentleman, formerly transformed by Circe into a lion and then
made man again, seeks refuge at the court of Charles I; and Circe,
who pursues him there, voluntarily surrenders her wand of enchantment to Minerva. The moral is set forth in terms that might be commended to critics of Milton's Lady:

> That divine *Beauty* accompan'ed with a troope of Stars of a
> happy Constellation ioyning with Heiroicke vertue should
> dissolue the inchantments, and *Circe* voluntarily deliver her
> golden rod to *Minerva,* is meant that a divine Beame comming
> from aboue, with a good inclination, and a perfect habit of
> vertue made, by the *Harmony* of the Irascible and concupis-
> cible parts obedient to the rationall and highest part of the
> soule. Making man onely a mind vsing the body and affections

as instruments; which being his true perfection, brings him to all the happinesse which can be inioyed heere below.

Professor John G. Demaray's *Milton and the Masque Tradition* (Harvard University Press, 1968) has demonstrated the absolute importance of *Tempe Restored* in the shaping of Milton's *Comus*. Not least enlightening is his revelation that five of the Egerton children – Penelope, Catherine, Alice, John, and Thomas – were seasoned troupers in masques at court. Lady Penelope had performed in *Chloridia*, Lady Catherine and Lady Alice in *Tempe Restored*, and Masters John and Thomas in *Coelum Britannicum*. Henry Lawes, the family music teacher, had been part of the music production staff and a performer in all three of these masques. The children's father, the Earl of Bridgewater, having been commissioned in 1631 to the office of Lord President of Wales, was scheduled for installation at Ludlow Castle on 29 September 1634; and Mr Demaray believes that the Earl will early have asked Lawes to prepare a brand new masque, with leading roles for his boys and girls, to be performed at the time of his installation. The beast-headed costumes used for Circe's rout in *Tempe Restored* could be borrowed from the Revels storeroom for the occasion. If, as Demaray surmises, Lady Penelope (the eldest sister) was chosen for the role of Sabrina, then four of the five children will have been used. Lawes himself played the part of the Attendant Spirit.

Demaray suggests what is virtually another type of analogue for Milton's *Comus*, namely, a Jonsonian masque, like *Hymenaei* (1606), which, while quite different in episode, proceeds from an initial condition of lawless immorality to a final state of virtue, dominated by reason, as the proper condition of man. In this final supremacy of virtue, there comes the perfect reconciliation of heaven and earth. The main masque presented persons of virtue and the antimasque the incarnations of vices; and the triumph of the former constituted the ultimate objective of the whole work. A prologue, antimasque, and main masque spectacles, with or without speeches, were always followed by a *deus ex machina* solution, this in turn by a main masque dance (figured and ballroom) to signify the triumph of virtue, and finally by an epilogue. The whole structure of the Stuart court masque was framed by the spectator arts of scenery and ballet. For the past two hundred years, critics of *Comus*, wholly ignorant of its complex but specific genre, have been finding fault with it because it failed to fulfil some other pattern of their choice.

The structure just cited was common to all six of the court masques in which Henry Lawes took part before he teamed up with John Milton to plan and produce *Comus*, namely, Jonson's *Loves Triumph through Callipolis* (1631) and *Chloridia* (1631), Aurelian Townshend's *Albion's Triumph* (1632) and *Tempe Restored* (1632), James Shirley's *The Triumph of Peace* (1634), and Thomas Carew's *Coelum Britannicum* (1634).

Co-37 (English)

THOMAS CAREW. *Coelum Britannicum. A Masque at White-Hall in the Banqueting-House on Shrove-Tuesday-Night, the 18th of February, 1633*. London, 1634. Available also in Rhodes Dunlap's edition of Carew (Oxford University Press)

Begins: MERCURY
          From the high Senate of the gods, to You
          Bright glorious Twins of Love and Majesty ...
   Ends: CHORUS
          Propitious Starres shall crowne each birth,
          Whilst you rule them, and they the Earth.

This performance begins, like *Comus*, with the descent of a heavenly messenger, in this case Mercury, whose message is that the very Olympians have been shamed into virtue by the high moral standards of the court of Charles I and his queen. Momus interrupts the proceedings with cynical impertinence, and no fewer than seven antimasques are summoned up, chiefly by Mercury, before Momus suddenly retires (at line 842). The antimasques are those of (1) loathsome monsters, (2) retrograde stars, (3) the vices, (4) country folk, called up by Plutus, (5) gypsies, called up by Poenia, (6) a battle, called up by Tyche, and (7) the five senses, called up by Hedone. Mercury adds on eighth antimasque of the ancient Picts, Scots, and Irish, by way of contrast to the entry dance of "the Masquers, richly attired like ancient Heroes," preceded by "a troope of young Lords and Noblemens Sonnes" (including Lord Brackley and Mr Thomas Egerton, who next year played the parts of the two brothers in *Comus*). After songs by a chorus and symbolical figures, the masquers dance their main dance; then come more songs; then the masquers (who include the King) dance the Revels with the Ladies "a great part of the night"; then follow more songs and a final dance by the masquers. The progressive triumph of virtue over vice, which is the standard theme of almost every court masque, is climaxed in the song of Eternity:

> Brave Spirits, whose adventrous feet
>   Have to the Mountaines top aspir'd,
> Where faire Desert, and Honour meet,
>   Here, from the toyling Presse retir'd,
> Secure from all disturbing Evill,
> For ever in my Temple revell.

In this masque, Inigo Jones outdoes himself in the devising of spectacular effects, but there is no "hinge" of plot, such as Ben Jonson desired and Milton employed in *Comus*. Carew studied at Merton College, Oxford, and graduated BA in 1612.

Carew based the text of his masque on Giordano Bruno's philosophical dialogue, *Spaccio de la Bestia Trionfante* (1584), itself derived from Lucian. Some authorities believe that Henry Lawes supplied the music.

Co-38 (English)

THOMAS RANDOLPH.   *The Muses' Looking-Glass.* Oxford, posthumously, 1638

Begins: MISTRESS FLOWERDEW
>   See, brother, how the wicked throng and crowd
>   To works of vanity! Not a nook or corner ...
Ends: ROSCIUS
>   We do not doubt but each one now that's here,
>   That has a fair soul and a beauteous face,
>   Will visit oft the Muses' Looking-Glass.

Thomas Randolph (1605–1635) entered Trinity College, Cambridge University, in July 1624, seven months before Milton was enrolled at Christ's. He wrote a number of plays and died young. His satiric, pseudo-dramatic comedy, *The Muses' Looking-Glass*, was written at some time in the period 1632–4 and has been referred to as "a provocative source" of *Comus*. A careful reading of the play, however,

finds very little ground for such a conclusion. The scene is a theatre
where two Puritans, Bird, the Featherman, and Mistress Flowerdew,
are shown a succession of vices, presented in pairs as the extremes on
either side of a virtue (e.g., Asotus the prodigal and Aneleutherus
the miser, as extremes of true liberality). All see themselves as they
are, in the Muses's looking-glass (i.e., the theatre) and are confounded. In Act v, Mediocrity (the *aurea mediocritas* of Horace) expounds true virtue in terms of temperate proportion, and there follows "The Masque, wherein all the Virtues dance together." The two
Puritans are highly edified and Mistress Flowerdew exclaims:

> Most blessed looking-glass
> That didst instruct my blinded eyes today!
> I might have gone to hell the narrow way!

Co-39 (English)

JOHN MILTON. *An Apology for Smectymnuus.* London, 1642

AN AUTOBIOGRAPHICAL STATEMENT by Milton, excerpted from
this work, will be found hereunder.[28] In it he tells of the profound
enthusiasm that he had known in his youth for Dante (cf. Co-13) and
Petrarch (cf. Co-14), for the chaste ideals of knighthood in the romances,
and for the exaltation of virtue by Plato (cf. Co-5 and Co-6)

> ... and above them all, I preferr'd the two famous renowners
> of *Beatrice* and *Laura,* who never write but honour of them to
> whom they devote their verse, displaying sublime and pure
> thoughts, without transgression ... Next, (for heare me out
> now, Readers,) that I may tell ye wether my younger feet
> wander'd; I betook me among those lofty Fables and
> Romances, which recount in solemn canto's the deeds of
> Knighthood founded by our victorious kings, & from hence
> had in renowne over all Christendome. There I read it in the
> oath of every Knight, that he should defend to the expense
> of his best blood, or of his life, the honour and chastity of
> Virgin or Matron. From whence even then I learnt what a

28 For a fuller text of this passage, the reader is referred to the Columbia
Milton, Vol. III, pt. i, pp. 302–6, or to the Yale University Press's
Complete Prose Works of John Milton, ed. Don Wolfe and others.

noble vertue chastity sure must be, to the defence of which
so many worthies, by such a deare adventure of themselves,
had sworne ... Thus, from the Laureat fraternity of Poets,
riper yeares, and the ceaseless round of study and reading
led me to the shady spaces of philosophy, but chiefly to the
divine volumes of *Plato* and his equall *Xenophon*. Where if I
should tell ye what I learnt of chastity and love, I meane that
which is truly so, whose charming cup is only vertue which
she bears in her hand to those who are worthy. The rest are
cheated with a thick intoxicating poison, which a certain
Sorceresse, the abuser of loves name, carries about; and how
the first and chiefest office of love, begins and ends in the
soule, producing those happy twins of her divine generation,
knowledge and vertue ...

❧ PART II: Analogues of *A Monody* (*Lycidas*, 1638)

Ly-1 (Greek)

THEOCRITUS. *Idyll I, Daphnis*. About 275 B.C. From *Bucolici Graeci*, ed. Udalricus de Wilamowitz-Moellendorff, Oxford, 1905

Begins: (THYRSIS)
'Ἁδύ τι τὸ ψιθύρισμα καὶ ἁ πίτυς, αἰπόλε, τήνα
ἁ ποτὶ ταῖς παγαῖσι μελίσδεται, ἁδὺ δὲ καὶ τύ ...
Ends: (GOATHERD)
ὧδ' ἴθι Κισσαίθα, τὺ δ' ἀμελγέ νιν. αἱ δὲ χίμαιραι
οὐ μὴ σκιρτασεῖτε, μὴ ὁ τράγος ὕμμιν ἀναστῆι.

Theocritus was probably born in the majestic Sicilian city of Syracuse, but spent most of his life in the gracious little Aegean island of Cos and part of it in megalopolitan Alexandria. Of his 28 major poems, the so-called "Idylls," only some eleven (Nos. I, III–XI, and perhaps XXI) may be classed as "pastorals," with their settings among the shepherds and neatherds of his native Sicily. Most of these are in the broad Doric speech of that island and were composed in epic hexameters. Himself an urban poet at the end of several centuries of Greek glory in epic, lyric, didactic, and dramatic poetry, he opened up a new genre for the Hellenistic world by his return to the simplicities of rural life. In a sense he is as erudite as Robert Bridges or T.S. Eliot and his pastorals are posed and synthetic; even his semi-Doric diction is as invented as Spenser's; and yet, by a miracle of imagination and style he presents country life with a freshness that charms the jaded city-dweller. He is the father of the pastoral, and his *Daphnis* became the progenitor of thousands of elegies, from Moschus' *Lament for Bion* down to Milton's *Lycidas*, Shelley's *Adonais*, and Arnold's *Thyrsis*. This Idyll is presented below in English translation. Many devices that were with him a happy rococo novelty became the mimicked mannerisms of later generations: the shepherd and neatherd participants, the appeal to *Sicilian* Muses for inspiration, the patterned use of a cyclic refrain, the failure of the nymphs to guard the dying neatherd, the sympathetic sorrow of flocks, herds, wild birds and beasts, flowers, hills and rivers, the procession of questioners, including deities, and a farewell by the singer. Much of the pathetic fallacy in all this was as artificial as the stage conventions of drama, but we more willingly suspend disbelief in the case of Theocritus than in that of many of his successors, with whom the addition of far-fetched allegory made the genre still more remote from reality.

Daphnis appears in four of Theocritus' *Idylls* (I, VI, VIII, and IX), in Vergil's 5th *Eclogue*, and in almost innumerable later pastoral poets in many countries. It is one of the minor miracles of poetic inspiration that Giosuè Carducci returns to Daphnis with such freshness and charm in the Doric section of his "Primavere Elleniche" (1872), rendering a passage from the 8th *Idyll* (lines 53–6) as two rhymed Italian Sapphics and going on to voice his own sense of the immortality of the ancient world: "The other gods die; the deities of Greece know no setting" (*Muoiono gli altri dei: di Grecia i numi non sanno occaso*). Enrico Carrara expressed the same sense of enduring tradition when he referred to Carducci's quotation as coming from the poet-herd of Sicily: "Daphnis, the deathless spirit of love, sings the sweet oblivion that our Italian race has made immortal in three languages."[1]

In translating into English from Theocritus, the *fons et origo* of all European pastoral, one faces a fundamental problem of method. Shall one use prose or verse? If one accepts Benedetto Croce's verdict that "Art is form, and nothing but form," then the reduction of Theocritus' exquisitely modulated hexameters to prose removes nearly everything that made his pastorals memorable. On the other hand, it may be objected that no form at all is preferable to an inadequate or a distorted form. Theocritus can be lost in an awkwardly moulded vase no less than in the pulverized crockery of prose. The English reader needs to be reminded that the original was immortal poetry. In the Loeb Classical Library (*The Greek Bucolic Poets, With an English Translation by J. M. Edmonds*, London and New York, 1928), the dialogue between Thyrsis and the goatherd is rendered by English prose, but the Greek text is also there to vouch for the poetic quality of the original. When one reaches the Song of Thyrsis, however, even this edition feels compelled to use rhymed fourteeners (a form of ballad measure), since every hint of its heightened quality would have been lost in prose. Similarly, in J.H. Hallard's translation of the Greek bucolic poets (*The Idylls of Theocritus, With the fragments of Bion and Moschus*, London and New York, 1924), a task to which he devoted thirty years of toil, the dialogue in *Idyll* I is rendered by

---

1 *La Poesia Pastorale* (Milan, 1909), p. 477. In other words, the Greek of the Sicilian Theocritus, the Latin of the Mantuan Vergil, and the Italian of the Tuscan Carducci are all part of one long and glorious literature in the region now called Italy.

blank verse and the Song of Thyrsis by heroic stanzas in rhymed hexameters. In the case of J. Banks (*The Idylls of Theocritus, Bion and Moschus*, London and New York, 1893), the volume provides a complete prose version by Banks (pp. 1–201) followed by a complete metrical rendering by M.J. Chapman (pp. 205–324), who uses heroic couplets for some idylls and Spenserian stanzas for others.

The choice of metre (if any metre is employed) is evidently yet another problem. In Greek and Latin pastoral, as in Greek and Latin epic, the universal metre is the dactylic hexameter. Theocritus differs slightly from Homer in caesura and both from Vergil (who is using a different language medium) in caesura and the amount of enjambement. The entirely different texture and flow of the English language have given the iambic pentameter (with or without rhyme and stanzaic arrangement) a dominance almost equivalent to that of the hexameter in Greek and Latin. It is the basic metre of Chaucer's *Prologue* and later *Tales*, of Shakespeare's dramas, of Milton's epics, of Pope's satires, of Wordsworth's *Prelude*, and of Tennyson's *Idylls of the King*. In view of all the foregoing considerations, the present edition is rendering the bucolic dialogue in Theocritus' *Idyll* 1 by the pentameter of blank verse (to avoid the distortions imposed by rhyme) and the Song of Thyrsis by interwoven rhymed pentameters, together with a literal prose rendering facing them.

In view of the continuing importance of this first pastoral elegy, rather full footnotes have been added.

Idyll I. Daphnis[2]

THYRSIS[3]
Sweet is the whisper of that murmuring pine
Above the spring, O goatherd – sweet no less
The melody that issues from your pipe.
Yes, Pan[4] alone could win the prize before you.
If he should choose the buck, yours were the ewe;

2 In Greek myth, a neatherd, the son of the god Hermes and a nymph. According to the version given here, he was the mate of a nymph and boasted that Cypris (Aphrodite) could never subdue him to a new affection. In revenge, she cursed him with desire for a strange maiden, but he never surrendered to it and died a constant lover.
3 The setting is in the island of Cos, but Thyrsis is a visitor from Sicily.
4 An Arcadian woodland deity, the son of Hermes and hence the brother of Daphnis. In some myths he is the inventor of the shepherd's pipe. In this Idyll, Daphnis also bequeathes him his own pipe (see p. 88).

If his the ewe, your share would be the kid:
And dainty flesh have kids when still unmilked.

GOATHERD

Shepherd, your song is sweeter than the voice
Of yonder stream that tumbles down the cliff.
If as their prize the Muses claim the ewe,
The stall-fed lamb is sure to be your prize;
But if it pleases them to take the lamb,
The ewe herself were certainly your lot.

THYRSIS

I pray you, goatherd, in the Nymphs' own name,
Sit down among the bushy tamarisks
Upon the shelving bank, and pipe your fill;
And meanwhile I shall make your goats my care.

GOATHERD

Shepherd, it would be wrong to pipe at noon.
We then have dread of Pan, for in its heat
He tires of all his hunting and must rest.
Quick is that god to frenzies of resentment,
And ever on his nostrils passion sits.
But you were wont to sing the woes of Daphnis,
And you are favoured by the shepherds' Muse;
So come, and let us sit beneath that elm,
Fronting Priapus[5] and the fountain-nymphs[6]
Beside the oak trees and the shepherd's seat.
If you will only sing as once you sang,
Set in a match of song with Libyan Chromis,
I'll pay three milkings of a twinner goat.
Two kids she has, yet after suckling them
She'll fill two pails with milk; I'll give you also
A deep, two-handled bowl of wax-smeared wood,
Just finished and still smelling of the chisel.
Ivy is carved around its edge on top,
And, mingled with the ivy, helichryse,

5 Here, a phallic effigy of Priapus, a rustic god of fertility, often erected
  in fields and gardens
6 A natural spring or fountain

Whose twisting tendrils flaunt their saffron fruit.
Among these twigs, a maiden is engraved,
Fair as the work of gods' immortal hands.
In flowing robes and fillets is she dressed;
On either side, a man with fine long hair
Stands quarreling; but neither moves her heart;
She smiles on one, then ogles at the other;
The men are hollow-eyed with hapless love
But for the maiden's grace they strive in vain.
Beyond these, an old fisherman is carved
And a rough rock, from which, with might and main,
He drags along a mighty casting-net.
In heavy toil his mighty thews are strained.
The muscles of his neck and shoulders swell
As if he put forth all his lustihood.
Although his straggled hair is hoar with age,
His body is the body of a youth.
Close to this rude old man, a vineyard spreads,
Burdened with clustered grapes in purple rows.
And there a little boy must guard the vines,
Carelessly sitting on a boulder-wall.
Around the youngster there, two foxes skulk:
One prowls the rows to snatch the ripened fruit;
The other to his wallet turns her cunning
And seeks the lad of breakfast to beguile.
But he is plaiting him a locust-trap,
Fitting the slender stalks of asphodel
Into a frame of reeds; and as he weaves,
He disregards the wallet and the grapes.
Wreaths of acanthus run around the bowl;
For goatherds it must be a wondrous sight.
The price with which I bought this masterpiece
From a Calydnian boatman was a goat
And an enormous loaf of creamy cheese.
My lip has not yet soiled the wondrous dish;
There it still lies, unhandseled and unspoiled.
Gladly I'd give that bowl to you as yours,
If you would only sing your charming song.
I do not jest. Come now, good friend of mine.
You must not hoard your songs to sing in Hell.

A   THYRSIS sings:
      Begin, dear Muses, a bucolic strain!
      Thyrsis of Etna sings with honey voice.
      Where were ye, nymphs,[7] when Daphnis died in pain?
      Where were ye? Did you stray by Peneus'[8] vales
      Or beneath Pindus? Certainly your choice
      Was not Anapus'[9] mighty flood, nor yet
      Etna's high watch-tower,[10] nor again the plain
      Watered by Acis'[11] holy rivulet.

B   *Begin, dear Muses, a bucolic strain!*
      For him the jackals mourned, and sorrowing wails
      Came from the wolves, and roarings of regret
      The lion from the coppice made in vain.
      Begin, dear Muses, a bucolic strain!
      Beside his feet the heifers lowed in grief
      And many bulls and many calves were fain,
      With many kine, in moans to find relief.
      Begin, dear Muses, a bucolic strain!
      Then first came Hermes[12] from the hills and said:
      "Dear son, what passion has thy spirit slain?
      For love of whom art thou as good as dead?"
      Begin, dear Muses, a bucolic strain!
      The neatherds and the shepherds both drew near,
      And goatherds asked his grief and bent an ear.

C   Priapus[13] also came, and asked the lad:
      "Unhappy Daphnis, wherefore dost thou pine
      While by all fountains goes a maiden sad,
      Searching for thee? Dost thou her love resign?
      Fie on thee, bootless, and a laggard swain!
      A goatherd dost thou stand, on witless feet.
      Begin, dear Muses, a bucolic strain!
      For many a goatherd weeps and seems to dote,
      Watching his nannies covered, as they bleat,
      And grieving that he was not born a goat;
      So thou, when thou dost see the maidens laugh,
      Dost look with longing eyes, but like a calf
      Will scarcely dare to mingle in their dance."

D   *Begin, dear Muses, a bucolic strain!*
      These words the herdsman answered not again,
      But bore his bitter love with doggèd glance,
      Yea, to the end he bore his evil chance.

(A) THYRSIS sings: *Begin, dear Muses, begin the pastoral song!*
I am Thyrsis of Etna, and this is the sweet voice of Thyrsis.
Where were you, nymphs,[7] where were you when Daphnis
died? By the beautiful vales of Peneus?[8] Or below Pindus?
For surely you were not by the great stream of the Anapus,[9]
nor on the watch-tower[10] of Etna, nor by the holy waters of
the Acis.[11]

(B) *Begin, dear Muses, begin the cowherd song!*
For him, jackals and wolves wailed and even the lion from the
forest lamented him as he lay dying.
Begin, dear Muses, begin the cowherd song!
Many cows and bulls were at his feet, and many calves
bewailed him.
Begin, dear Muses, begin the cowherd song!
First from the hills came Hermes[12] and said: "Daphnis, who is
tormenting you? My good lad, whom do you love so much?"
Begin, dear Muses, begin the cowherd song!
The neatherds came, the shepherds and the goatherds. They
all asked him what ailed him.

(c) Priapus[13] also came, and said: "Unhappy Daphnis, why do you
pine away? The maiden is roving by all the springs, through
all the groves, seeking you. You are a useless lover, and ac-
complish nothing. You have been called a cowherd, and now
you are acting like a goatherd.
Begin, dear Muses, begin the cowherd song!
For the goatherd, when he sees the bleating she-goats being
covered, weeps teardrops because he was not born a buck.

7 Since, in myth, Daphnis' mother and wife were both nymphs, this
appeal comes more naturally here than in the imitative pastorals of
twenty subsequent centuries.

8 A river in Thessaly, rising in the Pindus range

9 A river in Sicily

10 Milton's subconscious may have recalled this σκοπιά of the nymphs on
Etna in his "great vision of the guarded Mount" (*Lycidas*, 161).

11 Acis, a little stream in Sicily formed by the nymph Galatea out of the
body of her dead lover Acis, who had been crushed under a huge rock
by his giant rival, Polyphemus. Cf. Handel's opera, *Acis and Galatea*,
with libretto by John Gay.

12 His own father is thus the first to come.

13 The god of fertility comes, because Daphnis, by his obduracy, has
flouted him.

Renew, ye Muses, your bucolic strain!
But sweetly smiling Cypris also came,
With crafty smile she came, but full of ire;
And said: "O Daphnis, with what dark disdain
Thou boastedst thou wouldst wrestle Love's desire
And throw it! Is not thine, instead, the shame
Of being thrown by Love and set on fire?"
Renew, ye Muses, your bucolic strain!
But Daphnis, to her words, replied again:
"Cypris implacable and dread of might,
Cypris detested by the sons of men,
Already dost thou see me doomed to night,

E   My life's last sun has set; but with delight
I'll take revenge on Love in Hades' den.[14]
Renew, ye Muses, your bucolic strain!
Of Cypris and the hind is Hell's refrain –
Get thee to Ida and Anchises'[15] love;
Oak trees are yonder, there the bedstraw thrives,
And sweetly hum the bees about the hives.
Renew, ye Muses, your bucolic strain!
Sure, thy Adonis[16] must his manhood train,
He herds the sheep, he slays the leaping hare,
And chases every wild beast to its lair.
Renew, ye Muses, your bucolic strain!
Nay, outbrave Diomedes,[17] boldly say:

F   'The herdsman Daphnis by my hand is slain;
Come thou, join battle with my strength today!'
Renew, ye Muses, your bucolic strain!
Ye wolves and jackals of the waste, farewell!
Bears in your mountain caves, I bid adieu!
Daphnis you'll see no more in any dell,
In groves and woodlands he is lost to you.
O fountain Arethusa[18] and ye streams
That pour down Thymbris'[19] vales your waters clear,
Farewell, a long farewell, from one in pain.

G   *Renew, ye Muses, your bucolic strain!*

14 Daphnis has been the friend of all wild things, and hints, by his reference to bees and boars, what the nature of his revenge may be.

15 In one legend, her lover Anchises was blinded by bees. She had met him on Mount Ida and there conceived Aeneas.

And you, when you see the girls laughing gaily, weep tear-
drops because you are not dancing with them."

(D)   To these words the cowherd gave no answer, but endured in
his bitter love and bore his doom to the end.

Begin, dear Muses, begin again the cowherd song!

Then came sweet Cypris laughing, with sly laughter but with
heavy anger in her heart, and said: "Daphnis, you boasted that
you would throw Love for a fall, and now have you yourself
not been thrown by grievous Love?"

Begin, dear Muses, begin again the cowherd song!

But to her Daphnis made reply: "Pitiless Cypris, revengeful
Cypris, Cypris an enemy to mortal men, do you think that all
my suns have already set?

(E)   Even in Hades, Daphnis will be an evil grief to Love.[14]

Begin, ye Muses, begin again the cowherd song!

Is not the cowherd said (to have won) Cypris? Be off to Mount
Ida! Be off to Anchises![15] Oak trees are there, and galingale;
and the bees are humming sweetly about their hives.

Begin again, ye Muses, begin the cowherd song!

Blooming also is Adonis,[16] when he shepherds flocks, and
casts darts at hares, and chases all sort of wild beasts.

Begin, ye Muses, begin again the cowherd song!

Go again, and confront Diomedes,[17] and say:

(F)   'I have beaten the cowherd Daphnis. Come now, and fight with
me.'

Begin, ye Muses, begin again the cowherd song!

Farewell, O jackals and wolves and bears with dens in the

16 Her lover, Adonis, was killed by a boar. Cf. Bion's *Lament for Adonis*,
    p. 97.

17 Diomedes, of Argos, was one of the principal Greek chieftains in the
    Trojan War. In battle, he actually wounds the goddess Aphrodite (cf.
    Iliad, v, 330–42). In Chaucer's *Troilus and Criseyde*, Book v, he is the
    man who succeeds Troilus in the favours of the heroine.

18 Arethusa is the most famous spring in Sicily, found on the island of
    Ortygia in the harbour of Syracuse. It is reputed to have been a nymph
    thus transformed by Artemis when pursued by the enamoured Pelopon-
    nesian river-god, Alpheus. The latter then flowed under the sea and
    joined her in Sicily. Cf. Milton's *Lycidas*, 85, 132–3.

19 The name usually refers to the Tiber River, but here apparently means
    some place in Sicily (mountain, valley, or stream).

20 Mount Maenalus, in Arcadia, was sacred to Pan.

21 According to one legend, Zeus was born on Mount Lycaeus, in Arcadia.

I am the Daphnis here who herds the cows,
Who waters here the calflings and the bulls.
O Pan, Great Pan, wherever you carouse,
On mighty Maenalus[20] or on the brows
Of high Lycaeus,[21] leave those pinnacles
And hasten to our dear Sicilian isle.
Forsake the tomb of Helice[22] the fair,
Leave that high cairn above Lycaon's son
That seems a spectacle surpassed by none,
As even high Olympus is aware.

H   *Leave off, ye Muses, your bucolic strain!*
Come to me, Master, take my pretty pipe,
Whose wax-stopped straws can breathe with honeyed breath.
How well it fits thy lip, for music ripe,
For I by Love am dragged away to death.
Leave off, ye Muses, your bucolic strain!
Bear violets now, ye brambles and ye thorns;[23]
On boughs of juniper let lilies blow!
Let all things be confounded here below,
A ripening pear the pine-tree branch adorns.
Daphnis is dying now, by Cypris slain!
Let stags pull down the hounds, let owls prevail
To overcome in song the nightingale."
Leave off, ye Muses, your bucolic strain!

I   So Daphnis sang, and ceased; Cypris would fain
Have called him back to life. But nay, the thread
The Parcae had assigned was fully spun;
Daphnis went down the River of the Dead.

22 Lycaon, the wolfish primordial king of Arcadia, had a daughter named
Helice or Callisto. She became, by Zeus, the mother of Arcas, the
legendary ancestor of the "Arcadians," living in the supremely moun-
tainous north-central part of the Peloponnesus. Nearly all translators
take *sama Lykaonidao* as "the cairn of the *son* of Lykaon," although
Arcas, to whom this would seem to refer, was actually his grandson.
In a simpler explanation, Herbert Kynaston (*Idylls and Epigrams
Commonly Attributed to Theocritus*, Oxford, 1892, in a note on p. 127)
treats the patronymic genitive *Lykaonidao* as feminine and the line as
a gloss on the preceding one on Callisto's tomb. He points out, moreover, that this tomb of Helice-Callisto was actually shown to Pausanias,
in the second century A.D., by the Arcadians (cf. *Description of Greece*,
Vol. VIII on "Arcadia").

hills! I, Daphnis the neatherd, shall no more be with you, neither in the oak-coppices nor in the glades. Farewell, Arethusa,[18] and ye rivers that pour your beautiful waters down Thymbris.[19]

(G) It is I, Daphnis, who here herds the cows, who waters the bulls and the calves.

Begin, ye Muses, begin again the cowherd song!

O Pan, Pan, whether you are on the high mountains of Lycaeus[21] or dwell on great Maenalus,[20] come here to the Isle of Sicily, leave Helice's[22] peak and the lofty tumulus of Lycaon's son (grandson), admired even by the blessed gods.

(H) *Cease, O Muses, cease your cowherd songs!*

Come King (Pan), and carry away this honey-breathed pipe of hardened wax, a beautiful instrument well fitted to the lip. For I am being dragged down to Hell by Love.

Cease, O Muses, cease your cowherd song!

Now bear violets, you bramble-bushes;[23] bear them, you thistles; and let the fair narcissus spread its blossoms on the juniper-bush. Let all things be transformed; let the pine-tree grow pears; since Daphnis is dying, and let the stags drag down the dogs and let mountain-owls contend with nightingales."

Cease, Muses, cease now your cowherd songs!

(I) As he was speaking thus, he stopped. Aphrodite would gladly have raised him up again, but all the threads from the Fates had left him, and Daphnis went down the river (of Acheron). The eddying waters closed over the man[24] who was dear to the Muses and no enemy to the Nymphs.

Cease, Muses, now cease your cowherd song!

---

23 This prayer, that the course of nature should be reversed, is imitated by the youthful Vergil in *Eclogue* iii, 89, and in *Eclogue* viii, 52–7. It crops up again in Nemesian (p. 129 below).

Though dear to Nymphs and Muses, he was done;
The eddying waters closed above his head.[24]
Leave off, ye Muses, your bucolic strain!

Pray give me now the goat; the bowl as well;
That having milked the beast, I may pour out
A due libation in the Muses' honour.
Farewell, again farewell, O gracious Muses.
Some other day, I'll sing still sweeter songs.

GOATHERD
May the fair mouth of Thyrsis have its fill
Of honey and the comb, and may you eat
The sweetest figs that come from Aegilus,[25]
For you sing better than cicadas do.
Here is the goblet. See how sweet it smells.
You'd think it dipped in fountains of the Hours.
Come here, Cissaetha. Do you milk her now.
Stop jumping, kids, or else the buck will get you!

---

24 Professor James Holly Hanford has suggested ("The Pastoral Elegy and
   Milton's *Lycidas," PMLA*, xxv, 1910, 403–47) that this figurative
   passage in Theocritus may have been the seminal concept that led
   Milton, in the case of an actual drowning, to choose the genre of
   pastoral elegy for his poem, in which "the remorseless deep Clos'd o're
   the head" of Lycidas. Compare also Propertius, *Elegies*, III, vii, 65, on
   the drowning of Paetus, "Eddying waves as he spoke dragged him down
   to the depths of the waters" (*subtrahit haec fantem torta vertigine
   fluctus*), on p. 124 below. Dr. Hanford also suggests a source in
   Theocritus for the appeal to the Muses and the reference to the threads
   of the Parcae; but these had been used a hundred times by elegists
   between Theocritus and Milton.

25 A town on the west coast of Attica, famous for its figs

Ly-2 (Greek)

THEOCRITUS. *Idyll* VII. *The Harvest Home. Ca.* 275 B.C.

Begins: Ἦs χρόνοs ἀνίκ' ἐγώ τε κὰι Εὔκριτοs ἐs τὸν "Αλεντα
    εἵρπομεs ἐκ πόλιοs· σὺν καὶ τρίτοs ἄμμιν 'Αμύνταs·
Ends: αὖτιs ἐγὼ πάξαιμι μέγα πτύον· ἁ δὲ γελάσσαι,
    δράγματα καὶ μάκωναs ἐν ἀμφοτέραισιν ἔχοισα.

The setting of the poem is in the Aegean island of Cos, and tells of the poet's personal experience in the company of friends but under the pastoral alias of Simichidas ("snub-nosed" or "son of a little monkey"). This Idyll is thus an ancestor of those pastoral elegies in which, as in Milton's *Lycidas*, the poet speaks in the guise of a shepherd and makes his personal comments on his contemporaries.[26] Some of the names in *Idyll* VII are regarded as real, e.g., Antigenes and Phrasidamus, his hosts; Asclepiades ("Sicelidas") and Philetas, his former teachers; and Aratus the poet, author of the *Phenomena* and the *Prognostica*, a line from whom was quoted in Athens by Saint Paul (Acts xvii: 28). Fictitiously pastoral are Eucritus, Amyntas, Lycidas, Ageanax, and, of course, Simichidas. The *Britannica* (s.v. "Theocritus") suggests that the "Lycidas" of this Idyll may well have been an actual Cretan poet, Astacides, "the goatherd." Harrison and Leon identify him as Leonidas of Tarentum, one of the best poets in the Greek Anthology.

In craftsmanship, *Idyll* VII differs greatly from *Idyll* I. Like Chaucer's *Miller's Prologue* and *Miller's Tale*, it is spontaneously natural, roguishly presented, and prosodically superb. The two set pieces, told in good-natured rivalry by Lycidas and "Simichidas," are tailored out of the same piece of cloth as the narrative overcoat, and call for no lyric heightening of style. Only the rich descriptive tapestry of the close brings in an element of sensuous beauty, distantly akin to Keats's ode *To Autumn* but given in a less formal idiom. Literal prose

26 A reading of W. Leonard Grant's *Neo-Latin Literature and the Pastoral* (1965) has discovered no fewer than 32 poets who have used the name "Lycidas" in their Latin pastorals: Amalteo, Andrelini, Angelio, Arco, Arcucci, Berni, Boccaccio, Broukhusius, Calpurnius, Camerarius, Cordus, Dousa, Francius, Geraldini, Halley, Heinsius, Hume, Leech, Lotich, Mario, Moisant de Brieux, Nemesianus, Patrizi, Remmius, Sabinus, Sannazaro, Schoonhoven, Secundus, Sluperius, Vergil, Vida, and Yvelin. Only Daphnis, Amyntas, and Thyrsis have rivalled this name in popularity.

would dissolve out all these qualities. Blank verse has therefore been used below, with occasional feminine endings and enjambement, scrupulously adding little to pad the Greek but seeking to maintain at least a hint of the rhythmic flow of the bucolic hexameters.

Idyll VII. The Harvest Home

It chanced one time that Eucritus and I
Sauntered from town to seek the Hales River,
And with us came Amyntas as a third.
A harvest feast was planned, to please Demeter,
By Phrasidamus and Antigenes,
Lycopeus' two fine sons, the noble shoots
Sprung from an earlier age's hallowed stock,
Even Clytia and that Chalcon long ago
Who caused Burina's spring to rise and gush
By planting his firm knee upon a rock;
Around that spring the elms and aspens tower,
Whose arching shadows form a dusky covert
To shield the pool with tresses of green leaves.
The tomb of Brasilas was not in view
Nor had we finished half our pleasant walk
When, by the Muses' grace, we chanced to meet
A traveller from far Cydonia,[27]
A Cretan by the name of Lycidas.
He was a goatherd, nor could eye or nose
Find any other trade to list him by.
Down from his shoulders hung a tawny skin
Torn from a shaggy goat, rank with fresh rennet;
By a broad belt about his breast was tied
A worn, old tunic; while his right hand bore
A crooked staff of strong wild-olive wood.
With merry eyes he spoke, and slyly grinned,
And laughter on his lips prolonged the smile:
"Simichidas," said he, "the noon is hot.
Where do you drag your feet along the road,
When pale, green lizards in the stone-wall sleep
And even crested larks are not abroad?

27 A town on the northern coast of Western Crete

Seek you some feast, an uninvited guest,
Or rush to tread some winepress hereabouts?
Beneath your hastening feet the cobble-stones
Ring to the onset of your hobnail shoes!"
    I answered him: "Friend Lycidas, men claim
That you have matchless skill upon the flute;
The herdsmen and the reapers praise your notes.
This word of theirs has filled my heart with joy.
And yet, in my opinion, I may hope
To be a match for you. The way we walk
Runs to a harvest feast, where friends of ours
Prepare to offer to fair-robed Demeter
The first-fruits of their crop, because her hand
Has piled their threshing-floors with ample barley.
But come, the way is common to us both;
We both have time; so let us, as we walk,
Sing each his pastoral lay, for thus, perhaps,
We each shall give the other happiness.
Through my clear voice, like yours, the Muses speak;
Men rank me among singers of the best;
But this, by Zeus, I cannot quite accept,
For to my mind, my singing is uncouth
To that of Samos' bard, Sicelidas,
And sweet Philetas' song is past my reach.
For me to vie with them would be as useless
As for a frog to brave the locust's song."
    I spoke thus purposely. But with a smile
He said: "I shall present you with this staff
Because you are a scion of true Zeus,[28]
A perfect model of integrity.
Just as I scorn a builder who would seek
To make his house outsoar Oromedon,[29]
So I despise those cuckoos of the Muses
Who cackle at the Chian nightingale[30]

28 Since Truth was the daughter of Zeus, Lycidas means that Simichidas
   is an honest man.
29 The highest mountain in the island of Cos, where they are talking
30 The poet Homer, according to one tradition, was born in the island of
   Chios, although there were many other places that claimed the honour,
   such as Smyrna, Colophon, Kyme, Salamis, Rhodes, Argos, Athens,
   Ithaca, Ios, and Pylos.

But strive in vain to match his melody.
But come, Simichidas, let us begin
Our pastoral singing. I shall be the first.
See if you like this ditty that I sing,
A song I fashioned on the mountain-side."

(Lycidas sings)
"The voyage to Mitylene will be fair
For Ageanax, though the Kids[31] are riding
Across the abysses of the western sky
And though the southern tempests chase the waves
And though Orion[31] strides upon the sea,
If he sets free the heart of Lycidas
Whom Aphrodite burns with hot despair,
For ardent love of him consumes my soul.
Then shall the halcyons[32] make still the waves
And calm the stormy winds of east and south
That toss the seaweed on the topmost shore –
The halcyons, who of all birds that soar
And dive to seize the minnow in their mouth
The sea-green Nereids cherish as their own.
As Ageanax makes his peaceful way
To Mitylene, may the sky be kind
And may he come at last, beyond all perils,
To reach his haven. Upon such a day
I'll crown my brow with fennel and the rose

31 Two adjacent star-groups rising late in the autumn sky and once
regarded as signs of winter and stormy weather were (a) "the Kids"
(Haedi), represented along with their mother the She-goat (Capella) in
the left hand of the Waggoner (Auriga) and (b) Orion, the gigantic
hunter, wearing a belt of three stars and carrying a club and a sword.
These constellations contain three of the twenty brightest stars in the
whole sky (Capella, Betelgeuse, and Rigel), and were carefully watched
by the star-conscious ancients.

32 The legend of Ceyx and his wife Alcyone, transformed into seabirds
and nesting on the waves during fourteen "halcyon days" at midwinter
(cf. Aristophanes, Birds, 1594, and Ovid, Metamorphoses, xi, 410–748),
is of course apocryphal. Their identification with the kingfisher (North
American Megaceryle alcyon or European Alcedo ispida) is entirely
false, for these birds nest, early in the year, in a deep tunnel that they
excavate in an earth or gravel bank.

Or with white violets, and drain the wine
Of Ptelea from the bowl as I stretch out
Beside the hearth, and someone, for my comfort,
Is roasting beans among the glowing embers.
My easy pallet shall be elbow-deep
With fleabane, parsley-curls and asphodel;
There, lying at my ease, I'll drink right freely,
Thinking of Ageanax as I drink
And drain my brimming chalice to the dregs.
Two shepherds there shall play the flute for me –
One from Acharnae, one from Lycope –
While Tityrus shall sing beside them there
How once the neatherd, Daphnis, fell in love
With Xenea, and how the mountain grieved,
And how the mountain's oak-trees made lament,
The oaks that grow beside the Himera,
While Daphnis wasted like the snows that melt
On lofty Haemus or on Athos' brow
Or Rhodope or far-off Caucasus.
And Tityrus shall sing how long ago
A fierce and savage master penned a shepherd
Inside a cedar box while still alive,
And how, in his captivity, the bees,
Snub-nosed and friendly, from the meadow came
And fed him with the honey of soft flowers
Because the Muse poured nectar on his lips.
O blest Comátas, what a meed of fame
You won by your adventure in that chest,
Nourished with honey and the honey-comb
Until the spring's release returned again.
I wish you were alive in this my time;
Then in the mountains I would tend your goats
While listening to the music of your voice;
And you, divine Comatas, there would lie
And sing sweet songs beneath the oak or pine.

(Lines 90–127. Simichidas- Theocritus responds with a pastoral song
of the love of Aratus and Simichidas for Philinus)

Thus had I sung, and with a merry laugh

Lycidas handed me his staff again,
A gift of friendship for the songs we sang.
Then turning to the left-hand road, he went
His way to Pyxa; Eucritus and I
And pretty young Amyntas walked ahead
And soon turned in at Phrasidamus' farm;
And there we lay on couches made of boughs,
Of rushes sweet and fresh-cut leaves of vine.
Above us, many an elm and aspen swayed;
The sacred rill, near by, gushed into sunlight
With murmurs from the water-nymphs' cool cave;
The dusky-hued cicadas shrilled unceasing
On shady branches, and the tree-toad shy
Aloof in bramble thickets raised his voice.
The larks and linnets sang; the doves made moan;
The golden bees above the waters hummed;
And all the air was heavy with the scent
Of mellow summer and the fragrant breath
Of orchards in the season of their fruit.
Pears lay about our feet, and at our side
The luscious apples rolled in plenty down.
The burden of the plum-trees all about us
Bore down their heavy branches to the earth.
The four-year seals of pitch were broken loose
Out of the wine-jars' mouths to grace our feast.
Nymphs of Castalia's fountain, you who haunt
Parnassus' lofty peak, I pray you, tell
If ancient Chiron offered such a cup
In Pholus' rocky cave to Herakles?
And was that shepherd by Anapus' stream,
Strong Polyphemus, who in mighty strength
Hurled hills at ships, enticed by wine like this
To dance with joy upon the sheepfold floor,
Even such potions as you Nymphs poured out
For us that day to crown the threshing-floor
Beside Demeter's altar? On her mound
Of heaped-up grain may I some day once more
Plant a great winnowing-fan, and may she smile
With sheaves and poppy-blooms in either hand.

Ly-3 (Greek)

BION.   *Adonidos Epitaphios.* About 150 B.C. From *Bucolici Graeci,* ed.
Udalricus de Wilamowitz-Moellendorff, Oxford, 1905

Begins: Αἰάζω τὸν "Αδωνιν· 'ἀπώλετο καλὸς "Αδωνις.'
       'ὤλετο καλὸς "Αδωνις' ἐπαιάζουσιν "Ερωτες ...
Ends: λῆγε γόων Κυθέρεια τὸ σήμερον, ἴσχεο κομμῶν·
       δεῖ σε πάλιν κλαῦσαι, πάλιν εἰς ἔτος ἄλλο δακρῦσαι.

Born near Smyrna about 175 B.C., Bion is best known as an imitator
of Theocritus. According to a dirge ascribed to Moschus (Ly-4), he
died as a result of being poisoned. His most remarkable poem is his
Lament for Adonis, regarded by some as having been written for reci-
tation at the Adoniazusae or festival of Adonis. A fragment of another dirge, for an earlier stage of the same great festival as that held
in Alexandria, is given in Idyll xv, lines 136–44, by Theocritus. Bion's
Lament is a moving piece of poetic rhetoric, passionate and uncon-
trolled in its reiterated grief. It would probably take the emotions of
simple-minded worshippers by storm. His use of a refrain was borrowed from Theocritus and bequeathed to hundreds of successors.
Original with Bion is the tradition of bringing flowers to the bier or
the grave. Thus the poet commands Aphrodite to "Throw on him
fragrant wreaths and lilies white."

This magnificent dirge is compounded of shining imagery and a
hypnotic iteration of phrase. There is no narrative framework of
setting, and we are swept out at once into its purple stream of rhetoric. A prose translation would destroy nearly everything of its
emotional effect; and yet so much perverse manipulation of English
phraseology is necessary in even remotely reproducing the incanta-
tory effect of Bion's poetry that we are in danger of straying from
the meaning of the original. The only solution for a translator is to
supply, as is done here, both a verse translation for the general reader
and a literal prose rendering for the scholar.

Lament for Adonis

J   I sorrow for Adonis: He is dead,
Even the fair Adonis. And the Loves[33]
Echo my plaint for that beloved head.
    Sleep no more, Cypris, on your peerless bed
Amid your purple coverlets. Arise,
O wretched one, put on a cloak of gloom
And beat your breast; tell all, with grievous sighs:
"Dead is the fair Adonis, dark his doom."
I mourn Adonis, and the Loves make moan!
    Low on the hills the fair Adonis lies,
With the boar's tusk his snowy thigh is torn;
Leaving the sorrowing Cypris all forlorn,
He softly breathes his ebbing life away.
Down his white skin the scarlet blood-stream drips,
And dimness overcomes his dark-browed eyes;
The rosy hue is fading from his lips,
The very kiss of Cypris on them dies.
She fain would kiss the boy-mouth's ebbing breath;
He knew not that she kissed him at his death.
I mourn Adonis, and the Loves make moan!

K   Though grievous is the tusk-wound in his thigh,
More grievous is the wound in Cypris' heart.
His faithful dogs have howled to see him die,
The nymphs are wailing on the hills apart,
And Cypris, with her tresses backward thrown,
Goes wandering through the woodland in her woe,
With hair unbraided and with unshod feet;
Thorn-bushes wound her and her blood must flow.
With piercing cries she rushes to and fro
Through the far valleys; and her wails entreat
Her young Assyrian lord, the lovely lad.
But the dark blood about his navel spouts,
His bosom is made red with bloody gouts,
The streams that from his thigh their colour add
To stain his breast that once like snow was known.
"Alas for Cypris," all the Loves make moan.

L   That lovely man she lost, and with him went
The beauty of her own celestial face.
While her Adonis lived, her form was fair.

(J)   I bewail Adonis; the beautiful Adonis is dead. "The
beautiful Adonis is dead"– the Loves[33] join in the wail.

Sleep no more, Cypris, in purple garments; rise, wretched
one, put on sable robes and beat your breast, and say to
everyone: "Beautiful Adonis is dead." I wail for Adonis: the
Loves join in the wailing.

Beautiful Adonis lies low on the mountains, his white thigh
torn by a boar's tusk, a white tusk, and he brings anguish to
Cypris, as he feebly breathes out his life; but the black blood
trickles down his white skin; his eyes grow glazed under
their lids and the rose flees from his lip, on which dies also
the kiss that Cypris will never forego. To Cypris indeed the
kiss is dear, even though he is not living any longer; but
Adonis did not know that she kissed him as he was dying.
I bewail Adonis: the Loves join in the wailing.

(K)   A cruel, cruel wound Adonis has in his thigh, but Cytherea
bears a greater wound in her heart. Around that youth his
dear dogs howl, and the nymphs of the mountains weep, but
Aphrodite, having loosened her braided tresses, wanders up
and down in the woods, wretched, unkempt, unsandaled; the
brambles rend her as she passes, and draw her sacred blood.
Then shrieking she goes through the long valleys, calling
out for her Assyrian spouse and crying out for the lad. But
the black blood welled up about his navel, and his breasts
grew scarlet from his thighs, and the white parts beneath the
breasts of Adonis grew crimson.
Ai, ai, for Cytherea, the Loves join in wailing.

(L)   She has lost her beautiful man, and lost with him her own
holy beauty. Cypris had beauty, so long as Adonis lived, but
her form perished along with Adonis. All the mountains say
"Ai, ai, for Cypris" and the oak-trees say "Ai ai, for Adonis";
and the rivers grieve for the sorrows of Aphrodite, and the
springs on the hills shed tears for Adonis, and flowers
grow red from sorrow, and Cytherea sings sadly by every
mountain-shoulder and through every glen: "Ai, ai, for
Cytherea, beautiful Adonis is dead." And Echo answered:

---

33 Apparently a covey of Aphrodite's little, naked, winged children (like
the "Cupid" of Roman mythology and modern valentines), all armed
with bows and arrows

But with his dying perished all her grace.
"Alas for Cypris," all the mountains say;
"Woe to Adonis," all the oaks lament;
For Cypris' sorrow all the rivers wail;
The mountain springs for dead Adonis pray.
The flowers on the hill are red with pain,
And Cytherea, through each mountain vale,
Is singing amid sobs the piteous strain:
"Alas for Cypris, since Adonis dies."
"Adonis dies," the echo answers back.
Who would not greet her grief with like replies?

M   As she beheld Adonis' unstaunched wound
And saw the blood that on his torn thigh lay,
She stretched out both her arms and sadly crooned:
"O stay, Adonis, luckless lover, stay,
That for a last time I may hold you tight
And mingle lips with lips before the night.
Awaken but a little, O my dear,
And to my stricken love this last kiss give;
Kiss me as long as such a kiss may live
Until your breath into my mouth may go
And give my very heart your overflow,
That I may drink the magic of your love
And treasure up the kiss that you bestow
As ever in my heart I shall approve
My luckless darling, though your soul has fled.
Afar you flee, my dear, among the dead,
To Acheron and that harsh, hateful King;
But here above I must be lingering,
For, as a goddess, I to earth must cling
And in the realm of Hell may never tread.
Persephone, accept the lord I lose;
Stronger are you to seize on all I use,
For every lovely thing to you descends.
Forlorn am I, and bear unceasing pain;
I weep for my Adonis, who is slain,
And I must fear the realm in which he ends.
You fade, my lover, from a man's estate,
And all my love has fled me like a dream.
Cypris is widowed; and all desolate
Are left the Loves who linger by my side.

"Beautiful Adonis is dead."Who would not have bewailed the grievous love of Cypris,"Ai, ai"?

(M) When she saw, when she beheld the unstaunched wound of Adonis, when she saw the purple blood on his drooping thigh, stretching out her arms, she moaned: "Stay, Adonis; stay, ill-fated Adonis; that for the last time I may possess you, that I may embrace you and mingle lips with lips. Rouse but a little, Adonis, and kiss me again this last time, kiss me as long as there is life in your kiss, until the breath may flow from your soul into my mouth, even into my heart, and I shall drain your sweet love-philtre, and drink down your love, and I shall treasure the kiss as I will yourself, Adonis, since you, hapless one, are fleeing from me. You are fleeing far off, Adonis, and are coming to Acheron and its hateful and cruel king; but I, wretched one, live on, for I am a goddess and cannot follow you. Persephone, take my spouse, for you are much stronger than I; and everything beautiful must go down to you. But I am all-unfortunate and have unceasing sorrow, and wail for Adonis, for he dies to me, and I am afraid of you. Are you dying, thrice-regretted one? Then all my yearning has fled like a dream, Cytherea is widowed, and the Loves are desolate along my halls. Along with you, my magic girdle has perished. Why did you rashly go hunting? Fair as you were, why did you madly fight with a wild animal? Thus Cypris and the Loves joined in the wailing:"*Ai, ai, for Cytherea; beautiful Adonis is dead.*"

(N) The goddess of Paphos sheds as many tears as Adonis sheds drops of blood; and all these become flowers on the ground. The blood brings forth a rose, the tears the anemone. *I mourn for Adonis, the beautiful Adonis is dead.*

Cypris, mourn no more in the woods for your man. A lonely couch of leaves is no proper bed for Adonis. Cytherea, let dead Adonis now occupy your bed. Though he is a corpse, he is a beautiful, beautiful corpse, as if sleeping. Lay him down in the soft coverlets, among which he used to sleep, on which with you throughout the night he used to take his sacred sleep, on a couch all of gold; the bed yearns for Adonis, even though he is gloomy of face. Cast wreaths and blossoms upon him. All things, even all flowers, have died along with him, since he is dead. But sprinkle him with Syrian ointments, sprinkle him with perfumes. Nay, let all

My magic belt is lost with you, I deem.
Why did you go a-hunting, rash in pride?
Fair as you were, why did your soul not dread
To fight a savage beast? Then to her theme
The chorus of the little Loves replied:
"Alas for Cypris, and Adonis dead!"

N   As many teardrops does the Paphian shed
As blood-drops from Adonis stain the lea.
As flowers on the ground their colours spread:
Blood blooms, the rose; tears, the anemone.
I mourn Adonis, for the youth is dead.
Weep for your lover in the woods no more.
A lonely couch of leaves befits him not;
Then lay him, Cypris, in your own soft bed.
Lovely is he, though dead; like one that sleeps.
Above him let soft covers lie in heaps,
The sheets in which he slept when through the night
He shared your sacred sleep in happy lot
Upon a couch all gold. The bed now yearns
For dead Adonis, in his doom's despite.
Throw on him fragrant wreaths and lilies white.
All things with him have died, as he is dead,
And all the flowers have withered in their turns.
With Syrian unguents anoint him now,
Sprinkle his flesh with perfumes, breast and brow.
Nay, let all perfumes perish in their stead,
Since he who was your fragrance is no more.

O   Dainty Adonis lies in crimson quilt,
And round about his bier the Loves lament,
Cutting their long, fair locks to grieve more sore.
One Love around him has his arrows spilt,
One casts his wings and quiver, one his bow.
To loose the corpse's sandals, one has bent;
Water from golden basins others pour
To wash his bloody thighs; with wings alone
Another fans Adonis, sad and slow.
"Alas for Cypris," all the Loves make moan.

P   There at the doorposts Hymenaeus[34] quenched
All torches, and tore up the wedding wreath.
No more he chanted "Hymen," his own song,
But "Woe be to Adonis," as he blenched

perfumes perish, since Adonis, who was your own perfume, is dead.

(o)   Dainty Adonis reclines in a purple coverlet, and around him the weeping Loves raise their wail, cutting off their locks for Adonis. And one has thrown his arrows over him, another his bow, another his wing, another his quiver, and another has loosened the sandal of Adonis, others bring water in a golden basin, another washes his thigh, still another, from behind, fans Adonis with his wings.

Ai, ai, for Cytherea, the Loves join in wailing!

(p)   Hymenaeus[34] has quenched every torch on the door-lintels and has torn the bridal wreath to shreds, and no more sings "Hymen, Hymen," no more his own song; but he chants "Ai, ai, for Adonis" more than the bridal song. The Graces bewail the son of Cinyras, saying to one another "Fair Adonis is dead." They shriek "Ai, ai" more piercingly even than the paean of joy. And the Fates loudly bewail Adonis in Hades, and invoke him in song, but he does not heed them; and the Maiden[35] will not let him go.

(q)   Cease from your laments, O Cytherea. Refrain from breast-beating. You must mourn him again, and shed tears for him again, in another year.

(end of prose translation)

34 Or Hymen, the Greek god of marriage, who here cancels his rites and turns to mourning.

35 *Kore*, the Maiden, is Persephone, the Queen of Hades. Her counterpart in old Babylonian epics is Ereshkigal, the utterly horrifying elder sister of Ishtar. The rivalry of earth's fertility goddess (Aphrodite) with the Queen of Death (Persephone) goes back as far as the strife in Semitic myth between Ereshkigal and Ishtar for possession of Tammuz, the youthful spouse or lover of Ishtar. See Sir James George Frazer, *The Golden Bough* (abridged edition, London, 1925), pp. 324–56, and especially chapter xxix, "The Myth of Adonis." Sir James draws attention to an Old Testament reference in Ezekiel 8:14: "Then he brought me to the door of the gate of Yahweh's house which was towards the north [i.e. towards Lebanon, the ancient home of Tammuz-Adonis-worship]; and behold, there sat women weeping for Tammuz." The Greeks, when they imported Tammuz-worship, mistook his Semitic title *Adon* ("Lord") for a proper name, added Greek inflectional suffixes, and so unwittingly disguised him for us as *Adonis*; but it is the same deity. By the same process, they turned the Hebrew *Moshe* and *Elijah* into *Moyses* (Moses) and *Eleias* (Elias).

> To see the martyred mortal underneath
> Who rather to a bridal should belong.
> For Cinyras's son the Graces wail;
> Adonis' death is now their constant tale.
> They sing no paean, but a sad lament.
> Aloud in Hades do the grey Fates weep
> For dead Adonis, but he heeds them not.
> Perchance he might desire to make ascent
> Up to the daylight by a stairway steep,
> But Hell's Queen[35] will not loose him from his lot.

Ω   Cease, Cytherea, from your grief today,
> And beat no more your breast in anguish drear.
> Another time you'll mourn his buried clay,
> For you must weep when comes another year.

Ly-4 (Greek)

MOSCHUS. *Bionos Epitaphios*. About 150 B.C. From *Bucolici Graeci*, ed., Udalricus de Wilamowitz-Moellendorff, Oxford, 1905

Begins: Αἴλινά μοι στοναχεῖτε νάπαι καὶ Δώριον ὕδωρ,
     καὶ ποταμοὶ κλαίοιτε τὸν ἱμερόεντα Βίωνα ...
   Ends: καὶ σὲ Βίων πέμψει τοῖς ὥρεσιν. εἰ δέ τι κἠγὼν
     συρίσδων δυνάμαν, παρὰ Πλουτέι κ' αὐτὸς ἄειδον.

Moschus terms himself a pupil of Bion, and both were imitators of Theocritus, writing over a century after his death; but some scholars dismiss the *Lament for Bion* as by a weaker hand and leave its authorship uncertain. There is a pedantic Silver Age prettiness about the style, as when Bion is called "the Dorian Orpheus" and the sisters of Orpheus are "Oeagrian damsels." Moschus' closing passage about Persephone, however, is one of the pastoral felicities that the poets of Europe were destined never to forget. He was also the first pastoral poet to contrast the immortality of nature with the brief mortality of man. His chief achievement, however, was the establishment of the pastoral elegy as a genre to lament the death of a real, non-pastoral person. Nevertheless, his style marks the decline of the pastoral from its first flowering in Theocritus; and presently the original creative impulse was to peter out in the *technopaegnia* ("art games") of Dosiadas, Simmias, and Besantinos. It remained for Vergil, a full century later, to rejuvenate and transform the pastoral into a stylistic instrument on which anyone could play, even without being versed in pastoral or bucolic life.

Lament for Bion

Mournfully wail with me, ye woodland glades
And Dorian waters, weep for lovely Bion![36]
Lament with me, ye rivers and ye plants,
Cry out, ye forest groves, shed tears, ye flowers,
And sigh your lives away in sorrowing clusters;
Rose and anemone, grow red in grief;
And O ye hyacinths,[37] with deeper voice
Speak forth the letters graven on your petals!
Bion, the sweet musician, is no more.
  Begin, Sicilian Muses, your lament!
Let nightingales, that in thick foliage mourn,
Tell the Sicilian spring of Arethusa
That Bion, the dear cowherd, now is dead,
And with his death all music has departed
And all the gold of Doric song is spent.
  Begin, Sicilian Muses, your lament!
Wail by the waters, ye Strymonian[38] swans,
Chanting your dirge with melancholy note,
The lay he uttered with a voice like yours.
To the Oeagrian maidens[39] be it said,
To all Bistonian nymphs[40] the word proclaim:
"Alas, the Dorian Orpheus has perished."
  Begin, Sicilian Muses, your lament!

36 This is the first pastoral elegy that honours a real person, and that describes him as a shepherd, who also has achievements as a poet. This leads naturally on to an account of the author's relations with the dead poet (cf. *Lycidas*, 23–36), and opens the way for digressions. Hanford, in *PMLA*, xxv, stresses this dawn of "the personal elegy in pastoral form."
37 Cf. *Lycidas*, 106, and Sannazaro's *Mammilia*, p. 169.
38 The Strymon was a river in Thrace.
39 Orpheus' sisters, the daughters of Oeagrus, King of Thrace
40 Thracian. Thracian princesses and nymphs and a Thracian river are all invoked, because Orpheus, the legendary poet, lived and died in Thrace. Cf. *Lycidas*, 58–63.

To his beasts no more he sings, that herdsman dear,
Sitting beneath the solitary oak;
Nay, in the nether dark, by Pluto's side,
He sings a ballad of forgetfulness.
And so the hills are voiceless, and the heifers
Wander beside the bulls in silent sorrow
And will not go to pasture, out of grief.
  Begin, Sicilian Muses, your lament!
Even Apollo mourned your sudden fate,
O Bion, and the Satyrs[41] wept your end,
And all the sable-robed Priapuses[41]
And every Pan[41] made sorrow for your song;
The fountain-nymphs[41] bewailed you in the wood
Till every rill's cold waters were their tears.
Echo, among the rocks, was mute with grief:
Since you were still, she could not shape your voice.
The trees have dropped their fruitage at your dying,
And all the flowers have withered at your fall.
After your death, the ewes gave no good milk
And honey from the hives came not at all;
Deep in the comb it perished in its pain,
For since the honey of your song was spent,
Honey from bees mankind must now forego.
  Begin, Sicilian Muses, your lament!
Less sadly sang the Siren[42] on the beach,
Less mournfully the cliff-side Nightingale,[43]
Less sad the Swallow on the lofty hills,
Or Ceyx' cry for grieving Halcyon[44]
Or her reply among the grey-green waves,
Less sad the hovering bird of Memnon[45] sang

41 The effigies of these spirits, set up in the pasture-fields
42 Not the bewitching Siren of the *Odyssey*, Bk. xii, but a figure, half-bird
   and half-woman, that bewailed the dead
43 For the story of Philomela and Procne, the tragic daughters of Pandion,
   who were transformed into the Nightingale and the Swallow, see Ovid,
   Metamorphoses, vi, 428–670.
44 See n. 32, p. 94 above.
45 Memnon, the son of Tithornus and the Dawn, led an Ethiopian detach-
   ment in the Trojan War and was killed by Achilles. According to legend,
   his tomb was visited every year by birds known as "Memnonidae." In a
   much later legend, a colossal statue of Amenophis iv, near Thebes, in
   Egypt, was supposed to represent Memnon and to salute his mother
   with a musical note at daybreak.

Above the tomb where lay the Dawn's dead son
In valleys of the East, than all of Nature
Mourned in compassion at the death of Bion.
 Begin, Sicilian Muses, your lament!
All nightingales and swallows, whom of yore
He gladdened, as he taught them all to speak,
Sitting on branches, sang in antiphons
And said: "Sad birds, lament; and so will we!"
 Begin Sicilian Muses, your lament!
O thrice-regretted soul, who now will sing
To this your flute? Who would be rash enough
To set his lips upon your pan-pipes' reeds?
For in them still your lips and breath are living
And in these straws your music echoes yet.
Shall I give Pan the pipe? Yet he may fear
To lip it, lest he turn out second best.
 Begin, Sicilian Muses, your lament!
And Galatea,[46] too, bewails your lay,
She whom you once delighted as she sat
Beside you on the margin of the sea.
For not like Cyclops did you voice your song –
From such as he, fair Galatea fled,
While you she cherished like the sea itself.
But now, unmindful of its waves, she sits
Sad on the lonely sands and guards your cows.
 Begin, Sicilian Muses, your lament!
O neatherd, with your death have also died
All of the gifts the Muses can bestow:
 Begin, Sicilian Muses, your lament!
The charming kiss of maids, the lips of boys.
The sad-faced Loves lament about your corpse
And Cypris yearns more deeply for your love
Than, but the other day, she craved the kiss
With which she kissed Adonis as he died.[47]
 Most musical of rivers, Meles' stream,[48]

---

46 Bion is supposed to have written a serenade-style pastoral, sung as by a
 neatherd lover to the sea-nymph, Galatea. The four hexameters of his
 Fragment xii fit this pattern.
47 See Bion's *Lament for Adonis*, p. 100.
48 The Meles was a river at Smyrna, a city that was the birthplace of Bion
 and one of the alleged birthplaces of Homer.

This is your second grief, your second loss.
Homer died long ago, the honeyed mouth
Of sweet Calliopè, and you, they say,
Mourned your fair son with waves of many woes
And filled the whole salt ocean with your voice.
Now, for another son, you weep again,
And melt away in yet another sorrow.
Both men were dear to fountains: one of them
Drank at the mountain spring of Pegasus,[49]
The other took his draughts from Arethusa.
One sang the lovely daughter of Tyndareus,[50]
And Thetis' mighty son,[51] and Menelaus,[52]
The son of Atreus; but the other sang
Neither of wars nor tears, but songs of Pan;
The pleasant praise of cowherds did he sing,
And as he sang, he tended lowing herds,
And fashioned pipes, and milked the gentle cows;
The kiss of boys he taught, and in his bosom
He nourished up a playful little Cupid
And stirred the tender heart of Aphrodite.
    Begin, Sicilian Muses, your lament!
O Bion, every famous city mourns you,
And every little town. Ascra bemoans you
Much more than Hesiod; Boeotia's woodlands
Have never grieved so much at Pindar's death,
Nor Lesbos mourned so much to lose Alcaeus;
The town of Teos wailed her poet[53] less;
More than Archilochus are you to Paros;
While Mitylenè mourns your silenced voice
Instead of Sappho's song. To Syracusans
You were Theocritus come back again;
But I shall chant Ausonia's lament,
This song that I am singing in your honour,
Not as a stranger to the pastoral Muse
But as inheriting the Doric lay
You taught your pupils. You have honoured me,

49 Hippocrene, struck out on the crest of Helicon by the hoof of **Pegasus**
50 Helen
51 Achilles, the hero of the *Iliad*
52 King of Sparta and husband of Helen
53 Anacreon

By leaving some your wealth, but me your singing.[54]
   Begin, Sicilian Muses, your lament!
Alas, when mallows wither in the garth
And tendriled anise and green parsley die,
They rise again and grow another year;[55]
But we, great men and wise and strong of thew,
When once we die, sleep, lapped in hollow earth,
An endless, soundless sleep, and waken not,
As now you, too, are silent in the earth.
Nymphs to the frogs undying songs have given,
But theirs is raucous immortality.
   Begin, Sicilian Muses, your lament!
But poison came, O Bion, to your mouth,[56]
A fatal poison. How could venom come
To lips like yours and not be turned to sweetness?
What ruthless mortal could have heard your voice
And yet mixed poison as an evil gift?
The villain had no music in his soul.
   Begin, Sicilian Muses, your lament!
Though Justice took them all, I still must weep
In sorrow for the pity of your end.
Had only I been able, I had gone
With speedy purpose to the House of Pluto –
Even as Orpheus once made his way
To Tartarus below, and as of yore
Odysseus and Alcides ventured down –
Hoping to see you, if perchance you sing
To Pluto, and to hear what song you chant.
Come now, and offer a Sicilian strain,
A pastoral song, to please the awful Maiden.[57]
    For she, too, is Sicilian; on the shores

54 This is the first pastoral *elegy* into which the poet enters personally, as
in Theocritus' earlier non-elegiac *Harvest Home.*
55 This contrast between the cyclic return of plant life, year after year,
and the black finality of human death, still holds no hope. A change
seems to come with the apotheosis of Daphnis in Vergil's *Eclogue* v
and attains prominence in Christian elegies, including *Lycidas.* For the
Hebrew version, see *Job*, 14: 7–10.
56 See Shelley's *Adonais*, stanza xxxvi, and his use of four lines of
Moschus' Greek (111–14) as a motto at the beginning of his poem.
57 Cf. *Paradise Lost*, iv, 268–72; Arnold's *Thyrsis*, lines 81–90; and
Sannazaro's *Mammilia*, p. 171 below.

By Etna once she sported long ago.
She knew the Dorian strain. Not unrewarded
Will be a song that moves her memory.
Even as once, when Orpheus sang so sweet,
She granted his Eurydice's return,
So, Bion, she will send you to your hills.
If I had had such power with the flute,
To Pluto's face I should myself have sung.

Ly-5 (Latin)

PUBLIUS VERGILIUS MARO. *Ecloga* v. *Daphnis*, 42 B.C. From *P. Vergili Maronis Opera*, ed. Fredericus Arturus Hirtzel, Oxford, 1900

Begins: MENALCAS
Cur non, Mopse, boni quoniam conveniunt ambo,
tu calamos inflare levis, ego dicere versus ...
Ends: MOPSUS
non tulit Antigenes (et erat tunc dignus amari)
formosum paribus nodis atque aere, Menalca.

Sicilian shepherds, in the pastorals of Theocritus, were sometimes actual shepherds, though portrayed in the mellifluous verse of a sophisticated city poet who found refreshment and delight in this literary return to nature.

When the youthful Vergil, after steeping himself in the Greek of Theocritus, set out to reproduce the bucolic genre in Latin, he became both an imitator and an innovator. The German scholar Ribbeck has cited over eighty major borrowings (and a host of lesser ones) by Vergil from Theocritus; the *Eclogues* were as synthetically erudite as T.S. Eliot's *Four Quartets*. In a fundamentally new treatment, however, he used the apparent shepherds to represent actual non-shepherd people in the contemporary life of Rome. Thus the "lament for Daphnis" in *Eclogue* v is actually a tribute to the dead Julius Caesar, and is alleged to have been written for the anniversary of Caesar's birthday, 4 July 42 B.C., when the name of the month Quintilis was first changed to Julius. This pastoral is in two instalments, the first a song by Mopsus, who tells how all nature mourned the dead shepherd, and the second a song by Menalcas, who tells of the apotheosis of Daphnis – a passage with no parallel in Theocritus and one very relevant to the official deification of the "Divus Julius." Incidentally, it was imitated scores of times by later poets who found Christian consolation (as in *Lycidas*, 165–81) in the translation of a deceased friend to a place in Heaven. The flattery to the Caesarian house was gross but may have helped (along with the more direct appeal to Octavian in *Eclogue* IX) to win Vergil back his confiscated farm near Mantua.

For a literal prose translation by Harry Joshua Leon, see *The Pastoral Elegy*, ed. T.P. Harrison Jr and H.J. Leon (Austin, 1939), pp. 41–5.

Daphnis[58]
(Interlocutors: Menalcas and Mopsus)

MENALCAS
Since, Mopsus, we have met, both men of skill,
You on light reeds to play and I to trill
My verses, shall we not sit here, my friend,
Where elm-trees with the hazel bushes blend?

MOPSUS
You are the elder, and I must obey,
Whether we seek the shade where Zephyrs play
Or choose the cave. See how the gadding vine
Has marked the cave-mouth with its clusters fine.

MENALCAS
Here in the hills, only Amyntas tries
To rival you in singing for the prize.

MOPSUS
He might as well endeavour to outdo
Great Phoebus in a contest set for two.

MENALCAS
Begin, then, Mopsus, if you favour lays
Of love for Phyllis, or in Alcon's praise,
Or Codrus' scorn. Sing, as your fancy bids,

---

58 The title was supplied by ancient commentators. Nearly all of Vergil's names of shepherds are borrowed from Theocritus.

And Tityrus will tend your browsing kids.

MOPSUS

Nay, I will try some verses that of late
On a green beech-tree's bark I did narrate
And set to music, marking well the beat.
Then you may bid Amyntas know defeat.

MENALCAS

The olive-tree the willow bush outgoes,
The spikenard is inferior to the rose,
So much Amyntas at your song is dumb.
But peace, my lad, here to the cave we come.

MOPSUS sings

The Nymphs made moan for Daphnis in his death
By cruel fate; and you, ye hazel glades
And rivers, heard them utter mournful breath
When his sad mother[59] in your leafy shades
Embraced the hapless body of her son
And called upon the gods and cruel stars.
In those sad days, no rural work was done;
No neatherd drove his kine to slake their thirst
In the cool streams; no forest creature durst
Drink of the rill or touch a blade of grass;
The mountains and the forests heard the jars
Of bellowing grief as Afric lions curs'd
The death of Daphnis and roared out: Alas!
Daphnis it was who once taught men to yoke
Armenian tigers to the chariot
Of Bacchus, led his bands of dancing folk
And twined their pliant wands with bergamot.
As vines adorn the trees, as grapes the vines,

59 To a scene of mourning borrowed largely from the *Daphnis* of
Theocritus, Vergil has added the mourning Aphrodite of Bion's *Lament
for Adonis*, and this primarily as a compliment to the Julian family,
whose ancestress was alleged to have been the goddess Venus. As
Edward K. Rand has pointed out (*The Magic Art of Virgil*, 1931, p. 92),
"Virgil, then, is mingling the legends of Daphnis and Adonis in the
interests of a purpose different from either." His later *Aeneid*, the epic
of the son of Anchises and Venus through whom the lineage of Julius
Caesar was allegedly traced, spells the flattering theme out further.

As bulls the herds, as wheat in harvest shines,
So you were all the glory of your land.
Now that the Fates have taken you away,
Pales has left the fields, Apollo too.
Often the barley, planted by our hand,
Comes up as darnel in a luckless day
And sterile oats to mock our baffled view.
We seek soft violets and daffodils;
But thistles come, and brambles with their quills.
Spread leaves upon the ground, erect a shade
Over the flowing springs on his behalf.
Such are the honours Daphnis would be paid.
Build, too, a mound, and rear an epitaph:
"Here Daphnis rests, whose fame has reached the sky.
My herd is fair, but fairer still am I."

MENALCAS

O heavenly bard, your song has come again
Like slumber on the grass to weary men,
Or cooling water in a shady nook,
Quaffed in hot summer from a dancing brook.
You match your master, not with pipe alone
But with voice also. And you shall be known,
O happy lad, as second after him.
Yet shall I now reply in accents trim
And shall exalt your Daphnis to the stars.
He loved me too, and love my tongue unbars.

MOPSUS

What greater favour could your talent raise?
The lad was worthy of a song of praise,
But Stimichon has long since lauded you
For sweetest melody and accent true.

MENALCAS sings

Fair Daphnis, now divine, in wonder views
The unfamiliar threshold of the gods;[60]
He sees the clouds and stars beneath his feet.
And at the sight a thrill of pleasure sweet

60 This apotheosis of "Daphnis" is the wholly original part of *Eclogue* v
(see introductory note on p. xviii).

Runs through the forests, while all nature nods
In sudden joy; Pan and the shepherds muse,
With all the Dryads, in his grace complete.
The wolf now plots no ambush for the flock;
No hunter for the stag prepares his net;
Daphnis loves peace. With smiling face of rock,
The unshorn mountain shouts its joy to heaven;
The very cliffs and thickets now beset
The sky with song:"A god, a god is he!"
Be kind, I pray, and gracious to your folk!
Behold four altars: two for you are built
And two for Phoebus' sacrifice will be.
Each year two cups of milk I'll dedicate
And two of olive oil, and shall convoke
A banquet where the flowing wine is spilt,
Before the hearth if winter winds are cold;
But in the pleasant shade in harvest's heat
Out of the flagons I shall pour the bold
And new-made nectar of Arvisian wine.
Damoetas there shall sing a carol sweet,
And Lyctian Aegon chant a song divine;
Alphesiboeus there shall imitate
The dancing Satyrs. Thus we'll celebrate
To honour you forever, both each year
When to the Nymphs we pay our friendly vows
And when we cleanse the glebe-land and the ploughs.
As long as to the boar the hills are dear,
While fishes love the stream, and bees the thyme,
And on the dew the dark cicadas feed,
So long shall you in honour be sublime,
So long shall praises for your name abide.
As we in Bacchus and in Ceres trust,
So in your grace the farmers will confide,
And you will find their souls with vows august.

MOPSUS
What shall I give you for so sweet a song?
My spirit has not felt a joy so strong
In hearkening to the south wind as it rises,
Or to the billow that the shore chastises,

Or to the vocal brooks that downward flow
Through rocky valleys beneath peaks of snow.

MENALCAS
I'll first reward you with this slender pipe;
It taught me tunes like "Corydon is ripe[61]
With passion for Alexis" or, to free us,
"Who owns the flock? Could it be Meliboeus?"

MOPSUS
Take you this crook, for which Antigenes
Sued me in vain, though frequent were his pleas,
And though he then was worthy of my love.
Its even joints and brass, Menalcas, prove.

Ly-6 (Latin)

PUBLIUS VERGILIUS MARO. *Ecloga* x. *Gallus.* 38 B.C.

Begins: Extremum hunc, Arethusa, mihi concede laborem:
          pauca meo Gallo, sed quae legat ipsa Lycoris, ...
Ends: Iuniperi gravis umbra, nocent et frugibus umbrae.
          Ite domum saturae, venit Hesperus, ite capellae.

The allegorical incongruities of *Eclogue* v are outdone in *Eclogue* x, written by Vergil to console his friend and former fellow-student, Cornelius Gallus, for the unfaithfulness of his mistress, "Lycoris" (actually an actress named Cytheris), to whom Gallus, himself a poet as well as a high officer under Octavian, had addressed a number of poems in elegiac couplets. With awkward contradiction in Vergil's poem, Gallus is represented both as a soldier in camp in Italy (lines 44–5) and as a shepherd in the shadow of a cliff in Arcadia (lines 11–15). The debt to Theocritus (especially to *Idyll* I) is very heavy, and the same passages seem to have been mediated, in their Vergilian form, to *Lycidas*. For a literal prose translation by Harry Joshua Leon, see *The Pastoral Elegy*, ed. T.P. Harrison Jr and H.J. Leon (Austin, 1939), pp. 45–9.

61 Menalcas significantly claims as his own these quotations from Vergil's first two eclogues, thus apparently equating Menalcas and Vergil.

Gallus

Grant me, O Arethusa, this last song.
For Gallus must some song be sung indeed
Such as Lycoris by herself may read.
A gift of verses must to him belong,
For to deny them would be grievous wrong.
So, when beneath Sicilian waves you speed,
May bitter Doris[62] never intercede
And mingle with your stream her waters strong.
Therefore begin: Of Gallus' anxious love
Should be our discourse, while my flat-nosed goats
Browse on the tender bushes as they rove.
To no unhearing ears I tune my notes;
From every tree, below me and above,
The echoing forest all my verses quotes.

Where were ye, Nymphs, when Gallus dying lay[63]
Of hapless love? What groves or shadowy glades
Were you frequenting? For you did not stray
By high Parnassus nor the cold cascades
Of Pindus, or Aonian Helicon.
The laurels wept for him, the myrtles too,
And pine-clad Maenalus, and in the blue
The snowy peaks of cold Lycaeus shone
In sorrow as he lay beneath a cliff.
His sheep, too, stand about him, mute and stiff:
They scorn us not, and scorn not you the flock,
O godlike poet. Fair Adonis deigned
Likewise to feed his sheep by stream and rock:
The shepherds came; slowly the swineherds came;
Menalcas, from the steeping acorns stained,
Likewise drew near. "Will you give love a name?"
They all demand. Apollo spoke as well:
"Why, Gallus, are you crazed? Your faithless lass

62 The wife of Nereus, the seagod, is here used to personify seawater in
general. The fresh spring-water of Arethusa ran the risk of brackish
pollution as it fled on sea-bottom from Elis to Sicily.
63 The next 29 lines are modelled closely after Theocritus' *Daphnis*.

Has gone through campaign snow and mountain pass,
There with another friend in love to dwell."
Silvanus[64] came with chaplet on his brow
And fennels and broad lilies in his hand.
And Pan, Arcadia's god, drew near us now,
Whose visage bright and ruddy we have scanned,
With blood-red elderberries stained and decked.
"Is there no limit to your tears?" said he.
"Never has cruel Love for weeping recked,
Thirsty as grass for water, bees for thyme,
Or wanton she-goats for fresh greenery."
But sadly he gave answer: "Song sublime
Will you Arcadians sing in these your hills,
For you alone are skilled in tuneful song.
How gently would I rest, released from ills,
If your soft syrinx should my theme prolong.
I wish indeed I had been one of you,
To tend your flocks or dress your ripened grapes;
I would have found a rustic love most true,
Some Phyllis or Amyntas, pleasing shapes
(And if they should be dark, I should not care,
For hyacinths are dark, and violets),
Among the willows they my rest would share,
Beneath the creeping vine; while Phyllis gets
A garland for my head, Amyntas sings.
Here, my Lycoris, there are cooling springs;
Here is a grove; here velvet meadows lie;
Here by your side I could wear out my life
With time alone. But a mad love for Mars
Keeps me in arms, grasping the tools of strife
And face to face with foemen and their wars;
While you, alas, far from your native land
(Let me not credit such a dreadful tale!)
Alone, without me, gaze on Alpine snows,[65]
O cruel maid, and on Rhine's frozen strand.
Ah, may the cold not harm you! May no woes
Of jagged ice on your soft feet prevail!

64 The Roman god of the woods (*silvae*)
65 Lycoris has gone off "campaigning" to Switzerland or Gaul with some
   soldier.

I will depart; the measures I have framed
In verse of Chalcis[66] I shall not attune
To the soft pipe of the Sicilian swain.
In forests with the beasts I shall remain,
Young tree-trunks with my love-tale shall be maimed.
The trees will grow; and I, who shall commune
With them, shall find my passion likewise grow.
Meanwhile, through heights of Maenalus I'll go
With bands of nymphs, or hunt the fierce wild boar;
No frost shall check me and my faithful hounds
From ranging thickets of Parthenius;[67]
I fancy even now I sally thus
With speed through echoing woods and rocky bounds,
And loose Cydonian[68] shafts from Parthian bows! —
As if, indeed, this were an antidote
To all my frenzy, and that god of Love
Could soften at a stricken lover's woes.
My joy in nymph and dryad grows remote;
Even in song no pleasure can I prove.
Even ye woods, a second time farewell!
No sufferings can work on Love a spell,
Even if cold midwinter saw me drink
From icy Hebrus and the snows of Thrace;
Or if, where lofty elm-trees parch and shrink
Beneath the star of Cancer, I should pace
The pastures of the Ethiopian race.
Love conquers all; let us, too, seek his grace."

Pierian maids, may these, my songs, suffice,
Sung as a creel of mallow-stems I wove.
May their delight my Gallus' heart entice;
Like alder-shoots in spring aspires my love.
Before the deepening shadows let us rise,
Lest darkness to my song a peril prove.
Shade to the growing crop may be severe.
Home, then, my well-fed goats! The night draws near.

66 Gallus had translated some of the Greek poetry of Euphorian, a scholar
   from Chalcis, in Euboea.
67 A mountain in Arcadia
68 Cydonia, the Cretan home of "Lycidas" in Theocritus' *Harvest Home*,
   was apparently famous for the manufacture of arrows.

Ly-7 (Latin)

L Y G D A M U S (T I B U L L U S ?) . "Dying for Neaera" (*Lygdami Elegiae,*
ii). About 19 B.C.

Begins: Qui primus caram iuveni caramque puellae
         eripuit iuvenem, ferreus ille fuit ...
  Ends: Lygdamus hic situs est. Dolor huic et cura Neaerae
         coniugis ereptae causa perire fuit.

Published as a third book of the Elegies of Tibullus (about 54–19
B.C.) are six elegies ascribed to an unknown Lygdamus, once identified as a *nom de guerre* for Tibullus himself but now almost universally rejected as being an obviously inferior poet. In his Second
Elegy, he is dying (like Gallus or Daphnis) because of love. He
dreams of how, after his death, his lost sweetheart will come to his
cremation:

> Thus when I change, and have become a shade,
> And black ash cloaks the white my bones have made,
> Let sad Neaera weep beside my pyre,
> With hair dishevelled and in dark attire ...

Ly-8 (Latin)

P U B L I U S O V I D I U S N A S O . *Amores*, III, ix. About 19 B.C. ("Lament
for Tibullus")

Begins: Memnona si mater, mater ploravit Achillem,
         et tangunt magnas tristia fata deas ...
  Ends: ossa quieta, precor, tuta requiescite in urna,
         et sit humus cineri non onerosa tuo!

One of the early poems of Ovid (43 B.C.–A.D. 18) was his elegy on
the death of the elegiac poet, Tibullus, in 19 B.C. In it he laments the
deaths of all poets, from Orpheus and Homer down to Catullus, and
meditates, like Milton, on the questions that such human extinction
must raise. Their poetry itself may perhaps achieve immortality
(*defugiunt avidos carmina sola rogos*), but for the dead poet his

only word of consolation is the presence of loved ones at his cremation and the faint possibility of fellowship in Elysium with the blessed spirits of Catullus and "Gallus." Extracts from the "Lament for Tibullus" are printed below. Ovid, like Propertius, is clearly not in the pastoral tradition.

Lament for Tibullus

In truth death's hands profane all sacred things,
And plunge in gloom all human reckonings!
When Orpheus fell, what parent[69] cured his wrong?
What help were beasts once conquered with his song?
Linus[70] was mourned for by the same sad sire,
Deep in the woods with unresponsive lyre.
To these add Homer, to whose living source
The lips of bards have ever had recourse;
Him, too, to hell a final day once gave,
For only song escapes the hungry grave ...
Be just, you perish; seek the gods' own room,
Death from their temples drags you to the tomb;
Or trust in verse – Tibullus now lies dead,
A little ash is left us in his stead.
Is it your breast, O bard, so rapt anon,
That funeral flames have dared to feed upon?
A fire that shrank not from such awful odds
Would burn the golden temples of the gods! ...

If more than name and shadow shall abide,
Tibullus through Elysium will glide;
There may you meet him, crowned with ivy leaves,
Learnèd Catullus,[71] while your Calvus grieves;
And you, O Gallus, if devoid of stain,
So prodigal of heart's blood and of brain.
With these your ghost consorts; if ghost there be,

69 Though his parents were Apollo and the Muse Calliope
70 A mythological Greek hero whose untimely death was sung every year
     at harvest-time. Folk etymology may have created him out of the refrain
     of that song, taking *ailinon* as *Ai Linon* ("Alas for Linus"). He is
     believed to personify, like Daphnis or Adonis, the soft vegetation of
     springtime that perishes under the summer sun of the Mediterranean
     world.
71 One of the finest brief poems of Catullus (No. xcvi) was his six-line
     tribute of sympathy "To Calvus, on the death of [his wife] Quintilia."

Tibullus, you must grace their coterie.
Lie quiet, bones, placed here in quiet trust;
And may the earth be light above your dust![72]

Ly-9 (Latin)

SEXTUS PROPERTIUS. *Eclogues*, III, vii, *The Death of Paetus*. Rome, 16 B.C.

Begins: Ergo sollicitae te causa, pecunia, vitae!
       per te immaturum mortis adimus iter ...
 Ends: at tu, saeve Aquilo, numquam mea vela videbis:
       ante fores dominae condar oportet iners.

This poem, like *Lycidas*, laments the death of a friend by drowning at sea. Paetus, however, was not the victim of obscure misadventure but rather of shipwreck in a severe storm. His desire for money-making in foreign trade is the underlying cause of his untimely death. There is no pastoral make-believe in the poem, and Paetus, instead of any consolatory transformation, merely becomes "strange food for far-off fishes" (*nova longinquis piscibus esca*). The only hint of poetic artifice is when the north wind and the sea are addressed by name and when Thetis and the Nereids are upbraided for not saving the drowning youth; but almost in the same breath Propertius says bluntly: "There are no gods in the sea" (*non habet unda deos*). The metre throughout is the elegiac distich.

For a literal prose translation, see H.E. Butler, *Propertius* (London and New York, 1916), pp. 195–201.

For a critical note, see F.R.B. Godolphin, "Milton, *Lycidas*, and Propertius, Elegies III, 7," *Modern Language Notes*, XLIX (1934), 162–6.

The Death of Paetus
(Elegiac couplets)

You, then, O gold, are the cause that our pitiful life has
    found evil!

---

72 This imaginative touch is found again, a century later, in Martial (v, xxxiv), where he mourns the death of the little girl, Erotion, almost six years old, and petitions, at her graveside," "Be not heavy on her, O earth, for she was not so to you."

Seeking for you, we go down, sentenced to death ere our
time.
You give the vices of men the dark fodder that brings them
to trouble;
You are a fountain of grief, source of the seeds of our woe.
Thrice and four times you plunged Paetus in thundering
waves of disaster,
Setting his sails on the deep, seeking for Pharos[73] as port.
Following you, the poor wretch, he was cut off in season
untimely;
Strange food for fishes he floats, far from the land of
his sires.
Even the mother he loved could not give him the rites of
sepulture,
Laying his bones in the earth, close to the dust of his kin.
Only the birds of the deep by your bones on the seashore are
standing;
All the Carpathian Sea[74] serves as your desolate tomb.
Furious wind from the North, the deep dread of your raped
Orithyia,
What were the spoils that you sought, smiting so wretched
a man?
Neptune, how could you delight, to join in so sorry a
shipwreck?
Righteous were all of the men, borne in that pitiful barque.
Paetus, why number your years, as you swim in the surf
of the billows?
Why on your mother cry out? Gods in the sea there are
none.
Cables were bound to the rocks, but the terrible tempest of
night-time
Wore through their impotent strands, carrying all to the
deep.

Give back his body to earth, for his soul has been lost in the
ocean;
Drift at your will, barren sands! Cover our Paetus at last.

73 An island and lighthouse, part of the great port of Alexandria, then one
of the largest cities in the world and focus of the Mediterranean
commerce that held out a promise of wealth to traders like Paetus
74 South of Rhodes and the nearby island of Carpathus (Karpathos)

Sailors that pass by his grave, let them say as in horror they
    tremble:
    "Even in him who is brave, terror your fate can inspire."
Go, and create crooked vessels, and weave us new causes of
    dying:
    This is the fashion of death, framed by the craftwork of
    man.
Earth was too small for destruction, we added the billows;
    Thus by our arts are we slain, widening highways of fate.
You whom your home could not hold, could the fluke of an
    anchor preserve you?
    What would you say he deserves, finding his homeland too
    small?
That which you build by your toil is the pitiful sport of the
    tempest;
    Keels were not made to grow old; treacherous, too, is the
    port.
Nature with guile has provided the sea as a path for the
    greedy:
    Scarcely, for once in your life, gain from the sea is your lot.
Yonder are shores that bear witness to ills that once smote
    Agamemnon,
    Here where Argynnus was killed, branding the Mimian
    waves;
Here, for the loss of this youngster, calm-stayed were the
    ships of Atrides;
    Here, for the navy's delay, Iphigenia was slain.
Rocks of Caphareus[75] shattered the fleet that sailed homeward
    triumphant;
    Shipwrecked Greece was engulfed, deep in the waves of
    the sea.
One after one, as they perished, Ulysses bewailed his
    companions;
    Only when faced by the sea, all of his guile was as naught.

Paetus, if he had been willing to plough with his father's
    stout oxen,
    Giving my words due weight, still would be living today,
Would have been feasting in joy by his household's ancestral
    Penates,

75 A rocky promontory on the southeast coast of Euboea

Poor, but with naught to beweep, save but the absence of
wealth.
Paetus could never endure the shriek of the gale in the rigging,
Marring his delicate hands, hauling the cordage in pain.
Dreaming of chambers of marble, intent on Illyrian couches,
Propping his head upon down, tinted with glorious hues,
Him, while he lived, did the billow torment, tear the nails
from his fingers,
Flooding his mouth while he gaped, dashing the sea in his
throat.
Frail was the plank that he clutched, as the wild night beheld
him borne headlong:
So many evils conspired, plotting the death of our friend.
Yet he laid charge on the sea, as he wept in his last
lamentation,
Even while billows of black muffled his mouth as he died:
"Winds, and ye gods of the sea that prevail in your might on
the waters,
Every wave of the deep, dragging my head to the depths,
Where do you tear me away, in the years of my youthful
affliction?
What was the guilt of my hands, brought in despite to
your seas?
Sharp rocks, alas, where the kingfisher nests, shall with
rending afflict me!
Neptune, the blue sea's god, smites me to death with his
fork.
Ah, may the tides at the least cast me up on Italian beaches.
Little of me may be left; grant that my mother may know."
Eddying waves as he spoke dragged him down to the depths
of the waters;
Language and life, all at once, passed from the sorrowful
man.

Hundredfold daughters of Nereus, compassionate maids of
the ocean,
Thetis whom motherly love drew long ago from the deep,
You should have placed your white arms as supports to his
chin as he faltered;
Such a light burden was he, naught to your rescuing hands.

Furious wind of the North, you shall never see sails of my
   venture.
Close to my mistress's doors, there is the harbour I seek.

Ly-10 (Latin)

SEXTUS PROPERTIUS. *Elegies*, Book IV, vii. Rome, 16 B.C.

Begins: Sunt aliquid Manes: leta non omnia finit,
      luridaque evictos effugit umbra rogos ...
  Ends: haec postquam querela mecum sub lite peregit,
      inter complexus excidit umbra meos.

The elegies of Propertius are in an entirely different tradition from
those of the Theocritean-Vergilian pastoral. It is not merely that
he uses the elegiac couplet (alternating hexameter and pentameter)
instead of the bucolic hexameter. He has no artificial conventions
of shepherds or neatherds, rural or allegorical, but presents his own
experiences, especially his amorous adventures with Cynthia, a
beautiful golden-haired prostitute whom he loved deeply but could
not legally marry. In the seventh elegy of his fourth book, after the
death of Cynthia, her ghost comes to him in a dream. She recalls
their former days of passionate love and reproaches him with lack
of concern for her tomb at Tibur. She had been true to him (after her
fashion) –"if I lie, may a serpent hiss on my grave and sleep above
my bones." Two of her servants had poisoned her, but she begs him
to provide for her aged nurse, Parthenie. Soon he, too, will die, and
then his bones will mingle with those of his cremated sweetheart.

Ly-11 (Latin)

M. AURELIUS OLYMPIUS NEMESIANUS. *Eclogue* I: *Meliboeus*
About A.D. 290. From *Minor Latin Poets*, ed. J. Wight Duff and Arnold M.
Duff (London and Cambridge, 1934)

Begins: TIMETAS
      Dum fiscella tibi fluviali, Tityre, iunco
      Texitur et raucis immunia rura cicadis ...

Ends: TITYRUS
> Sed iam sol demittit equos de culmine mundi,
> Flumineos suadens gregibus praebere liquores.

The white-haired old shepherd, Tityrus, urges the young shepherd, Timetas, to sing a song in honour of their friend, Meliboeus, who has died recently of extreme old age. Previous elegies had celebrated lives cut off untimely, and Nemesianus has shown marked originality in extending the genre to cover death in ripe old age. Otherwise the elegy is a mosaic of adaptations from Vergil. Assuming personal allegory, we do not know any of the persons involved. Nemesianus was a native of Carthage and lived in Rome during the reigns of Carus and his sons. Eleven centuries later, Petrarch referred (*Eclogue* x, 199–201) to his pastorals in complimentary fashion.

For a literal prose translation by Harry Joshua Leon, see *The Pastoral Elegy*, ed. T.P. Harrison Jr and H.J. Leon (Austin, 1939), pp. 50–4.

Meliboeus
(Interlocutors: Timetas and Tityrus)

TIMETAS
While, Tityrus, you weave a creel of rushes,
And in the fields no high cicala shrills,
Begin some song that from the thin flute gushes;
For Pan has taught you how in reeds to blow
With vocal lips, and Phoebus, too, fulfils
Your prayer that gifts of verse he might bestow.
Begin, while kids all munch on willow-boughs
And cows on grass, while dew and early sun
Urge you to let them at their pleasure browse
The meadows of a morning just begun.

TITYRUS
Neighbour Timetas, do you, young in years
And favoured by the gods, ask songs of me,
Whose years are many and whose head is hoar?
I made up songs, and sang, in years of yore,
When love did with my carefree youth agree.
But now my head is white, love disappears
And seethes in me no longer. Sure, my reeds

To rustic Faunus have been hung away.
It is with you the fields resound today,
For lately, with myself as judge, your deeds
In song made mock of the discordant lay
And scrannel pipes of Mopsus in the meads.
Old Meliboeus hearkened to you both,
Beside me, and he praised you to the skies.
He now has closed a life both good and wise,
And so the quiet heaven of the just
Must hold him in its bosom, nothing loath.
Therefore proceed, if to his soul august
There linger any thanks within your heart.
Honour his shade with all your sweet flute's art.

TIMETAS
Obedience to your will shall please me well;
What you request is welcome. That old man
Deserved the tribute of Apollo's song,
Of Pan's own pipes, of Linus with his lyre
And Thracian Orpheus, that their praise should swell
The many glories of his earthly span.
But since from my own music you desire
The praises that to such a soul belong,
Hear now the verses that the cherry tree
Beside the river-bank records for me,
Cut in its bark, upon this very theme.

TITYRUS
Declare them then; but lest this chattering pine
Disturb our peace beside the gentle stream,
Let us beneath the elm and beech recline.

TIMETAS
Here it is sweet to sing: for meadows lush
Spread their green grass and all the grove is still:
See how the bullocks in the noonday hush
Crop in the meadow on the distant hill.

He sings:
All-gendering Heavens, and ye Waters, too,
The source of being, and thou Mother Earth

And vital Air, sustainers of our birth,
Accept these songs, and waft them through the blue
To greet our Meliboeus, if consent
Be granted for the silent shades to know,
After their death, our utterance below.
For if sublimer souls of men frequent
Celestial realms and far-off starry homes
And live in heavenly joy, give gracious heed
To this my plaintive measure as it roams,
For once you cherished it, and praised my deed.
Your life was long, and well approved by all;
And happy years were yours, till at the last
The closing cycle of a natural
And righteous life was added to the past.
Yet none the less our grief bewailed that time
Than if harsh death had plucked you in your prime,
Nor did life's common fate check our laments:
"Alas, good Meliboeus, stark you lie
In death's cold rigour by the lot of man,
Worthy in hoary age to seek the sky
And fellowship with gods where life began.
Your breast was full of just authority.
Rustic disputes you oft would arbitrate,
Soothing their quarrels with a soul sedate.
A love of right prevailed beneath your sway,
Respect for justice under you would be:
Disputed fields received a boundary-stone.
A kindly gravity was in your face
And mild tranquillity was on your brow;
Yet kinder than your face your heart was known.
At your behest, reeds to our lips we'd place
And, joining them with wax, would disallow
Harsh care, for your instruction set us free.
You did not let our sluggish youth lie slack,
But often offered gifts of high degree
To lure our talent on. Despite your age,
Lest we should be reluctant to perform,
You would yourself recall some ditty back,
Some reed-song of Apollo's heritage.
O happy sage, farewell! With homage warm,
Rural Apollo, plucking laurel boughs,
Offers their leafy fragrance as a gift.

The Fauns, according to their strength, uplift
Clusters of ripened fruitage from the vine,
Grain from the fields and fruits from every tree.
Then venerable Pales from the cows
Offers you vessels full of milk a-foam;
The Nymphs bring honey; Flora's hands combine
Blossoms of many colours from the lea.
These are the final honours they bring home
To grace your ghost. The Muses give their songs,
Such songs as Muses give, and we proceed
To tune them to the flute. The grove prolongs
Our tribute as the plane-tree murmurs low
And pine-tree whispers to your name give heed;
Echo repeats the notes that from them flow
And all our herds cry out your treasured name.
Sooner will seals in our parched meadows feed,
Sooner will shaggy lions haunt the sea,
Yew-trees ooze honey, or, in shattered frame
Of muddled seasons, the frigidity
Of winter give us wheat, soft summer days
The ripened olive, autumn bourgeon flowers,
And springtime yield us grapes in sheer amaze,
Than will my fluting leave your praise unsung."

TITYRUS
Go on, my lad, do not leave off the lays
That you have thus begun. So sweet the hours
In which you sing, surely Apollo's powers
Will lead you kindly to earth's capital.
Already here, in forest walks, your fame
Has opened up a pathway for your name,
Cleaving the clouds of envy with her wing.
But now the evening sun, about to fall,
Drives down his horses from the firmament
And bids us offer, as the day grows spent,
The river to our flocks' low murmuring.

Ly-12 (Latin)

PASCHASIUS RADBERTUS. *Ecloga duarum sanctimonialium.* About
A.D. 826. J.P. Migne, *Patrologia Latina*, cxx (Paris, 1879)

Begins: GALATEA
    "Plangite, quaeso, viri, mecum pie plangite patrem,
    Omnis et inploret veniam provectior aetas ...
Ends: GALATEA
    Sparge viam violis, virtutum floribus arvam,
    Pinge rosis callem, plateis lilia sterne."

Born in or near Soissons about 790, Radbertus, around the age of 22, entered the Corbie monastery near Amiens. As a monk, in"the Carolingian Renaissance"of the age of Charlemagne, he studied classical authors as well as Scripture and the Latin Fathers. From before 790 until 826, Saint Adalhard was the abbot of his monastery and the founder of another one, New Corbie, in Saxony. In Radbertus' pastoral elegy on the death of his former superior, he personifies the Old Corbie (Gallic) monastery as an agèd nun, the spiritual spouse of Adalhard, and the New Corbie (Saxon) monastery as a young nun, their spiritual daughter. The echoes of Vergil are numerous, as well as the patching in of passages from *Isaiah* and *Ecclesiastes*. Radbertus himself left an extensive key to his allegory, written in Latin prose, and this helped to persuade Petrarch, five centuries later, that this was a proper function of the pastoral. The dirge for Adalhard embodied both a protest against Death and an exaltation of Adalhard's achievements and virtues. The consolation to be found in a Christian heaven is added to the tradition, as well as the representation of a priest (here the abbot) as the shepherd of a flock.

For a literal prose translation by Harry Joshua Leon, see *The Pastoral Elegy*, ed. T.P. Harrison Jr and H.J. Leon (Austin, 1939), pp. 55–64.

An unexpected outburst of pastoral song in the same period is a lyric by Alcuin (735–804), blending the countryside of his native England with the spirit of the classical humanism of which he was the supreme expression at the court of Charlemagne:"Plangamus cuculum, Dafnin dulcissime, nostrum ..."[76] Nearly four centuries later, but still two centuries short of Petrarch, the unidentified

---

76 Raby, F.J.E., ed., *The Oxford Book of Mediaeval Latin Verse* (1959), pp. 107, 466. Tr."Dearest Daphnis, let us lament our Cuckoo." In this poem sent to a favourite pupil, whom he had nicknamed"Daphnis," Alcuin lamented the disappearance into a non-academic world of another well-loved pupil whom he had nicknamed"The Cuckoo."He was a Scholar Gypsy – but roving in pursuit of Bacchus.

"Archpoet" gave voice to the verbal magic of the greatest mediaeval lyric: "Dum Dianae vitrea sero lampas oritur ... Fronde sub arboris amena, dum querens canit philomena, suave est quiescere ..."[77] And an even more anonymous poet satirized the pastoral tradition in a spirit of gaiety: "Gregis pastor Tityrus, / asinorum dominus, / noster est episcopus."[78] Evidently the Dark Ages were quite familiar with the classical pastoral, even if, until the fourteenth century, few poets felt impelled to reproduce the genre.

Eclogue of the Two Nuns
(Interlocutors: Galatea and Phyllis)

In this laudatory l'envoi to a Latin life of Saint Adalhard, these two nuns represent allegorically the two monasteries that he had founded, Corbie (*Phyllis*, the elder), before A.D. 813, near Amiens, France, and New Corbie (*Galatea*, the younger), in A.D. 822, on the Weser River, in Westphalia. The former presents herself as his spouse, the latter as his spiritual daughter.

GALATEA
Bewail, I pray you, in a pious dirge
The worthy father, and let everyone
Advanced in age now pray to be forgiven.
Sprinkle the earth with tears, and deck the field
With flowers for our Father's funeral;
Therefore make all things damp with lamentations.
Let moanings from the heart so aid the tongue
That even stars may echo back our grief.
Let rustic Roman speech and Latin tongue
Proclaim his obsequies; and let the Saxon,
In his own language, mourn instead of singing.
Hither let all men turn, and, as of old
That mighty poet bade us, "Rear a tomb,
And to the tombstone add an epitaph."
Bear now the blessèd limbs of this old man

77 Ibid., pp. 322–3. Tr. "While the crystal lamp of Diana is rising late ... it is sweet to rest under the kind branch of a tree, while Philomela sings her lament." The ascription is uncertain, but Helen Waddell (*The Wandering Scholars*, 1927, pp. 147–60) puts the poem in her chapter on "The Arch Poet."

78 Ibid., p. 309. Tr. "Tityrus, shepherd of the flock, master of asses, that's our bishop." The poem was doubtless written for the Feast of Fools.

To this famed spot, even of him who toiled
To show our eyes the gleaming veins of ore.
Here at his burial let the clergy sing
Poems divine with alternating voice,
Thus mingling in the echoing antiphon.
Let shepherds in the voice of verse proclaim
That he was great, a fair flock's faithful keeper,
Himself more fair, and let the crowd reply:
"O God, Creator dear, grant favour now
To this Thy servant; we beseech and pray
That he may be endowed with Paradise:
Grant Thy compassion to this agèd man,
And on ourselves have mercy, for Thou knowest
How worthy was this man of Thy compassion."
Give voice then to your loving pain and sorrow;
Let boys seek virtue, and the old due praise.

PHYLLIS
Who then, I beg you, would not weep and wail
Because a man whose merit reached the stars
Is now but ashes, in hard marble sealed;
That he whose merit speeds through all the earth
Among all peoples and the race of kings
Is food for worms? Alas, what shall we do,
Faced in our wretchedness with ruthless Death?
We wail, we groan, but cannot call him back.
His call from Death has come, and he is gone,
And cannot hear the voices of his friends.
We rend our breasts, our hearts are torn with grief;
But neither tears nor sorrow touch him now.
Because we suffer, we are all confused;
Grief rends our souls, but deaf Death pays no heed.
We may preserve his body's earthly dust,
But his translated soul, among the stars,
Rejoices in the choir of the blest.
Therefore I wish that men and lads and girls
Shall mightily lament; from pious hearts
Let salty fountains of your sorrow flow,
In order that, since our sad human birth
Ordains a mortal destiny for all,
The one sure fate of all who went before us,

We all should feel this common plight together.
Therefore let weeping, grief and hapless tears
Break in one utterance forth; through lips of monks
Let but a single lamentation flow.

GALATEA
I ask that you, the elder of us Corbies,
Should duly lay the old man in the tomb.
Thereafter I, the younger, thus bereaved
Of such a loved protector, shall compose
A dirge that may be sung in antiphons.
When you, a happy mother, gave me birth,
A happy daughter, by your only spouse,
You gave me your own name and gladly said:
"Lovely am I, and I have brought you forth
A lovely daughter to the end of time."
Rejoicing, three times blessèd, he begot me
And uttered many saving prophecies.
For then the devil raged; his wicked worship
Defiled the land; he cast the altars down
And all the holy sheepfolds of Christ's flock.
Then did our father, cutting far and wide,
The very timbers of the rooted grove,
Establish there a holy monastery
And fill its quiet corridors with monks.

PHYLLIS
Too happy have I been – what sorrows now
Must I endure! Though as a gift of God
Rich benefits were heaped upon your work,
O holy shepherd, first on Amiens' soil,
Where your own merit destined you to lead
The flock of Corbie; then the Saxon land
Hailed you as father, that you might restore
A doubled talent to the hand of God.
But you, O treacherous Death, all-venomous,
Pity no mortal, least of all ourselves,
And cannot be assuaged by any gift.
You love not man, and will not save our masters.
One sad, inevitable hour awaits
The ghosts of all men; for Death's sudden hand

Has snatched away from us this blessèd man
Whom in one chorus of complaining tongues
We weep and wail and, in our mourning, love:
But you, O ruthless Death, no pity know,
Not even upon us, the pitiful.
The pity of it all! In utter envy
You drag all men away, and swallow up
All the experience that our lives have known.

GALATEA

How kind of word and gentle was our master!
Why have you gone from us so suddenly,
Weak as we are? You, through your death, will be
Throughout all ages blessèd; as for me,
An uncouth virgin, stained by many wars
And dripping with a rainy fount of tears,
In loud laments I beat my guilty bosom;
Hence I shall wash with tears my sin-blotched face,
So that however dark and scummed with poisons
My countenance may be, I shall grow fair
With heavenly roses on my snowy cheeks.
My beauty shall blaze forth, though moist with tears;
And happy in your love I yet shall weep
For such a span of years as fate ordains.

PHYLLIS

Never will you outdo me in your grief
And lamentation, or in echoing songs
And uttering vows of honour to the dead.
Mix honey therefore, while I gather flowers;
Pluck me pale violets, while I pick lilies,
And we shall deck his grave with sweetest herbs.
Most worthy was he of such gifts as these,
For he himself endowed us with delights
And had baptized you with the blood of Christ.
Isaiah had foretold this long ago:
See, now, the holy trees of glory come,
Clapping their hands; the myrtle here is glad,
The fir-tree joins the pine in exultation;
The vineyard and its grapes are flourishing;
The shining olive too; like paradise

And gardens of delight will you be nourished
By flowing waters from the peaks of heaven.
A desert have you been, a path to Hell,
And have become a portal of the sky
And now stand open as the gate of life.
Nor shall the treachery of Death suffice
To countervail you in so swift a course
In which with soaring head you touch the stars
And in your glory flame across the world.
Soon shall no earlier nurse of monks display
A richer harvest under all the sky.
Therefore, instead of song, make due lament,
For scarcely eighty years had he completed,
And never yet with milk your breasts had flowed.
Lo, suddenly he died; and with that death,
The pitcher has been broken at the fountain.

BOTH
He was his country's trusted counsellor,
Filled with the sapience of Jesus Christ.

GALATEA
Alas, my mother, why would you renew
Our grief by telling it? Or why recall
The harshest day that we have ever known
Or can endure in all the years to come?
Our founder's death today has robbed us quite
Of every good, and cut his virtues off.
How pitiful we are, deprived of him,
For we are vanquished by an evil lot;
When he was with us, we were hard beset
To make our way to heaven; 'twere better far
To die with him than linger in our weakness.

PHYLLIS
Therefore, O people, whom baptizing streams
Have washed from sin, bring from your inmost hearts
A stream of living grace; and let us mourn
My spouse's death, because the man was prudent,
Sober and chaste and filled with charity,
Gentle, and just, and kindly, and most modest;

Noble, moreover, and in wise discourse
Surpassed by none; for in his sparkling speech
The wisdom of the Lord came springing forth,
A sermon of salvation to us all.
His character was notable, quite filled
With virtue's own instruction, fond of peace,
Gentle and merciful and very meek –
These qualities of soul were his by right,
The fragrant assets of my bridal dower.
Therefore my blessèd love of such a saint
Increases like the flowers that grow in spring.
But all the more my grief from hour to hour
Must follow me, because my love for him
Blazes unquenchably, and no kind cure
Avails my grief if I am not permitted
At least to celebrate his holy name.

GALATEA

Begin to lay your anxious griefs aside.
Perhaps the Muses at our funeral rites
Are so amazed that words and tunes are parted.
At these your dirges, all of Nature grieves,
Even the stones. Oh, might his love return,
That we who have been plunged in waves of tears
Might be revived to know his honeyed breath!
May we some day, together, hand in hand,
Go to the citadel, the mansioned home
To which he summons us across the years.
May we feed always in those heavenly fields
Where old Menalcas, that most happy man,
Deserved to enter, he who took with him
Our long enduring love and faithful sighs.

PHYLLIS

The laws of prayer are sure to reach to heaven,
Though now before us, right athwart our path,
The sad tomb stands. But if we constantly
Knock at the door and ask, there is no doubt
That after death we shall attain the city
Where piety and virtue ever reign,
Where peace and light and plenty shall prevail.
There joy, fruition, rest and pleasure shine;

There every good thing gleams, and concord sweet
Shall soothe us; glory, honour and high praise
Flow from one fountain; there eternal life
Rejoices in the fields where virtue grows;
Flocks of angelic sheep proclaim their thanks;
The heavenly meads are green; rewards at last
Are ratified with never-failing gifts;
For God himself is ever in their midst
And rich rewards shall bless the regiments
Of the apostles and the patriarchs;
Heaven's fragrance is more sweet than any herb;
In open, mossy plots the martyrs lie;
The city of the prophets there exhales
Sweetness unspeakable; the shining ranks
Of all the saints wax gold in virgin flower;
Pleasure devout shall all souls celebrate,
Re-echoing their songs as with one heart,
Each singing thus with honey in his tones.

GALATEA

Cease your description, mother, for perchance
We shall with better justice sing it all
When we have seen it, and our happy lot
Shall be in heaven with the blessèd host.
And meantime let us roam our earthly fields
In search of lilies, till the heavenly chorus
Echoes around us. Strew with violets
The way we tread, bedeck the fields with flowers,
The streets with lilies, and the roads with roses.

Ly-13 (Hebrew)

EZEKIEL. *Denunciation of the Shepherds (Ezekiel 34: 2–10).* About 593–571 B.C.

Begins: Ben-'adam hinnabhe' 'al-ro'ei yisrael ...
  Ends: wehissalti soni mipihem welo-thihyeyan lahem le'akhlah.

A prophetic denunciation of the "shepherds" of the nation, in the spirit of *Lycidas* 108–31, goes back at least as far as Ezekiel, "in

Chaldea, by the River Chebar," early in the sixth century B.C. The word of the Lord (Yahweh) comes to him:"Son of man, prophesy against the shepherds of Israel. Prophesy and tell them: 'Shepherds, this is what the Lord God says: Trouble waits for the shepherds of Israel, who feed themselves! Shepherds should feed their flock, but you have fed on their fat, have clothed yourselves in their fleeces, have slaughtered the fattest sheep, but have failed to give food to the flock. You have not made the weak sheep strong, nor cared for the sick sheep, nor bandaged up the wounded sheep ...' "Ezekiel's slightly older contemporary, Jeremiah, had used the same allegory of the unfaithful shepherds and the untended flock (*Jeremiah* 23: 1–6) and a late portion (about 350 B.C.) of *Zechariah* (11: 4–17) echoes this phraseology. All three probably referred to kings and other civil rulers; but Christian poets like Dante (Ly-14), Petrarch (Ly-16, Ly-17), Mantuan (Ly-28), Spenser (Ly-70), and Milton sensed the applicability of such language in their own day to those whose very titles in the Church identified them as "shepherds" (*pastores*). For a discussion of this analogue, see E.L. Brooks, "*Lycidas* and the Biblical Pastoral," *Notes & Queries*, new series, iii (1956), 67–8.

Ly-14 (Italian)

DANTE ALIGHIERI. *Paradiso*, xxvii, 10–66. Completed by 1321. From *Le Opere di Dante Alighieri*, ed. E. Moore and Paget Toynbee, 4th edition, Oxford 1924

Begins: Dinanzi agli occhi miei le quattro face
            stavano accese, e quella che prima venne
            incominciò a farsi più vivace ...
  Ends: E tu, figliuol, che per lo mortal pondo
            ancor giù tornerai, apri la bocca,
            e non asconder qual ch' io non ascondo.'

Very relevant to *Lycidas*, lines 108–31, is a famous passage in the 27th canto of Dante's *Paradiso*, where St Peter, his face purple with indignation, denounces the current pope as one"who has turned my cemetery into a sewer of blood and filth"(*fatto ha del cimitero mio cloaca del sangue e della puzza*), to the great delight of the Devil. Looking down from Heaven, St Peter sees wolves in shepherds' clothing ravening in all the sheepfolds. Similar denunciations of the clergy by Dante may be found in *Inferno*, xix, 90–120, and in *Paradiso*, xxix, 103–26. It remained for Petrarch to devote an entire eclogue (see Ly-16) to St Peter's denunciation of corruption in the Church.

At the very close of Dante's career, he exchanged epistolary Latin eclogues (two each way) with a young Italian scholar at Bologna, Johannes de Virgilio. These were the very last works from his hands, and represented, some decades before Petrarch's eclogues, an interesting revival of the pastoral form. Neither of Dante's two eclogues is an epicedium and neither shares in his invective against ecclesiastical corruption.

For a literal prose translation of the present passage, see H.F. Tozer, *Dante's Divina Commedia* (Oxford, 1904), pp. 417–18.

For the influence of Dante on Milton, see C.H. Herford, *Dante and Milton* (Manchester, 1924); Paget Toynbee, *Dante in English Literature* (New York, 1909); and Kenneth McKenzie, "Echoes of Dante in Milton's *Lycidas*," *Italica*, xx (1943), 121–6.

George R. Coffman[79] casts his net still farther to include the parable of the Good Shepherd (St John, iv, 1–28), Pope Gregory the Great's sermon on this parable, Bernard of Morlais' *De Contemptu Mundi*, the Prologue to John Gower's *Confessio Amantis*, and Chaucer's portrait of the "povre Persoun of a toun" (*Canterbury Tales*, Prologue, 477–514).

Saint Peter Denounces the Church

Before my eyes four torches[80] stood alight
   And that which had advanced beyond the rest
   Began to make its radiance yet more bright:[81]
The semblance of its visage might suggest
   An interchange of Mars and Jupiter
   If both were birds, each like the other dressed.
The Providence whose powers here confer
   On every soul his time and service due
   Now hushed the blessèd choir from sound and stir,
When thus I heard: "If I should change my hue,
   Pray marvel not, for, while your soul I greet,
   You will see all these spirits changing too.

79 *ELH*, III, ii, 101–8
80 Adam and three Apostles (St John, St James, and St Peter)
81 St Peter's light grows fierce with holy anger.

He who on earth usurps my holy seat,
 My holy seat that in the eyes of Christ
 Is vacant, by depravity complete
Has made my burial-place a sewer, spiced
 With blood and filth, at which the Reprobate
 In Hell below to pleasure is enticed."
Such colour as the sun in low estate
 At morn or eve casts on the clouds now went
 The whole of heaven to illuminate.
And like a virtuous woman, confident
 In her own merit, when she hears of shame
 That stains another with its excrement,
The face of Beatrice grew dark with blame,
 Such darkness as, I deem, on earth was shown
 When the Almighty to his Passion came.
The mighty words went on, as changed in tone
 As was the transformation in his face
 While he denounced the fouling of his throne:
"The spouse of Christ was not nursed up in grace
 With blood of Linus, Cletus and my veins
 To prostitute her soul for money base;
But to arrive at these celestial planes
 It was, that Pius and Calixtus bled,
 That Sixtus toiled and Urban suffered pains.
It was no aim of ours that, badly led,
 Half of our flock upon the right should stand,
 While others on the left should have their stead;
Nor that the keys, committed to my hand,
 Should be an emblem on a battle-flag
 To war on the baptized; nor had I planned
That on some venal and mendacious rag
 My likeness should be added as a seal,
 At which I often in my anger gag.
In all the pastures, ravening wolves now steal,
 Disguised as shepherds in destructive glee.
 Weapons of Heaven, have you lost your zeal?
The sons of Cahors and of Gascony[82]

82 Pope Clement v was a Gascon, and the Avignon Anti-Pope, John xxii,
a native of Cohors (in southwestern France), a notorious centre of
usury.

> Prepare to drink our blood. And must the end
> Of fair beginnings sink to this degree?
> But providence sublime, that did defend
> Rome's empire by the strength of Scipio,
> Will soon, I deem, a hand of help extend.
> But you, my son, who must return below
> Because of mortal weight, open your lips
> And do not hide what I have deigned to show!"

Ly-15 (Latin)

FRANCESCO PETRARCA.   *Aegloga* II. *Lament for Argus.* Written at Vaucluse, 1346. Available in *Il Bucolicum Carmen*, ed. Antonio Avena (Padua, 1906)

Begins: IDEUS
> Aureus occasum iam sol spectabat, equosque
> Pronum iter urgebat facili transmittere cursu ...

Ends: IDEUS
> Solus ego afflicto moerens in littore mansi.

A bridge between the classical pastoral and that of men like Spenser might seem to be found in the sequence of twelve Latin eclogues by Petrarch, but it is a bridge almost blocked with cobwebs of pedantic allegory and allusion. In the second Eclogue, we have three shepherds – Ideus (Barili), Pythias (Barbato), and Sylvius (Petrarch) – bewailing the death of the shepherd Argus (King Robert of Naples). The grief of all nature at his passing is given its traditional emphasis:

> Believe me, shepherds, it is death to live
> After the death of Argus. You will see,
> Already now, the ponds and lakes grow dry,
> The fountains, and the very sea itself.

There is also the familiar note of pious resignation near the close, as they think of their dead friend, now living in heaven.

But when we turn to Petrarch's *Letters*, where a very detailed exposition of his eclogues is given, we find this seemingly simple pastoral shot through with cryptic trivialities. It is more in need of a key than Joyce's *Ulysses*.

Ly-16 (Latin)

FRANCESCO PETRARCA. *Eclogue* VI: *Pastorum Pathos*. Mostly before
1352. Available in *Il Bucolicum Carmen*, ed. Antonio Avena (Padua, 1906)

Begins: PAMPHILUS
    Quis nemus omne vagis lacerandum prebuit hircis?
    Quid silve meruere mee, quas rore superno ...
Ends: MITIO
    Men verbis terrere paras? Presentia fortes
    Despiciunt; timidos etiam distantia terrent.

The cryptic allegory of this pastoral covers a violent attack on the
Papacy-in-Exile, at Avignon. Two shepherds, Pamphilus (Saint
Peter) and Mitio (Pope Clement VI) discuss the present state of the
flock (the Church). Mitio boasts of his vast quantities of gold, secured by the sale of young lambs (a reference to simony) and of the
queenly splendour of his wife (the Church). Pamphilus retorts that
if he will lift up his drunken eyes and look around, he will see that
wolves and thieves are preparing to attack the fold:

                        lumina tolle
    Immodico depressa mero; lupus instat ovili,
    Antraque pervigiles circumstant ditia fures.

Mitio replies that he is protected from thieves and wolves by a contract drawn up on the devil's altar and signed with pigs' blood. Pam-
philus-Peter ends by threatening Mitio-Clement with the imminent
return of their Master, who will turn wicked joy into grief.

The State of the Shepherds

PAMPHILUS [83] (alone)
Who has consigned the entire grove to ravage
By wandering goats? What have my woods deserved
That Jove once watered with celestial dew,
That his pure wife endowed with foaming streams,
Like saintly Pyroes [84] and Phanios?

83 St Peter, one who "loves all men"
84 St Paul, in one tradition "burned" to death

What secret frenzy fed on unripe crops,
Has foiled the hopes and profit of the field,
For which fair Hiberus,[85] our pride and joy,
In that far plough-time did not fear to add
Hot, living embers to his crackling laurels,
And would have been consumed, had not Apollo
Stretched forth his right hand to the dying martyr
And borne him safely to the lofty mountains?

MITIO [86] (to himself)
Harsh is the shepherd's lot! – restraining goats,
Forcing compulsion on the untamed flocks,
And making udders always flow with milk ...
For this we have no magic! Now, alas,
This fierce old fellow is preparing quarrels
And dark reproaches, bearing in his hand
His blessed Rock[87] and knotty regulations;
He mobilizes curses past deserving,
To sentence me to poison and the sword.
But I shall try him out with flattery. –
(To Pamphilus)
Whence do you come, O Pamphilus? And whither
Might you be going? Tell me where you dwell.
Sure, late you are in visting your fold!
Why are you angry now? And for what cause
Have you a seething soul, a face austere?

PAMPHILUS
Ha, are you here, you arrant gallows-rogue?
Has earth not swallowed up your guilty carcass?
No marvel is it if the grove and harvests
And all else have made mockery of my hopes.
Ha! To whose care was all this plough-land given?
Who was to feed the flock on tender grass?
The lambs have perished in untimely death;
The cows have starved and died; while goats survive,
And filthy hogs whose bellies are blown up
With luxury and leisure, such rude mobs
As hurtfully and lawlessly spread out

85 St Lawrence, a native of Ibera, tortured by fire
86 From Latin *mitis*, "slack, permissive," Pope Clement vi
87 Cf. Matt. 16: 18

Their insolence through every field, destroying
The copses with their rapine, while their stench
Assails the mountains and disturbs my peace.

MITIO (aside)
Insults, not unexpected, I endure;
Because, communing with my silent heart,
I saw them coming, and was well aware
That this tempestuous fellow would return,
Well taught to flog a servant's cringing back
And foul the reputation of a friend,
All with no hint of pity on his brow. –
(To Pamphilus)
How easy, Pamphilus, it is to blame
Another's life, how hard to mend one's own!
Perhaps when you were shepherd long ago
Death and the wolf assailed the snowy flock
None the less actively? In vain you came,
Threatening those enemies with crook and frown;
Nor did harsh winter (though it seemed to yield
To your austerity), nor dubious spring,
Nor pestilence upon the southern wind,
Nor scorching summer willingly obey you;
Birds would not spare the crops, nor shade the grapes,
Nor goats the trees, nor cows the springing grass.

PAMPHILUS
Was I not shepherd when dark Nereus,[88]
The vilest and most truculent of men,
Feeding his bulls upon the hill before me,
Cast earth across my path, and was prepared
To seize with violence on all my flock?
I strove against him, till his greater strength
Tore off my shaggy cloak and left me naked.

MITIO
How I should like to tell the grisly story
How many of our flocks were then cut down.
The vale is still manured with their blood,
Their bones are piled in sightless catacombs;

88 Nero

The very spot appals the beholders' eyes.
And neither you nor others were permitted
To take the beef and mutton to the market;
For wolves and lions scattered them abroad.

PAMPHILUS
May heaven be your enemy! Their masters
Did not lie dead; the hoarse dogs were not mute;
Whatever cruel Fortune brought to pass:
They stripped the fallen saints of all their sins
And rendered snowy fleeces to the city
And to their lord. What have you saved for me
But bullocks' horns torn harshly from their heads?

MITIO
I have saved gold, because I sold the lambs;
But did not deign to tap the cork-tree's bark
And was embarrassed at my humble parents.
And you may add, that through my leadership
The shepherd's art has flourished, for behold,
A Tyrian buskin in the newest style
Makes gay my ankle and upon my brow
A dainty crown of shining jasper sits.
White fleeces I have stained three times and more
With lush Sidonian purple; and have spared
Great friends who plied me with a gift of milk.
My wife is bright with gems; she decks her throat
With a jewelled necklace, and she lolls at ease
In dusky shadows at my amorous side;
Not stiff with ice and snow nor scorched by sun
As your old woman always used to be
When all the fields were yours. Look at my wife,
And you will see how queenlike she appears.
The kids are playing in the grassy valleys,
And inborn pleasure rolls the lazy swine
In foul hog-wallows; the intrepid shepherd
Will not set foot within their moist abode.
Meanwhile I sit, or sprawl upon my back,
Singing whatever carol love dictates,
And for tomorrow take no thought at all.
As for the flock committed to my charge,

I watch their sports and fights. But you complain
And look severe this morning; you are ready
With a dog's tooth of enmity to bite
Whatever fault your madness has proposed.

PAMPHILUS
You foul one, would you set your guilty gold
Beside my thorns? And does your wife present you
With shameful garments, burdened with her business?
Do you lie down on a luxurious bed
And snatch with wakeful eyes at anxious sleep
That wearies you with chaos in your dreams?
Your cups entice your thirst; your handsome house
And furniture give cause for you to fear.
What folly to gain peril at a price!
What frenzy to obey a crazy wife!
Base man, can you conceal adulteries
And all the sins that stain your marriage-bed?
Doubtless these men, whom you regard as friends,
Have stol'n the easy virtue of your wife
And even now lay plots against yourself.
Lift up your eyes, besotted with much wine:
The savage wolf is threatening the fold,
And wakeful thieves surround your wealthy cave.

MITIO
Nay, I have signed a contract with the thieves,
Written in pigs' blood and devised upon
The devil's altar; such an act may prove
Hateful to heaven, but its purpose stands,
Accepted by the gods of hell, whose queen
Has promised our agreement due success.
Let hungry tigers raid my well-stocked folds,
Let raging hail come streaming from the sky
And let harsh weather slaughter all my flock,
No poor man shall I be: my trust is firm
In the black powers of the nether world.

PAMPHILUS
Revoke that iron bargain, foolish wretch,

At which both Sun and planets surely blushed
And all the stars as well! I leave unsaid
A tale that would be bitter in the telling.
A shepherd you began, but now amass
A merchant's wealth, and fail in either trust.
Dare now to leave the woods, to see far cities,
To unfurl your sails, to face the rising winds.
Your wife once strayed on unfamiliar hills,
Leaving her father's home, her virtuous bed,
But now, a whore notorious, she draws
A train of ardent paramours behind her
And stinking goats who love a foreign marsh.

MITIO

Why, O my father, do you fill our hearts
With hidden riddles? Why would you destroy
Our lingering leisure with untimely strife?
Cease to disturb the joy of cheerful men
With gloomy words. Come, tell me quickly now
The purpose of your unprovoked attack.

PAMPHILUS

You have deserved both chains and crucifixion,
And flogging and the sword. Too brief a doom!
Nay, rather, endless torment deep in hell
Or any other torture grimmer still.
You faithless slave, you ingrate to your Master!

MITIO

You rude old man! As if you did not know
The way to bear a cross or walk in chains! –
That was *your* fate. The tale is spread abroad
Through every valley, how through utter terror
Of Nereus you would fain have left the flock
Had not Apollo ordered you to halt,[89]
There in the street, and to turn back again.
Nor shall I hold my peace of other times
How little faith you mustered for your lord,
In times of peril, when the flock was stricken.

89 From the story of *Domine Quo Vadis?*

PAMPHILUS

I fled, but I came back; I feared the lash
That flogs an unjust shepherd for his crime;
No epoch has condemned a natural fear.
But soon I washed my stains off in the river
And so was white again. What cause have you
To leave your post, to flee a quiet fold?
Why, following things far off, do you despise
The oak-trees that your forbears sought with pride?
Where do you take the apostolic keys,
You madman? Better cast them both away
If care for things of hell oppresses you.
Leap from the sheepfold wall, and force the flock
Back from its wandering to turn home again.

MITIO

Great things now please my heart; must I forever
Remain the servant of a shabby fold?
Having obtained a mistress who sings sweetly,
I would grow handsome; since I hate the sun,
I choose a shady cave, and freshen there
My hands and forehead in a cooling spring.
This mirror, where I view myself with pride,
Byzantine Corydon[90] has given me,
A pleasant gift; all this my wife has known,
This she permits, since gladly in my turn
I yield to all her onerous demands.
Your boast may be of unknown mistresses;
Let Epy fold me in her arms forever.

PAMPHILUS

Then let an ill-famed woman cherish you!
She brought disaster to her many husbands.
Your predecessor, Epycus,[91] once fell
Into her bad embrace and sang with joy
Through fields and cities that his spouse was kind.
In gaining her, he gave his sorry self

90 The Patriarch of Constantinople
91 Pope Boniface VIII

And his well-watered gardens to her hand;
All creatures mocked him as he lived and died;
Dogs ate his corpse and staled upon his tomb.
After his end, to others in their turn
She brought no less bad luck; to you, perhaps,
Her faith is likewise faithless; but of course
You have your pretty mirror to enjoy.
And may that wretch who first gave courtly gifts
To simple shepherds groan in hell for ever!
While you are seeking to be deemed a beauty,
And putting wreaths upon your snow-white head
(None of your forebears carried such a weight),
And while, you fool, you deck your cave with flowers
And wreathe wild roses round your holy crook,
May all things perish; since unholy stars
Prevail aloft and evil chance on earth!
And may your pastoral care be likewise doomed,
And rural toil, and all your zeal for gold!

MITIO
Perhaps another will succeed me here –
I prophesy that he is close at hand –
Whose sluggish purpose will excuse all wrong,
Banish all harshness from the shepherd's life,
And bring Alverno's filth to Roman fields.

PAMPHILUS
Can you foreshadow such a man as this
Unless you have begot him in your heart?
Is this your total faith? Is this the climax
Of all your praise! If this our earth should bear
A man still worse than you, then you yourself
Will be the best, O harmless Mitio.
Will you purge crime with crime? Live loosely then,
Glad in the shadow of still greater vice.

MITIO
I shall live happy, and regret to die;
But you, austere and stern in life and death,
Some vague old vision may preserve at last.

PAMPHILUS

Alas, you should remember through what perils
The Master once provided all these things.
We saw him torn with thorns of bitterness.
With what great pity did the merchant come
From high Olympus to redeem the lost!
How lean a living and devoid of pride
Inherited the master of the field!
You live in luxury upon his lands,
Where he himself was hungry and a-thirst.

MITIO

He cared not for himself and, truth to tell,
Was greedy,too! He fears to lose a few,
When many more will perish in the process.
He fills his shepherds' throats with grating voices;
This you have surely learned; and always dips
The sick sheep in the fountain, shears their fleece,
Lest burrs be tangled in their snowy coats;
So, too, he drives the goats from off the fence,
But shows them bramble-bushes as their food
And sterile myrtles (at such provender
Even wild beasts would baulk); he wastes his servants
With fasting and with penitential cold,
Hunger and sleeplessness and parching thirst;
To this he adds the thunder of his threats;
Forbidding all things pleasant, he ordains
Harsh things instead; your footsteps must avoid
Soft ploughland, you will walk through desert wastes,
Will cross the cruel hills; with naked feet
Your soul will tread upon tormenting thorns.
Will any offspring of the blood of men
Consent to ways like these? Or if he does,
How may he marvel that he has no friends?
I, for my part, am ready to remember
The power of my lord; though I recall
That I thereby have lost a glorious one,
The honour that I choose has pleased full many.
And where no force compels, who would endure
The toil of heavy harvests? And what flock

Would nibble through a wilderness of grass?
You should permit the wanton flocks to wander,
The goats obscene to couple in their lust.
I, too, shall have my sport. And while my wife,
My own dear Epy,[92] honours me, do you
Live out your life and leave me to my own.

PAMPHILUS
Unhappy man, do you thus mark your Master?
You think you stand here safely in the shade,
But he will come, and turn your joy to weeping.

MITIO
Is it with talking that you try to scare me?
Brave men despise the dangers they can see,
While far-off dangers terrify the timid.

Ly-17 (Latin)

FRANCESCO PETRARCA. *Eclogue* VII: *Grex infectus et suffectus.* Before 1352

Begins: MITIO
    Dulcior his silvis, et gramine dulcior arvi,
    Gratior his antris, et gratior amne sonoro ...
Ends: EPY
    Multa quidem curis dedimus, iamque hora quietis
    Nos vocat. Accelera; glacies premat hispida colles,
    Brachia nos nexi, molli iaceamus in ulva.

This sequel to Eclogue VI continues the attack on corruption in the Church. "The Pilot of the Galilean Lake" has disappeared and the two collocutors are Mitio (Pope Clement VI) again and Epy (his mistress, the papal court at Avignon). It transpires that Mitio has been properly alarmed by the threats of Pamphilus; and he therefore proposes to Epy that they count their sheep (bishops) and goats (cardinals) so as to be ready for the Master's return. She replies that death and disease have laid waste the flock; that fever, itch, and vio-

92 His wife, the Church, the "Epicurean" one

lent coughing dominate the fields. She then goes on to describe a dubious procession of goats, the identifying of whom as unsavory cardinals of the time has fascinated researchers ever since. Petrarch's symbolic presentation of the Church as a neglected and infected flock achieved instant fame and encouraged a whole tribe of imitators, from Boccaccio down to Spenser and Milton, to use comparable symbolism in their attacks on clerical corruption.

Ly-18 (Latin)

FRANCESCO PETRARCA. *Ecloga* xi, *Galatea*. After 1348

Begins: NIOBE
    Duc, soror, ad tumulum gelidique ad saxa sepulcri.
    FUSCA
    Quid lacrimis alimenta petis, germana? Quid optas?
Ends: NIOBE
    coniugium turtur, predam lupus, arbuta capre,
    custodita dolos mulier, mendacia servus.

In this pastoral elegy, Petrarch laments the death of Galatea, i.e. "Laura," the object of his most profound affection, who had died of the Black Death on 6 April 1348. She seems to have been buried at Avignon, in the church of the Grey Friars. The elegy represents a visit to her tomb by three sisters, representing in allegory three aspects of Petrarch's own spirit: (a) Niobe, whose heart is turning to stone with grief, (b) Fusca, the human faculty of reason, which despairs of all salvation, and (c) Fulgida, a hope that reaches out to immortality. In argument, Fulgida prevails, and Niobe glories at last in the celestial transubstantiation of Galatea, clothed in the glory of a heavenly body. The elegy ends with a bucolic conceit of impossibility as in Verg. *Ecl.* i, 59–63, "ante leves ergo pascentur in aethere cervi ... Quam nostro illius labatur pectore vultus" (tr. "therefore nimble stags shall graze in the sky ... before his face fades from my heart"). John Addington Symonds declared that the death of Laura "was the turning-point in Petrarch's inner life." The intensity of the experience vibrates in this pastoral. Even in this poem, however, there are traces of his inveterate allegorizing. Thus the "knotted halters" (*nodosa capistra*) of "the bullocks" at Laura's resting-place are the strict rules of the Franciscans, and the "grey hounds" (*gilvi molossi*) are the Grey Friars themselves. Freed from the shackles of his pastoral cryptics, this eclogue's tribute to Laura is spelled out freely in Italian in his *Trionfo della Morte*:

> Questa leggiadra e gloriosa Donna
> Ch' è oggi nudo spirto e poca terra ...

> "That charming and glorious Lady
> Who is today a bare spirit and a little earth ..."

For a literal prose translation by Harry Joshua Leon, see *The Pastoral Elegy*, ed. T.P. Harrison, Jr and H.J. Leon (Austin, 1939), pp. 71–6.

Galatea

NIOBE
Lead, sister, to the grave, the stone-cold tomb.

FUSCA
Why seek out food for tears? Why choose this gloom?

NIOBE
Groaning gives comfort to a mighty grief;
Afflicted souls in sighing find relief.
Pent sorrow slays the mind, but open woe
Is the best medicine a heart can know.
If my mute spirit caught from tears no hint,
Torpor would turn my bosom into flint.
A total silence is a death to keep;
But lead me, as I wish, where I may weep.

FUSCA
Come by this road where bullocks may be found
Whose necks with knotted halters have been bound;
By many dogs the threshold here is barred,
By grey Molossian hounds the cloistered yard.
This place conceals your loss; this spot revere,
For Galatea has been buried here,
Fairer than whom was no created thing,

Unless deep love confused our reasoning.
Lay down your load; embrace the sepulchre;
Here kiss the stones; with the mute ghost confer.

NIOBE

Too close, too dark a house for one so fair!
Is this your resting-place? The sun, aware
Of how you shone, his senses overthrown,
Confessed your beauty greater than his own,
And so beneath the waves he hurried prone.
Is this your place? Stars, do you keep your quest?
Boötes, stands your wagon in the west?
Jove, do you watch the sky with shining face?
Are Saturn and Orion in their place?
Moon, do you keep your cycle? Hermes swift,
Do you and wayward Venus westward drift?
Already, Galatea, here you lie,
Already pale cold dust, like all who die!
Unless, perchance, your spirit lives above,
Watching your weeping friends with eyes of love.
Can you no answer to my ear remit,
Half of my soul, the better half of it?
At my petition, lend me your right hand,
If any faith survives in all the land
Or any ancient pieties endure.
Alas, my sister! In what strength secure
Shall I roll back the stone that guards the tomb
And find her sacred body in the gloom?
Into her mouldering arms I fain would haste,
And kiss her, place my arms about her waist,
Carry her past the portals of this shrine,
And to a secret crypt her bones assign.
Perpetual honours should prepare their lights,
Virgins I'd bring and venerable rites,
The honours of a goddess; neither torch
Nor chanting should be lacking at her porch,
To make the world accept this lady's praise.
Alas, I find the stone too hard to raise,
A hopeless load. I fail beneath its weight,
And from the effort I must abdicate.

FUSCA

Rise, sister, rise; and do not seek to smutch
Your sacred body with a corpse's touch.
Accept the present; vainly would you long
For what is past. Oblivion's force is strong
To soothe the sorrow in a lover's heart.
The past comes not again, by any art;
Death removes cares, death loosens all our chains.
Enough you've wept, since death your love arraigns.

NIOBE

I would that death had quelled my sorrows too,
As to the blessed past I bade adieu.
My hope that pain had paused soon mocked relief,
My spirit is reserved for every grief.

FUSCA

Be still! For lo, sad Fulgida draws near,
And blames your sorrow by her brow austere.

FULGIDA

Why, wretch, thus blind of soul do you bewail
Things of mortality to no avail?
Why weep, O Niobe? For shame, begin
To accept your mortal lot without chagrin.
Me, too, lost love torments; I, too, must yearn
For this dear creature who will not return.
But what would you propose? The hope is vain
To kick against the goad of earthly pain.
Patience is better for a soul oppressed;
Bearing our burdens will at last bring rest.
Why, then, lament? Our friend was born to die,
And now she is immortal in the sky.
To waste away with loss is not to love;
To mourn another's blessedness above
Is wrong indeed. We know what we have lost
And an ungrateful world may sense the cost,
While we endure it. Cease in grief to grope:
To heaven, not to earth, assign your hope.

FUSCA
A fable that! Can mortals fly so high?

FULGIDA
On heavenly wings, for there our course must lie.

FUSCA
The things I trust in must admit of proof.

FULGIDA
Fusca, in worldly thoughts you dwell aloof.
But we are destined to the heights by birth
And gaze serenely upon heaven and earth.

NIOBE
Leave off these ancient riddles and the knot
Of truth that none may loose. That quest allot
To those who follow in the age to come.
Rather, dear Fulgida, make for this tomb
An epitaph the rural Muse may heed,
And that a later age may gladly read.

FULGIDA
Fair Galatea here her body left,
And high in heaven, of that corpse bereft,
Frequents the royal mansion of the Lord
And all the feasts and choirs about his board.
Death touched her rosy limbs, her snowy throat;
Her cheeks and starry eyes his sceptre smote;
In the dark earth her tranquil face is laid.
Can love still cling to mortal things that fade,
Or hope to plant enduring footsteps here
Where every grace must end upon the bier?
Of what avail are ancestry or truth?
Or wealth? or beauty? or the bloom of youth?
Or gracious manners? or a glorious name?
All these were hers; to these death laid his claim.
Naked, ascending to her home afresh,
She fled the well-loved prison of the flesh.

NIOBE
Naked? Not so! Behold a shining dress
In heaven clothes her radiant loveliness,
A garment still more glorious through the years.
Sure, every living lady who endears
By beauty or by mind, by song or speech,
Should let this blessed saint her spirit teach.
And we, while in these members life abides,
And even if our steps the future guides
Among the shades below, by Lethe's stream,
Shall her the pattern of all virtue deem,
The model of all merit in our heart.
Not from our bosom will your name depart,
O Galatea, till the star-host flees
Out of the welkin, till the buzzing bees
Abandon honey, doves their nests betray,
The turtle leave his mate, the wolf his prey,
The goat the arbutus bush, her feigning smiles
A guarded woman, and a slave his wiles.

Ly-19 (Latin)

GIOVANNI BOCCACCIO. *Eclogue 14: Olympia.* About 1361. From
Boccaccio: Opere Latine Minori, ed. A.F. Massèra, Bari, 1928

Begins: SILVIUS
Sentio, ni fallor, pueri, pia numina ruris
Letari et cantu volucrum nemus omne repleri ...
Ends: SILVIUS
Vos, pueri, vitulos in pascua pellite: surgit
Lucifer et mediis iam sol emittitur umbris.

This long elegy, consisting of 285 hexameter lines, was written as a
memorial to Boccaccio's five-year-old daughter Violante (named in
heaven "Olympia"), who had died not long before. In terms of genre,
it is not so much a pastoral as a mediaeval vision, whose later influence on the Middle English alliterative poem, *The Pearl*, has been

shown by W.H. Schofield.[93] Vergil and Petrarch are both drawn upon
for bucolic elements, but there are major debts to Dante, particularly
in Olympia's description of heaven in terms of the earthly paradise
in the *Purgatorio*.

For a complete literal prose translation by Harry Joshua Leon, see
The Pastoral Elegy, ed. T.P. Harrison Jr and H.J. Leon (Austin, 1939),
pages 77–91.

Olympia

(Lines 170–91. In a vision, his dead little daughter describes
her new home in Paradise)

In a retired spot a mountain stands
Beyond the reach of flocks from earthly lands;
Bright is that hilltop with perpetual light
Where Phoebus issues forth to human sight;
Upon its topmost crest a forest lies,
Raising its leafy branches to the skies,
High palms, and happy laurels, and the shade
Of noble cedar-trees that never fade,
And shining olive-trees, to Pallas dear,
Sacred to peace throughout the human sphere.
Who could describe the flowers of every hue,
And who the odours that the winds pursue,
Who streams like silver in their winding course
That murmur softly of their sylvan source?
The golden apples on the heavenly trees
Outshine the fruit of the Hesperides;
Here there are birds whose plumes are flecked with gold;
Here, goats with golden horns, and does untold
And lambs whose snowy fleece has golden tints;
Cows, bulls and heifers hues of gold evince;
Lions and griffins, gentle both, pass on
With radiant manes in which red gold has shone.
Our moon is silver but our sun is gold;
And greater stars than yours our skies enfold.
Spring is perpetual; no storms intrude;
The region is with temperate airs endued ...

93"The Nature and Fabric of the Pearl," *PMLA*, XIX, 154–215

Ly-20 (Latin)

MATTEO MARIA BOIARDO. *Phyliroe.* 1465. Available in Solerti, Angelo, ed. *Le Poesie Volgari e Latine di Matteo Maria Boiardo,* 1894

Begins: TITYRUS
   Vos eritis, silvae, testes, vos flumina, vosque
   Numina silvarum, tuque, o clarissime Titan ...
Ends: BARGUS
   Phyliroemque tuam meritis tollemus ad astra
   Laudibus: Alterno resonabunt carmine valles.
   TITYRUS
   Perge, sequar; forsan melior fortuna paratur.

Best known for his Italian epic, *Orlando Innamorato,* Matteo Maria Boiardo (1441–1494), Count of Scandiano, was educated at the University of Ferrara and had a distinguished career as an administrator and a diplomat. Almost all of his poetical works were written for the entertainment of Duke Hercules d'Este and his court at Ferrara. With Vergil as his model, he began his output with a set of ten Latin eclogues. In the second of these, two shepherds, Lynces and Bargus, listen to the lamentations of a third, named Tityrus, over the untimely death of his sweetheart, Phyliroe. He threatens to commit suicide, but they finally persuade him to face life with resolution. Boiardo is superior to Mantuan in the Latinity of his verse. He also wrote a sequence of ten eclogues in Italian, in the eighth of which Melibeo and Menalca bewail the death of a young girl, Nysa. The metre in these Italian eclogues is *terza rima.*

Ly-21 (Italian)

LORENZO DEI MEDICI. *Lamento di Corinto Pastore.* About 1480. From *Antologia della Poesia Italiana,* ed. Ottaviano Targioni Tozzetti, 21st ed., Livorno, 1927

Begins: La luna in mezzo alle minori stelle
   Chiara fulgea nel ciel quieto e sereno ...
Ends: Ninfa, che sei senza pietate alcuna.
   Ma, lasso a me! non è la voce udite!

Unique among the Maecenases of history, Lorenzo "the Magnificent" (1448–1492), tyrant of Florence, was not only the generous patron of artists, poets, and men of letters (Michelangelo, Pulci, Ficino, Poliziano, Pico della Mirandola, and indeed all members of the Platonic Academy) but was himself an active and distinguished participant in their labours. The love-lament cited here constitutes lines 1–36 of his poem *Corinto*, written in imitation of ancient classical eclogues. A shepherd, Corinto, bewails among beech trees the flinty heart of the shepherdess Galatea. The bright moon is shining among the lesser stars (a literary echo from Horace's Epode xv, 1–2) and his sheep are cropping the soft grass (an imitation of Vergil's Eclogue vi, 53–4), all unconscious of his sorrow. The metre is fluent *terza rima*.

Ly-22 (Italian)

ANGIOLO AMBROGINI POLIZIANO. *La favola di Orfeo*. June 1480. From *Antologia della Poesia Italiana*, ed. Ottaviano Targioni Tozzetti, 21st ed., Livorno, 1927

Begins: MERCURIO
      Silenzio. Udite. El fu già un pastore
      Figluol d' Apollo, chiamato Aristeo ...
Ends: BACCANTE
      Ognun segua, Bacco, te.
      Bacco, Bacco, eù oè!

According to the Italian scholar, G.B. Picotti,[94] this pastoral drama was almost miraculously drafted out and composed in two days in June 1480, "intra continui tumulti." This sudden birth of the poem may help to account for some of its prosodic irregularities, regarded by Richard Cody[95] as the culpable faults of a Socratic-Orphic theory of poetics, a deliberate harshness designed to drive away all but Platonic initiates. Cody analyses the play at considerable length[96] and terms it a ritual of love, in which the "Passion" of Orpheus, the founder of poetic theology, is duly celebrated. Elsewhere,[97] he finds a community of pastoral consciousness amongst Poliziano in the

94 *Sula data dell' Orfeo* (Rome, Reale Accademia dei Lincei, 1915), pp. 21–3
95 *The Landscape of the Mind* (Oxford, 1969), pp. 38–9
96 Ibid., pp. 30–42
97 Ibid., p. 14

Orfeo, Tasso in the *Aminta*, Shakespeare in *A Midsummer Night's Dream*, and Milton in *Lycidas*. In Milton's case, this is not primarily the stress on the Orpheus-story (lines 58–63) as a mighty symbol behind the fate of "Lycidas," but rather the Orphic hint of death as a divine mystery: "For Lycidas, your sorrow, is not dead." At the close of Poliziano's poem, after a Bacchant exults over the "gory visage" of a dismembered Orpheus and a chorus of Bacchants calls on the audience in the theatre to drink and dance in honour of their deity, the final mood in the "revels" is one of joy in the sacrifice of "questa vittima" to Bacchus. Edgar Wind,[98] after examining the Orphic beliefs of the Renaissance Platonists, suggests that the *Orfeo* ought to be analysed again in the light of the Orphic revival. Love and death are inextricably intertwined, and Plato's theory of love in the *Symposium* is also "the key to a philosophy of death."

Poliziano, or "Politian" (1454–1494), was one of the most notable scholars and poets of the Italian Renaissance. At the age of sixteen he had been taken into the household of Lorenzo dei Medici as tutor to his children, and presently became the most distinguished professor in the University of Florence and counted among his pupils the Italian Michelangelo, the German Reuchlin, and the Englishmen Grocyn and Linacre. He spoke and wrote Latin and Greek with incomparable freedom and composed poetry of the first rank in both, as well as in his native Italian. In the Platonic Academy at Florence, he was closely associated with Marsilio Ficino (1433–1499) and Giovanni Pico della Mirandola (1463–1494). Gretchen Finney[99] has argued that *Lycidas* was influenced by a later version of *La favola d' Orfeo*, redrafted by Alessandro Striggio as a libretto (1607) and set to music by Claudio Monteverdi.[100] This thesis must assume that Milton had somehow encountered this musical drama in England before November 1637, when *Lycidas* was completed, six months before he left for Italy.

Ly-23 (Latin)

GIOVANNI PONTANO. *Melisaeus*. Naples, 1491. Mi: Harvard Library

---

98 *Pagan Mysteries in the Renaissance* (Peregrine, 1967), pp. 152–63
99 *HLQ* xv (1952), 325–50; *PMLA* LVIII (1943), 657
100 See William Riley Parker, *Milton: A Biography* (Oxford, 1968), pp. 180–1, for the possibility that this was among the "choice music-books" that Milton had shipped home to England in the spring of 1639.

Begins: C I C E R I S C U S
    Hic cecinit Melisaeus, et haec quoque signa doloris
    servat adhuc Corylus: Vidi tua funera coniunx ...
Ends: C I C E R I S C U S
    cortice quoque etiam lentescat vulnus, et udo,
    quae super ipse linens imponat glutine libro.

In the Theocritean setting of a dialogue between two shepherds, Ciceriscus (Pontano himself) and Faburnus, the author laments the death of his wife, Adriana Sassone. This poem was probably the most famous pastoral dirge of Renaissance Italy – the natural and spontaneous outpouring of a poet who was as fluent in Latin as in his mother-tongue. Giovanni Pontano (1424–1503) of Cerreto was the first among Italians to put the epicedium to natural use, unencumbered by Petrarchan pedantry and complexity.

Ly-24 (Latin)

G I O V A N N I   P O N T A N O . *Maeon*. Naples, about 1491. Mi: Harvard Library

Begins: S Y N C E R I U S
    Ipse vides, quo tot Zyphyree inventa, sepulchrum
    cuncta tulit, superat vix ah, vix est super umbra ...
Ends: S Y N C E R I U S
    Quid segnes? eia ite, eia, nox advenit, eia
    ite domum; insidiis nox opportuna luporum est.

In the guise of a pastoral lament by Syncerius and Zephyreus, the poet grieves over the death of Paolo Artaldi, a physician. After lamenting that the only reward for his professional labours is oblivion, the "shepherds" decide that they will therefore enjoy themselves and they enter upon a cheerful interchange of appreciative comments on love and life.

Ly-25 (Latin)

P U B L I O   F A U S T O   A N D R E L I N I . *Eclogue* III. "The Death of Menalcas." About 1496. In *Bucolicorum autores ... farrago eclogarum*, ed. Johannes Oporinus. Mi: Bodleian

Begins: M O P S U S
>   Heus, heus, o Lycida, tacito quid solus in antro
>   Dulcia contemnis festi consortia pagi ...

Ends: M O P S U S
>   Ducere. Quod superest, cum crastina fulserit hora,
>   Accipies; iam, iam caeco surgamus ab antro.

Andrelini was an Italian humanist who spent most of his life at the University of Paris. He was a close friend of Erasmus and did much to bring the New Learning to France. In this, his third eclogue, Lycidas (an unidentifiable French scholar) laments the death of the shepherd Menalcas (also unknown), while Mopsus (Andrelini himself) complains of the enmity of a foreign shepherd who has arrived recently.

Ly-26 (Latin)

S I M O N   N A N Q U I E R . *Bucolicon de funere Caroli Octavi.* Paris, 1498. Mi: Bibliothèque Nationale (*De lubrico temporis curriculo*, Paris, 1560)

Begins: P R I M U S   P A S T O R
>   Candida sublimi non semper vertice florent
>   Lilia: nec violis semper contexta corona ...

Ends: O mors, tu generi humano non parcis, at illud
>   Obruis in vasto semper telluris hiatu.

Simon Nanquier seems to have been a Benedictine monk in Paris. Of his two Latin poems, one, cited here, is an eclogue on the death in 1498 of Charles VIII of France, a deluded youth who had set out for Naples at the age of twenty-five, stuffed with dreams of conquering the Turk and becoming "emperor of the East." Nanquier was closer in spirit to Juvenal than to Vergil or Theocritus, and he is moved to inveigh against the follies of human ambition. His monkish style has plenty of errors in quantity, syntax, and rhythm, but his rude sincerity is preferable to the smooth but vapid flatteries of many of his contemporaries.

Ly-27 (Latin)

B A P T I S T A   M A N T U A N U S . *Ecloga III. Amyntas: De insani amoris exitu infelici.* Mantua, 1498. From *The Eclogues of Mantuan*, ed. W.P. Mustard

Begins: FAUSTUS

Illa hesterna ruens Baldi de vertice grando,
Fortunate, fuit nobis innoxia (divis ...

Ends: FORTUNATUS

dum cadit, agricolis vicinos nuntiat imbres;
cogere et ad caulas pecudes convertere tempus.

Giovanni Battista Spagnuoli ("Baptista Mantuanus") was born in Mantua in 1448, and by the close of his career (in 1516) was almost as famous for his Latin poetry as that earlier"Mantuan,"Vergil. The fame has not survived to our day. In the third eclogue, cited here, Faustus and Fortunatus, after discussing recent hail damage, go on to lament the sad death of their young shepherd friend, Amyntas. While Mantuan's Latin poetry totalled some 55,000 lines, or four times Vergil's complete output, it was his ten eclogues (like Vergil's ten) that were school texts for centuries and stimulated the schoolmaster Holofernes' apostrophe to"good old Mantuan!" (*Love's Labour's Lost*, IV, ii, 97).

The first formal pastorals in the English language would seem to be *Certayne Ecloges* by Alexander Barclay, written and published about 1515, while he was a Benedictine monk at Ely. They consisted of two satirical eclogues in rhymed couplets, paraphrased from Mantuan (the latter's fifth and sixth eclogues) and three from *Miserae Curialium* ("The Miseries of Courtiers", Rome, 1473) by Aeneas Sylvius Piccolomini (Pope Pius II). About fifty years later, there were similar English translations from Mantuan by George Turberville, a facsimile of which was edited by Douglas Bush in 1937.

Ly-28 (Latin)

BAPTISTA MANTUANUS. *Ecloga* IX. *Falco, sive de moribus curiae Romanae*. Mantua, 1498

Begins: FAUSTULUS

Candide, quo casu patriis procul actus ab oris
haec in rura venis? hic pascua nulla nec amnes ...

Ends: FAUSTULUS

si favet iste, mane. quod si negat iste favorem,
Candide, coge pecus melioraque pascua quaere.

As a satire on clerical corruption, this eclogue shares with the extracts quoted from Dante (Ly-14), Petrarch (Ly-16, 17) and Spenser (Ly-70) in supplying precedents for Milton's attack on the "corrupted clergy" in *Lycidas*, lines 108–31. For example, "the grim Wolf with privy paw" echoes lines 141–45 in Mantuan's *Falco*:

> mille lupi, totidem vulpes in vallibus istis
> lustra tenent et, quo dirum ac mirabile dictu est,
> ipse homines (huius tanta est violentia caeli)
> saepe lupi effigiem moresque assumere vidi
> inque suum saevire gregem ...[101]

but the whole eclogue arraigns the papal court.

Falco
(lines 120–52)

FAUSTULUS
Rome preys on men, as upon birds the owl:
Upon a tree she sits, a queenly fowl,
And with proud nods invites them from afar.
They gather round, dull creatures that they are,
And marvel at her ears and two big eyes,
Her ugly head and beak of threatening size;
And while about the boughs they lightly flit,
Now here, now there, dark nets some feet outwit
While twigs with birdlime other birds betray
And all are soon consumed as hapless prey.

CANDIDUS
Well said! No utterance could be more apt.
But lo, a serpent, in sly coils enwrapt,
Approaches on his twisted thoroughfare
And with his thirsty tongue assails the air.

FAUSTULUS
Keep in your mindful heart what I indite:
When through the woods you walk, protect your sight
With a stout cap, for brambles there unsheath
The savage lancets of their spiny teeth

---

101 For translation see p. 166.

And with their curving sword-points tear your cloak.
Hold fast your staff, to deal some sturdy stroke;
Still in your cloak-fold carry many a stone,
Lest some unlooked-for foe should knock you prone;
Next with a heavy boot your foot protect
For in some thorny bush you may expect
An adder's onslaught on the life of men
When summer's heat has maddened it again.
A thousand wolves, and foxes in a horde,
Are kenneled in these valleys' evil sward;
And, strange to tell, my eyes have often seen
Men who assume the character and mien
Of ravening wolves (so dreadful is this spot)
That rage against the sheepfold they have got,
And pour their flock's dear life-blood on the ground;
At deeds like these, a ribald laugh goes round;
The folk here feel no horror at the crime,
And offer no restraint at any time.
Often strange portents from the earth appear,
That evil forces from the depths uprear.
Dogs become rabid, to such fury stirred
That more than wolves they rend the fleecy herd;
Thus trusted watch-dogs, with a flock to keep,
Grow murderous and slay the gentle sheep.

Ly-29 (Latin)

GIANO ANISIO. *Eclogue* I. *Melisaeus.* Naples, about 1503. Mi: Bodleian

Begins: AEGILUS

Unde Mycon quaesita diu, longumque vocata
Omnibus e tumulis, tua tandem armenta revisis? ...
Ends: AEGILUS

Mecum eris, atque istaec dominis armenta relinques.
Nox ruit, ad fluvium pastae properate capellae.

In this first of six eclogues by Giano Anisio (*ca.* 1475–*ca.* 1540), he laments the death of his fellow Neapolitan Giovanni Pontano (1424–1503), one of the very greatest of the Neo-Classical poets of Italy. The title, "Melisaeus," is the one that Pontano had applied to himself in a famous Latin elegy on the death of his wife, Adriana Sassone (see Ly-23). At the outset, the shepherd Aegilus rebukes the cowherd Mycon for wailing in the graveyard when he ought to be tending and protecting his beasts. Mycon replies that he has been singing an original dirge in honour of their dead friend Melisaeus. Aegilus urges him to sing it again: Let us sit in the shade of the spreading beech-tree. The zephyrs summon us and the moaning doves invite us. Mycon complies in the style of Vergil's *Gallus* or Milton's *Epitaphium Damonis*. In the first part of his song, the refrain is: "Dicite Pierides, dic fistula flebile carmen."[102] In the second part, it changes to "Dicite pastores Melisaeum, dicite Musae."[103] Aegilus thanks him and as a reward gives him a she-goat, three kids and six little cheeses. "I'm a poor man, and it's the best that I can do."

Ly-30 (Italian)

JACOPO SANNAZARO. *Eclogue 5: Ergasto sovra la Sepultura*. From *Arcadia di Jacopo Sannazaro*, ed. M. Scherillo, Torino, 1888

Begins: Alma beata et bella
          Che da' ligami sciolta ...
Ends: Quercie frondose et folte,
          Fate ombra alle quiete ossa sepolte.

Immensely popular in the sixteenth century was Sannazaro's pastoral romance, *Arcadia* (1504), a narrative mélange of prose and verse in which a never-never land of nymphs and shepherds became a sort of Golden Age region of escape from the horrors of contemporary warfare and violence. Sannazaro was one of the great humanists of his time and his style was a mosaic of reminiscences from the Greek and Latin classics, stirring all the chords of memory in a learned generation yet charming in itself to the ordinary reader. The work was seminal for the pastoral romance in Spain, France, and England. In Spain, where a translation appeared in 1547, its chief offspring were Jorge de Montemayor's *Diana* (1560), Cervantes' *Galatea* (1584), and Lope's *Arcadia* (1598). Its chief descendants in French were Belleau's *Bergerie* (1565) and Honoré D' Urfé's *Astrée*. When Sir Philip Sidney wrote *The Countess of Pembroke's Arcadia* (1590),

102 Tr. "Utter O Muses, utter O reed-pipe a tearful song."
103 Tr. "Speak of Melisaeus O shepherds, speak O Muses."

he is believed to have modelled it more on Montemayor than on Sannazaro. The pastoral elegy is only incidental to the more expansive pastoral romance and not a necessary part of it.

Sannazaro was also the author, in Latin, of one of the very greatest New Testament brief epics – *De Partu Virginis* (1526) – a distinguished forerunner (in genre only) of Milton's *Paradise Regained* (1671). Towards the end of the sixteenth century came the crowning achievements of the Italian pastoral in Tasso's *Aminta* (see Co-18) and Guarini's *Pastor fido* (see Co-20), which made the pastoral drama a fashion (with local modifications) as far afield as England in Daniel's *Hymen's Triumph*, Fletcher's *Faithful Shepherdess*, Randolph's *Amyntas*, and Jonson's *Sad Shepherd*, and even in the pastoral elements in *Arcades* and *Comus*.

In the present extract from Sannazaro's *Arcadia*, ten cowherds are found about the tomb of the shepherd Androgeo. Their leader sings the praises of the buried man and plays sweetly on a bagpipe, to whose accompaniment another cowherd, Ergasto, sings a melancholy song, telling how all nature had wept at this piteous death.

The revised 1514 Venetian edition of the *Arcadia* rans to 89 pages. The extent to which this comparatively short work was a cento of lifted or adapted phrases will be made clear by the number of its borrowings from earlier poets: Vergil 248, Boccaccio 164, Ovid 136, Petrarch 119, Theocritus 41, Longus 32, Pontano 27, Statius 26, Calpurnius 26, Homer 24, Horace 24, Claudian 23, Tibullus 23, Dante 19, Catullus 19, Propertius 17, Nemesian 17, Moschus 16, Poliziano 8, Bion 6, Tatius 5, Silius Italicus 5, Martial 3, and lesser numbers from Anacreon, Apuleius, Ausonius, Boethius, Hesiod, Valerius Flaccus, Juvenal, Lactantius, Lucan, Meleager, Persius, Seneca and Terence.[104]

There was actually very little prosodic originality in Sannazaro's *Arcadia*. Its mixture of prose and verse may be traced back through Boccaccio's *Ameto* and Dante's *Vita Nuova* to Boethius's *De Consolatione Philosophiae*, while its spirit owes much to Ovid and to the *Daphnis and Chloe* of Longus. Neither do its metres show any innovation. In general its twelve eclogues consist of one sestina (vii), one double sestina (iv), two canzoni (iii, v), and eight poems in *terza rima*; but these latter are frequently diversified with *rime sdrucciole* (dactylic rhymes), *rimalmezzo* (in which the end of one line rhymes with the middle of the next line) and even long passages in *canzone-*

104 These figures were arrived at by my taking a census of the notes in the Scherillo edition.

measure. All of these verse-forms antedate Sannazaro. The *sestina*, the *canzone* and *terza rima* seem to have had their roots in popular Provençal poetry, but were raised to a literary level, first by Dante and then by Petrarch. Boccaccio used *terza rima* for eclogues in his *Ameto*. The *rima sdrucciola* in tercets had been used in eclogues by Matteo Maria Boiardo, Jacopo Fiorino, and Francesco de Arsochis; and even Dante (slightly) and Petrarch (more abundantly) anticipated Sannazaro in their use of the Provençal *rimalmezzo*. It was the good fortune of the *Arcadia*, formed of these familiar elements, to catch a great tide of public favour, in which a deep urge to escape from an age of war was blended with a rising pride in poetic achievement in the vernacular Italian as over against the classical and neo-classical traditions in Latin and Greek.

Ly-31 (Italian)

JACOPO SANNAZARO. *Eclogue* XI: *Mamillia* (from *Arcadia*, A.D. 1504)

Begins: Poi che 'l soave stile e 'l dolce canto
Sperar non lice più per questo bosco,
Ricominciate, o Muse, il vostro pianto ...
Ends: Quel duro eterno inexcitabil sonno
D'haverti chiusa in così poca fossa:
Se tanto i versi miei prometter ponno.

Again from the *"Arcadia"* is this long (160 pentameters) dirge by Ergasto (Sannazaro himself) over the death of his mother Massella ("Mamillia"). The metre is *terza rima*. He calls on hills and caves, beech-trees and oaks, rivers and fountains, echoes and valleys to come and mourn with him. Let earth paint her lilies and her violets black. All the flowers are asked to help him persuade Death to release him from life. He wishes that as Orpheus' song could persuade Pluto to let Eurydice go, so his own song could persuade Heaven to let his mother return. Finally he prays that the eternal sleep of Death will not be able to keep her forever within the narrow limits of the grave.

A literal prose translation by Harry Joshua Leon may be found in *The Pastoral Elegy*, ed. by T.P. Harrison Jr and H.J. Leon (Austin, 1939), 98–105.

Mamillia

Delightful style and golden song are spent;
    This forest to those tones no more may hark.
    Begin once more, O Muses, your lament.[105]
Weep, sacred hill, so shadowy and dark;
    Ye hollow caves and grottoes full of gloom,
    Come, join our ululations, sad and stark.
Weep, mountain oaks, in accents of the tomb;
    Beeches with weeping to these rocks declare
    The lamentable rigour of our doom.
Lament, ye rivers, of all sweetness bare;
    Ye streams and fountains, stay your onward force
    And move no more upon your thoroughfare.
Sad Echo, in your vocal intercourse,
    Joint with my woe in sorrowful duets
    And on the trunks of trees my grief endorse.
Cry out, abandoned valleys, your regrets;
    Upon your mantle, Earth, let there be blent
    Dark lilies and the black of violets;
Because with sudden fury Death has sent
    For wise Egeria and the Theban dame.
    Begin once more, O Muses, your lament.
And if, O river-bank, you know the claim
    Of human feeling, join with me, I pray,
    To help my flutings in their mournful aim.
Grasses and flowers that in some far day
    Were mighty monarchs but by destiny
    Must now among the ponds and rivers stay,
Come, all of you, to beg of Death with me
    That he, if possible, may end my woe;
    That wearied of my outcries he may be.
Weep, Hyacinth; grief's trophies with you grow;[106]
    Redouble from of old your sad complaint
    And on your leaves my gloomy sorrow show.
Blest shores and sunny slopes, renew the taint

105 Moschus' *Lament for Bion* was first printed in 1495 in the Aldine edition
    of Theocritus, and its impact on Sannazaro led to much imitation in
    the present poem. One such feature is the cyclic refrain of lamentation.
106 An appeal to the flowers, as in Moschus

Of sad Narcissus in his grieving heart,
  If ever from my prayers you felt constraint.
No more let blooms and grasses green upstart,
  Nor rose nor amaranth their hues augment
  To show the world bright beauty's counterpart.
Alas, what hope of praise can life present?
  For faith and faithful judgement both are dead.
  Begin once more, O Muses, your lament.
And while my unavailing sighs are said,
  Come, little birds, so loving and so gay,
  Out of the well-loved nests to which you fled.
O Philomel, who, from that far-off day
  Renew each year your woe with accents warm
  And fill the woods and caves with sad affray;
And Procne, if, in truth, your change of form
  Has left your soul unchanged and full of grief,
  So that your woes still vex you in a swarm;
Leave off your piercing cries; let me be chief
  And only mourner till my throat is numb;
  Then only, may you give your hearts relief.
Ah me, though thorns dry up, a time will come[107]
  When all their former strength will be restored
  And each in its own place be mettlesome,
But us, when once we fall to death abhorred,
  No wind nor sun nor rain nor spring avails
  To raise us from our grave beneath the sward.
The sun, moreover, towards the evening pales,
  Leading our lives and days along his course,
  But in the dawn, his pristine strength prevails;
Happy was Orpheus,[108] whose transcendent force
  Availed to venture down the steep descent
  To where the Powers of Darkness have their source;
Conquering Rhadamanthus, down he went;
  Megaera and Inferno's King he swayed.
  Begin once more, O Muses, your lament.
Why could not I, alas, the flute have played
  With such a blend of melancholy notes
  As might have won from Hell that dearest shade?

107 He repeats the contrast in Moschus between Nature's revival and the finality of human death.
108 The descent of Orpheus is worked in, as in Moschus

Weaker than his, my tribute downward floats,
     And yet the pity of the gods above
     Surely to Heaven's ears my song devotes.
But if our human state be scorned by love
     And she comes not, then would I gladly find
     That no returning path my feet can prove.
What vain desires afflict my restless mind!
     All human spells and herbs are impotent
     To change the immortal law that mocks mankind.
The ivory gate of dreams was surely meant
     To bring again her converse and her face.
     Begin once more, O Muses, your lament.
And yet it brings not, to her former place,
     Her whose removal blotted out my sight;
     It cannot lure from heaven her starlike grace.
But you, O River,[109] noble-born and bright,
     Summon your nymphs to gather in your deeps
     And there renew your gracious ancient rite.
A fame throughout the world the Siren keeps
     Because you fashioned here so proud a tomb.
     Here, for a second time, your sorrow weeps.
Grant that another trumpet here may boom
     Her ringing praises, that all men may hear
     Those echoes fill an ever-widening room.
And if rough showers never interfere
     With your fair current, aid my humble style
     Until sweet pity shall my words revere;
Not that my measures may some book beguile,
     But that on beech-tree trunks they may abide,
     Artless and loving in the forest aisle;
Hither may other shepherds turn aside
     To read upon the rough and savage bark
     Of acts and customs fit for noble pride.
Then through the hours and years mankind may mark
     Her ever-growing fame throughout these hills
     While grasses wave and starlight gilds the dark.
Beasts, birds, and shady caves and bubbling rills
     And men and gods will chant with high intent
     That holy name in verse of gracious skills.

109 Just as Moschus invoked the Meles River of Smyrna, so Sannazaro
    invokes an Italian stream, probably the Sebeto, adjacent to Naples.

And since at last my song must seek ascent,
  Leaving behind the humble shepherd's guise,
  Begin once more, O Muses, your lament.
From me, ill-sounding notes no more arise
  But songs so clear and fair that they may reach
  That proud and gentle spirit in the skies.
May her high radiance my spirit teach,
  May she stoop down to grant me timely aid,
  And grant my soul the pity I beseech.
And if your ways the power of speech evade,
  Forgive my vain attempts and merely grant
  That honour to your name my page has made.
But yet a time shall come, all-jubilant,
  When Muses shall be honoured and all mist
  Out of our eyes new glory will supplant.
Then each of us from evil must desist,
  Purging himself of tainted thoughts of earth
  And setting in the sky his hopeful tryst.
Then shall I know my rhymes have little worth,
  And yet I hope for praise from shepherd-folk
  Who in this humble forest have their birth.
Many whose praise, before, no poet spoke
  Will see their names in red and yellow flowers
  Amid the meadows like a starry cloak;
And springs and rivers through these vales of ours
  Will murmur as they give my song assent
  With crystal waters through their leafy bowers;
And saplings that I plant in glad content
  Will give a whistling answer to the breeze.
  Bring to an end, O Muses, your lament.
Happy the shepherds who to heights like these
  Have hoped to soar, and therefore put on wings,
  Although we cannot tell of time's decrees.
But you, a soul beyond all reckonings
  Forever fair, hear me in heaven perchance
  And deem me equal to your choir that sings;
Grant that these laurels with their thick expanse
  Of foliage ever green may shroud us both,
  Here in our tombs, in shady vigilance.
May pleasant bird-song in the undergrowth
  Join the sweet sound of sparkling waters clear

That every charm may blend in holy troth.
Then, if indeed my days shall persevere
Till, as I wish I yield your name due praise
(And may the God of heaven my wishes hear),
I hope that in the narrow grave's cold clays
No hard, eternal, never-waking sleep
Shall have the power to seal you through all days:
This is the promise that my verses keep.

Ly-32 (Latin)

BALDASSARE CASTIGLIONE. *Alcon*. About A.D. 1505. Mi: Harvard

Begins: Ereptum fatis primo sub flore juventae,
            Alconem nemorum decus, et solatia amantum ...
  Ends: " '... Collacrimant duri montes, et consitus atra est
            Nocte dies; sunt candida nigra, et dulcia amara.' "

The author of "Il Cortegiano" also wrote one of the greatest of Latin elegies, this lament for his intimate young friend, Matteo Falcone. Like Milton in *Epitaphium Damonis*, Castiglione seems to have chosen Latin as a freer and less openly self-revelatory medium for expressing his grief. Although much of the poem is nourished by Vergil and Moschus, it is not slavish imitation and does not smell of the lamp. In the wholly original second part (lines 83–129), in which he laments his absence while Alcon died and wistfully remembers how he had even then been dreaming of poetic achievement and happiness together hereafter, we have a pattern borrowed by Milton in his *Epitaphium Damonis* 135 years later. The resemblance is too close to be accidental. Incidentally, Castiglione's emphasis on the long intimacy between the mourning shepherd and his dead friend was to extend the scope of the genre.

I have rendered the poem by the canzone-measure of Milton's *Lycidas*. For a literal prose translation by Harry Joshua Leon, see *The Pastoral Elegy*, ed. T.P. Harrison Jr and H.J. Leon (Austin, 1939), pp. 112–19.

Special reading is recommended in J.H. Hanford, "The Pastoral Elegy and Milton's *Lycidas*," *PMLA*, xxv (1910), 403–47, and T.P. Harrison, Jr, "The Latin Pastorals of Milton and Castiglione," *PMLA*, L (1935), 480–943.

Alcon

Snatched by the fates in the first flower of youth,
Alcon, the meadow's grace, the lover's stay,
Whom Fauns and Dryads have heard sing, in sooth,
While Pan and Phoebus praised his roundelay,
Alcon the shepherds wept. Beyond them all,
His loved Iolas, whom a sad face mars
With flowing tear-drops, warm and tragical,
Called to the cruel gods, the cruel stars.
Just as the nightingale in dark bemoans
Her brood in mournful tones,
Or as the turtle-dove, who mourns his mate,
Slain by a cruel shepherd who has spied
Her perch incautious, on a towering oak,
And with keen arrow has achieved her fate;
So neither resting on the leafy branch
Nor on the gracious grass, nor turned aside
His grievous thirst in the smooth stream to stanch,
His wailing outcries in his bosom choke,
Filling the lofty groves with sad complaints.
For not a day Iolas came upon
Without a tear at sunset or at dawn;
He never thinks to drive the flock to grass,
Or the sleek bulls; he uses no constraints
To urge them to the river for a drink;
Nor in the pinfold, when the sun has gone,
Does he take care his charges to restrain;
Only amid the woods or on the brink
Of some far lake, alone with his despair,
Unmindful of the gloom of midnight there,
He to the cliffs poured out these words in vain:

"Alcon, to Muses and Apollo dear,
Alcon, my soul's true half, the major part
Of all my grieving heart,
Destined to leave my eyes an endless tear,
What god or luckless chance has torn you hence?
Does ruthless fate steal from us, year by year,
All that is best? Is some divinity

Harsh only to the good? No reaper would commence
To sickle springing corn, nor from the tree
Will the rude farmer pluck the unripe fruit.
But brutal death has plunged you ere your time
In black Avernus, laying greedy hands
Upon your years still tender in the shoot.
O luckless lad, who perished in your prime,
With you has died the solace of the fields,
Love dies, the Graces perish in our lands,
Now fades the joy that man's existence yields.
The trees have lost their tresses; woods, bereft
Of all their glory, do not grant their shade
For shepherds; by the dying grasses left,
The meadows lose their splendour; springs grow dry
And parching rivers in their course are stayed.
The sterile fields their harvest now deny,
For evil rust devours the growing wheat.
Sad squalor holds the herds, the shepherds too,
In spite of all we do;
The hungry wolf is savaging the flocks;
Tearing the lambkin from its mother's teat,
It rends the helpless young, it rends the ewe,
Even the shepherds and their dogs it mocks
And carries off its prey on fearless feet.
Mournful are all the sounds of woodland places;
The pastures and the rivers join their sighs;
The fountains, as they rise,
Murmur your funeral rites with gentle graces
That woods and rivers echo to the skies.
O luckless lad! Your death untimely moves
The sylvan gods. Throughout the leafy groves
The farmers have beheld the wood-nymphs weep
Along the forest steep,
Pan, and Silvanus, and the little faun
With cloven foot. And yet cold, impious fate
By tears and lamentation is not drawn
To cancel out your spirit's endless sleep;
Death will not heed my wailings desolate.

"Though cut down by the plough the grasses die
Throughout their fields, yet will they spring again;
But cruel Fates refuse a knot to tie

In once-cut threads that held the lives of men.
The setting sun is sinking in the sky;
And as it sinks, it sets the stars alight;
Still, having washed its car in waves of night,
It will revisit all our lands once more
When dawn shall day restore;
But when in inky waters of chill death
We render up our breath,
And when the door of that harsh realm is shut,
No stair leads ever to the light above,
An everlasting sleep subdues our eyes
And bitter shadows all our senses glut.
Then vain are tears and vows of human love,
Fruitless are all the prayers that mortals say;
Vows, tears and prayers the tempest bears away.
O luckless lad, stolen by envious skies,
Never again shall I behold you stand,
Erect at my right hand,
A victor with the arrow or the spear
Or besting comrades, wrestling in the sand.
Never again, when summer days are clear,
Shall we in soft, green meadows lie at ease,
Escaping the fierce heat of summer suns
Where shade the dog-day shuns;
Nor will your piping all the hillside please
Nor vales prolong your carol as it runs.
No more shall your Lycoris, she whose name
So often you have carved on beech-tree bark,
Nor Galatea, once my constant flame,
To love-songs of us twain together hark.
For you and I, up from our tender years,
Have lived together, braving heat and cold,
And by our common labours of the fold
Pastured our sheep and goats, our cows and steers.
My fields were yours as well: we lived as one.
What life is left me, now that you are gone?

"Alas, that heaven's wrath should me dispatch
Far from my native shores! So, in that hour,
I could not close my comrade's dying eyes
With tender hands, nor with my own mouth catch
The last breath of his spirit as it flies

Or kisses from his icy lips devour!
Leucippus, I must envy you, my friend;
Good Alcon saw your sorrow at his end,
Gave you his final charges, full of trust,
And looked upon your face with failing eye.
Thus, when he came to die,
It was your hands that laid him on his bier,
Your tear-drops that were shed above his dust.
Then after all due rites and weeping here,
You followed Alcon to the world of shades,
His glad companion, for you would not stay
To walk without him through these friendless glades.
Now, strolling gladly in Elysium
With Alcon, you enjoy his comradeship
And will enjoy him for all time to come.
Perhaps upon a river's flowering lip
Some kindly shepherd will have laid your bones
In the same grave with him, with pious praise
And equal reverence to your spirits twain,
While equal grief a double tribute pays.
But far away from home, I made no moans
Nor paid just reverence to the buried swain.
But rather, unaware of his sad state,
I fashioned idle dreams, in folly great:

" 'Here in these glorious pastures shall I dwell;
And hither shall my dear friend, Alcon, come,
Leaving the rugged rocks, the ragged fell,
The pestilential waters, and the food
With death envenom'd; hither Alcon good
To gentle meads and rivers frolicsome
Will come to visit. I shall run from far
To meet him; I shall be the first to know
My friend as he approaches, I the first
To give him my embrace and weep for joy.
Discourse long hoped for we shall then employ;
We shall delight in telling all the worst
That we have suffered since the long ago,
And find new joy in converse jocular.
Then, as we talk, we slowly shall renew
Our old affection; pleasure shall not cease;
Sweet pastoral delight our eyes shall view

And we shall pass our lives in gentle peace.
These wheatfields, Ceres loves; Bacchus, these hills;
Apollo, all these pastures; Pales' hand
Gives grasses for the flock, and for the lambs
The milk they love. Beside these mountain rills
The dainty nymphs go hunting through the land
And often dance their morrice. Here the Tiber
Imbued with sacred glories from the past,
Washes the ruined walls of ancient Rome
And all the monuments that circumscribe her.
Here springs abound; here woodland shade is vast,
Here vales are cool; and here, by waves a-foam,
The shepherd Corydon once sang his love
For beautiful Alexis. Therefore, pray,
Come, well-loved youth; the pastures and the streams
Await you; all the nymphs make holiday
To crown you with a wreath of living flowers.
To see you come, their simple hearts make gay,
And earth brings forth new blossoms for these hours.'

"Such visions I was fashioning, alas,
   Wretch that I was, led on by baseless hopes,
   Not knowing Fate and death can overpass
   Our little dreams by crimes unspeakable.
   But since my broken prayers, all sorrowful,
   Are lost on fleeting winds down Hades' slopes,
   And I was not permitted to behold
   The living features of my friend of old,
   And living words with him to interchange,
   Hither at least may his dear shade make haste,
   Winging across the void in gentle flight,
   And with compassion for my grief tonight
   Accept at last, as through the gulf I range,
   The tears and sighs my bosom has embraced,
   The cries these hollow caves give back again.
   With my own hands, upon the Anio's bank,
   I'll raise an empty tomb in sight of men;
   This as a solace for my grief will rank,
   My pious incense on the flames I'll throw
   And shall invoke his spirit from below.
   Join with me, boys, in casting fragrant flowers:
   Soft roses and narcissus and the blooms

Of sweetly blushing hyacinth be ours
To blend with ivy and the laurel's leaves.
Let twigs of pungent cassia be brought
And cinnamon with sweet amomum mixed,
So that the night-wind, breathing through the glooms,
May spread the gracious odours it has caught
Till nostrils by the incense are transfixed.
For Alcon loved me much; and of my love
The man was worthy; thus was honour due.
Meantime the Nymphs will weave the violet
And amaranth, and on the grave will set
Blossoms and garlands, and with face of gloom
Will write this epitaph upon the tomb:

'Since wicked fates have stolen Alcon's soul,
Rough mountains wail his death in deep distress.
The day by utter night is swallowed whole:
White turns to black, and sweet to bitterness.' "

Ly-33 (Latin)

HELIUS EOBANUS HESSUS. *Epitaphium Iolae.* About 1509. Mi: Bodleian (in Johannes Oporinus, *Bucolicorum autorum ... farrago eclogarum,* Basel, 1546)

Begins: MELETURNUS
    Nunquid adhuc ardes formosan Daphni Calypso,
    Dic precor? an dulces liquisti fortiter ignes? ...
Ends: MELETURNUS
    Et nunc Oceano proprior sol: plura canemus,
    Olim, cum puerum matremque videbimus ipsam.

The shepherd Meleturnus asks his friend Daphnis the reason for his grief. The latter answers by lamenting the death of Iolas (*i.e.,* Wilhelm II, Margrave of Hesse, died 1509). Meleturnus seeks to console him by pointing out that Iolas's later successor, Eurynomus (i.e., Philip of Hesse, 1504–1567) will prove equally effective in protecting "the flocks" by driving out thieves and by killing wolves. Philip was, in fact, deeply involved in the Protestant-Catholic wars of the next half-century.

Eobanus (1488–1540) was professor of Latin at his Alma Mater, Erfurt, in 1517–26. His 17th eclogue laments the collapse of that university during the turbulence of the Reformation. His chief contribution to his generation was probably his translation of the *Idylls* of Theocritus into Latin hexameters in 1531, while he was a professor at Marburg. There were, of course, many scholars and poets of the time for whom this introduction to the *Idylls* was superfluous. Sannazaro, for example, was completely versed in Greek, and Theocritus was a required author for all students of Greek at Wittenberg from 1547 on. If Hamlet and Horatio may be imagined as undergraduates at sixteenth-century Wittenberg, they would doubtless have been so instructed.

Ly-34 (Italian)

LUIGI ALAMANNI. *Eclogue* I. About 1518. Available in *Versi e prose di Luigi Alamanni*, ed. Pietro Raffaelli, 1859

Begins: TIRSI
　　Dolce è l'acuto suon degli alti pini
　　Contrastanti coi venti, e dolce ancora ...
Ends: MELIBEO
　　O s' altro augel più dottamente piange.
　　Prendi ora i premi al tuo cantar promessi.

Luigi Alamanni (1495–1556) attended the University of Florence but seems to have been influenced still more by a sort of Platonic Academy at the home of Bernardo Rucellai. Here he came to know and to have affection for Bernardo's grandson, Cosimo Rucellai, who suffered untimely death by the plague in 1518. In the sequel, Alamanni wrote four Italian eclogues in his memory. The first of these, listed above, is modelled closely on the first Idyll of Theocritus, but with the substitution of Fortune for the implacable Cypris in the Greek original. For metrical reasons, Cosimo becomes "Cosmo" in Alamanni's poems. In his Italian pastorals, totalling fourteen in all, he was one of the earliest poets to use blank verse. He also wrote two "hunting eclogues" in rather wooden Latin hexameters.

For a literal prose translation by Harry Joshua Leon, see *The Pastoral Elegy*, ed. T.P. Harrison, Jr and H.J. Leon (Austin, 1939), pp. 120–27.

Eclogue I

THYRSIS
Sweet is the high, shrill tone of those tall pines
Contending with the wind, and no less sweet
I judge your pipe; next to the gods themselves,
The universal verdict of us shepherds
Awards to you the proudest praise of all.

MELIBOEUS
Sweet, shepherd, is the water's murmuring
As from the lofty cliff it splashes down,
And yet far sweeter is your charming voice.
Next to the Muses, our fair Tuscany
Awards to you the utmost of its praise.

THYRSIS
If you consent to linger here with me,
Pray you, bring out your pipe, and in this spot,
Bedecked with myrtle, crimson blooms and roses,
Make glad with music all the fields about us,
While I in silence give the flocks my care.

MELIBOEUS
Do not request me that at noon's high hour
I interrupt with piping the sweet slumber
Of our god Pan, who in the grassy fields
Must rest his body, breathless from the chase.
His anger is too greatly to be feared!
But you, who with your song, like Orpheus' self,
Can stir the woods and hills, and stay the streams,
And tame the barbarous wolves among our flocks,
And who with skill to match our Tuscan bard,
Aiolle, can make all the vales rejoice –
Matching Aiolle, in whom Florence finds
Whatever harmony and vocal art
Comes from Terpsichore among mankind –
Sing me, with softened utterance (as you sang
The other day at old Damoetas's)
The miserable death that Cosmo died,

He whom we shepherds hold in honour still
And whom all Tuscany adores and weeps.
As a reward, to pay you for this favour,
I shall reserve a she-goat, snowy-white,
Who suckles now two young ones like herself
And fills two pails each morning with her milk.
I also have a rich vase kept for you,
Packed in sweet juniper, and round its sides
Are green acanthus and green ivy wound.
Within their folds, artistically shaped
By hands of skill, are all the seasons set.
The peasant here is seen who from low vines
Prunes useless branches, trims the trees' high boughs,
And for their growth a strict new law ordains.
Next, underneath the summer sky he stands,
With the curved sickle in his eager hand,
Reaping the harvest of his heavy labours.
Next, joyful in new vintage, bathed and stained
By trampling in the wine-press, see him offer
His sacrificial gifts to kindly Bacchus.
Then, when the vanquished sun lays down its arms
And yields to ice and tempest, here he sits
In greater joy beside the household fire
With his small family, and files and sharpens
The curving plough-share and his other tools
Made dull by constant use, preparing thus
In the sweet hope of warm new days to come.
And one would vow, of all these ornaments,
That, were it not that powers of speech are lacking,
These were a work of nature, not of art.
This master-work is yours, if you but grant
Your honeyed singing, that should not be hoarded
Since presently eternal death will come
And leave us mute and deaf for evermore.

THYRSIS
Since your request and these your gifts of worth,
Compel me to recall our sad affliction,

Begin, O Muses, your unhappy song.
Where were you, all ye Graces at that time,

Ye Virtues and Ye Muses, at the time
When Cosmo's radiant spirit soared to Heaven?
Not on his crystal Arno's soft, cool banks
Could you be found, nor in the grassy hills
Of his beflowered nest; rather, alas,
You were so distant that you came too late
To rescue your belovèd lad from death.

Begin, O Muses, your unhappy song.
The flocks then wept; alas, the herds made moan;
The birds and beasts, the rock and plants all wept;
The Sun was veiled; the sky, that had been gay,
Grew sorrowful and dark, and turned to rain.

Begin, O Muses, your unhappy song.
Apollo from Parnassus then descended
And in his weeping said: "Alas, poor Cosmo,
Where would you go? Who robs the world of you?
Where is the winsome speech, the gracious song,
And all those other arts and virtues rare
I set in you, as in their proper home?

Begin, O Muses, your unhappy song.
Pan also came, with shepherds by the thousand;
His face was doleful, and he muttered low:
"Alas, how Death has cancelled our high hopes
For fair young Cosmo! Many a time I said:
'Our beauteous Tuscany shall one day grow
So famous through this lad that Sicily
And fair Arcadia will yield him fame!'
With what good reason do the flocks and herds
Weep for his loss, for had he lived perchance
No plundering shepherd-thieves nor ruthless wolves
Would come to gulp their milk and eat their young."

Begin, O Muses, your unhappy song.
Last of them all there came the fickle goddess
Who turns the world. Our name for her is Fortune.
Her heart was happy, but she cloaked its joy
In false, dissembling sorrow as she spoke:
"What god, alas, is stealing you from us?
Who brings you to an end before your time?"

Begin, O Muses, your unhappy song.
Cosmo, at point of death, had held his peace,
But, overwhelmed with wrath at her deceit,
He broke his silence with indignant words:
"Deceitful goddess, full of treachery,
  Turning this poor, blind world to ceaseless trouble!
  Well do you know that you have caused my fate.

Begin, O Muses, your unhappy song.
"By hapless proof, I know your perfidy,
  Raising the guilty up and trampling down
  The righteous, and with evil art confounding
  The issue of all honourable plans.

Begin, O Muses, your unhappy song.
"But if my soul must leave this present life
  With less of fame and praise than I desire,
  Let still my warrant be the brevity
  Of time allotted to my thread of life
  By the false, greedy Fates; and may my friends,
  With whom I often shared my purposes,
  All vindicate my name. Alas, how wrong
  The edicts of your kingdom, how capricious,
  That for another's fault, I pay the price!
  But let my lot be sealed; for even today
  I hope to rise to heaven, if good intentions,
  Regardless of my weakness, be a virtue.

Begin, O Muses, your unhappy song.
"O woods and hills, O green and sunny slopes,
  Delightful fields and groves, where I disclosed
  The tender wounds of love in all my song,
  Alas, I now must leave you! Rest in peace.

Leave off, O Muses, your unhappy song.
"Fair fountains, and the beauteous stream of Arno
  Who bathe and cleave the nest where I was born,
  Alas, I now must leave you! Rest in peace.
Leave off, O Muses, your unhappy song.
"And rest you here in peace my dearest friends,
  And do not mourn; yet let some memory
  Of me, my noble thoughts and high designs,

Cut short by death, come back to bless your hearts.
And you, my fair Elisa, rest in peace."
As thus he spoke, his naked soul broke free
From its terrestrial veil and soared to heaven,
To dwell in joy, leaving us here in sorrow.

Leave off, O Muses, your unhappy song.
Give me, forthwith, the white goat and the vase,
That I may render pious sacrifice
And offer prayer to the nine gracious Sisters.
O holy Muses, see how oft I bend
To you my knees and soul, and hope that soon
I'll call on you again with sweeter song.

MELIBOEUS
All that this world of ours has ever owned
Of light and sweetness in your song abides;
Henceforth let Philomel and Procne hush,
Or any bird that mourns with greater art.
Take now the promised prizes for your singing.

Ly-35 (Italian)

LUIGI ALAMANNI. *Eclogue* II. About 1518

Begins: Lasciate, o Ninfe, i freschi erbosi fondi
    De' liquidi cristalli, e i chiari fiumi ...
Ends: Lui chiamando ad ognor che non risponde.
    Piangete sempre omai, sorelle tosche.

In his second eclogue, Alamanni follows with equal exactitude the
Lament for Bion by Moschus. There is, however, a deliberate transfer to a setting in Tuscany: The river Arno, "il tosco fiume," flowing
through Florence, replaces the Greek Meles; Cosimo, the dead poet,
is "il nuovo tosco Orfeo"; and even the Muses become "sorelle
tosche." Both in his close imitation of the Greeks and in his use of
blank verse, Alamanni pointed the direction for the French Pléiade,
who followed half a century later.

Ly-36 (Latin)

MARCO GIROLAMO VIDA. *Nicê*, 1525. Mi: Bodleian (*Carmina minora*, Basel, 1534)

Begins: Coniugis amissi sinus pulcherrima Nicê
           Flebat, et in solis errabat montibus aegra ...
  Ends: Sistite, correptamque domum deducite nymphae,
           Sola dies poterit tantum lenire dolorem.

Marco Girolamo Vida (1485–1566), of Cremona, was best known for his religious epic, the *Christiad* (see PR-13) and expository Latin poems on the *Game of Chess*, the *Silkworm*, and the *Art of Poetry*, but three eclogues were included in his *Carmina minora*. The third of these was a pastoral lament in which a woman called Nicê (Greek for the Italian "Vittoria" Colonna) is inconsolable for her lover Davalus (i.e. Hernando *d'Avalos*, Marquess of Pescara, who had died in 1525). The obvious model in style is Moschus's *Lament for Bion*.

Ly-37 (Latin)

FRANCESCO BERNI. *Amyntas*. About 1525. Mi: British Museum

Begins: Sederat argutae pastor Meliboeus ad umbram
           Ilicis, et medio pecudes collegerat aestu ...
  Ends: Donec eum occiduo propior iam vesper olympo
           Admonuit gregis, et serae decedere nocti.

Superb in their Latinity were twelve Latin poems by Francesco Berni (1497–1535), of Lamporecchio, near Florence. Only one of these was a pastoral elegy, namely *Amyntas* (73 hexameters), in which the shepherd Meliboeus sings, in the noonday shade, of the sorrow of Lycidas, who had been scorned by Amyntas and died of grief. Its model is Vergil's *Gallus*. Berni was even more famous for his *rifacimento* of Boiardo's *Orlando Innamorato*, a clever refake that for a time eclipsed the less polished original in popular favour.

Ly-38 (Latin)

JACOPO SANNAZARO. *Phyllis*. Naples, 1526. Available in *The Piscatory Eclogues of Jacopo Sannazaro*, ed. W.P. Mustard, Baltimore, 1914

Begins: LYCIDAS

Mirabar, vicina, Mycon, per litora nuper
Dum vagor exspectoque leves ad pabula thynnos ...

Ends: LYCIDAS

Tu socios invise, escas nam quaerere tempus
Et tibi nunc vacuae fluitant sine pondere nassae.

By virtue of five eclogues published in 1526, Sannazaro was hailed by his contemporaries as the inventor of the "piscatory eclogue," in which the principal characters were not shepherds (neatherds, goatherds) but fishermen. It has been protested that the 21st Idyll of Theocritus, eighteen centuries before, had been a piscatory and that Sannazaro actually borrows from his forerunner. His originality remains unimpeached, however, since Theocritus' piscatory is not a lament for the dead but a grumbling-match between two discontented fishermen in their hovel before dawn, while Sannazaro's *Phyllis* is a Vergilian epicedium in the style of *Daphnis*, but with fisherfolk instead of shepherds occupying all roles in the poem. He published, moreover, a sequence of five piscatories, which established the fame of the genre beyond all cavil. W.P. Mustard[110] analyses more than a score of subsequent poets who cultivated the piscatory style, including John Donne in his deliberate change into piscatory terms of Marlowe's pastoral song, *The Passionate Sheephearde to his Loue*. James Holly Hanford has identified at some length[111] the echoes of *Phyllis* in Milton's *Lycidas*. Thus Sannazaro's fisherman, Lycidas, invoking the spirit of the dead girl, wherever it may be, to look back on her friends (*Phyllis*, 91–8; *Lycidas*, 154–63) declares that she will be "the genius of the shore" (*Phyllis*, 97–100; *Lycidas*, 183–5). Among the sea-nymphs, both poets mention the rather rare mermaid Panope (*Phyllis*, 86; *Lycidas*, 99).

For a literal prose translation from Sannazaro's Latin by Harry Joshua Leon, see *The Pastoral Elegy*, ed. T.P. Harrison, Jr and H.J. Leon (Austin, 1939), pp. 105–11.

110 In the Introduction to the edition mentioned in the headnote above
111 In *John Milton: Poet and Humanist* (Cleveland, 1966), pp. 149–51

Phyllis

LYCIDAS
Mycon, I marvelled, as I lately wandered
Along the neighbouring coasts, watching the while
To find swift tunnies at their feeding-beds,
In wonder why the raven greeted me
With curious outcries, why the dripping coots,
Perched here and there among the cliffs and caverns,
Filled all the mournful rocks with grievous cries,
And why the curving dolphin leaped no more
Nor led his wonted bands among the waves.
And lo, the day had come on which in earth
We buried our dear Phyllis and lamented
Her ever-blessèd shade beside her grave.
My grief is great, and yet I do not cast
My sad existence off; and rough Pylemon
Does not disdain to offer consolation.

MYCON
That doubtless was the reason why I heard –
As all night long beside Posilipo[112]
I wandered to and fro and my swift skiff
Skirted the shores of fishy Nisida[113] –
The gulls complaining with a doleful cry.
Phyllis was calling them; Phyllis it was
(If we may credit it), dear Lycidas,
Who summoned them to come with lamentation
And chant a funeral dirge above her tomb.

LYCIDAS
Alas, dear Mycon, with these very eyes
What solemn rites I saw – I now recall it –
What hands of hers, what lips, as these my eyes
Beheld her funeral in all my grief!
And yet no savage sorrow drove me on
To cast my body from the rocks and cliffs,

112 A rocky cape, a town and a long mountain, fronting on the Bay of
     Naples west of the city
113 A little rocky islet, once volcanic, just west of the Collina di Posilipo

Nor did the same fierce force of fire consume me,
On the same pyre, nor did some god consent
At least to drown my anguish in the sea.

MYCON
And do you not consider, Lycidas,
How far more fortunate has been her fate
Than if the smoky cave of Lycotas
Had been her home or she had joined the hut
Of shaggy-haired Amyntas and, alas,
Were seeking out the bait to serve the hook
Or mending broken creels with pliant withies.
But if you can recall some fitting song
To mourn a former flame and bear your witness
To a ghost and ashes that you loved of old,
Begin to sing, while now the beach spreads out
Its soft sands at your feet, and frantic waves
Have laid aside their mournful murmuring.

LYCIDAS
Nay rather, I shall now begin these verses
That lately for her shade I formed in haste,
As from the harbour's end I cast my gaze
Along the curving shore and paid due honour
To the white marble of her snowy tomb.
Cast cypress now upon her sepulchre,
And spread green myrtle on the burial mound.

MYCON
See, we have brought the blue sea's clammy moss;
Behold these purple shells and corals, sought
From all the deep and with an effort torn
From off the lowest rocks. Begin, my friend;
Begin your solemn chants. Milcon of Baja[114]
Is spreading out his nets before the sun
And coiling in his boat his dripping ropes.

114 A little town on the west coast of the Gulf of Pozzuoli, some four miles
northwest of Nisida. As the ancient Baiae, it was one of the most famous
watering places and resort towns of the Roman world, but in the sixteenth century it was only a humble fishing village. About a mile to the
north is the ancient Lake Avernus, a flooded volcanic crater, in a grotto
near which Vergil located the entrance to hell.

LYCIDAS (sings)
Goddesses, daughters of old Nereus, pray
What rocks, what caves will you display before me?
What herbs from hidden shores, O Father Glaucus,[115]
What grass with magic juices will you show me,
That by their might I may leave earth behind,
Wretch that I am, and in the watery deep,
With altered body in the midst of waves,
May follow you and with a forkèd tail
May smite the sounding marble of the billows?
For why, alas, in all my misery
Would I be left alone, bereft of Phyllis?
What hope of happiness is left to me
When she, my light, is gone? What can I hope for?
Why should I linger in my misery?
Is it that lying on this worthless seaweed
I may see only dried-out shrubs, and shores
By man abandoned, and in bitterness
Offer my utterance to a thankless tomb?
Is this the marriage and the happy bridal
I hoped to celebrate? Does Venus thus
Bestow a nuptial torch and all its joys?
And does Lucina[116] give such anxious fears?
Who, tell me, who has snatched you from my arms,
O sweetest Phyllis, Phyllis once my peace,
My life's one hope, but now my sorrow rather,
An everlasting woe within my breast?
For fate forbade that I should join with you
In longed-for sleep or pluck the pleasant gifts
Of youth's first years or with you should prolong
The happiness of life to grey old age.
And now – who would believe it? – this cold stone
Possesses you, and you are nowhere now.
Nowhere on earth is Phyllis; but her shade
And memory delude my nights with dreams.
Wretch that I am, where shall I search for you,
Throughout what region? Whither shall I follow?
Earth, in times past, pleased me, because of you,
With all its peoples and its happy towns,

115 A sea-god, the prophet of the Nereids
116 The goddess of childbirth

Girdled with ramparts; but my only wish
Is now to roam across the boundless deep,
To wander madly through the stormy billows,
Among the troops of Tritons, and the monsters
That lurk among the rocks, and uncouth seals
With bristling bodies, that I might not see
The land again forever. Now, O earth,
That I have cherished for so many years,
Farewell, with all your cities and your peoples;
Farewell, dear shores; farewell, beloved Phyllis.
Here in your honour, fronting on the surges,
We shall build seven altars, and each year
Shall offer you accustomed sacrifice –
Some seven monsters of the mighty sea,
Sea-calves all shaggy; and to honour you,
Gay oyster-shells shall hang in seven wreaths,
Mingled with murex and with snowy pebbles.
Here will Nisaea and Cymodyce
With flowing golden tresses and the gentle
Palaemon with his loving mother Ino
And Panope[117] and sister Galatea,
The guardian of the salt Sicilian deep,
All join in solemn dances in your honour
And sing the songs that Proteus once taught them,
That bard divine, when he bewailed the death
Of great Achilles, soothing Thetis' grief.
But you, my dear, whether you dwell in bliss
In heaven above or mid Elysian shades
And the revered sweet fellowships of Lethe
You chase the darting fish in limpid pools
Or with fair fingers pluck immortal flowers –
Narcissus, crocus, dateless amaranth –
And blend fine seaweeds with pale violets,
Look down on us, and come to us with favour;
You will be goddess of the waves forever,
A gracious omen to the fisher-folk.
To you as to the Nymphs and Nereus
And Amphitrite with her golden hair
Shall the triumphant boats pour out libations.
Meanwhile, accept, I pray, this final song

117 Mentioned in *Lycidas* (*99*), "Sleek *Panope* and all her sisters play'd"

That hails your tomb, a song the fisherman
Who ties his line upon a slender pole
May scan from far away and heave a sigh
Of sorrow from the cape: "Here Phyllis lies,
Lapt in the bosom of the well-loved Siren.
Rejoice, Sebeto[118] in a double tomb."[119]

MYCON
Sweet has your lay resounded, Lycidas,
Nor would I rather hear the halcyons
Nor on a grassy bank beside a stream
Listen to swans that flute their sweet laments.
But sing again – and may Megaria[120]
Ever provide you shellfish in abundance
And nearby Mergellina[121] give sea-urchins
And oysters for you from the rocky cliffs –
Since evening still postpones its twilight shadows
And since the Sun still measures out the sky,
Begin again, repeat your song for me;
Reiterated song repeats its charm.

LYCIDAS
Force me not so, dear Mycon, in my grief;
My eyes and cheeks have had enough of tears.
Behold how grief has choked my parching throat
And how my bosom is convulsed with sobs
And my weak voice dies in my panting breath.
Yet at another time I'll sing for you,
This, and still other songs, and even better,
If the kind Muse comes favouring my song.
Rather, that sailing-ships some day hereafter
May view my words from under Procida[122]

118 A small stream, once the eastern boundary of Naples
119 The other tomb being probably that of Vergil, whose mausoleum at
Naples was long regarded with almost religious veneration
120 A small island (Megaris), just off the shore of Naples. It was later joined
to the city by a causeway and on it was built the Castello dell' Ovo,
completed about 1550, twenty years after the death of Sannazaro.
121 Formerly a seashore town at the western edge of Naples, but now a
subdivision of the city. It was while living in his villa here that Sannazaro wrote his piscatories, including *Phyllis*.
122 A coastal town, an island, and a tufa mountain, all about ten miles west
of Naples

Or Cape Miseno,[123] I shall write my verses
In huge green letters that the passing sailor
May view from out the deep and say aloud:
"This poem is the work of Lycidas!"
But since your comrades, shouting here and there,
Call you along the beach and seek your strength
To help them with the nets, let us arise.
Here by the tomb, I'll stay; but you must go
To join your fellows; bait must now be sought;
And now your empty creels unburdened float.

Ly-39 (Latin)

ANDREA NAVAGERO. *Iolas.* 1530. Mi: Bodleian

Begins: Pascite, oves, teneras herbas per pabula laeta,
Pascite, nec plenis ignavae parcite campis ...
Ends: Praesidio umbrarum fretus malus ingruat hostis,
Jam pasti secura greges in ovilia abite.

One of the few important neo-Latin poets produced by Venice was Andrea Navagero (1483–1529). The librarian of St Mark's, he also served his city as an ambassador to Madrid and to Paris. His second eclogue, *Iolas* (88 hexameters) was regarded by W. Leonard Grant as the most beautifully finished of all neo-classical pastorals, with a consummate sense of *le mot juste*. Navagero's notes to a complete edition of Ovid's poetry survive, and he had evidently saturated himself in the prosodic art of the Roman poet. In essence, *Iolas* is a love-poem, avowing fidelity to an absent Amaryllis and declaring that the gifts and overtures of Alcippê leave him cold. It is cited here as the probable model for George Buchanan's *Desiderium Lutetiae* (Ly-49).

Ly-40 (French)

CLÉMENT MAROT. *Complainte* IV. Paris, 1531

123 An isolated rocky mass, forming a promontory about four miles west of Nisida. Vergil here located the tomb of Misenus, the trumpeter of Aeneas.

Begins: THENOT
>En ce beau val sont plaisirs excellens,
>Un cler ruisseau bruyant pres de l'umbrage ...

Ends: THENOT
>Puis le soleil tombe en ces bas limites.
>Et la nuict vient devers l'autre coste.

This elegy was formerly listed as a lament "for Madame Louise of Savoy, Mother of the King, in the form of an eclogue." Clément Marot (1496–1544), writing at the court of Francis I, was successful in acclimatizing the traditions of Theocritus in his own intimate French, not without influences from Moschus, Boccaccio, and Sannazaro. He is actually homelier than Theocritus: Thyrsis, who watches the sheep, becomes a simple sheep-dog, and the gift of an elaborately fashioned bowl becomes the gift of a dozen quinces. His use of the pathetic fallacy and of a catalogue of flowers is wholly in the Theocritean tradition. Entirely original, however, is a portrayal (lines 65–92) of the way in which "Loyse de Savoye" had grouped the young ladies of the court about her and instructed them in ways of industry and usefulness. His prosody employs a quatrain adaptation of the *terza rima*, with stanzas rhyming abab, bcbc, cdcd, dede, etc. When Spenser, in the "November" eclogue of his *Shepheardes Calendar* openly made it "in imitation of Marot his song," he used this identical rhyme scheme in his first 52 lines, but then shifted into elaborate 10-line strophes of his own.

Ly-41 (Latin)

JULIUS CAESAR SCALIGER. *Napaea.* Agen, Lot et Garonne, France, 1533. From *Poemata Omnia*, Paris, 1621

Begins: Aestivam praeceps annus sublegerat horam;
>Vitrea cum tepidis coquitur vindemia saxis ...

Ends: Tu modo, diva, tuis aspira lenior aris:
>Aeternumque meo salve, ac vale inclyta luctu.

In this pastoral eclogue, Julius Caesar Scaliger (1484–1558), one of the most famous classical scholars of the sixteenth century, represents his father ("Aelinus") as mourning the death of his mother.

The characteristics of the genre are strictly reproduced. An odd feature of the poem is that his father actually predeceased his mother and that both were long dead when the elegy was written by the 49-year-old son. Its full title was "Napaea, sub cuius persona Divam Berenicam Lodroniam matrem flet D. Benedictus Scaliger pater."

Ly-42 (Spanish)

GARCILASO DE LA VEGA. *Égloga* I. In *Las Églogas de Garcilaso de la Vega*, Ed. Jorge Rubió y Balaguer, Barcelona, 1945

Begins: El dulce lamentar de dos pastores,
    Salicio juntamente y Nemoroso,
    he de cantar, sus quejas imitando ...
Ends: el fugitivo sol, de luz escaso,
    su ganado llevando,
    se fueron recogiendo paso a paso.

Striking similarities mark the careers of the Spaniard, Garcilaso de la Vega (1503–1536), and the Englishman, Sir Philip Sidney (1554–1586). Both trained in Latin and Greek, blended with the idealism of Castiglione's *Courtier*; spending most of their brief lives in close association with the court and in political missions abroad; influential in mediating Italian literature into their own national lifestreams, especially Sannazaro (whose eclogues deeply influenced Garcilaso's and whose *Arcadia* was the model (through Montemayor?) for Sidney's *Countess of Pembroke's Arcadia*); each meeting untimely death in warfare in a foreign land and as the result of tragically quixotic impulses; both dying at almost exactly the same age (33 and 32); they were fantastically famous with the people of their respective countries. The poetry of both men, moreover, was published posthumously.

Of Garcilaso's three *Églogas*, the first, cited above, and written in 1534, is the most relevant to the present study. The second, while also an epicedium, runs to 105 pages and lacks artistic structure. In the first eclogue, two shepherds, Salicio and Nemoroso (both now believed to represent the poet himself) declaim long dirges in eloquent and highly patterned verse. The lament of Salicio, for example, consists of twelve 14-line stanzas, with a complicated but rigidly uniform pattern of rhyme and varying line-length, and with each of the first eleven stanzas ending in an identical refrain: *Salid sin duelo, lágrimas, corriendo*. In the dirge by Nemoroso, the stanzas are doubled in length and there is no refrain. The eclogue laments a Spanish lady referred to as "Galatea" or "Elisa," concerning whose identity (as with Petrarch's "Laura" and Sidney's "Stella") there has been a good deal of discussion by the peepers and priers of this world. His poetry was limited in quantity – three eclogues, five canciones, a verse epistle and thirty-eight sonnets – but their quality is incomparable and places him among the very greatest of Spanish poets.

Ly-43 (Spanish)

FRANCISCO DE SÁ DE MIRANDA. *Nemoroso*. Written in 1537. In *Poesías*, ed. Carolina Michaëlis de Vasconcellos, Halle, 1885

Begins: PELAIO

    Di me, pastor de cabras alquilado,

    (No te me enojes por la tal demanda ...

  Ends: SALICIO

    El mal todo es de España

    Si enriquecen tus huesos tierra estraña.

Equally a poet in Spanish and in his native Portuguese, Francisco Sá de Miranda (1485?–1558) was a pioneer, independently of Garcilaso, in acclimating Italian influences into the poetry of the Iberian peninsula. Of his 212 poems, some 85 were written in Spanish. Five of these were eclogues, and of these, *Nemoroso*, an epicedium on the death of Garcilaso de la Vega in 1536, merits very high praise. The 533-line poem is a pastoral dialogue amongst six shepherds: Pelaio, Sancho, Rodrigo, Salicio, Blas, and Serrano. The final tribute to Garcilaso, whose bones "make rich a foreign soil," is put on the lips of Salicio, one of the two shepherds in Garcilaso's First Eclogue, the other being Nemoroso, now mourned by Sá de Miranda as synonymous with the dead Garcilaso himself. According to Señora Michaëlis de Vasconcellos, the poem was written in the autumn of 1537, for the first anniversary of the death of Garcilaso. Although Garcilaso's poetry was not *printed* until 1543 (in the same collection with the poetry of Juan Boscán), Sá de Miranda had received a manuscript copy as early as 1534–5 from the hands of Antonio Pereira, to whom he therefore dedicates his *Nemoroso*. Sra. Michaëlis de Vasconcellos also shows that Garcilaso and Sá de Miranda were kinsmen and that their families were country neighbours in Asturias.

Ly-44 (Latin)

GIAMBATTISTA GIRALDI. *Daphnis. Ecloga* II. *In funere Ioannis Manardi praeceptoris optimi, et Ludovici Bonactioli.* Ferrara, 1537. Mi: Bodleian

Begins: Quid Damone mihi, quid nunc mihi Daphnide rapto
Aut spei, aut vitae superest? quae pabula? quasve ...
Ends: Hic Daphnis iaceo, satis hoc tibi nosse, viator:
Caetera fama tulit super et Garamantas et Indos.

Giambattista ("Cinzio") Giraldi (1504–1573) was a citizen of Ferrara, Italy. In this Latin epicedium, his former professor, Joannes Manardus, is identified as "Damon" and Ludovicus Bonactiolus as "Daphnis." There are few pastoral characteristics apart from these names.

Ly-45 (Latin)

BASILIO ZANCHI. *Meliseus.* Rome, 1550. Mi: Bodleian (in *Basilii Zanchi Poematum Editio Copiosior*)

Begins: Vix primum roseo spargebat lumine terras
Aurora Oceani exurgens natalibus undis ...
Ends: Donec summa dies dissoluerit artus;
Et tenuem Melisee tibi coniunxerit umbram.

One of the most skilful Latin poets in Italy in the early sixteenth century was Basilio Zanchi (1501–1558) of Bergamo, in Lombardy. His poetry early won the favour of Pope Leo X at Rome, but he later ran foul of the terrible-tempered Pope Paul IV; was incarcerated in the dungeons of the Castel Sant' Angelo; and died very quickly. His *Meliseus* is an epicedium on the death in 1503 of Giovanni Pontano of Naples (see Ly-23, 24). As Zanchi was only two years old when Pontano died, his elegy was evidently a work of literary piety written in cold blood many years later. This poet is not to be confused with the Protestant theologian, Girolamo (Jerome) Zanchi (1516–1590), born at Brescia and teaching in German universities from 1551 till 1590. It is this latter author whom Milton frequently cites with approval (as "Zanchius") in his *De Doctrina Christiana*, e.g., in chapter xxvii, "Of the Gospel and Christian Liberty."

Ly-46 (Latin)

BASILIO ZANCHI. *Damon*. Rome, 1550. Mi: Bodleian

Begins: LYCIDAS
    Quid tantum insano foedantem pectora luctu
    Funesta te Thyrsi iuvat tabescere in umbra ...
  Ends: Aeternum et salve singultibus intermistis,
    Aeternumque vale dicent ò maxime Damon.

This is a pastoral elegy in honour of Baldassare Castiglione (see Ly-32), who had died in 1529. The shepherd Lycidas asks his friend Thyrsis the reason for his sobs and wails. Thyrsis tells of the death of luckless Damon, who has drowned in a whirlpool in the river. During the two days before his death, nature had been full of portents of disaster. Damon had been a supreme singer, and now only grief is left for Thyrsis.

Ly-47 (Latin)

BASILIO ZANCHI. *Licmon*. Rome, 1550. Mi: Bodleian

Begins: Forte sub Autumni extremum intractabilis imbrem
    Tristior, et partes animum diductus in omnes, ...
  Ends: Torserat: ast illi circum cava tempore serpsit
    Blanda quies furtim: atque oculis se immisit apertis.

This pastoral epicedium laments the death of his poet-friend, Giovanni Cotta, of Vangadizza, near Legnano, in Lombardy, who died in 1520. Giano Anisio's elegy, *Meliseus* (Ly-29), on the death of Giovanni Pontano, had been placed on the lips of this same Cotta. In a striking passage in Zanchi's elegy, he congratulates Cotta on having died before the appalling sack of Rome in 1527 by the 30,000 ruffians of an invading imperial army.

Ly-48 (Latin)

LUIGI PASQUALE. *In Morte Ludovici Pontani*. In *Carmina illustrium poetarum Italorum*, ed. Giovanni Bottari, Florence, 1719–26, eleven volumes. Mi: Harvard

Begins: CALIDORUS
    Aspicis, ut saturae ludant per prata Capellae,
    Nec dulcem Cythisum, aut Salices pascantur amares ...
Ends: CALIDORUS
    Sidera somnifero Grylli stridore salutant.
    Surgamus laetisque domum repetamus ab agris.

Luigi Pasquale lived in Rome and flourished about 1550. The Pontanus lamented in this epicedium is not Giovanni, the great Latin poet. The goatherd Calidorus asks his friend Arganthys the reason for his sorrow. The well-fed goats are sporting; the dogs are standing with pricked-up ears; yet you have a grief-stricken face. Arganthus replies that Pontanus is dead, and sings a long tribute to his worth. The Dalmatian woods then wave their branches in applause, even as the Thracian woods had applauded Orpheus and the Aracynthean woods had marvelled at Amphion.

Ly-49 (Latin)

GEORGE BUCHANAN. *Desiderium Lutetiae*. Coimbra, Portugal, about 1551. Mi: Bibliothèque Nationale, Paris

Begins: O formosa Amarylli, tuo jam septima bruma
    Me procul aspectu, jam septima detinet aetas:
Ends: Illa meum rudibus succendit pectora flammis,
    Finiet illa meos moriens morietis amores.

Scotland's greatest humanist in the sixteenth century, and a poet sometimes termed the Latin laureate of Europe, was George Buchanan (1506–1582). Much of his life was spent abroad as a teacher in Paris (where Montaigne was one of his pupils), Bordeaux, and Coimbra (where he fell for a time into the hands of the Inquisition). About 1560 he returned to Scotland and soon professed himself a

Protestant. He became principal of St Leonard's College, St Andrews, in 1566–70 and moderator of the General Assembly in 1567. His four Latin tragedies are outstanding and his Latin versions of the Psalms were used in Scotland's schools for nearly two centuries. His Latin poetry was given high praise by J.J. Scaliger, Sir Philip Sidney, John Dryden, Samuel Johnson, and William Wordsworth. Paris long held the affections of his heart and his homesickness for that city, during his incarceration in Coimbra, welled over in his *Desiderium Lutetiae* ("Longing for Paris"). The model is Navagero's *Iolas* (Ly-39), but its stock phrases and traditional manner are used figuratively to express intense personal emotion. The speaker, Daphnis, cries out for his darling Amaryllis (Paris) and disdains the advances of the Portuguese girls, Lycisca and Melaenis.

Ly-50 (Latin)

GERVAIS SEPIN.   *Alexis: Epicedium Henrici Bellay.* 1555. Mi: British Museum

Begins: CORYDON
> Damoeta, ecquid agit Mopsus? quem more ferarum
> Nuper ego obstupui silvarum habitare latebras ...
Ends: CORYDON
> Nulla etiam, si sit, pellat vim grandinis umbra.
> Surgamus, iam sponte fugit pecus ocyus imbrem.

Elaborate poetical rhetoric went into the making of this elegy in memory of the poet's thirteen-year-old pupil. Gervais Sepin (*fl.* 1550) of Saumur, near Tours, had been well grounded in Cicero and Vergil. In due time, he became tutor to Henri, the little son of François du Bellay de Lire, and moved with the family to Paris. The boy died young and this neo-Latin lament, though conventional in form, reveals genuine affection on Sepin's part. Two shepherds, Damoetas and Corydon, exchange laments in their grief for the youthful Alexis. At the close of the eclogue, a hailstorm comes, and their panicky beasts lead the pell-mell rush for shelter.

Ly-51 (French)

IAN ANTOINE DE BAÏF.   *Eclogue* II. *Brinon*. Paris, 1555

Begins: Pucelles, qui aimez les verdoyans riuages,
   Et pres du bruit des eaus la Fraicheur des embrages ...
   Ends: Leuons- nous, il est nuit, petit troupeau refet,
   Le Soleil est couché, sus retournez au tet.

Born in Venice, the natural son of the scholarly French ambassador to that state, Ian Antoine de Baïf (1532–1589) was given a thorough training in Latin and Greek and became in Paris one of the most highly educated members of the Pléiade. Ronsard was his pupil in Greek. The Maecenas of the Pléiade was Jean Brinon, who almost bankrupted himself in showering gifts and hospitality on the little group. On Brinon's death in 1555, the poets of the time piled flowers on his grave and wrote elegies in his honour. Baif's *Brinon*, cited here, is a free paraphrase of Vergil's tenth eclogue. He uses the closed heroic couplet throughout, but in keeping with his reformist theories he has *vers mesurés* supplant natural accentuation. In other eclogues, he uses various patterns of stanza and metre, a practice that was to be adopted by Spenser in his *Shepheardes Calendar*.

Ly-52 (Latin)

JOANNES (MONTANUS) FABRICIUS. *Orion*. About 1557. Mi: British Museum

Begins: Ereptam terris Threnem lugebat Orion,
   Assiduo gemitu silvas montesque fatigans: ...
   Ends: Omnia narrarunt Limago, qui dicta probavit,
   Misit et Oceano per conscia flumina Rheni.

Fabricius' (1527–1566) family was Swiss, but he happened to be born at Metz. He was first educated in Switzerland and then at the University of Marburg. Returning to Switzerland, he married a twenty-year-old girl. After a year of idyllic mutual happiness, she died in childbirth. As a shepherd named"Orion,"he mourns his "Threne"in this eclogue, but without the illusions of the pathetic fallacy. All nature is resplendent with blossoms and bird-song, while he alone is broken-hearted.

Ly-53 (Latin)

JEAN DORAT. *Tumulus Mellini Sangelasii.* 1558. Mi: British Museum

Begins: Carylus et Darylas Mellinum nuper ademptum
Pastorum florem, florens, tunc pastor uterque ...
Ends: Laetos terque sonos, pro maesto carmine dantes
Nunc quasi Mellinum, quam flebant nuper, adorent.

Praised by Mark Pattison and W. Leonard Grant as a very accomplished Hellenist, Jean Dorat (1502–1588), a professor at the Collège Royal in Paris, undertook in 1558 to write an elaborate memorial to his dead friend, Mellin St-Gelais. A vast sequence of balanced quatrains is bandied back and forth between the shepherds, Dorylas (Dorat) and Carylus (Lancelot de Carle). Even elegance, in excess, can be hard to endure.

Ly-54 (French)

PIERRE DE RONSARD. *Angelot* (Eclogue I in *Bergerie*). About 1559

Begins: Quand le bon Henriot par fiere destinée
Auant la nuict venuë accomplist sa journée ...
Ends: Plus forte que la mort, fleurissante en tout temps
Par ces grandes forests comme fleurs au Printemps.

Written to commemorate the death in 1559 of King Henry II of France, this piece of courtly compliment is largely based on Vergil, Sannazaro, and Marot. One would never gather from its flattery that Henry had been bigoted, cold, dull, haughty, melancholy, and merciless. At his death, says Ronsard, the sun hid his head in rusty crape; rocks, caves and woods wept for him, and even the wolves and lions lamented him. Since the death of "Henriot," the ploughlands have grown only weeds, the grass has lost its greenness, and the flowers have all turned black. His royal spirit now inhabits heaven, amid the perpetual spring of a better land. On earth, his renown will endure for ever. Ronsard's poetic tribute was as undeserved as

Germain Pilon's monumental tomb to Henry and his queen in the Abbey Church of St-Denis, Paris, with its poignant Manneristic contrast between the kneeling bronzes of the royal pair on top of the tomb and their marble *gisants,* or nude corpses, inside it, the king in the guise of a Dead Christ and the queen as a Dead Venus.

For a literal prose translation by Harry Joshua Leon, see *The Pastoral Elegy,* ed. T.P. Harrison, Jr and H.J. Leon (Austin, 1939), pp. 153–7.

Angelot

After good Henriot[124] in death grew dumb,
Ending his journey before night had come,
Our flocks, foreseeing danger dark and dank,
Pined in the fields, and neither ate nor drank:
They cried and bleated; to the earth they cowered,
As by a clap of thunder overpowered.
All things on earth were weeping in dismay;
The sun was veiled, lest he that death survey,
And hid his golden head in rusty crape,
Detesting earth, where evils thus take shape.

    The Nymphs, with mournful voice, made loud lament,
The caves made moan, the woods, and steep ascent.
Ye forests, in your groves, this too you know,
That wolves and savage lions voiced their woe.

    This was that Henriot whose reign of ease
Restored the cult of banished deities,
Who won in civil arts the highest prize,
And raised his army's glory to the skies.

    Just as the grape-vine is the elm-tree's glory,
And as the grape fulfills the grape-vine's story,
As the flock's glory is the goat that leads,
As the field's glory is the grain it breeds,
And as the orchard's glory is its fruit,
So Henriot's fame for us stood absolute.

    How often, since his cruel death brought dearth,
Our ploughs with yearly toil have cleft the earth,
And yet, instead of grain, by field and coppice,

---

124 A pastoralized form of Henri (i.e. Henry II, King of France)

We harvest only darnel, pinks and poppies.

The grasses at his death their verdure lost,
Roses and lilies were with midnight crossed,
The marguerite assumed the hues of grief,
Dianthus wrote its woes upon its leaf.

Shepherds, to praise him, strewed the earth with flowers,
And veiled the brooks with vines and ivy-bowers;
They built of turf a tomb on his behalf,
And to his honour reared this epitaph:

"The soul whose virtue ranked beyond the best,
Left here its cloak in passing to its rest;
Ye oak-trees, cast your shade on his demise;
And manna, rain from heaven where he lies."

O Shepherd Henriot, how better far
Than earth, so full of fear, deceit and war,
Is yonder Heaven, where in peace you find
Beneath your feet the planets and the wind,
Beneath your feet the stars and clouds in bands,
The air, the sea, the old, familiar lands;
These, like a perfect Angel, you behold,
Freed from the cares that mortal life enfold.

O regal spirit in the highest heaven,
To you our lives and thoughts for scorn are given,
And worldly pleasures, whose too sudden course
Yields us the bitterness of long remorse.

Like a fair Sun among celestial souls,
By lightnings flanked, flames and bright aureoles,
You shine in Heaven, and, from fear exempt,
You laugh at earthly wiles in calm contempt.

Where you have come, the spring is always green,
There are no storms, no heat or cold are seen,
But only clear, pure air; your evening sun
Will never set, as here on earth is done.

You gaze on other woods and other shores,
On higher cliffs, on glades with greener floors,
And grassier meadows, where your dear sheep lie
By other, fairer blooms that never die.

Therefore our woods and plains and grassy nooks,
Our streams and leas, our flowers and our brooks,
Are full of plaudits, from both wave and sod,

That the good Henriot is now a god.

Accept our vows: of ivory and stone
Beside the Loire a temple you shall own;
And there, when April days are long and new,
I shall have shepherd contests held for you;
Leaping and wrestling, will our lads dispute;
As prize upon a pine will hang a lute.

Your Janot will be there to sing your deeds,
Your wars, your battles and your conquering steeds,
All that you did, by matchless hand and lance,
To raise again the shepherd-staff of France.

Farewell, great Shepherd; and as long as we
Shall mark birds swim the winds and fish the sea,
We'll love your name; and by this hermitage
Your glory shall live on from age to age.

Each year we shall rear altars in your name,
As we with sods build aegipans the same,
Satyrs and fauns, and offer sacrifice.
Your Perrot first will sing the chant precise,
In long, white surplice and with cypress crowned;
And with the horn we'll make the woods resound
With your just honours; thus your praise will range,
Year after year, exalted without change,
Stronger than death, and in all seasons bring
To these great woods perpetual flowers of spring.

Ly-55 (Latin)

JACOBUS SLUPERIUS. *Iolas.* In *Delitiae poetarum Belgicorum*, ed.
Jan Gruter, 1614, Vol. IV, pages 352-4. Mi: Harvard

Begins: O dolor, ô lachrymae, quo tam felicia quondam
             Tempora: quo placidis aetas tam grata Cicutis? ...
Ends: Humentem rosca pepulisset lampade noctem,
           Et nitidum rotulo monstrasset lumine Solem.

Perhaps the earliest of the Dutch neo-Latinists was Jacobus
Sluperius, or Jakob de Sluyper (1532-1582), of Herzele. The sample
of his poetry listed here is pioneer work only. In the first 45 lines,
the shepherd Iolas invokes his dead friend. In the next 36, Phoebus

and the Muses come to comfort him. Then follows "the Heliconian Dream" (*Somnium Aonium*). It is night, with a full moon, bitter frost, and howling winds. He dreams that he is sitting beside the hearth, trying to warm himself and reading famous annals and passages on death. After brief rest, and still asleep, he sees a venerable man with a shining face standing beside his bed. It is the god Mercury, sent by Apollo, to upbraid him for his poetic idleness. In the last few lines, the poet awakens and obeys the heavenly vision.

Ly-56 (Latin)

PETER LOTICH. *Daphnis*, 1560. Mi: British Museum

Begins: Irrigui iuxta fontem Acidis, ilice tecti,
   Myrtilus et Celadon occasum insontis amici ...
 Ends: Spectandum, ut celebri praetexat honore sepulcrum,
   Aeternum vestri monumentum, et pignus amoris.

Praised by W. Leonard Grant as the greatest of the neo-Latin bucolic poets in Germany, Peter Lotich the Younger (1528-1560), of Schlüchtern, in Hesse, was associated with the universities of Wittenberg (from whose disorders he fled in dismay), Marburg, Montpellier, and Heidelberg. His Latin poetry, published posthumously at Leipzig in 1586, included six eclogues. In the fifth of these, entitled *Daphnis*, a fowler named Myrtilus and a hunter named Celadon lament the death by drowning in the Rhine of their friend and fellow-poet, Hilarius Cantiuncula (Hilaire Chansonette).

Ly-57 (Latin)

FRANCESCO VINTA. *Amyntas* (about 1560). In *Corpus Illustrium Poetarum Italorum*, Vol. XI, pp. 249–52. Mi: Harvard

Begins: MAENALUS
   Frondibus exuras sylvas, et gramine campos
   Tristis hiems, gelidasque nives, aut alpibus imbres ...
 Ends: ALCON
   Jam silice abstrusos Campillius excitat ignes,
   Crebrique victricis fumant mapalia turris.

This dirge by Francesco Vinta, of Volterra, Tuscany, is written in readable but undistinguished Latin hexameters. It laments a deceased abbot, Joannes Baptista Bava. Two shepherds, Maenalus and Alcon, narrate in turn the sad changes in nature that express grief for the dead Amyntas. Then evening comes. They raise fish-traps from the river and call on Campillius (who has no speaking part) to start a fire from the flint so that they may cook their supper.

Ly-58 (Portuguese)

LUIS DE CAMOENS. *Egloga*. Written before 1564, published posthumously in 1595. From *The Oxford Book of Portuguese Verse*, ed. Aubrey F.G. Bell, Oxford, 1925

Begins: Que grande variedade vão fazendo,
         Frondelio amigo, as horas apressadas ...
  Ends: que a pesar de los hados enojosos
         tambien para los tristes hubo muerte!

The death of Tionio is lamented in long amoebic interchange between two shepherds, Umbrano and Fidelio. Most of their elegy is in *ottava rima*, but Fidelio uses long passages in *canzone*-measure, though with a much greater proportion of short lines than may be found in *Lycidas*. In the traditional fashion, the water-nymphs share in the "silencio triste" of universal grief. The dialogue is ended with 43 lines in *terza rima* by the shepherdess Aonia. The genre is Vergilian rather than Theocritean. Camoens was born about 1524 and died in 1580, but he had written practically all of his significant poetry before the age of forty.

Ly-59 (Portuguese)

LUIS DE CAMOENS. *Elegia*. Written before 1564, but published posthumously in 1595. From *The Oxford Book of Portuguese Verse*, ed. Aubrey F.G. Bell, Oxford, 1925

Begins: O poeta Simonides, falando
         com o capitão Themistocles um dia, ...
  Ends: me não entrega ao duro Radamanto,
         se para tristes ha tam leda sorte.

This melodious elegy consists of 218 flowing lines in *terza rima*, a poem nearly twice the length of a canto of Dante's *Commedia*. It is not in the tradition of Theocritus and Vergil, but rather in that of Propertius or Ovid; but he has deliberately chosen *terza rima* instead of couplets (elegiac or heroic), because the latter, with their brief, self-contained quanta of verse, would not produce the solemn, sonorous, never-ceasing, richly blended current of poetry that he desires. His youth had been nourished on the classics at Coimbra University in its golden age under King João III, and the "Elegy" is full of classical allusions as he describes his "passage to India" or meditates on the solemnity of Death and the assured immortality of his verse. He begins by invoking Simonides and ends under the shadow of Rhadamanthus.

James H. Sims, in an essay, "Camoens' *Lusiads* and Milton's *Paradise Lost*: Satan's Voyage to Eden," pp. 36-46, in *Papers on Milton*, ed. P. Makone and L.F. Zimmerman (1969), finds that Milton was familiar with Camoens' epic since he borrowed certain nautical-maritime imagery to describe Satan's voyage to Eden. There is no textual or other evidence that Milton was aware of Camoens' *Elegia*.

Ly-60 (Latin)

GEORGE BUCHANAN. *Ioannis Calvini Epicedium*. Edinburgh, 1564. Mi: Bibliothèque Nationale, Paris

Begins: Si quis erit nullos superesse a funere manes
        Qui putet, aut si forte putet sic vivit ut orcum ...
  Ends: Vulturibus jecur exesus, cava dolia lymphis
        Frustra implens, Ixioneum distentus in orbem.

The Scottish Presbyterian Buchanan here pays elegiac tribute to his friend and slightly younger coeval, John Calvin, who had died in Geneva in May 1564 at the age of 54, worn out by his scholarly and administrative labours. This 48-hexameter elegy (*epicedium*) should be read in conjunction with Ly-49, written 13 years before, when he was a prisoner of the Inquisition in Portugal. In the earlier poem, he could gracefully adapt Navagero's Latin pastoral, *Iolas*, in order to express his deep longing for the city of Paris. His elegy on Calvin, however, is written *in propria persona*. It was doubtless impossible for him to imagine the austere 54-year-old author of the *Institutes* and himself, the 58-year-old translator of the *Psalter*, as a pair of young Sicilian shepherds. His poem, however, like Vergil's *Daphnis* and Milton's *Lycidas*, has a flavour of apotheosis. Calvin's great theological works will waft him heavenwards. Pluto, Charon, and Cerberus cannot touch him.

Ly-61 (Latin)

PIETRO ANGELIO. *Varchius*. Rome, 1565. Mi: Harvard (*Poemata omnia*)

Begins: Nec tamen interea, ni mens mihi laeva fuisset
Signa dabant obitus Superi non clara futuri ...
Ends: Mitteret ut dulci memorabile munus amico:
Supremumque vale, Varchi vale optime, dixit.

Pietro Angelio of Barga, Italy, is best known for a formidable twelve-book Latin epic, the *Syriad*, telling the story of the First Crusade. Of his four eclogues, the fourth, *Varchius*, is a lament by an Etruscan nymph, Daphne, at the tomb of the neo-Latin poet, Benedetto Varchi (1503-1565), here Latinized as Varchius. Maurice Kelley has proved that Milton owned a copy of Varchi's *Sonetti* (Venice, 1555), now in the New York Public Library bound into a single volume with his personal copies of Dante's *L'Amoroso Convivio*, and Giovanni della Casa's *Rime et Prose*.

Ly-62 (Latin)

GIOVANNI BATTISTA ARCUCCI. *Ecloga I: Olympias*. Naples, 1568. Mi: Harvard, in *Odarum libri ii*, Naples 1568

Begins: Germanae extinctae fatum deflebat Amyntas,
Atque has infelix iactabat ad astra querelas ...
Ends: Perge dolor, dulcesque iocos, risusque sororis
Saepius in mentem revoca, meminisse iuvabit.

This Neapolitan poet here laments the death of his sister. The Latin style is simple but eloquent. The description of the actual death scene is rather unusual in this type of epicidium. He refers to himself as a shepherd, Amyntas by name. We know very little about Arcucci, apart from an editor's assertion, in the preface to the 1568 edition of his Latin poetry, that he was "Theologus gravissimus, Orator eloquentissimus, et Poetarum (ut nomen indicat) Princeps, natus ad immortalitatem suis carminibus."[125]

Ly-63 (Latin)

GIOVANNI BATTISTA ARCUCCI. *Eclogue* II: *Epicedium*. Naples, 1568. Mi: Harvard, in *Odarum libri ii*, Naples, 1568

Begins: LYCIDAS
    Quis tibi tam pulchros calamos dedit? An Meliseus?
    AMYNTAS
    O Lycida nondum genetrix me dulcis in auras ...
Ends: AMYNTAS
    Discedit coelo sensim, nostraeque vagantur
    Huc illae fusae nullo costode capellae.

Two shepherds, Amyntas (again the poet himself) and Lycidas, engage in highly formalized amoebean dialogue. Amyntas praises the poetic skill of his former mentor, Uranius, who has written expository poems on orange-culture and on astronomy; while Lycidas lauds the charm and beauty of Phyllis (perhaps Ippolita, of the princely house of Gonzaga). Amyntas bewails the death of Uranius, and Lycidas the death of Phyllis.

Ly-64 (Latin)

GILES FLETCHER, the Elder. *De Morte Boneri*. Cambridge, 1569. Mi: Bodleian

Begins: Jam nova fulcatus reparaverat horrea messor
    Quae prior emensi victus consumpserat anni ...
Ends: Pyraque, quae nuper ramis fragrantia legi:
    Et jam suadet oves sub culmina ducere vesper.

125 Tr. "A most weighty theologian, a most eloquent orator, and (as the name indicates) the Prince of Poets, born for immortality through his songs."

Giles Fletcher the elder (1546–1611) was an older contemporary of Edmund Spenser at Cambridge. His first Latin eclogue, *De morte Boneri* (1569), is in memory of Edmund Bonner (or Boner), who had just died in the Marshalsea Prison, London. Bonner had been Bishop of London under Henry VIII, fell out with the Church of England under Edward VI, was reinstated as a Roman Catholic bishop under Mary I, and finally, having refused the oath of supremacy under Elizabeth I, spent the last ten years of his life in the Marshalsea. Fletcher's poem begins with poor, hungry Thestilus, guardian of a scanty herd, fishing on a river-bank, with only his faithful dog sitting beside him. His reed-pipe is hanging on a branch, his bullocks are cropping the grass, and he himself has just lowered a baited hook into the stream when he sees his friend Palaemon approaching. They engage in a long, sad discussion of the religious strife of their time. At last Thestilus announces that he has caught some fish and has picked some ripe pears from nearby branches. Evening is summoning his herd to make for home.

Ly-65 (Latin)

POMPEIO ARNOLFINO. *Thyrsis*. In *Carmina illustrium poetarum Italorum*, ed. Giovanni Bottari, Florence, 1719–26, eleven volumes. Mi: Harvard

Begins: Fistula quae dulces Pastorum ludere Amores,
          Et solita et curas pellere corde graves ...
  Ends: Haec Thyrsis, moestae responsant undique valles
          Dum deflet moestis Daphnin arundinibus.

Arnolfino flourished at Lucca about 1570. Little is known about the poet or his work. This epicedium, *Thyrsis*, is written in elegiac couplets instead of the Theocritean and Vergilian hexameters. In it, the shepherd Thyrsis sings a lament for his dead shepherd-friend, Daphnis (Giulio Bruto).

Ly-66 (Latin)

FRANÇOIS TILLIER. *In obitum Regis Caroli* IX. Paris, 1574. Mi: Bibliothèque Nationale

Begins: GALLUS

    Ah, miser infestus, quid agam? quo pauper abibo?

    Rarane vah! quondam spreto mihi grata relinquam? ...

Ends: DAMON

    Atque duas super hanc capras mactabimus albas,

    Tunc florum dabimus duo plena canistra quotannis.

This hollow epicedium laments the death in 1574 of Charles IX of France, under whose weak and ill-balanced rule his mother, Catherine dei Medici, had engineered the murder of 50,000 Huguenots in the Massacre of Saint Bartholomew (1572). Haunted and fever-ridden, he died at the age of twenty-four. In Tillier's eclogue, two rustics, Gallus and Damon, exchange laments over the death of Charles. The poem is highly conventional, ending, however, in the bizarre suggestion (in the context) that they match alternate songs, with forfeits to be paid by the loser. François Tillier (*ca.* 1515– *ca.* 1580) was a lawyer in his native city of Tours. This poem is his only known composition.

Ly-67 (Latin)

ANTONIUS FUMAEUS. *Livia*. Lyons, 1574 or 1575. Mi: Bibliothèque Nationale

Begins: Livia defuncta est, pulcher, suspirat Iolas,

    Indoluit Venus, et lacrymas fudistis Amores ...

Ends: Livia iam vivit, iam Livia facta columba est,

    Solvitur e somno, atque armenta revisit Iolas.

When Charles IX of France was succeeded in 1574 by his younger brother, Henry III, the president of the Breton *parlement*, Antoine Fumée (1511–*ca.* 1575), launched out into a brief literary career, including a panegyric in French and three eclogues in Latin. *Livia*, the third of these latter, laments the death of the new king's mistress, Marie de Clèves. As a shepherd, Iolas, lies dreaming beside a spring, he sees his shepherdess-sweetheart, Livia, sad and pale of face. When he tries to embrace her, she disappears. Then he sees a funeral cortège of birds, carrying, by cords around their necks, a coffin containing her dead body. He breaks out into a lament, then awakes and goes to look after his flocks. The style is correct but uninspired. Perhaps it was hard to wax poetic over a monarch whom the *Britannica* characterizes as indolent, vicious, and corrupt.

Ly-68 (Latin)

GILES FLETCHER, the Elder. *Adonis*. London, 1576. Mi: British Museum

Begins: Extinctum Lycidas nuper deflebat Adonim
            Venator, gemituque lacus fluviosque replebat ...
Ends: Blanditu cupiunt domini lenire dolorem,
            Sic lacrimans excessit agris, urbemque petebat.

Walter Haddon (1516–1572) was a friend of Roger Ascham and a Latin poet in his own right. During his career, he was vice-chancellor of Cambridge University, 1549–50; master of Trinity Hall, Cambridge, 1552; president of Magdalen College, Oxford, 1552–3; M.P. for Thetford, 1558; and a judge and an ecclesiastical commissioner. He died in January 1572, and only four months later his son Clere was drowned in the Cam River at Cambridge. In 1576, a two-volume edition of Walter Haddon's Latin *Poems* was published in London. Bound in with this work, as a sort of supplement, were six Latin poems by other hands: (iii) a lament by Haddon's son, Clere, on the death of his father; (iv) a reply to Clere Haddon's lament, by Osmund Lakes; and (i, ii, v, and vi) four poems by Giles Fletcher the Elder, namely, elegiacs on the death of Walter Haddon, on Haddon's willow-tree and on Clere Haddon's lament, and a pastoral elegy, in hexameters, printed simply as"Adonis Eiusdem Fletcher," on the death of Clere Haddon himself, in which the poet, as "Lycidas,"grieves over Clere as"Adonis."Much space is given to upbraiding the treacherous river in which the young man had been drowned. This epicedium and Fletcher's slightly earlier *De morte Boneri* (see Ly-64) are probably the first examples of this genre in England's neo-Latin poetry. His posthumous poem, *De literis antiquae Britanniae* (1633), has"Father Camus"telling the shepherd "Lycidas"the story of early English history, including the metamorphosis of Sabrina into the goddess of the Severn River. Fletcher's elder son, Phineas (1582–1650), published in his *Piscatory Eclogues* (1633) stanzas on the death of his father as"Thelgon"(see Lloyd E. Berry, *The English Poems of Giles Fletcher the Elder*, 1964, p. 49).

Kenneth Muir has summarized[126] the possible echoes in *Lycidas*

126 *John Milton* (London, 1955), p. 47

of *The Purple Island* (1633), the *magnum opus* of Phineas. The parallels are a passage on ambition, another on the death of Orpheus, and the penultimate lines that run"Home then my lambes; the falling drops eschew;/To morrow shall ye feast in pastures new, ..."

R. Blenner-Hassett[127] has analysed Milton's"deft rewriting"of the original Sabrina-story as recorded by Geoffrey of Monmouth and in Milton's own *History of Britain*. Sabrina had been the issue of adultery by Locrine and had been murdered by his lawful wife, Guendolen, who drowned her in the Severn River. Milton, seeking to exploit local geography at the inauguration of the highest judicial officer of Wales, therefore stresses Sabrina's innocence and purity, refers to Guendolen as her"step-dame,"emphasizes the respectability of Locrine's ancestry, and represents Sabrina as voluntarily seeking death in the river as she flies from"the mad pursuit"of Guendolen.

See also W.B. Austin,"Milton's *Lycidas* and Two Latin Elegies by Giles Fletcher the Elder."[128]

Ly-69 (Latin)

M A R C O   P U B L I O   F O N T A N A . *Eclogue* VI, *Caprea, sive deploratio capreae suavissimae*. Bergamo, 1578. Mi: Harvard (edition of 1752)

Begins: Aeriae rupes, et vos juga plurima circum
            Dissita, sola feris sedes fidissima capris, ...
   Ends: Rura petis; pluresque simul cum moenibus urbes
            Te proprium accipiunt repetita ad limina civem.

The North-Italian town of Bergamo is famous not only for the Tasso family but also as the birthplace of the copious neo-Latin poet, Marco Publio Fontana (1548–1609). The poem cited here is a happy parody of the pastoral epicedium, gracefully burlesqueing all of the stock phrases and situations of the genre, in a lament over the death of"the sweetest little she-goat,"belonging to his friend, Bartolommeo Fino, of Bergamo. For example, instead of the deification of the classical hero we have the stellification of the darling goat to shining eminence in the sky. Just out of focus for possible comparison with Fontana's *Caprea* is the First Eclogue, entitled *Lycidas*, of Giambattista Amalteo (1525–1573), suggested by Sir J.E.

127 *MLN* (1949), 315–18
128 *SP*, xliv (1947), 41–55

Sandys[129] as a possible source for Milton's *Lycidas*. In Amalteo's poem, a North Italian, given the name Lycidas, is about to take ship for Spain and bids a regretful farewell to Italy and especially to his pet he-goat, the leader of his flock. This is not an epicedium, no one is dead, and there is little in common with Milton's poem except the name. Even this is applied to the speaker, and not to someone else.

Ly-70 (English)

EDMUND SPENSER. *The Shepheardes Calendar*. London, 1579

Begins: COLIN CLOUTE
  A shepherds boye (no better doe him call)
  When winters wastful spight was almost spent ...
Ends: COLIN CLOUTE
  Adieu, good Hobbinol, that was so true:
  Tell Rosalind her Colin bids her adieu.

Spenser, at the age of twenty-seven, emulated Vergil by beginning his poetic career with pastoral poetry, in this case twelve "eclogues" patterned after the twelve months of the year. The May eclogue is a dialogue between Piers and Palinodie concerning unfaithful "shepherds," and ends with a fable of the Fox and the Kid. The complaint against corrupt clergymen is repeated in the July eclogue. In September, Diggon Davie tells of "wolves" that prey privily on "the flock." In October, Spenser deplores the neglect of poetry by potential patrons, while he asserts its high honour. In the "Epistle" prefixed to *The Shepheardes Calendar*, he mentions his poetic debts to Theocritus, Vergil, Petrarch, Boccaccio, Mantuan, Sannazaro, Marot, "and also divers other excellent both Italian and French poetes, whose foting this author everywhere followeth, yet so as few, unless they be well sented, can trace him out." While "November" is wholly a pastoral dirge for "some mayden of greate bloud," it is avowedly modelled, not after the ancients but after the French elegy of Clément Marot (Ly-40) on the death of Queen "Loys" of France. While, at this time, thousands of Theocritean poems were current in neoclassical Latin, Spenser was instrumental, like Marot, Tasso, and Camoens, in helping to initiate the pastoral in the vernacular.

129 *TRSL*, xxxii (1914), 233–64

Ly-71 (Latin)

THOMAS WATSON. *Amyntas*. London, 1585. Mi: British Museum

Begins: Phyllida formoso raptam sub flore iuventae
           Assiduo gemitu tristis lugebat Amyntas ...
  Ends: Rupes, et gelidae valles, montesque, lacusque
           Ruricolae frustra quaerunt, et vana queruntur.

In a sequence of eleven flowery "querelae," totalling some 1140 hexameters, the shepherd Amyntas bewails the dead shepherdess, Phyllis. One senses a maximum of rhetoric and a minimum of genuine emotion. In style, the influence of Ovid and Petrarch appears to be strong. This Vergilian eclogue has sometimes been mistakenly described as a translation of Tasso's pastoral drama, *Aminta* (cf. Co-18 above), to which it shows no resemblance and owes no debt.

Ly-72 (Italian)

TORQUATO TASSO. *Il Rogo di Corinna: Poemetto Pastorale*. Written about 1586. First published in Venice in *Le Opere di Torquato Tasso*, 1612. Now read in separate edition of E.G. de Povèda, Florence, 1824

Begins: Piangea dolente, e sospiroso Aminta
           Lungo le rive del famoso fiume ...
  Ends: LE MUSE
           Là v'è chi gode e luce,
           Lieta lasciando lacrimosa luce.

When the poet of the *Gerusalemme Liberata* writes for his noble friend, Don Fabio Orsino, a pastoral dirge in honour of "Corinna," a "bella Donna a lui cara," we would expect the thing to be done with a flourish, and this is indeed the case. Its models are Vergil's fifth Eclogue and the first Idyll of Theocritus. There are two shepherd interlocutors, Amintas (Orsino) and Thyrsis (Tasso); but whereas Vergil has no procession of deities and Theocritus brings on only Hermes, Priapus and Cypris, Tasso has a march-past of sixteen major and nine minor gods and goddesses, all of whom are given speaking parts, at "the pyre of Corinna." If we count the Graces as three and the Muses as nine, there are actually 35 deities in the parade. After the Vergilian model, Thyrsis announces the apotheosis of Corinna and proposes the building of four altars, two for her and two for Diana. The poem totals 719 lines, partly in blank verse and unrhymed *canzone*-measure and partly in rhymed strophes that help to give form to the short speeches of the deities. It is of biographical interest that both Torquato Tasso and Giambattista Marino (see Co-32) were befriended in their sore misfortunes by Giovanni Battista Manso, Marquis of Villa, the distinguished Neapolitan Maecenas to whom Milton addressed his *Mansus* in 1638-9, praising him for his kindness to these two poets, as also to himself (*missus Hyperboreo iuvenis peregrinus ab axe*). While F.T. Prince has analysed in depth[180] the prosodic influence on *Lycidas* of Dante, Tasso, Guarini, Rota, Sannazaro and Spenser, Ants Oras[181] has argued that Milton's rhyme-scheme in the poem was shaped by the madrigals of Pietro Bembo (1470-1547) and the rhymes that are found in Tasso's *Il Rogo di Corinna*.

Ly-73 (Latin)

WILLIAM GAGER. *Exequiae illustrissimi equitis D. Philippi Sidnaei.* London, 1587. Mi: Bodleian

Begins: BELLESITA
 Extinctum flevit pulchrum Bellesita Daphnim,
 Nobilis Australes inter Bellesita Nymphas ...
 Ends: Commiscent, luctusque suos cum flumine miscent,
 Maesta ubi formosas habitat Bellesita sedes.

The poet, William Gager (1555-1622), was educated at Westminster and at Christ Church, Oxford, where he received an MA in 1580 and a DCL in 1589. He was best known for five Latin plays, performed at Oxford, and was ranked among comic dramatists in Meres's *Palladis Tamia* (1598). He was chancellor of Ely in 1606 and vicar-general to Bishop Andrewes in 1613, 1616, and 1618. Like many other Englishmen of his time, he wrote pastoral laments in Latin, Ly-73 and Ly-74, on the untimely death of Sir Philip Sidney. The first of

130 *The Italian Elements in Milton's Verse* (Oxford, 1954), pp. 71-88
131 *MP*, lii (1954), 12-22

these, *Bellesita*, sets the stage for the more intimate and personal *Daphnis*, which follows. The University of Oxford is represented as the fair nymph, Bellesita ("Beautiful-for-situation"), the mother of the most noble and heroic youth, Daphnis. Before making her lament, bare-footed and bare-breasted, she puts on her long cloak and wreathes her brow with cypress. Her pride in her son and her grief for him will endure forever

> qua se Cherwellus et Isis
> Commiscent, luctusque suos cum flumine miscent
> Maesta ubi formosas habitat Bellesita sedes.[132]

Ly-74 (Latin)

WILLIAM GAGER. *Daphnis*. London, 1587. Mi: Bodleian. For an English verse translation, see below, pp. 220–25

Begins: Pastorem pastor Daphnim Melibaeus acerbo
         Funere correptum, Shotoveri in vertice flebat ...
Ends: Daphnidis ad charam Nutricem consedit, illa
         Excepit flentem, flens ipsa, toroque locavit.

Since William Gager (1555–1622) and Sir Philip Sidney (1554–1586) had been fellow students at Christ Church, Oxford, it is natural for the former to picture himself (Melibaeus) bewailing the latter (Daphnis) beside the Cherwell and "the fishy Isis" and "on top of Shotover Hill," three miles east of Oxford, for this was a favourite student walk, then even as in Shelley's day. Richard Milton, the poet's grandfather, is alleged to have been a ranger in the royal forest here. This resort, along with Stowe Wood, Beckley, and Blenheim Park, were familiar to my own student days at Oxford, and I am indebted to the late Dean of Christ Church (C.A. Simpson) and his librarian (J.F.A. Mason) for identifying the *lucum sacrum tibi Bartholomaee* as being probably a now vanished grove in the area of Bartlemas Close, Cowley.

It is interesting to compare Vergil's *Gallus* with its later derivatives, Gager's *Daphnis* and Milton's *Lycidas*, in terms of prosodic structure. *Gallus*, written entirely in Latin hexameters, has an 8-

---

132 Tr. "Where Cherwell and Isis mingle, and mix their dirges and their
     waters, where sad Bellesita dwells in her beautiful abode."

line prologue and an 8-line epilogue, bracketing the pastoral lament "sung" *in propria persona*. *Daphnis*, also in hexameters, has a 14-line (sonnet-length) prologue and a 4-line epilogue. *Lycidas*, with its pastoral lament in *canzone*-measure, also has a 14-line *canzone*-measure prologue, but its 8-line epilogue is an *ottava rima* stanza and serves as a *commiato* or coda to the series of twelve stanzas in *canzone*-measure. In both *Daphnis* and *Lycidas*, the sonnet-length prologue is organized symmetrically in syntax, seven lines plus seven, rather than according to the standard sonnet pattern of eight-plus-six, although in *Lycidas* this syntax-break after line 7 is superimposed on an enjambed *chiave* rhyme-division after line 5, producing a hidden tension between the two systems. Readers interested in the fundamentals of Milton's prosody should turn to a basic study by F.T. Prince.[133] Among the matters of technique that *Lycidas* has borrowed or adapted from such Italian poets as Dante,[134] della Casa, Bembo, and Tasso we may note the following: (a) the great predominance of long lines over short fulfils Dante's rule for a "tragic" canzone; (b) Milton made free to use the *chiave* type of rhyme-line as a principle of articulation between rhyme-groups within his paragraphs, rather than only for transitions between major syntactical units; (c) he creates a counterpoint between the ebb and flow of syntax and the recurrent pattern of a "rhetoric of rhymes"; (d) a short line is always followed by a long one; (e) an unrhymed final syllable (and there are several in *Lycidas*) must always be a heavy one, followed by a pause; (f) rhymed couplets are often used to give quiet finality at the end of a stanza, and these are the only true closed couplets in the whole poem; (g) there is a careful attempt to produce the effect of Vergil's vocabulary and manner by a manipulation of diction and word-order, producing a sort of *latinità in volgare*.

Daphnis

For shepherd Daphnis, stol'n by bitter Death,
The shepherd Melibaeus made lament
Upon the height of high Shotover Hill;

133 F.T. Prince, *The Italian Element in Milton's Verse* (Oxford, 1954), especially chap. 5, on "Lycidas," pp. 71–88

134 Most of the principles listed here may be found in Dante's *De vulgari eloquentiae*, Bk. II, chaps. x, 29–50, xii, 11–14, 67–72, and xiii, 28–30, 50–52

There Daphnis with his sheep long days had spent
And in the nearby valley, where the still
Smooth waters of the fishy Isis flow
And Cherwell wanders slow,
Even as fair Adonis had been wont
The leafy fields to haunt,
And fair Apollo there would tend his sheep.

Declare, O Nymphs, the shepherd's doleful song;
For all of you have heard it, who belong
To those glad fields that close to Oxford sleep.
It was of Daphnis that the shepherd sang;
And all his woeful countenance grew pale
Like his whose heedless foot amid the swale
Has trodden on a snake, and felt its fang.
His hair and forehead with dark yew were bound,
And fixedly he gazed upon the ground
While in your honour, Daphnis, sadly mute
He fashioned for the flute
A wistful air, and tender verses found:

"Alas! how harsh is War, where death will strike
The brave man and the craven, both alike,
The sons of gods and nurslings of the earth,
The leader and the humblest veteran.
And what had you to do with savage Mars,
O Daphnis? By what fact of rank or birth
Had he the right to end your earthly span?
Much better had it been, avoiding wars,
To loiter in the oak-grove's pleasant shade,
To feed the flock, in some cool cave to sing,
And be their poet by the shepherds made!
There is no sense in War's dark harvesting,
And you, like the first violet and rose
And mournful hyacinth, a youth most rare,
This harsh day carries off with sudden snows
In the prime honour of your early spring.
A lengthy lifetime should have been your share;
Your youth was worthy of abundant years.
But you, O Daphnis, lie, a piteous ghost;
Utter injustice rules that all is lost

Except a mortal body without strength,
A head without a mind or charming glance;
And to your loved ones you have left at length
Nothing but tears and suits of solemn black.
Thus have we lost, by evil circumstance,
The angelic honour of your starry brow,
Your gaze serene, a god's majestic grace,
The lovely hands of Bacchus, and the face
And locks of Phoebus, with a gentle soul,
And knowledge of sweet song at your control.
How can we mortals trust in destiny,
If evil is permitted in your case,
O Daphnis, for whom every hope lies dead,
Slain in your April days by fate's decree?
Thus have I seen a mountain-ash-tree torn
Up by the roots, once offering in vain
A nest for birds and shelter for the swain.
Wrenched ruthlessly from earth and overborne
By the brief fury of the hurricane,
It strews across the earth its topmost boughs.
Shepherds, bewail a great tree's mighty fall,
Within whose shade a herd might hope to drowse
And where you shepherds have been wont to sprawl,
By fluting to enthral
The verses of your rustic roundelay;
Your cups and satchels at its foot would stay
And on its branches you would hang your flute
When weary. But the grain is slashed away;
The poets' crowning harvest is laid low;
And now let worthless ferns possess the field!

    "Like rest to soothe the body that is tired,
A breeze when all perspired,
Like sounds of springing waters, low concealed,
Like summer shade to reapers in the sun,
Like winter suns to shepherds on the hills,
Water to thirsty mouths, to thrifty bees
The flower, spring to birds from overseas,
And dew to the cicada, by his arts
Was Daphnis to our hearts,
And even more delightful than all these.

Control your sheep, O shepherds, and your steers,
Lest they with wanton teeth the laurels bite
That Daphnis planted in the bygone years
With his own hands, and left for our delight.
Let them grow up, for wreath and woven crown,
And let each shepherd shape his oaten pipe.
For Daphnis merits such regard as this,
Because he was the poet's archetype,
The poet's proper theme in his renown;
Yet in himself he carried off the skill
Of singing and the theme for shepherds' flutes;
Low in the tomb, he guards them with him still.
Make offerings at his grave, as him besuits,
And blend your grief and music, with a will.

"There is no need to strew bright flowers here;
Out of the earth, where Daphnis' bones are resting,
White lilies and blue violets appear.
In pious obsequies your love attesting,
Sum up the youth's great soul in mighty song;
No braver Englishman in arms was strong,
And he in piping was beyond compare.
No other flute on earth could sound so sweet;
That it was Orpheus singing, you might swear,
Or Linus, whom Calliope once bore
And whom a gaping company would greet
As on a grassy hill he sat of yore.
But at the song of Daphnis I have seen
(True, though amazing!) beasts in pleasure leaping,
Birds lingering, the rocks and oak-trees keeping
Due time with swaying summits, tall and green;
I have seen rivers pause, and nymphs in chorus
Stir up their ecstasy in steps before us,
The woodland deities attentive stood,
And Pan let down his ringlets in the wood.
Shall we no more hereafter, Daphnis, hear
Your carol loud and clear,
And love the well-known sweetness of your voice?
Therefore, each twy-formed satyr and each faun
Laments the singer gone,
As many mourners as Shotover knows

Or Stow or Beckley or great Woodstock too
Or spirits that repose
In groves made sacred to Bartholomew,
Or gods on all the mountains there in view.

"On every side, the Muses are complaining
That with your death their beauty is impaired,
Since you, who praised it best, are not remaining.
Past others, Galatea feels the curse
And wastes away in sorrow undeclared.
She was the nymph, O Daphnis, whom your verse
Would often celebrate; she would have proved
Vainglorious but for knowing she was loved.

"The fairest Nurse of men draws near in grief;
Once Wolsey's daughter, but ennobled now
With Christ's own title, and her halls endow
A breed of noble sons beyond belief:
'O gracious Nurse indeed, your rolls attest
He once was nourished at your agèd breast.
But Harpy-hearts, our queen has understood,
Have slain your nursling in their thirst for blood.'

"That Tityrus of yours who cultivates
The richest genius with his matchless tones
Bewails you, and in deep concern debates
The honour of a tomb above your bones.
The sheep, by bleating, have expressed their sorrow;
The Cherwell seems to borrow
Its heavy freshets from the landscape's woe;
The Isis within banks can scarcely flow;
The Thames is rising with its flood of tears,
And all the swans its bears have wept your loss,
And all the spirits of the streams and weirs.
The woods have shed their tresses; many a tree
On your behalf distills from its hard bark
Slow sap instead of tears of sympathy.
Without your presence, nothing sweet remains;
There is no grace in nature, cold and stark.
So let the ewe forget to fear the wolf,
And let the fish unlearn to love the stream,
Before a loss of memory shall engulf

The shepherds' love for Daphnis; still supreme
Deep sorrow for your death my fluting fills,
And I shall wander by the woods and hills
And each familiar spot will speak your name.
Neither the swan nor Philomel will sing
(The former as he chants his dying dirge,
The latter as she mourns her bloody loss)
As sweet a song as issues from my grief.
Moreover, I shall carve in bold relief
The name of Daphnis on the mountain's verge
And on the trunks of trees amid the moss;
The trees will grow, and so will Daphnis' name;
The elm, the vine's true friend, will spread his fame;
The beech-tree do the same;
So, too, the yew-tree, which men shape as spears;
So, too, the poplar, which in shields appears;
And so the alder, which in boats will dash;
And everywhere the hillside mountain-ash
Will testify to you; likewise the oak,
Outspeeding ash-wood in the rowers' stroke.

"I shall hang up my verses on the briars,
And scatter my devotion, written plain,
By pathless walks where love of you aspires,
By every highway and by every lane.
Only, O Daphnis, may your spirit know
The duty that I offer by my acts;
My pipe may lack true music in its woe,
But do not scorn the service it transacts.
And if its pastoral best my pipe shall play,
The shepherds shall remember you each day,
While spring succeeds to winter, and in turn
Summer and autumn follow after spring,
And while our English glories brightly burn,
And England, among nations, stands, a king."

Thus far did Melibaeus' flute rehearse
Its tribute until midnight was abroad;
Then, raising up his body from the sod,
He made his way to Daphnis' ancient Nurse.
She welcomed him; some mutual tears they shed;
And with her blessing, he went up to bed.

Ly-75 (Latin)

JANUS DOUSA. *In obitum Daphnis Ecloga, 1587.* Available in *Delitiae poetarum Belgicorum*, ed. Jan Gruter, 1614, Vol. II, pp. 177–9. Mi: Harvard

Begins: Forte pedo stabat Lycidas innixus agresti
          Ad Thamesis ripas, quam plurima fagus ob umbras ...
 Ends: Dixit cras solitum repetet mea tibia carmen,
          Dixit et agrestem repetit cum Thyrside villam.

One of the most gifted of Dutch neo-Latinists was Janus Dousa (1571–1597), born near Leyden, where he studied under Justus Lipsius. At the age of 20, he was made librarian there. In 1594–96, he lived in England. His one pastoral dirge, *Daphnis,* was written on the death of Sir Philip Sidney. It is given very high praise by W. Leonard Grant.

Ly-76 (Latin)

THOMAS WATSON. *Meliboeus.* London, 1590

Begins: CORYDON
          Tityre, iam quoniam prati per amoena vireta
          Sparguntur pecudes, et nos consedimus ambo ...
 Ends: TITYRUS
          Ire domum libeat, pecudesque includere septis,
          Discam paulatim rigidos dediscere luctus.

This dialogue between Corydon and Tityrus is an elegy on the death of Sir Francis Walsingham. The poem is uninspired and conventional.

Ly-77 (English)

EDMUND SPENSER. *Daphnaida.* London, 1591

Begins: Whatever man he be, whose heavie minde,
          With griefe of mournefull great mishap opprest, ...
 Ends: As if that Death he in the face had seene,
          Or hellish hags had met upon the way:
          But what of him became I cannot weene.

The poem was written in memory of Douglas Howard, daughter of Henry Lord Howard and wife of Arthur Gorges, Esq. She died in August 1590. The bereaved husband,"clad all in black"like the similar figure of John of Gaunt in Chaucer's *Book of the Duchess*, is described as having been formerly

> Alcyon he, the jollie shepheard swaine,
> That wont full merrilie to pipe and daunce,
> And fill with pleasance every wood and plaine.

Worthy of note is the haunting music of a new stanza, formed out of the orthodox rhyme royal by the transposition of the fifth and sixth lines. Arthur and Douglas had been married in 1584, when she was 13 and he was 27; and she was not quite 19 when she died, leaving him a baby daughter,"Ambrosia."Spenser's elegy is named *Daphnaida* after the poetic nickname"Daphne"that Gorges had used for his young sweetheart in the courtship poems that he had shown to Spenser in 1584.

For the rank of *Daphnaida* in English elegy, see F.T. Prince's verdict as quoted in Ly-81.

Ly-78 (Latin)

MAFFEO BARBERINI. *Iulus.* Paris, 1592. Mi: Harvard Library

Begins: Infelix Galatea vagas Minionis ad undas,
    Seu solis fugeret radios, seu ferret opacas ...
  Ends: Oceani coelo, vaga sidera volvebantur,
    Cum tandem madidos irrepsit somnus ocellos.

Pope Urban VIII, who ruled from 1623 to 1644, during Milton's visit to Italy was a poet, Maffeo Barberini (born 1548 at Florence), before he became a bishop, and celebrated in a pastoral epicedium in 1592 the death, as a result of wounds before Caudebec, of Alexander Farnese (1545–1592), duke of Parma and governor-general of the Netherlands for Philip II of Spain. By an irony of fate, Alexander Farnese's grandson, Odoardo, was destined to defeat the 96-year-old pope's own troops at Palestrina, a few miles from Rome, in 1644. It was the old poet-pope's nephew and chief counsellor, Cardinal Francesco Barberini, who singled out an amazed 30-year-old John Milton for special honour at the door of the Barberini Palace in Rome on 27

February 1639, when the young Englishman had come by special invitation to witness a pastoral opera, *Chi soffre speri*, with words by Giulio Rospigliosi (later to be Pope Clement IX, 1667–9), music by Virgilio Mazzocchi, and staging by Bernini. Cardinal Mazarin of France was also present at the performance in the great hall of the Palace and the audience totalled 3500. Barberini's poem is a lament by the hapless nymph Galatea, sitting on the banks of the Minio[135] and bewailing her dead brother, Iulus. At last the chariot of Phoebus dips beneath the western waves (of the Tyrrhenian Sea) and the wandering stars are wheeling in the sky.

Ly-79 (Latin)

BERNARDUS PRETORIUS. *Ecloga funebris.* About 1592. Mi: British Museum

Begins: Alma per Erigonae proles Hyperionis astrum
        Ignavo mos agitans rapido temone iugales ...
  Ends: Attegiisque; procul Cerealia culmina fumant.
        Ergo domum ite boves; iam sufficit; ite iuvencae.

This is a pastoral dirge to end all dirges, for it marches almost interminably through 158 pages of small type and its 5500 hexameter lines never quicken their gloomy pace. Its author, Bernardus Pretorius, wrote it dutifully in memory of Wilhelm, Margrave of Hesse, who died in 1592. At the beginning of the poem, the cowherd Sylvanus meets the shepherd Faunus and asks for news. Faunus replies that he lives in such seclusion that he has heard nothing worthy of report. Sylvanus then reveals that civil war and treachery have racked the state and resulted in the death of "Wilhelmus." "O scelera! O mores! O tempora flagitiosa!"[136] cries Faunus. At last they call on God to grant the son and heir, Mauricius, a double portion of his father's noble spirit. They then drive their beasts home for the night.

Ly-80 (English)

MICHAEL DRAYTON. *The Ninth Eclogue.* In *The Shepheards Garland*, London, 1593

    135 A small Italian river, now the Mignone, flowing into the Tyrrhenian
        Sea about 50 miles northwest of Rome
    136 Tr. "O crimes! O (what) behaviour! O shameful times!"

Begins: What time the wearie weather-beaten sheepe,
   To get them fodder, hie them to the fold ...
Ends: The faithfull swayne, here lastly made an end,
   Whom all good shepheards ever shall defend.

This is a homely variant of Theocritus' *Song of Daphnis*. It records the dying song of the shepherd, Rowland, heart-broken by the ingratitude of men, rather than by the love-curse of Aphrodite. Instead of being mourned by jackals and wolves, cows, bulls and calves, he knows rather the sympathy of his faithful dog, Whitefoote:

Which, though as he his masters sorrowes knew,
   Wag'd his cut taile, his wretched plight to rue.

In a revised edition, in 1606, this became "The Tenth Eclogue."

Ly-81 (English)

EDMUND SPENSER. *Astrophel*. London, 1595

Begins: Shepheards that wont on pipes of oaten reed,
   Oft times to plaine your loues concealed smart: ...
Ends: The which I here in order will rehearse,
   As fittest flowers to deck his mournfull hearse.

This elegy in memory of Sir Philip Sidney served as a sort of prologue to a little anthology of elegies written by the Countess of Pembroke (1590), Lodowick Bryskett (1587), Matthew Roydon (1589), and Sir Walter Ralegh (1591). Spenser apparently furnished it on request and paid the Countess the compliment of using her stanza-form, ababcc. All were published in 1595 in the same volume with *Colin Clouts Come Home Again*.

F.T. Prince, in *The Italian Element in Milton's Verse* (1954, 1962), p. 83, affirms that this and *Daphnaida* (Ly-77) were "the finest pastoral elegies written in English before *Lycidas*." Both differ basically from *Lycidas*, however, in being built of regularly formed stanzas. While Milton might have learned something from their flow of melody, Berardino Rota and Torquato Tasso had taught him how to put his long waves of rhymed verse in tension with a submerged pattern, in this case a series of irregularly formed *canzoni*.

Ly-82 (English)

MARY HERBERT, COUNTESS OF PEMBROKE. *To Astrophel.* London, 1595

Begins: Ay me! to whom shall I my case complaine,
That may compassion my impatient griefe? ...
Ends: Thus do we weep and waile, and wear our eies,
Mourning in others our owne miseries.

This pastoral lament by Sir Philip Sidney's sister, the Countess of Pembroke, was printed in the same little volume with Spenser's *Astrophel* in 1595. The countess was a poet in her own right, and when Sir Philip, at his death, left English verse renderings of 43 of the Psalms, his sister versified the remaining 107 with great skill and power, in a wide range of metres. Their joint achievement was published in 1963 by New York University Press as *The Psalms of Sir Philip Sidney and the Countess of Pembroke.*

Ly-83 (English)

LODOWICK BRYSKETT. *The Mourning Muse of Thestylis.* London, 1595

Begins: Come forth, ye Nymphes, come forth, forsake your watry bowres,
Forsake your mossy caves, and help me to lament ...
Ends: Yet wish their verses might so farre and wide thy fame
Extend, that envies rage, nor time, might end the same.

Included in the same collection of pastoral laments for Sidney as Spenser's *Astrophel* and the Countess of Pembroke's companion piece, is this dirge by another member of their circle. Lodowick, or Lewis, Bryskett was educated at Trinity College, Cambridge; accompanied Sidney on his continental tour in 1572–5; and held government appointments in Ireland, 1577–1600.

F.T. Prince (*The Italian Element in Milton's Verse*, n., p. 83), states that this and the following poem (Ly-84) by Bryskett show that, like Spenser, he was familiar with the forms then developing in Italian pastoral. "Both [poems] are written in continuous but irregularly placed rhyme; the second shows also an attempt to obtain Virgilian movement by strong pauses within the lines."

Ly-84 (English)

LODOWICK BRYSKETT. *A Pastoral Aeglogue upon the Death of Sir Phillip Sidney, Knight.* London, 1595

Begins: LYCON
    Colin, well fits thy sad cheare this sad stownd,
    This woful stownd, wherein all things complaine ...
  Ends: COLIN
    Warnes us to drive homewards our silly sheep.
    Lycon, lett's rise, and take of them good keep.

This more strictly pastoral epicedium laments Sidney under the name "Phillisides." All of the Theocritean stereotypes are faithfully reproduced. This poem, also, was included in the *Astrophel* volume.

Ly-85 (English)

MATTHEW ROYDON. *An Elegie, or Friends passion, for his Astrophill.* London, 1595

Begins: As then, no winde at all there blew,
    No swelling cloud accloid the aire ...
  Ends: And here my pen is forst to shrinke,
    My teares discollors so mine inke.

Another friend and poet who contributed to the *Astrophel* volume was Matthew Roydon (*fl.* 1580–1622), an MA of Oxford and intimate with Sidney, Marlowe, Spenser, Lodge, and Chapman. Pastoral traditions are often included in his lament for Sidney:

    Within these woods of Arcadie
    He chiefe delight and pleasure tooke ...

Non-pastoral companion pieces in the same volume were an *Epitaph* by Sir Walter Ralegh and another by Fulke Greville, Lord Brooke.

Ly-86 (Latin)

DAVID HUME. *Ecloga prima, cui nomen Philomela.* London, 1604. Mi: British Museum (in *Poemata Omnia*, Paris, 1639)

Begins: Formosam moestae lugent Amaryllida sylvae
          Extinctam: Coryli tenues, tenuesque muricae ...
  Ends: Ora rursus: floreat natis, solo, coelo, charis, gratus annos
          multos. Amen, Aeque Amen: Amen, Amen, Amen.

One of the earliest and most rhetorical of Scottish neo-Latinists was David Hume (*ca.* 1560–*ca.* 1630), who studied at St Andrews and later won fame as a controversialist and historian. His *Philomela* is an elaborate and highly traditional lament over the death of Queen Elizabeth I in 1603. All Nature grieves and there is even a vociferous mourning choir of animals. The Scottish courtier then passes on almost inevitably to flattery of his fellow-countryman "Daphnis" (James I) and a prophecy of a new Golden Age under his beneficent rule.

Ly-87 (Latin)

DANIEL HEINSIUS. *Thyrsis.* Leyden, 1609. Mi: Harvard (edition of 1621)

Begins: Amissum tristi longaevum funere Thyrsin
          Thyrsin, delicias pastorum, et gaudia ruris ...
  Ends: Talia cantabant pueri, cantantibus illis
          Hesperus extremam veniens abrupit avenam.

Written when the author was nineteen, this pastoral lament is a tribute by Daniel Heinsius (1590–1655) to his well-loved Leyden professor, Joseph Justus Scaliger (1540–1609), the greatest scholar of his time. The poem is elaborate and in the traditional manner, but the poet's intense personal feeling saves it from being mere rhetoric. Daniel's son, Nikolaes Heinsius (1620–1681) was a more accomplished Latin poet but wrote no epicedia. Many of his Latin letters, taking Milton's part against their common enemy, Salmasius, were published in Pieter Burmann's *Sylloges Epistolarum a Viris Illustribus Scriptarum* (Leyden, 1727).

Ly-88 (Latin)

JOHN BARCLAY. *Daphnis*. London, 1610. Mi: Harvard (*Poematum libri ii*, Cologne 1626)

Begins: Texerat horrentes furva caligine vultus
         Sol Pater, et toto squalebant sidera coelo ...
  Ends: Frangite jam multos risus, jam fingite crinem,
         Hic aget hic vestras patrio de more choreas.

This pastoral dirge on the assassination of Henry IV of France was written by a young Scottish Latinist, John Barclay (1582–1621). Born at Pont-à-Mousson (in Northern France), where his father, William Barclay, was professor of civil law in the local university, he lived in London 1603–5 and 1606–16, but spent the last five years of his life in Rome. He is known chiefly for two prose works in Latin, the *Satyricon*, a Petronius-style satire on the Jesuits, and the *Argenis*, a long-winded romance on political intrigue. In the present eclogue, two shepherds, Corydon and Tityrus, bewail the murder of Daphnis (Henry IV), whose reign had brought in a Golden Age. The quality of its Latin verse is mediocre.

Ly-89 (Latin, Greek, Italian, French, English)

Epicedium Cantabrigiense, In obitum immaturum, semperque deflendum, Henrici, Illustrissimi Principis Walliae. Cambridge, 1612. Mi: Cambridge University

In 1612, Henry Frederick, Prince of Wales, eldest son of James I of England, died of typhoid fever at the age of eighteen and was buried in Westminster Abbey. The above memorial volume was forthwith published by undergraduates, fellows, professors, and graduates of Cambridge University. It included 128 poems (110 in Latin, 4 in Greek, one each in Italian and French, and 12 in English) by 94 poets.

Unlike its later analogue, Ly-101, it did not contain any single poem of the stature of *Lycidas*; but the quality of some of the verse is far from indifferent. The most notable contributor (two Latin poems, one in hexameters and one in Alcaics) was George Herbert (1593–1633), public orator of the university in 1619–27 and the author of a posthumous volume of religious lyrics, *The Temple*.

Poets who were to be senior members of the university in Milton's time at Cambridge were Andrew Downes, one of the translators of the Authorized Version of the Bible and regius professor of Greek, contributed two elegies in Greek; Samuel Collins, provost of King's and regius professor of divinity, gentle but profound; Matthew Wren, master of Peterhouse, whose unflinching support of Laud was later to bring him eighteen years (1642–60) in the Tower of London; and Samuel Walsall, master of Corpus Christi, author of a Latin hexameter dirge, "In morbum et diem fatalem," and himself destined to die young in 1626. Other contributors to the volume were Richard Moundeford, president of the Royal College of Physicians; (b) Thomas Young, presently to be a tutor of Milton in his boyhood, in 1618–20; and (c) Thomas Walkington, author of *The Optick Glasse of Humors* (1607), a forerunner of Burton's *Anatomy of Melancholy*.

None of the English poems in the volume are pastorals and most of the Latin poems are in non-pastoral elegiacs. There are, however, three rather mediocre Latin pastoral elegies in the traditional hexameters: (a) a *Daphnis* by an unnamed "fellow of King's," (b) an *Iulas*, signed "Sa. Savel. Regal," and (c) an amoebic epicedium by John Shotbolt of King's, with Theophilus and Philocrates as the collocutors.

For the phenomenal public tribute to the dead prince, see E.C. Wilson's *Prince Henry and English Literature* (1946), also Ly-90, Ly-91, Ly-92, Ly-93, Ly-94, and Ly-96.

Ly-90 (Latin)

D A V I D   H U M E . *Henrici principis Iusta*. London, 1612. Mi: British Museum Library, in *Poemata Omnia* (Paris, 1639)

Begins: Dextra Patris, Matris decus, Amborum alma voluptas,
         Amborum observans, Natus pius, et pius idem ...
  Ends: Magnus erit mihi: Te qui vero amplexus amore est;
         Aeterno (quod possum unum) amplexabor amore.

This is a competent but undistinguished memorial tribute to Henry Frederick Prince of Wales (eldest son of James I of England), who died 6 November 1612, at the age of eighteen. The author was a 52-year-old Scottish historian, controversialist, and prolific Latin poet.

Ly-91 (Latin, Greek, etc.)

UNIVERSITY OF OXFORD. *Iusta Oxoniensium*. London, 1612. Mi: Bodleian (2 Reg. 3. 38."Num ignoratis quoniam Princeps et Maximus cecidit hodie in Israel?")

The most elaborately staged of all the collections of elegies published in memory of Henry, the Prince of Wales, was"The Obsequies of the Oxford Men,"issued formally by the University. Here were 184 poems, written by 157 poets. Two were in Greek, one each in Hebrew and French, and all the rest in Latin, overwhelmingly in elegiac couplets. Every college head contributed his poetic tribute and the heavy artillery of the funeral salute included a full range of professorships: Robert Abbot (divinity), Sebastian Benefield (divinity), John Budden (civil law), Samuel Fell (divinity), Edmund Gunter (astronomy), John Harris (Greek), Richard Kilbie (Hebrew), Edward à Meetkerke (Hebrew), John Prideaux (divinity), Robert Sanderson (divinity), and John Spenser (reader in Greek). Of the foregoing, Kilbie of Lincoln and Spenser of Corpus Christi had been among the translators of the King James version of the Bible; the former lamented Prince Henry in Hebrew and the latter in Latin.

The higher ranks of the Church of England were actually or potentially among the elegists. William Laud (Latin elegiacs) was to become Archbishop of Canterbury and to be executed for"high treason"in 1645, and Accepted Frewen (Latin elegiacs) would be Archbishop of York after the Restoration, because Charles II remembered that he had taken the lead in presenting the University's plate to the coffers of Charles I. Other poetic bishops, then or thereafter, were Robert Abbot (Salisbury), John Bancroft (Oxford), Richard Corbet (Oxford, Norwich), Brian Duppa (Chichester, Salisbury, Winchester), William James (Durham), Henry King (Chichester), John King (London), John Prideaux (Worcester), and Robert Sanderson (Lincoln).

Elegists of 1612 who were to play an active part in public affairs were (a) Sir Thomas Lake, who became secretary of state in 1616 and was ruined by a suit for slander by the Countess of Exeter; (b) Sir John Glanville the Younger, who took a leading part in the impeachment of Buckingham and was the Speaker of the Short Parliament; and (c) Sir William Waller, who was a general in the Civil War.

The most learnèd among the authors in the volume was Isaac Casaubon (1559–1614), a classical scholar of European stature, who had been professor of Greek at Geneva and Montpellier, royal librarian in Paris, editor of famous Renaissance editions of Persius, Suetonius, Athenaeus, Theophrastus, and Polybius, a close friend of Joseph Scaliger, and an academic guest in England from 1610 on. He was buried in Westminster Abbey. More familiar to English readers today is Robert Burton, author of *The Anatomy of Melancholy*. Less important authors in the *Iusta's* roster are Richard Corbet (collected poems, 1647), William Crosse (translator of Sallust), Thomas Goffe (author of *The Tragedy of Orestes*), John Heath (*Two Centuries of Epigrammes*), Edmund Gunter (advanced works in mathematics), John Reinolds (*Epigrammata*), Thomas Sutton (sermons), Joseph Swetnam (*The Araignement of lewd, idle, froward and unconstant Women*), Thomas Williams (a Latin-Welsh dictionary), Thomas Wilson (a concordance to the Bible), and Richard Zouche (*Elementa Jurisprudentiae*). Of the 157 poets in the *Iusta Oxoniensium*, 49 are in the *Dictionary of National Biography*. In terms of genre, however, it remains unhappily true that there is not a single pastoral elegy in this great tribute from the University of Oxford.

Ly-92 (Latin, Greek, etc.)

MAGDALEN COLLEGE, OXFORD. *Luctus posthumus*. Oxford, 1612. Mi: Bodleian

A separate collection of laments was prepared by Magdalen College, Oxford. Since it was here that Prince Henry had matriculated in 1605, at the age of eleven,[137] the president and fellows felt that the Prince of Wales had belonged to them in a very special way. The result was a total of 120 poems by 71 poets. Some five of these were in Greek, one in French, one in Italian, and 113 in Latin; and of these latter, 82 were in elegiac couplets, 18 in hexameters, 5 in iambic senarii, and 8 in various lyric measures. The volume began with a dedication to the memory of the Prince by William Langton, the

---

137 One is reminded of Grotius at eleven, studying under Scaliger at Leyden, or of Francis Bacon at twelve, studying under Whitgift at Trinity College, Cambridge. Henry's father, James I, from the age of four to the age of twelve, had been the pupil of Europe's greatest Latin poet of the time, George Buchanan, and was now ambitious for his own brilliant eldest son. But typhoid fever was no respecter of princes.

president of Magdalen, and ended with a prose *oratio funebris* by Accepted Frewen, destined to be president in 1626–43. There were no pastoral elegies in the volume, although Michael Oldsworth contributed a Latin "epicedion" in hexameters, followed by an "epitaphium." Ten of the Magdalen poets were also represented in the *Iusta Oxoniensium*, namely, John Budden, Henry Bust, Robert Cooke, John Drope, Accepted Frewen, William Langton, Thomas Loftus, Samuel Smith, A. Warters, and John Wilkinson. None of the 71 Magdalen poets achieved fame as a writer, but Edward Blunt (or Blount) was one of the chief publishers of the age, being responsible for Montaigne's *Essays*, Marlowe's *Hero and Leander*, Shelton's *Don Quixote*, and (with Isaac Jaggard and others) the First Folio of Shakespeare's *Works*. Two of Magdalen's elegists who were in the very centre of English history three decades later were John Hampden and his close college friend, Arthur Goodwin. The former led the opposition to Charles I in the Short Parliament, raised a regiment of foot at his own expense, and died of battle-wounds in 1643. The latter was also an M.P. from Buckinghamshire, was parliamentary commander-in-chief in 1643, and was present at Hampden's death.

Ly-93 (Latin, Greek, etc.)

BROADGATES HALL. *Eidyllia in obitum fulgentissimi Henrici*, etc. Oxford, 1612. Mi: Bodleian

Much more exciting than either the *Iusta Oxoniensium* or the *Luctus Posthumus* is a collection of memorial verse prepared by Broadgates Hall (converted into Pembroke College by James I in 1624). It begins in startling fashion with dedicatory couplets in Chaldaic, Syriac, Arabic, and Turkish by "Josephus Barbatus Arabs Memphiticus Cophteus," apparently a wandering Coptic Arab scholar from Cairo. Then follow eight Asclepiadean stanzas and nine elegiac distichs, all in Latin, by "Jacobus Aretius, Germano-Britannus."[138] Almost all of

138 Identified by Anthony à Wood in *Fasti Oxonienses* (3rd ed., 1815, p. 355) as "a young man, Jacobus Aretius, who stiles himself Germano-Britannus." That he hailed from the domain of Frederick V, elector palatine of the Rhine, seems evident from his four chief Latin poems published in England: (i) a panegyric on the prince palatine himself; (ii) a Carmen Saeculare on the inauguration of James I of England, father-in-law of the elector; (iii) an epithalamium on the wedding of

the remaining contributors are blanketed (after three and a half centuries) under the virtual anonymity of initials. The central substance of the volume consists of three authentic *eidyllia*, or full pastoral elegies, *Amyntas*, *Tityrus*, and *Daphnis*, written in the traditions of Theocritus and Vergil. *Amyntas* is composed by the Jacobus Aretius mentioned above, and *Tityrus* and *Daphnis* by two collaborating authors, "C.F." and "G.L.F." The first and third pastorals are structured after Vergil's *Gallus*, while the second is of the amoebean type, with Maeris and Daphnis as collocutors. The Latin style of all three is surprisingly good. Of the 249 Oxford poets who contributed collectively to the three memorial volumes, only Jacobus Aretius, C.F., and G.L.F., all of Broadgates Hall, dared to string the Odysseus-bow of the pastoral elegy; and these three individuals did so triumphantly. Their work contrasts happily with the "versus cancrini seu tessellati" of T.C. and the fragmental lines of E.H., both comparable to the fantastic style of *Tristram Shandy* at its most perverse. In *Amyntas*, the shepherd Alexis invokes the dead swain and calls on all nature to grieve. The snowy-feathered swans and all birds that dwell in the wood will re-echo a long farewell to Amyntas. The bald simplicity of the dirge suggests how much Milton's *Lycidas* owes to its "digressions." In *Tityrus*, Daphnis and Maeris interchange laments over their dead friend and there is a parade of Nereids, Oreads, Dryads, Naiads, Fauns, Satyrs, and Pan, the guardian of the flocks. Even Ceres joins the general sorrow with a failure of the harvest. In *Daphnis*, Alexis mourns his lost comrade and there is a plangent refrain: Dicite Phoebeum mea carmina dicite Daphnin.[139]

It may be indicative of a gradual shift to the vernacular that, while

Frederick v and Princess Elizabeth Stuart, both aged sixteen, on 1 February 1613; and (iv) his pastoral lament, *Amyntas*, on the death of her brother, Henry, the Prince of Wales, on 6 November 1612. The first three were published in London in 1613. The fourth, while ceremoniously dated at Oxford in the year of Henry's death, doubtless took more than seven weeks in the composing, editing, and printing of the collective volume by the men of Broadgates Hall, and would also really belong in 1613. Wood further lists Aretius in *Athenae Oxonienses* (1817 ed., vol. III, 269) among visiting "outlander" scholars associated with Dr John Prideaux, rector of Exeter College, Oxford, and sometime chaplain to Prince Henry, "that have been eminent in their respective countries, wherein afterwards they have lived."

Help in supplying me with relevant photocopies from Anthony à Wood came from Irene Cornock and Peggy Cordy of Pembroke College, Oxford.

139 Tr. "Speak of Apollo-like Daphnis, speak, my songs"

there was not a single elegy in English in any genre among the 334 poems in the three Oxford collections for Prince Henry, there were 12 in English (out of 128) in the Cambridge University memorial volume (Ly-89), of 1612. In the elegiac collection published in 1638 by Christ's College, Cambridge, there were again 12 poems in English (out of 33) in tribute to the drowned alumnus, Edward King. It is perhaps to that change in linguistic emphasis that we are indebted for an English *Lycidas*, rather than an earlier Miltonic equivalent of the *Epitaphium Damonis*.

My careful checking of their initials with *The Dictionary of National Biography* has revealed that the two hitherto unrecognized joint authors of true pastorals in this volume were almost certainly (a) as"C.F.,"Charles Fitzgeoffrey (1575–1638), MA, Broadgates Hall, 1600, who published an English epic on Drake in 1596, also *The Blessed Birthday* in 1634, and a volume of Latin epitaphs and epigrams; had been mentioned in the *Palladis Tamia* of Francis Meres in 1598; and was quoted in *England's Parnassus* in 1600; and (b) as"G.L.F.,"George Fortescue (1578–1659), author of *Feriae Academicae* (Latin essays) in 1630 and *The Soules Pilgrimage* in 1650. A.B. Grosart edited *The Poems of Charles Fitzgeoffrey* in 1881. As John Crowe Ransom has reminded us,[140] *A Monody* (acknowledged seven years later and renamed *Lycidas*) was also originally published over bare initials and might, had Milton died before 1645, have remained"a poem nearly anonymous."It would not, of course, have been so to his college contemporaries. As Todd has pointed out,[141]"In a collection of this sort, the last is the place of honour," and the initials, subscribed to work of such superior merit, would hold no secret for them.

Ly-94 (English)

WILLIAM DRUMMOND. *Tears on the Death of Moeliades*. London, 1613

Begins: O Heavens! then is it true that thou art gone,
        And left this woful isle her loss to moan ...
  Ends: Moeliades sweet courtly nymphs deplore,
        From Thule to Hydaspes' pearly shore.

140 John Crowe Ransom,"A Poem Nearly Anonymous,"pp. 1–28 in *The World's Body* (New York, 1938)
141 H.J. Todd, *The Poetical Works of John Milton*, v, 3

William Drummond (1585–1649) was born at Hawthornden, near Edinburgh, and after graduating from the University of Edinburgh in 1605 and continuing with five years further study on the Continent, spent the last 39 years of his life as the studious laird of Hawthornden. When King James's eldest son, Prince Henry, died in 1612 in his nineteenth year, the young laird wrote the above elegy and gained considerable applause for it. While half of the poem cons over the familiar conventions of pastoral poetry, the other half (lines 35–70, 143–96) displays dignity and originality; and the final consolation is both Christian and Platonic:

> Rest, blessèd spright, rest satiate with the sight
> Of him whose beams both dazzle and delight,
> Life of all lives, cause of each other cause,
> The sphere and centre where the mind doth pause;
> Narcissus of himself, himself the well,
> Lover, and beauty, that doth all excel ...

Ly-95 (English)

WILLIAM BROWNE. *The Shepheards Pipe*. London, 1614

Begins: Under an aged Oke was WILLY laid ...
  Ends: Was never *Shepheard* lov'd more deere,
       Nor made a truer mone.

The youthful author of *Britannia's Pastorals*, the *Inner-Temple Masque* (see Co-29) and a famous epitaph on the Countess of Pembroke ("Underneath this sable hearse ..."), also published at 24 a tuneful collection of eclogues, *The Shepheards Pipe*. His fourth eclogue, cited above, is a pastoral lament on "Philarete," i.e. Thomas Manwood.

Ly-96 (Latin)

LEO AETSEMA. *Exequiae Funebres Illustriss. Princ. D. Hendrici Iulii, Ducis Bruns. et Luneb*. In *Poemata*, Franeker, 1617. Mi: Harvard

Begins: DAMOETAS
   Quid sibi pullatae vestes, obscuraque frontis
   Tegmina fari volunt, Lycida, quid taenia pendens ...
Ends: DAMOETAS
   Pascite jam tauros pueri velut ante feroces,
   Et resonare bonum Daphnin pineta docete.

Aetsema was a Dutch neo-Latinist of indifferent ability, who flourished *ca.* 1610–1620 and was praised by the great scholar, Daniel Heinsius. Unfortunately, this elaborate elegy, modelled after Vergil's fifth Eclogue, is notable chiefly as marking the persistence of the tradition. The collocutors are Damoetas and Lycidas.

Ly-97 (Latin)

JOHN LEECH. *Dorylas*. In *Musae priores*, London, 1620. Mi: British Museum

Begins: Si vacat, huc Stimichon, namque heic levis adstrepit unda:
   Heic Zephyrus placidis per saxa adremigat alis ...
Ends: Haec sunt e duris vix vulsa cor allia saxis,
   Haec sunt Balthiaco sudata electra profundo.

This is the second of Leech's *Eclogae Piscatoriae*, in which fishermen take the place of shepherds in the pastoral. In it a fisherman named "Lycabas" (John Leech himself) recites a dirge on the death of "Dorylas" (his father). The poet (*ca.* 1590–*ca.* 1630), who is associated with Montrose and Aberdeen (MA, 1614), was an elder brother of David Leech, DD, vice-principal of King's College, Aberdeen, and chaplain to Charles II. He Latinized his name as "Leochaeus."

Leech wrote eclogues ostentatiously in four styles (bucolic, piscatory, marine, and vinitory) but invented none of these variants of the genre. Theocritus had begun the bucolic and the piscatory, Grotius the marine, and Lorenzo Gambara the vinitory.

Ly-98 (Latin)

ARTHUR JOHNSTON. *De Gordoniis in arce Frendriaca combustis.* Aberdeen, 1632. Mi: British Museum

Begins: Vos supremi ignes, extremaque lumina mundi,
         Insomnesque faces, et ponto nescia mergi ...
 Ends: Vre, seca, nulloque virum discrimine saevi,
         Dum tormenta tibi, superest dum Scotica cervix.

A grim episode in highland feuding came in 1630, when two Gordon
chieftains, enticed as guests to the castle of Frendraught by James
Crichton and his wife, were there burned alive. Scotland's chief Latin
poet of the time, Arthur Johnston, soon to be rector of King's College, Aberdeen, denounced the crime in two tremendous poems: (a)
the present hexameter dirge for the dead Gordons, judged by Leices-
ter Bradner to be one of the greatest poems in modern Latin, and (b)
a lament, supposed to be spoken by Sophia Hay, widow of the
murdered Viscount John Gordon. Her elegiacs end with the stern
judgement:"Let mortals punish other crimes; this butchery has God
alone as its avenger." In 1625, Johnston had published a Latin elegy,
"On the death of James the Peacemaker"(i.e., James 1 of England),
but the genre was not the pastoral and the metre was the elegiac
couplet rather than the hexameter. His Latin version of the entire
Psalter, also in elegiacs, is one of the glories of Scottish scholarship.
"The Fire at Frendraught"is also the title of a famous ballad (No.
196 in F.J. Child's *The English and Scottish Popular Ballads*, where
several pages are devoted to an inconclusive weighing of the evidence for and against the Crichtons). Here Lady Frendraught is presented as a sort of Lady Macbeth, who locks the Gordons in a tower,
throws the keys down a well, and calmly watches her victims scream-
ing as they burn.

Ly-99 (German)

FRIEDRICH SPEE. *Mon des Himmels*, written before 1635. Pp. 147–9
in *Deutsche Barocklyrik*, ed. Max Wehrli, Basel, 1956

Begins: Mon des Himmels treib zur Weiden
         Deine Schäflein güldengelb ...
 Ends: Dann der Milchweg hinderlassen
         Ist wohl halb von solcher Bach.

A piece of pious sentimentalism is this baroque pastoral in which
Christ, in the Garden of Gethsemane, is portrayed as a mystical

Daphnis, lamented by the Moon, the shepherd of the stars. The pastoral correspondences are carefully worked out. Friedrich Spee was a Jesuit hymn-writer, famed for the tender grace of his hymnody; but its tenderness is sometimes overdone. He was born at Kaiserswerth-am-Rhein in 1591 and died at Trier in 1635 of a contagion incurred in nursing sick soldiers.

Ly-100 (English)

WILLIAM DRUMMOND. *Alcon.* Edinburgh, 1638

Begins: In sweetest prime and blooming of his age,
           Dear Alcon ravish'd from this mortal stage ...
  Ends: Friendship an earthquake suffer'd; losing him
           Love's brightest constellation turnèd dim.

Sir William Alexander, Earl of Stirling and the King's secretary for Scotland, was long a close friend of William Drummond of Hawthornden. When the former's young son, Sir Anthony, died in London in September 1637 and was buried in the church at Stirling, Scotland, Drummond was moved to present the grieving father with an appropriate elegy. His close model was Castiglione's *Alcon* and his laboured condensation of the Italian original is a rather unhappy performance. The father is best known as the Scottish knight to whom in 1621 King James I gave "Nova Scotia" or "New Scotland," a domain comprising the present Atlantic provinces of Canada.

Ly-101 (Greek, Latin, and English)

Justa Edovardo King naufrago ab Amicis moerentibus amoris et mneias charin. Cambridge, 1638. Mi: British Museum

This is the collection of memorial verse in which Milton's *Monody* (*Lycidas*), signed simply "J.M.," occupied the final pages. Of the 33 poems, three are in Greek, eighteen are in Latin, and twelve are in English. The classical languages occupy the first 36 pages, while the English laments, subtitled "Obsequies to the Memorie of Mr. Edward King," fill the last 25 pages. Milton's *Lycidas* is the only *pastoral* elegy in the entire volume and the only poem in *canzone*-measure.

In poetic stature, all the other elegists are pygmies by comparison, yet while a score are mere ghosts of names today, some eight have their record of achievement set down in the *Dictionary of National Biography*. Thus Joseph Beaumont (whose elegy was in English octosyllabic couplets) became master of Peterhouse and regius professor of divinity in Cambridge University, and published a philosophical epic, *Psyche* (PL-235 and PR-23) in 1648. John Cleveland (English heroic couplets) became a ferocious Cavalier poet. Michael Honywood (two poems in Latin elegiacs) became dean of Lincoln. Charles Mason (Latin hexameters) became a Royalist divine and a prebendary of St Paul's. Robert Mason (Latin hexameters) became secretary to the Duke of Buckingham. Henry More (Greek hexameters) was one of the Cambridge Platonists and a writer of philosophical poetry (see PL-232). John Pearson (Latin elegiacs) became bishop of Chester. Ralph Widdrington (Latin elegiacs) became regius professor of Greek in Cambridge University. Milton's *Monody* not only outsoared the elegies of all his fellow-mourners but did so on the pinions of an earlier poetic tradition. As John Carey has emphasized,[142] "Milton's Spenserian pastoralism in *Lycidas* contrasts markedly with the 'metaphysical' diction and imagery of the other contributors to the 1638 volume." A brief quotation from John Cleveland's contribution will underline the difference:

> – Our teares shall seem the Irish seas,
> We floating islands, living Hebrides.

The academic collection of elegies in memory of Edward King had had numerous forerunners. Thus Oxford University had published *Exequiae P. Sidnaei* (London, 1587), on the death of Sir Philip Sidney; *Funebre officium* (Oxford, 1603), on the death of Elizabeth I; and *Iusta Oxoniensium* (Oxford, 1612), on the death of Henry, Prince of Wales. Cambridge had published *Lachrymae tumulo P. Sidnaei* (1587), *Epicedium cantabrigiense* (1612) and, on the death of James I, *Dolor et solamen* (1625). Even individual colleges would issue their own collections of elegies, such as *Peplus P. Sidnaei* (New College, Oxford, 1587), *Luctus posthumus* (Magdalen College, Oxford, 1612) and *Eidyllia* (Broadgates Hall, later Pembroke College, Oxford, 1612).

142 *The Poems of John Milton*, ed. John Carey and Alastair Fowler (London, 1968), p. 234

Ly-102 (Latin)

JOHN MILTON. *Epitaphium Damonis.* London, 1640

Begins: Himerides nymphae (nam vos et Daphnin et Hylan,
          Et plorata diu meministis fata Bionis) ...
  Ends: Cantus ubi, choreisque furit lyra mista beatis,
          Festa Sionaeo bacchantur et Orgia Thyrso.

While Milton sets this lament on the lips of that Thyrsis who mourns Daphnis in the first Idyll of Theocritus, and while he borrows the structural device of a recurrent refrain from Bion, Moschus, and (above all) Vergil, he shows marked originality in weaving his own personal memories and ambitions into the fabric of the poem. Professor Thomas Perrin Harrison, Jr[143] has discovered in the *Epitaphium* some fourteen echoes from Castiglione's *Alcon* (Ly-32), fourteen from Vergil, eight from Theocritus, two each from Petrarch, Sannazaro, and Spenser, and one each from Moschus, Ovid, Marot, and Baïf. "Verbal parallels with Castiglione," he comments, "are less common than those of organization, idea and figure." Important organizational borrowings from *Alcon* are the long passages of regret that absence abroad prevented him from sharing in his friend's dying hours and that his absentee dreams of happy reunion were ironically doomed to frustration.

Don Cameron Allen[144] finds in the pagan Greek and Roman tradition of the *paramythia* and the *consolatio,* modified by Christian arguments of comfort set down by such writers as St Gregory Nazianzen and St Jerome, an ancient infrastructure common to all of Milton's epicedia, from his formal Latin laments at Cambridge down to his elegies for King and Diodati.

143 In the notes on this poem in his anthology, *The Pastoral Elegy* (1939),
     pp. 294–5
144 *The Harmonious Vision,* pp. 43–7

∾ PART III : Analogues of *Paradise Regained* (1671)

PR-1 (Hebrew)

ANONYMOUS. *The Book of Job*. Fifth century B.C.?

Begins: Ish hayah ve'ereç-'uç 'iyyobh shemo vehayah ...
  Ends: vayyamath 'iyyobh zaqen ûsbha' yamim.

This masterpiece of ancient Hebrew literature was cited by Milton in 1642 (in a personal digression in *The Reason of Church Government*) as a "brief model" of the epic that he was then considering as a genre for his poetic emulation. The recognition of *Job* as an epic was firmly vouched for by St Jerome, whose second Latin version of the Old Testament ("Iuxta Hebraeos") was translated direct from the Hebrew text. Its epic identity was further accepted by all Christian scholars and poets down to Milton's own day (see Introduction, p. xxiii).

In the original Hebrew, the prologue and the epilogue of *Job* are in prose, while the dialogue (including the speech of Yahweh, chapters 38–41), is in verse – chiefly the *mashal* type of couplet that characterized so much of the Wisdom Literature. While there is no conceivable Greek-style pattern of quantitative feet, Jerome and Origen, who sought to ascribe all virtues to the Scriptures, disingenuously declared that its couplets were in strict elegiac metre, made up of alternating hexameter and pentameter lines.

Even a casual reading of *Paradise Regained* will detect an infrastructure borrowed from *Job*. Satan comes to an assembly beside the River Jordan, hears the Son approved, and undertakes to test him, a resolve confirmed by a council of devils in the clouds. The ordeal is also approved by God the Father in a council in heaven, where he actually compares Christ to Job (*P.R.*, I, 150–67). Christ, alone in the desert, is as stripped of material support as was Job on his midden-heap, and lacks even food. The failure of Satan's first attack on Job had been followed by his second appearance at a council in heaven; while the failure of his first attack on Christ is followed by a second council of evil spirits. The unrelenting arguments by which Job's friends seek to undermine his integrity are paralleled by Satan's arguments seeking to seduce Christ from his beliefs regarding wealth, power, glory, and wisdom. The voice in the whirlwind in *Job* is perhaps paralleled by the terrors of the storm in the desert (*Paradise Regained*, IV, 409–15), which Satan tries to interpret as a sign of God's displeasure:

Whereof this ominous night that clos'd thee round,
So many terrors, voices, prodigies,
May warn thee, as a sure fore-going sign. (*P.R.*, IV, 481–3).

And of course the final vindication of Job and the doubling of his
wealth as a victor's reward are re-echoed in the vindication of Christ
by angelic choirs, who feed him on "Celestial Food" and sing "Heavenly Anthems of his victory."

PR-2 (Greek)

AESCHYLUS. *Prometheus Desmotes. Ca.* 460 B.C.

Begins: KRATOS
    Χθονὸς μὲν ἐς τηλουρὸν ἥκομεν πέδον,
    Σκύθην ἐς οἶμον ἄβατον εἰς ἐρημίαν.
Ends: PROMETHEUS
    ὦ μητρὸς ἐμῆς σέβας, ὦ πάντων
    αἰθὴρ κοινὸν φάος εἱλίσσων,
    ἐσορᾷς μ' ὡς ἔκδικα πάσχω.

Equally familiar to Milton, but less analogous to *Paradise Regained*,
is *Prometheus Bound*, a tragedy by Aeschylus (roughly contemporary with the author of *Job*), in which a lonely demigod, the incar-
nate spirit of Wisdom and Benevolence, bound to a rocky crag "in a
lonely waste where no foot has trodden," challenges the apparent
injustice of an Almighty Power, as cruel and vindictive as Satan.
Only 37 lines survive from its sequel, *Prometheus Set Free*, in which
the immortal martyr comes back, thirty thousand years later, to be
vindicated in a universal order based at last on reason.

PR-3 (Greek)

The Gospel According to Luke, iv: 1–13. About A.D. 100

Begins: Ἰησοῦς δὲ πλήρης Πνεύματος Ἁγίου ὑπέστρεψεν ἀπὸ τοῦ Ἰορδάνου,
    καὶ ἤγετο ἐν τῷ Πνεύματι εἰς τὴν ἐρήμον ἡμέρας τεσσεράκοντα
    πειραζόμενος ὑπὸ τοῦ διαβόλου.

Ends: Καὶ συντελέσας πάντα πειρασμὸν ὁ διάβολος ἀπέστη ἀπ' αὐτοῦ ἄχρι καιροῦ.

This is the version followed by Milton. In *The Gospel According to Matthew*, iv: 1–11, the second and third temptations are interchanged. All subsequent literary treatments of the Temptation of Christ are derived directly or indirectly from either *Matthew* or *Luke*.

The most powerful and imaginative use of this passage in any literature is to be found in the "Grand Inquisitor" chapter of Dostoyevsky's *The Brothers Karamazov* (1880). Although first published in Russian over two centuries after the death of Milton, its greatness demands its mention here. In Ivan Karamazov's prose-poem, Christ returns briefly to mankind, in Seville, Spain, at the height of the Inquisition, and is privately cross-examined, after arrest, by the Grand Inquisitor himself. "Do you believe," says the latter, "that all the wisdom of the world put together could have invented anything as deep and powerful as the three questions that were actually put to you by the wise and mighty spirit in the desert? From those questions alone, from the miracle of their affirmation, we can see that we have here to do not with the evanescent intelligence but with the absolute and the eternal ..." The Grand Inquisitor then proceeds to his justification of a terrorist régime based on miracle, mystery, and authority – the three "truths" affirmed by Satan in the wilderness.

THE TEMPTATION
(King James Version)

And Jesus, being full of the Holy Ghost, returned from Jordan, and was led by the Spirit into the wilderness, being forty days tempted of the devil. And in those days he did eat nothing: and when they were ended, he afterward hungered. And the devil said unto him, If thou be the Son of God, command this stone that it be made bread. And Jesus answered him, saying, It is written, That man shall not live by bread alone, but by every word of God. And the devil, taking him up into an high mountain, shewed unto him all the kingdoms of the world in a moment of time. And the devil said unto him, All this power will I give thee, and the glory of them: for that is delivered unto me; and to whomsoever I will give it. If thou, therefore, wilt worship me, all shall be

thine. And Jesus answered and said unto him, Get thee behind
me, Satan: for it is written, Thou shalt worship the Lord thy
God, and him only shalt thou serve. And he brought him to
Jerusalem, and set him on a pinnacle of the temple, and said
unto him, If thou be the Son of God, cast thyself down from
hence: For it is written, He shall give his angels charge over
thee, to keep thee; and in their hands they shall bear thee up,
lest at any time thou dash thy foot against a stone. And
Jesus, answering, said unto him, It is said, Thou shalt not
tempt the Lord thy God. And when the devil had ended all
the temptation, he departed from him for a season.

PR-4 (Old English)

AUTHOR UNKNOWN. *Christ and Satan* (lines 667–710). About A.D.
790–830? Cf. edition by M.D. Clubb, *Yale Studies in English*, LXX, 1925

Begins: Swylce he fæste   feowertig daga
         metod man-cynnes   þurh his mildsa sped ...
  Ends: ær twa seondon   tida agongene
         þaet þu merced hus   ameten hæbbe!"

This third part of *Christ and Satan* in the Junius manuscript (Bodleian Library) is essentially a separate poem in itself, as distinct
from"The Fall of the Angels"and"The Harrowing of Hell."Only
two of Satan's temptations are mentioned: the invitation to turn
stones into bread and the mountain-top request to worship him in
return for the kingdoms of the world as viewed from thence. The
most notable expansion in treatment is in the invective with which
Christ rejects the second proposal. Otherwise the Anglo-Saxon alliterative lines add little to the bare account in Scripture except perhaps their sonorous kennings for Christ (metod man-cynnes, Cyn-
ing, alwihta, ece Drihten, sigores Agend, liht lifigendum, Drihten
Hæland, Meotod alwihta), for the Devil (awyrgda, hearm-bealowes
gast, Satanus seolf), and for hell (hel-heoðo dreorig, grim græf-hus).

G.P. Krapp assigns this poem to the eighth century. He states
categorically that it belongs neither to Caedmon nor to the Caedmonian school, but is related rather to Cynewulfian poetry. As it
was included in the Junius manuscript, it is as likely (or unlikely)
to have been known to Milton as is the Caedmonian *Genesis* (cf.
PL-41 and PL-42).

Christis and Satan[1]

Forty days fasting, he fared in the desert;
Heaven's All-Highest was hungered past measure,
The king of all creatures, kind, in his mercy.
Soon to assail him, Satan was present –
Hurled out of heaven, to hell he once tumbled.
A tempter's enticements he tried on the Saviour,
Laying broad stones in the lap of the Lord;
Bade him turn boulders to bread for his hunger –
"If you have power such portents to work."
Answered the eternal and ageless Messiah:
"Rogue, have you read, what is written in Scripture,
'Warrant your ways by the word of Jehovah?'
In vain you revile the victor of heaven,
The light of the living that lasteth forever
In the kingdom of heaven the holiest joys."
    Then did the spiteful spirit of evil
Seize with his hands our Saviour and Lord,
Took on his shoulder in terrible scorn
And set on a summit, forsooth on a mountain:
"Look, if you like, on the land and its people;
The land and its folk under law I shall give
For you to possess, their cities and glories,
If yours is by right the rule of the heavens,
Of angels and men as your mind has desired –
If you will but kneel and acknowledge my lordship."
    Answered the eternal and ageless Messiah:
"Away with you, wicked one, work out your torment,
Doomed to a den in the darkness of hell.
Torture is ripe for you, ready to meet you
Kept from the joys of the kingdom of God.
But I command, by the mightiest Power,
That you hold out no hope to hell and its inmates
But that you should tell them the topmost of sorrows
Has crowned your encounter with the King of Mankind,
The greatest of Lords. So get you behind me.
Know also, most wicked, how wide and extensive

1 As in PL-41 (cf. *The Celestial Cycle*, pp. 19–43), an attempt has been
made to adapt the old alliterative line to the less inflected character of
modern English.

Is hell's dreary hall. Make haste to appraise it,
With your hands, as you mete it, lay hold on its depths,
Go near it with care till you know all its circuit,
First measure its range from the roof to the floor,
How deep are its densest and darkest of vapours.
You will know all the more by the gnaw of remorse
How once, long ago, with God you were stationed,
When your hands shall have measured how high and
    how deep
Are the bowels of hell, the horrible grave.
Go to your kingdom, ere called on once more,
A second sad time in the tale of the years,
To measure the house that is marked as your dwelling.

PR-5 (Old Saxon)

A N O N Y M O U S . *Heliand.* Composed about A.D. 830. Ed. J. Andreas
Schmeller. Munich, Stuttgart and Tübingen, 1830

Begins: dopislea drohtin the godo · an ena wostunnea waldandes sunu ...
    Ends: Geng in tho bi iordanes stade thar ina iohannes antfand.

This poem, literally "The Saviour," is a rambling narrative, composed of some 4000 alliterative lines. It is little more than a free
translation of the Scriptural story of the life of Christ, padded out
with a moralistic running commentary. The order of the three temptations is based on the account in *Matthew*, iv, 1–11, namely, bread-
temple-kingdoms. The passage cited above is limited to this episode.
The text is drawn from a collation of manuscripts in Munich (Bib-
liotheca Regia Monacensis) and in London (British Museum).

PR-6 (Middle English)

A N O N Y M O U S . *Cursor Mundi.* About 1325. (Available in Richard Morris, ed., *Cursor Mundi: A Northumbrian Poem of the XIVth Century*, 3
vols., London, 1874, 1893, pp. 1820)

Begins: Man yhernes rimes for to here
        And romans red on maneres sere ...
    Ends: And til his clarete he us ken,
        Thurgh prayers of his moder: Amen.

This massive rhymed chronicle is called *Cursor Mundi* because, as its unknown author explains, "it runs over the whole world." Its 24,000 lines cover human history, largely in Biblical terms, from Creation down to the Judgment Day; in other words, it presents in narrative form the same range of episode that was later to be presented, also in Northern England, in the cycles of the Mystery Plays. There are four comparatively complete surviving manuscripts, which differ considerably in form and language: (a) Cotton MS Vespasian A iii (British Museum Library); (b) Fairfax MS 14 (Bodleian Library); (c) Göttingen MS Theol. 107.r (Göttingen University Library); and (d) MS R.3.8 (Trinity College Library, Cambridge). In the Fairfax MS, the Temptation episode (lines 12916–12998) is subtitled "how ihesus was temptid with þe feinde," and the rhymer is rustically indignant at the devil: "Who ever heard of so bold a beast!" As the original has it:

> Qua herd euer best so bald!
> He hint his lauerd al in his wald,
> In armes his, and tok his flight
> To tun ierusalem ful right,
> And set him on þe hei pinion
> O þe temple o þe tun.

PR-7 (French)

La Bible et le Nouveau Testament Moralisés et mis en vers, par Macés de la Charité sur Loire, Curé de Cinquoins. Manuscript dated 1343. Original in Bibliothèque Nationale, Paris. Microfilm from the Mediaeval Institute, University of Notre Dame, Notre Dame, Indiana

> *Begins*: Dieu créa au comencement
> Le ciel et la terre ensement ...
> *Ends*: Couche te tart, leve matin,
> Soys curieux de ta besoigne,
> Et donc tu trouveras ta soigne.

This is a famous old rhyming version of the Bible, in the same tradition as the *Cursor Mundi*, with the Temptation of Jesus occupying a very small spot in the narrative. Since the whole work still remains in manuscript, it will have had no conceivable influence on the formation of *Paradise Regained*.

PR-8 (Icelandic)

EYSTEINN ÁSGRÍMSSON. *Lilja: Krists konungs drápa tirae*ð (edited by Guðbrandur Jónsson, Helgafell, Iceland, *sine dato*, pp. 183). Composed about A.D. 1350

Begins: Almáttigr Guð, allra stétta
         yfirbjóðandi engla og þjóða ...
Ends: lof sé þér um aldr og ævi,
         einig sönn í þrennum greinum.

This "heroic poem of one hundred stanzas in honour of Christ the King" was written by an Augustinian monk in the monastery of Thykkvabær, in southeastern Iceland, about the middle of the four-teenth century. Its one hundred stanzas, like the hundred cantos of Dante's *Commedia*, are numbered after the one hundred letters in the complete *Ave Maria*, and the poem itself is named "The Lily" in honour of the Virgin. Its metre, based on alliteration plus internal rhyme, was the standard court-measure or lord-song (*drottkvæði*) for poems addressed to royalty.

Stanzas 39 to 45 deal with the temptation of Christ by Satan, whose motivation is partly curiosity as to the true identity of Christ and partly a malicious desire to complete the overthrow of man that he had begun with Adam.

PR-9 (Middle English)

ANONYMOUS. *A Stanzaic Life of Christ*, edited for the Early English Text Society by Frances E. Foster, London, 1926

Begins: Ihesu, þat born was of a may
         In amendement of mankynde ...
Ends: ffrom heuen to hom hit lyght Adovn,
         As we in holy chirche can syng.

This 10,840-line poem would seem to be a fourteenth-century com-pilation, versified into English, with monkish patience, from two well-known Latin prose works, Ralph Higden's *Polychronicon* and Jacobus de Voragine's *Legenda Aurea*. Each of the 2710 stanzas is a quatrain of rude iambic tetrameter lines, rhyming *abab*. A sample stanza runs:

> Then was the deul adred ful sore,
> ffor atte forme ouercomen was he,
> but yet he thoght to fonde hym more
> the seconde time, as ye shyn se.

The story of the Temptation of Christ runs from line 5229 to line 5332. It points out that Satan's temptations involve the three deadly sins of gluttony, vain-glory (pride), and avarice. According to Professor Foster, this version of the Temptation is based on the *Polychronicon* and on a homily by Pope Gregory (*XL Homiliarum in Evangelia*, Lib. i, Hom. xvi), and is itself a probable source of the Chester Cycle Play No. xii (see PR-11, below). She thinks that the author of *The Stanzaic Life of Christ* was very probably a monk in St Werburgh's Abbey, in Chester. This would make him a forerunner there of the fifteenth-century monkish poet, Henry Bradshaw.

PR-10 (English)

ANONYMOUS. *The York Mysteries*. xxii. The Temptation. Fourteenth century

Begins: DIABOLUS
> Make rome be-lyve, and late me gang,
> Who makis here all þis þrang? ...

Ends: JESUS
> I knawe my tyme is faste command,
>   Now will I wende.

Considerable attention has been paid by Robert L. Ramsay[2] and Allan H. Gilbert[3] to the possible influence on Milton of the mediaeval guild plays. Neither has found any specific debt, but both feel certain of some indirect propagation of their mediaeval spirit.

Most of the parallels drawn by Gilbert are found in many other analogues on Milton's themes. An interesting item in the York *Temptation* is Satan's argument that by turning stones into bread

2"Morality Themes in Milton's Poetry," *SP*, xv, 2
3"Milton and the Mysteries," *SP*, xvii, 2

Jesus can help not only himself but "othir moo" (cf. *Paradise Regained*, I, 344–5).

PR-11 (English)

A N O N Y M O U S .   *Chester Plays*. XII. The Temptation. About 1447

Begins: S A T H A N A S
    Now by my soverayntie I sweare
    And principalitie that I beare ...
  Ends: Thus holpe the woman, in good faye,
    Our sweet lord Jesu.

Here Satan's doubt as to the identity of Jesus (cf. *Paradise Regained*, I, 79–97) is set forth clearly. In the Chester play he also reasons over his first failure and plans more carefully for the second attack.

PR-12 (English)

A N O N Y M O U S .   *Ludus Coventriae*. XXII "The Temptation." Before 1456. Edited for the Shakespeare Society by James Orchard Halliwell, London, 1841

Begins: S A T H A N
    Now belyard and belsabub, ye der wurthy devele of helle
    And wysest of councel amonges all the rowte! ...
  Ends: J H E S U S
    Shewe thi myght agens thi ffoo,
    Whan thi sowle partyth the froo,
     In blysse than xal it be. *Amen!*

According to Halliwell, these plays were long performed at Coventry on Corpus Christi Day by the Grey Friars of that town. Margaret of Anjou, the queen of Henry VI, witnessed them there in 1456, and they are alleged to have been performed before Elizabeth I at Kenilworth in 1575. They were composed in a rough-hewn but elaborately rhymed 13-line stanza. In the unique manuscript, dated 1468 and preserved in the Cottonian Collection in the Bodleian

Library, Oxford, one or more scribes have perpetrated many obvious errors both in the English text and in the numerous Latin passages that occur. The version of "The Temptation" printed below (pp. 259–65) is that of Halliwell, who reproduced these corruptions as a matter of principle.

At the opening of this play, there is a council of devils, somewhat comparable to those in *Paradise Regained* (I, 40–113, and II, 118–235). The only lieutenants given speaking parts are Beëlzebub and Belial. The latter recommends the tempting of Jesus by "sotyl why-lys." The infernal "parlement" expresses some uncertainty as to the true identity of Jesus (cf. *Paradise Regained*, I, 79–97).

The Temptation

SATHAN

Now Belyard and Belsabub, ye der wurthy devele of helle,
    And wysest of councel amonges alle the rowte!
Herke now what I sey, a tale I xalle yow telle,
    That trobelyth sore my stomak: thereof I have grett dowte.

BELYALLE

Syr Sathanas, owre sovereyn, syre, with the wol we dwelle,
    Alle redy at thi byddynge to the do we lowte;
If thou have any nede of oure wyse counselle,
    Telle us now this qwestyon alle out and oute;
        Sey al thi dowte be-dene.

BELSABUB

ya, sere, telle us thi dowte by and by,
    And we xul telle the so sekyrly,
That thou xalt know verryly
        What thi dowte dothe mene.

SATHAN

The dowte that I have it is of Cryst i-wys;
    Born he was in Bedleem, as it is seyd,
And many a man wenyth that Goddes sone he is,
    Born of a woman and she a clene mayd.
And alle that evyr he prechyth, it is of hevyn blys,
    He wyl lese oure lawe, I am ryght sore afrayd;
ffayn wolde I knowe who were ffadyr his,

ffor of this grett dowte I am sore dismayd
　　　Indede.
If that he be Goddys childe,
And born of a mayd mylde,
Than be we ryght sore begylde,
　　　And short xal ben oure spede.
Therefore, seres, sumwhat that ye shewe.
　　In this grett dowte what is best to do;
If he be Goddys sone he wyl brede a shrewe,
　　And werke us meche wrake, both wreche and woo:
Sorwe and care he wyl sone strewe,
　　Alle oure gode days than xulde sone be goo;
And alle oure lore and alle oure lawe he wyl downe hewe,
　　And than be we alle borne, if that it be soo,
　　　He wylle don us alle tene.
He wylle be Lorde over hevyn and helle.
And ffeche awey alle oure catelle,
Therfor shewe now sum good counselle,
　　　What comfort may best bene.

BELYALLE
The best wytt that I kan say,
　　Hym to tempte forsothe it is;
With sotyl whylys, if that thou may,
　　Asay to make hym don amys.
If that he synne, this is no nay,
　　He may not be kynge of blys:
Hym to tempte, go walke thi way.
　　ffor best counselle I trowe be this;
　　　Go forthe now and asay!

BELSABUB
The best wytt I hold it be,
Hym to tempte in synnys thre,
The which mankende is frelte
　　　Doth ffalle sonest alway.

SATHAN
So after your wytt now wylle I werke,
　　I wylle no lengere now here abyde;
Be he nevyr so wyse a clerke,
　　I xal opposyn hym withinne a tyde.

BELSABUB

Now, lovely Lucyfer, in helle so derke,
   King and Lorde of synne and pryde;
With sum myst his wittys to merke,
   He send the grace to be thi gyde,
   And evyr more be thi spede!

BELYALLE

Alle the develys, that ben in helle,
Shul pray to Mahound, as I the telle,
That thou mayest spede this jurney welle,
      And comforte the in this dede.

JHESUS

xLti days and xLti nyght
   Now have I fastyd for mannys sake;
A more grett hungyr had nevyr no wyght,
   Than I myself begynne to take;
ffor hungyr in peyn stronge am I pyght,
   And bred have I non myn hungyr for to slake,
A lytel of a loof relese myn hungyr myght,
   But mursele have I non my comfort for to make;
      This suffyr I, man, for the.
ffor thi glotenye and metys wronge,
I suffyr for the this hungyr stronge,
I am afferde it wyl be longe
     Or thou do thus for me.

SATHAN

The Sone of God if that thou be,
   Be the grett myght of thi godhede,
Turne these flyntes, anon lett se,
   ffrom arde stonys to tender brede.
More bettyr it is, as I telle the,
   Wysely to werke aftyr my reed,
And shew thi myght of grett majeste,
   Than throw grett hungyr for to be dede.
      These stonys now bred thou make.
Goddys Sone if that thou be,
Make these stonys bred, lett se,
Than mayste thou ete ryght good plente,
     Thyn hungyr for to slake.

JHESUS
Nott only be bred mannys lyff yitt stood,
  But in the wurde of God, as I the say,
To mannys sowle is nevyr mete so good,
  As is the wurd of God that prechid is alway.
Bred materyal dothe norche blood,
  But to mannys sowle, this is no nay,
Nevyr more may be a betyr food,
  Than the wurd of God, that lestyth ay.
          To here Goddys wurde therfore man love.
Thi body doth love materal brede,
Withoute the wurde of God thi soule is but dede,
To love prechynge therfore I rede,
          If thou wylt dwellyn in blysse above.

SATHAN
foor no grett hungyr that I kan se,
  In glotony thou wylt not synne;
Now to the temple come forthe with me,
  And ther xal I shewe the a praty gynne.
Up to this pynnacle now go we,
  I xal the sett on the hyghest pynne,
Ther I preve what that thou be,
  Or that we tweyn part a twynne,
          I xal know what myght thou have.

Hic ascendit Deus pinnaculum templi, dum diabolus dicit quoque
sequitur,
          Whan thou art sett upon the pynnacle,
          Thou xalt ther pleyn a gweynt steracle,
          Or ellys shewe a grett meracle,
                    Thysself ffrom hurte thou save.

His Satanas ponit Jhesum super pinnaculum, dicens,
          Now if thou be Goddys ssone of myght,
            Ryght down to the erthe anon thou ffalle,
          And save thisylf in every plyght
            ffrom harm and hurt, and scappys alle;
          ffor it is wretyn with aungelys bryght
            That ben in hevyn, thi faderes halle,
          The to kepe bothe day and nyght

Xul be ful redy as thi thralle,
      Hurt that thou non have.
That thou stomele not ageyn the ston,
And hurt thi fote as thou dost gon,
Aungelle be redy alle everychon,
      In weys the to save.

JHESUS
It is wretyn in holy book,
  Thi Lorde God thou xalt not tempte;
Alle thynge must obeye to Goddys look,
  Out of his myght is non exempt;
Out of thi cursydnes and cruel crook,
  By Godys grace man xal be redempt: —
Whan thou to helle, thi brennynge brook,
  To endless peyne xal evyr be dempt,
      Therin alwey to abyde.
Thi Lorde God thou tempt no more,
It is not syttenge to thi lore,
I bydde the sese anon therfore,
      And tempte God in no tyde.

SATHAN
Ow! in gloteny nor in veynglory it dothe ryght nott avayl
  Cryst for to tempt, it profyteth me ryght nought;
I must now begynne to have a new travayl, —
  In covetyse to tempt hym it comyth now in my thought.
ffor if I went thus away and shrynkyd as a snayl,
  Lorn were the labore alle that I have wrought;
Therefore in covetyse our syre I xal asayle,
  And assay into that synne yf he may be brought,
      Anon forthe ryght.
Syr, yitt onys I pray to the,
To this hygh hyl com forthe with me.
I xal the shewe many a cete,
      And many a wurthy syght.

Tunc Jhesus transit cum diabolo super montem et diabolus dicit.
  Into the northe loke fforth evyn pleyn,
    The towre of Babylony ther mayst thou se;
  The cete of Jerusalem stondyth ther ageyn,

And evyn ffast therby stondyth Galyle.
Nazareth, Naverne, and the kyngdom of Spayn,
 Zabulon, and Neptalym, that is a ryche countre,
Both Zebec and Salmana, thou mayst se serteyn,
 Itayl and Archage that wurthy remys be,
  Both Januense and Jurye.
Rome doth stonde before the ryght,
The temple of Salamon as sylver bryght,
And here mayst thou se opynly with syght
  Bothe Ffraunce and Normandye.

Turn the now on this syde and se here Lumbardye.
 Of spycery there growyth many An C. balys;
Archas and Aragon, and grett Almonye,
 Parys and Portynagale, and the towne of Galys;
Pownteys and Poperynge, and also Pycardye,
 Erlonde, Scottlonde, and the londe of Walys.
Grete pylis and castellys thou mayst se with eye,
 ya, and alle the wyd werld without no talys.
  Alle this longygh to me.
If thou wylt knele down to the grownde,
And wurchepp me now in this stownde,
Alle this world, that is so rownd,
  I xal it gyve to the!

JHESUS
Go a bak, thou fowle Sathanas!
 In holy Scrypture wretyn it is,
The Lorde God to wurshipp in every plas,
 As for his thrall and thou servaunt his.

SATHAN
Out, out, harrow! alas! alas!
 I woundyr sore what is he this?
I cannot brynge hym to no trespas,
 Nere be no synne to don amys.
  He byddyth me gon abakke!
What that he is I kannot se,
Whethyr God or man, what that he be
I kannot telle in no degre:
  ffor sorwe I lete a crakke.

Hic venient angeli cantantes et ministrantes ei: – "Gloria tibi, Domine!" Dicens.

JHESUS

Now, alle mankende, exaumple take
  By these grete werkys that thou dost se,
How that the devylle of helle so blake
  In synne was besy to tempte me;
ffor alle hise maystryes that he dyd make.
  He is overcom and now doth ffle;
Alle this I suffyr ffor mannys sake.
    To teche the how thou xalt rewle the,
      Whan the devylle dothe the assayle.
Loke thou concente nevyr to synne,
For no sleytys, ne for no gynne,
And than the victory xalt thou wynne,
      The devyl xal lesyn alle his travayl.
To suffyr temptacion it is grett peyn.
  If thou withstonde it thou wynnyst grett mede,
Of God the more grace thou hast serteyn,
  If thou with-sett the devyl in his dede.
Thow that the fende tempt the ageyn.
  Of his power take thou no drede;
ffor God hath the yovyn bothe myght and mayn,
    Hym for to with-sytt evyr at nede,
      Thou has more myght than he.
Whan the devyl doth tempte the thoo,
Shewe thi myght aghens thi ffoo.
Whan thi sowle partyth the froo.
      In blysse than xal it be.   *Amen!*

PR-13 (Latin)

MARCO GIROLAMO VIDA. *Christias.* Rome, 1527. Book IV, 647–98.
Xe: Harvard

Begins: Qui mare, qui terras, qui coelum numine comples
       Spiritus alme, tuo liceat mihi munere regem ...
  Ends: Protinus hinc populos Christi de nomine dicunt
       Christiadas. Toto surgit gens aurea mundo,
       Seclorum oritur longe pulcherrimus ordo.

So great already was the scholarly and poetic fame of 24-year-old Marco Girolamo Vida (1489?–1566), an Italian of Cremona, that Pope Leo x, on his accession in 1513, gave the young man a priory sinecure (the equivalent of a modern "grant in aid") and commissioned him to write a Latin epic on the life of Christ. Its contemporary reputation was prodigious. The Temptation episode, quoted below in full, was evidently regarded by Vida as only a minor event in the life of his hero. It has no artistic pattern of its own, beyond the triple onslaught of the Tempter, nor any architectural bearing on the structure of the epic as a whole. As a reward for his total achievement, he was made Bishop of Alba, in Piedmont.

A recent critic, Mario di Cesare,[4] quotes approvingly line 26 of Milton's early poem, The Passion: "Loud o're the rest Cremona's Trump doth sound;" and adds: "As an estimate of the Christiad compared to other attempts at Christian epic, this is clear, comprehensive and accurate." The whole of Cesare's chapter VII expands this judgment. C.S. Lewis,[5] however, gives his grounds for regarding Cremona's Trump as hopelessly out of tune. "Vida's Christiad," he says, "is the supreme example" of "endless labour to be wrong"... "One changeless and unmeaning glossiness spreads over every episode."

FROM *The Christiad*

Nor did Hell's King, our race's filthy foe,
Who strives to turn our souls aside from right,
Forbear to assail the blessed Lord, our God.
It chanced He fled the hubbub of his friends
And of the throng that sought to follow him;
Thus he forsook the company of men
And roamed in secret in the lofty glades.
Then forty days he spent devoid of food;
For forty nights he suffered hunger's pangs.
Lo, the night-potent Foe, considering
That now the time was ripe to do him wrong,
Drew near with many thousands of the fiends
That he had led from his Tartarean caves,
And on his bestial head shook locks of fire.

4 *Vida's 'Christiad' and the Vergilian Epic* (New York, 1964), p. 280
5 *English Literature in the Sixteenth Century, excluding Drama* (Oxford, 1954), p. 24

But now his cunning saw that open force
Would be in vain; therefore with hopeful guile
He assailed the Saviour in deceitful words:
"In truth, a heavenly Parent has begot you,
A god past doubt, and everything obeys you.
Why, with exhausted body, do you still
Endure such hunger? Why not suddenly
Transform the many stones around you here
Into the sustenance of wheaten loaves?"
His guile did not escape the man divine,
Who answered thus: "Instead of mortal gifts
Of baker's wheat, I cherish in my soul
My Father's conversations, holy words,
And when I con them over in my heart,
Straightway all pangs of hunger disappear
And all desire for feasting is forgotten."
Thus he had spoken, but the enemy,
Though plainly vanquished in his first attack,
Kept up the fight, pressed on with more assaults,
And slyly, though in vain, renewed his wiles.
Thus next he sought, though vainly, to pervert
His steadfast spirit with a love of power
And empty praise in ruling over kingdoms.
But as when winds stir up the smitten sea
With raging billows, thundering on the cliffs,
And still the broken waves retreat again,
So, knowing all, the faithful Son endured,
And yet did not forbid the foul attempt
To weave dark stratagems against himself.
Next, he permits the Fiend to carry him
Above the steeples of the marble temple,
Based on the rough foundations of a crag.
And when the Devil, dreaming he had conquered,
Gaped at his quarry with infernal joy,
Forthwith the hero was made manifest,
A very god, and dragged forth all dark wiles
Into the clear discomfiture of day.
In such a fashion does a mighty horse,
Who slips the reins, and gallops off in freedom,
Mock at the grooms who follow from afar;
Often he makes pretence, and vexingly

Loiters along the road and crops the grass.
But when he sees them rushing in to seize him,
He eludes them, gives a bound and thunders off
Across the broad expanses of the plain.
When therefore the fierce Enemy perceived
That all his false pretences were in vain,
Retreating in defeat, he left the god;
To whom a hundred flying messengers
Came, at his Father's bidding, on swift wings
And brought his hunger ample sustenance.

PR-14 (Italian)

THEOPHILO FOLENGO. *Della Humanità del Figliuolo di Dio.* Venice, 1533. Mi: Harvard

Book IV, lxx–lxxv
Begins: Finite ció dà l'Angel ricoperto
          De l'inconsutil manto, ouè la bella ...
  Ends: Distrutta fú dapó l'digiun sofferto,
          Per suo non giá, ma be per nostro merto.

This lengthy Italian poem on the life of Christ is composed in ottava rima and continually turns aside from straight narrative to moralize on human sin and error. Prior to the Temptation, there is a Council in Hell, dominated by Satan, who is described as a grotesque monster with a bull's horns and a hog's face. He is also referred to as the clever, treacherous Spider (*l'astuta insidiosa Aragna*) and the Wolf (*Lupaccio*). The three temptations take the order loaves-pinnacles-kingdoms, and there are continual marginal references to Scripture. Folengo was born of noble parentage near Mantua in 1491. At the age of seventeen, he became a Benedictine monk, but seven years later he forsook the Order for the companionship of a well-born young woman, with whom he wandered about Italy, supporting himself by his gift for verse, especially of the macaronic type. His broad humour was frequently quoted and copied by Rabelais. Ten years later, he returned to the Benedictines and wrote this versified life of Christ.

PR-15 (English)

JOHN BALE. *A brefe Comedy or enterlude concernynge the temptacyon of our lorde and sauer Jesus Christ by Sathan in the desarte.* London, 1538. Mi: Bodleian

Begins: JESUS
  Into this desert the Holy Ghost hath brought me,
  After my baptism, of Satan to be tempted ...
  Ends: ANGELUS ALTER
  Our manner is most highly to rejoice
  When man hath comfort, which we now declare in voice.

Bale was a bitterly controversial champion of the Reformation. In 1538, the year in which this play was written, he had been evicted from his pulpit for excessive vehemence and was touring the country with a company of actors to set his case before the common people of England. Todd[6] devotes considerable space to the influence of this play on *Paradise Regained*, finding in it a forerunner of the luxury spectacle (*PR*, II, 337–67) that, as Allan H. Gilbert has shown us,[7] belongs to the second temptation, not the first. Bale's version runs:

  Here is golde and sylver in wonderfull habundaunce,
  Silkes, velvetes, tissues, with wynes and spyces of plesaunce.
  Here are fayre women, of countenance ameable,
  With all kyndes of meates to the body dylectable.

Todd also finds some resemblance between Satan's disguise in *P.R.* I, 314, as "an aged man in Rural weeds" and the form of an ignorant old hermit that he assumes in Bale:

  Scriptures I know non; for I am but an hermite, I;
  I maye saye to yow, it is no part of our stody.

Parallels to Satan as Milton's "gray dissimulation" are also traced by Todd in Cornazzano's *Vita et Passione di Christo* (1518), Marlowe's *Tragical History of Dr. Faustus,* and Milton's own Guy Fawkes epic,

6 *The Poetical Works of John Milton,* ed. H.J. Todd (London, 1801), IV, xvi
7 "The Temptation in *Paradise Regained,*" *JEGP,* xv (1916), 599–611

In Quintum Novembris (lines 80–90), written in Latin at the age of seventeen.

PR-16 (Latin)

JACOBUS STRASBURGUS. *Christi victoris et Satanae pugna in deserto*. Leipzig, 1565. Ph: British Museum. For partial translation, see below

Begins: Dicere victoris Christi Satanaeque duellum,
    Montibus in vastis inter deserta ferarum ...
  Ends: Praecipitem in vallem deiecit, et aëre turpes
    Suffocante gulas, vitam hostibus ultor ademit.

This vigorous Latin poem long escaped the notice of Miltonists in the British Museum, where, along with PL-146 (*Hypotyposis divini judicii contra lapsum hominem*), it lurked under the non-committal title of *Orationes duae carmine heroico scriptae*. The title-page becomes more explicit in its subtitle:"In prima oratione describitur Christi victoris et Satanae pugna in deserto."The public declamation of the poem was made on 10 March 1565, at the University of Leipzig (founded 1406), apparently at the request of Victorinus Strigelius, dean of the Faculty of Arts; and the printed edition in that same year carried a complimentary dedication to Otho and Carolus, two young princes of the ducal branch of the House of Saxony.

This is the only brief epic in any language that deals specifically and totally with the same theme as *Paradise Regained*. In treatment, however, the two poems could hardly differ more. While Milton, with the format and argumentation of *Job* in mind, devotes most of his space to rhetorical thrust and parry"between the pass and fell incensed points of mighty opposites,"Strasburgus is wholly obedient to the demands of the neo-classical epic theory and seeks throughout to multiply the imagery of an actual battle. After each temptation has been briefly presented by Satan, dark Furies from hell and a swarm of personified Vices assail the Saviour. His personified Virtues, also equipped with the weapons of psychomachia, rally to his defence and rout the enemy. A typical example of the resourcefulness of Strasburgus in mobilizing his hosts comes when (following the third temptation) Blasphemy is befouling the countryside with her assaults. In ancient times, Isaiah and Hezekiah had by prayer brought about the destruction of the Assyrian host. It is these two "saints," therefore, who now issue forth from heaven at the head of a flying phalanx of angels.

Strasburgus describes Christ's whole Temptation experience as the training of a young warrior for a greater conflict to come in the Harrowing of Hell:

> Et quondam exuto stygium victurus Averno
> Praedonem, leuibus primum experiatur in armis
> Tyro rudimentum, et magnis se praeparet ausis. (See below,
>   p. 274.)

These very words seem echoed by God the Father in *Paradise Regained*, when approving of the testing of his Son:

> There he shall first lay down the rudiments
> Of his great warfare, e're I send him forth
> To conquer Sin and Death the two grand foes ...

That ultimate victory, again in physical terms, is foreshadowed in Strasburgus' concluding episode, in which the omnipotent Christ dashes the Furies upon the rocks.

The First Declamation
(The battle of victorious Christ and Satan)

A Godlike impulse spurs my mind to tell
The duel fought between victorious Christ
And Satan, won by speech and heavenly arms
In the vast mountains and the pathless haunts
Of savage beasts. Whence do we now begin,
Whence launch such mighty wrath? The task is great
And the presumption is beyond my strength.
But thou, O Holy Dove, whose mind and might
Suffuse all things, who from the Father art
And breathest forth his likeness on mankind,
Thou who didst nurse the sea, when the new world
Was fresh afloat, assist me to proclaim
Thy praises if upon thine altars laid
I consecrate the Muse's holy songs.
Be thou beside me, since with thee as guide

A mortal may ascend the rocky ridge
Of mountains inaccessible to man
And sing of strife and ranks in battle joined;
For thou dost know true causes from the first
And of so great a war the primal course.
  Therefore, angelic ministers, ye throng
That saw the fight, ye faithful warriors
In the victorious regiments of heaven
Beneath the unexhausted radiance
Of endless light; ye heralds of God's praise
And holy guardians of pious men;
Ye who still weave the poet's laurel wreath
And build the high memorials of peace
And the eternal rest that flourishes
At heaven's door; ye who mark holy days
For the remembrance of a later age;
Enwreath my brow with hands of victory,
And as you manifest the vanished deeds
Of ancient heroes in a by-gone day,
Unroll this battle to my gazing eyes.

(Lines 29–56: He also calls on the Muses and asks especially for the
kindly favour of Victorinus Strigelius, dean of the Faculty of Arts
at the University of Leipzig, and of the scholarly physician, Meurer)

After man dared to filch forbidden fruit,
Destined to bring down wrath upon his heirs
Through times remote, and from that primal Fall
Had merited an endless place in hell,
Thy everlasting mind, O gracious God,
Mourning the mishap of the human race
(To whom the serpent's treachery had brought
Dread poison from Avernus' stinking throat),
Made mild thine anger to a softer doom,
Granting salvation to a world made new
And restoration to a cancelled heaven,
Whence our race fell, and whence an earlier host
Of angels was cast down, for having sought
To thrust the Son from off the throne of God
And in excess of blasphemy to claim
This honour for itself in God's high realm.

Therefore the Christ was born, by a virgin birth,
Without the intromission of man's seed;
The immortal God, essence intangible,
Assumed man's flesh to comfort frail mankind.
For thus the Son then took upon himself
The body of our exile, yet remained
The Word that he had been since time began;
He assumed a form from the chaste maiden blood
Of his fair Dame, yet from this body's use
The Word did not degenerate at all
Nor lose its former powers (I do not know
How this could be, but simply rest in faith).
He is true God in honour, of like age,
The offspring of the eternal Father born,
The second Person of the mind divine
And the Creator of the world. True man
He also is, by virtue of the flesh,
Like to our nature in all natural things,
Rejoicing in our joys, tempted like us –
Yet without sin – the rest is integral
With the true fleshly character of man.
    Almost had Christ completed thirty years
Of human life, a Jewish citizen,
'Mid friendly kinfolk set. The time had come
For him to manifest himself indeed
As promised in the Garden long ago,
Which, when the gardeners had been driven out
After grim crimes, God blanketed in dark,
Barred the closed doors and set angelic guards
Before the primal threshold of the race.

(Lines 92–128: The prophet, John the Baptist, comes as the herald
of a Saviour soon to follow)

Now when Christ entered fields by Jordan's stream,
He halted on the banks where long ago
The Covenant's Ark had stood and Joshua
Across the river's channel walked dry-shod.
Raising his eyes and on the familiar shore
Watching the people eddy to and fro,
"Now it is right," said he," to accept God's gift

And to repair the ancient fall of man,
Lest his race perish, into darkness plunged
And the unholy depths of Phlegethon.
Our Father's will stands firm; thus He demands
The increase of His kingdom." Thus he spoke;
Then stooped, and showing John a steadfast face,
He by his presence and his act affirmed
The duty of obedience to God's will,
Since of his own accord and sinlessly
He yielded to the stream his sacred head.

(Lines 141–53: Christ approves of baptism as fulfilling his Father's word)

Down through the gleaming air a voice was heard:
"This is my Son, his Father's highest joy.
Since him I cherish, hearken to his words
When he shall teach you." Thus the Almighty spake,
And with loud thunder shook the vault of heaven.
Straightway the Spirit through the air flew down,
Shaped like a dove, and rested on Christ's head
And flew about him on its snowy wings.

(Lines 161–86: This was a mighty omen of Christ's identity and duty on earth)

While from these cares he soothed his heart and brow,
Glad in the hope of aid divine and faith
In high salvation, lo, a holy breeze,
Through swift air sweeping, caught the Saviour up
And carried him by ways circuitous
To empty forest glades and wild beasts' haunts,
So that he might frequent the monstrous ridges
Of the waste desert, and, some future day
Destined to strip Avernus of its spoil,
He here might learn his martial rudiments
As a beginner, in a tyro's fights,
And train himself for greater deeds to come.

(Lines 196–250: His enemy there was not a human foe, as in David's fight with Goliath, but Satan, the supreme spiritual adversary of

mankind, who seduced our first parents and is still our relentless
foe. The poet appeals to the Holy Ghost for inspiration)

Phoebus, the first-created, prince of light
And arbiter of time, now drove his steeds
Along the circuit of his lofty way
Past Capricorn, the Archer, and the urn
With which Aquarius stirs up the clouds:
When Christ, who had been moving on through haunts
Harsh and inhospitably rough with stones,
Now through God's influence began to stray
Among the pathless coverts of wild beasts.
Bright dawn had ushered in the fortieth day;
And now the moon, that rules the frosty night,
Had brought dim twilight to the frigid earth.
Harsh fasting had deprived his unfed veins
Of their due moisture, sucked his members dry
Through their own motions. What was he to do?
Hunger was long drawn out, and in the fields
No harvests stood nor farmers at their tasks.
The place was parched. If reason were to judge,
The threat of instant death was everywhere,
Void of all hope of safety. Such a day
Fulfilled his Foe's best prayers, and lent itself
To cunning fraud. His weapons now he seized,
His wicked weapons, and approaching nigh
He mocks the lonely man with friendly words:
"Hail! Are you not that Christ whom for the world
A virgin bore without the seed of man?
The world's Creator, God, and God's own son
Who still maintains the universe he made
From nothing, and who feeds all living things?
Now you yourself can see that lowing herds
Find their food here while none is left for you.
I well believe, nor is my faith in vain,
You are the Father's well-belovèd son,
The sole delight of His eternal heart,
And now stark hunger dooms you here to die,
A rotten corpse, food for the birds of prey
And carrion beasts; but if you are a shoot
That issues from the stock of ancient gods,

If fictive majesty exalts your name,
Either you can, or will, display a deed
To manifest your soul's omnipotence:
Therefore, I say, command these very stones
To soften into bread, that you may eat
And I may recognize your origin."
    Scarce had he spoken this when pale Despair,
Lurking in bramble-bushes, issues forth
And beats the rushing breezes far and wide.
Closed are her eyes and mournful is her face,
Of her own destiny not unaware.
Care follows closely; her capacious breast
Is girt with lust for gold or lust for food,
Slavish, importunate, in spoils rejoicing,
And, always ragged in the midst of wealth,
Given to theft, sad with perennial grief,
And the more coin she has, the more she seeks
To fill her pouch with money ill acquired.
Hence Fear, Anxiety and Pallor come
With sleepless Grief to share in her attack.
    When Christ beheld these monstrous Furies rise,
Whose very names are horrible to hear,
"Have I not come to battle thus," said he,
"That I alone, compassed by many foes,
May prove sufficient and with glorious praise
May triumph? With an omen most assured
God has established this and to our arms
Gives strength and power to wound. Why, Satan, then
Do you attempt most savagely to daunt
My spirit and pretend a source uncertain
From which my human origin has sprung?
Nor have I a beginning, for I am
The everlasting image of the Father,
Yet am I born, true man, of a chaste virgin.
Both facts are evident. By hidden power,
I, uncorrupted God, have still survived
This lingering fast. Yet gnawing hunger proves
My true humanity. To hope by bread
To save myself alive is surely right,
And yet to yield as slave to appetite
Is far from needful. Mightier still for me

Is every word that issues from God's mouth.
Upon that word alone I would depend,
When no external aid is here to bless me."
  He spoke; and monsters of the infernal crew,
Black Furies, urged in hate their blood-gorged veins
And readied for attack those fateful arms
With which they hitherto had conquered earth;
These weapons now they draw and threaten death.
  But when brave Faith and Faith's immortal sisters
Beheld these plots – for the loud uproar smote
The liquid breezes – swifter now they speed
Than gathering gales. And forthwith Faith alone
Before the rest displayed herself to view.
Seizing a shepherd's crook that chanced to be
There in the field, the solitary maid
In manly fashion smote the host of foes,
Amid such daring deeds unmindful quite
Of her own safety, though no helmet's crest
Upon her head received the foemen's strokes,
No heavenly corselet tired out their blows.
Her bare hand plied its muscles as she leapt
In zeal on their broad shoulders. With her staff
(For to her deeds no other arms were given)
Her indignation smote their cohorts down.

(Lines 334–52: Faith defeats and fetters a shameless monster)

    Nor does she linger, for her eyes perceive
How Avarice, intent on shady gloom,
Has fled through sterile fields to seek near by
A valley where a forest doubly dense
Casts shadows with its branches, and a brook,
Muddy with gold, inflames the wanton gaze,
While all its waters, poisonous to drink,
Cast shifting colours on the sandy shores.
    After the holy goddesses had come
More swiftly than the wind upon her trail,
Their eyes perceive her on the shady banks
Where golden shallows gild the little stream,
Fearing no foe as with her ancient gown
She dries the yellow pebbles that she finds.

They call her from afar; she flees away;
And still they follow: but the fatal weight
Of her untimely plunder drags her down,
Grown weary in mid-course, raising both hands
And asking for indulgence all in vain.
Then venerable Faith, first of the band
Of warrior maidens, seized the Fury's throat
And dashed her hands and freighted body down
To shatter upon Cyclopean oaks.
From her foul bones a noxious fluid flies;
Its evil touch pollutes the grassy fields,
Its very stench defiles the ambient air.
A lingering death wears out her wistful eyes
And the malignant groaning of her soul.
Her evil body then is buried deep
Among the thickets under piled-up stones;
An ash-tree, with its branches hewn away,
Serves as a trophy of the victory.
  Meanwhile, at break of dawn, the victor Christ
Salutes his Father with a suppliant prayer;
Casting his eyes aloft, he pours forth sighs
Out of a hungry heart; the shadowy waste
From rocky cliffs repeats his orisons.
But walking down the sandy mountain-side
Among the shadows that the willows cast,
The Enemy draws near, shaping new plots,
And hidden in the trees he terrifies
The harmless nestlings with a hideous shout,
For through the woods he sends his futile words
That breezes carry uselessly away:
"I am a soldier once again – at least
I hope this time for happier auspices –
I plan new warfare, though my earlier deeds
Brought me no praise at all. May fate permit
That Christ may be compelled to know retreat,
That I may thus insult the tyrant, God,
And celebrate a victory in hell.
But if indeed my strength, subdued before,
Still languishes too much for me to strip
His armour from the Robber-Lord of Heaven,
Yet had my primal force availed me still,
It would be joy to taste of such delights.

If strength for victory be still denied,
My will would strive for glory and deserve
To show its efforts in a doubtful cause,
Whether they wreck me or the battle's end
Greets me with favour. Where the cause is great,
It is most seemly to attempt great things!"
With shameless words like these, the Enemy
Advances through dense willows, and conceives
Swift enterprises in his crafty heart,
For cares encompass him on every side.
　　Christ lying on the grassy earth the Fiend
Happened to see, and to himself he said:
"Does not this time befit my enterprise?
Great frauds can be defeated by delay."
Therefore through air he bore the Christ aloft
Above strange lands and mighty mountain-tops
To seek a city's sacred walls, once deemed
Worthy of God as guest to worshippers
And holy prophets. There he set his feet
Upon the temple's topmost pinnacle,
A spire that soared above the frosty clouds.
Standing beside him there, the wily Devil
Begins with gentle words and friendship feigned
While he conceals sheer anger in his heart:
　　"If your loud reputation has not lied
About your lineage, if you come from heaven,
Your Father's darling and most certain Son,
Hurl yourself headlong down, for this will bring
The glory of an unaccustomed deed
And a most useful pledge of fame divine.
This novelty will win the people's love
And thus your name through eager ears will spread
Among the mighty rulers of the world,
Affirming the great future of your race
And giving of yourself a sign indeed.
For God himself has given his angels charge
Concerning you, lest on a rugged spot
You hurt your foot in falling; with their hands
They will sustain your weight where'er you go."
　　Thus Behemoth had spoken, hypocrite
And liar too, corrupter of the truth
And the appropriate author of all lies.

(Lines 432–58: The Devil in his plans is as variable as Proteus)

> Meanwhile insane Ambition, greatly striving
> In purblind lust for honour, follows them
> And leads swift squadrons into battle's heat.
> Her face in beauty shines; her golden tresses
> Are billowing down her back and ivory neck.
> Hung from her shoulders is a purple cloak,
> Foreign in fashion, with abundant folds,
> Which shines with gems (that waves of ruddy water
> And Tagus with its crystal sands beget);
> This with its sparkling rays outdoes the sun,
> Outshines the stars, and cleaves the clouds with splendour,
> And beckons on the dullards who delay.
> Preëminent in radiance of face,
> She tortures humankind with love of self,
> When still they know no evil nor a heart
> Broken with flattery (such is the force
> Of this pervasive madness), but at length
> The shameless harlot mocks the men who love her
> With a fallacious hope, and in a web
> Of doom inextricable snares her wooers
> And wears them out with bitter penalties.
> Behind her, Glory walks, seen from afar
> Yet a less lasting vision of delight;
> Her wandering gleam she rarely casts below
> But high above the clouds she rears her head,
> Tramping the sterile sand with ruddy sandals
> And wildly setting steps on distant fields.

(Lines 483–513: Still other Furies join in the assault on Satan's behalf)

> Without delay – for what else could they do? –
> These furious hosts, the progeny of hell,
> Assail his head high poised among the clouds,
> The Hero's body balancing in air;
> Some beat his generous brow with boisterous wings
> And hostile uproar, some with stooping neck
> Molest his shoulders and his sacred back.
> All on his various members pitch their camp,

With one dark impulse and one will to harm,
Whether by cunning craft or open war.

(Lines 523–96: Christ's virtues enable him to sustain the attack of
the infernal crew. Ambition, as she stumbles, drops an urn full of
stinking poison that spreads heresies across the countryside and
stirs up civil war)

But still the Demon-Tempter, whose allies
Had thus been driven off in various rout,
Voices vain hopes but deep within his heart
Bears griefs that breathe out stratagems and slaughter.
Lightly he flutters in the sunny air
About the steadfast Christ and urges him
With wiles of soft, insinuating words:
"Easy it is to throw your body down,
And safe, moreover, should you cast yourself
In solitary downfall through the air;
A deed like this by God's omnipotence
Befits his offspring's name and majesty;
All other miracles by common use
Grow stale in practice and appear to be
Examples of the normal course of nature."
Scarcely had Satan ceased, the futile author
Of wicked counsels, and delayed no more,
When Christ replied:"Wherefore do you suggest
So great a sin and such a useless proof
Of whence I come, an argument forsooth
To gain God's favour? For the thing you urge
Is not beyond my strength; yet it is wrong
For a simple man to go beyond the measure
That a common rule dictates; that way alone
Is safe to follow which our God ordained.
To wish by sinful daring to depart
From the just median of earthly conduct
Will perpetrate a crime by tempting God;
For proudly trusting in one's human strength
Often brings on a lamentable end
And risk for others. Wisdom, if elated
By its own deeds, thoughtless of the Creator,
Cannot be fortunate. Why should I cast

My body forth, into the empty void,
When a due staircase grants an easy way
Down to the inner nave within the temple?"
    When Satan saw that all elusive arrows
Had failed him in his impotent defeat,
That all his shafts were spent without a wound,
That nothing had been gained by such an effort,
That his militia had not held their line
And all his grim endeavour had been thwarted,
He shook himself three times into the air
And wheeling in a spiral through the sky
With one swift glance a fiery eye he cast
Across the far-flung regions of the earth.
Then as an eagle hovers in the heights,
Urged on by hunger as he gazes down
On open fields and scans the countryside
With eyes sagacious to pursue afar
Through clouds a dove that seeks familiar streams
And having settled on the sandy shore
Then hears the stridor of descending wings
And flies to hide among the willow-boughs
And so evades her cruel enemy,
The bird of prey, frustrated in his hope
Of sudden rapine, beats with flapping wings
Upon his breast, while pangs of hunger rouse
His anger and he fills resounding hills
And woods and grassy valleys with his cries,
Even so Satan with increasing rage
Wandered the desert ways irresolute
Uncertain what to do, what wicked plans
His cunning might stir up, what arms to employ.
Nor did he long delay: he snatched up Christ,
Swathed in soft cloudy vapour, through dim woods,
And bore him to a mighty mountain-top,
A peak that touched the stars; along its ridges
Altars to serve old gods were reeking still
In a consecrated temple, where a priest,
Deformed of body, with an oblong hood,
Gave service to dark customs and dark rites.
Upon the farther slope, which fronts the realms
Of Palestinian impiety,

Dread blasphemy within its horrid shrine
Gives wicked worship to a triple monster
That assails with empty words the threefold name
Of God's own self, the eternal Three-in-One.
Out of its mouth a hundred throats and tongues
Breathe a suffusion of Egyptian poison;
Flat floors are dark beneath erected trophies;
Consuming mouths smear blood on sweating posterns
That a new dogma spreads in infamy
Through flourishing, great cities. And the sin
That mankind has committed in the body,
This in the body suffers punishment;
And thus the blasphemy of teeming tongues
Is justly paid for by a broken neck
Or amputated jaws; such tapestries
Throughout that temple's chambers make their boast.
    Scarce had the Fiend, pressing through sharpest thorns,
Taken his stand upon the lofty hill
Whence the sea spread itself and all the earth
Surrounded by its watery limits lay,
Than he began to speak, with cunning words
That sought a gentle entry to his theme,
Though doomed to failure. Yet if on the earth
Only one man were left, and that man Christ,
The Devil might have stirred his mind heroic:
"You see the greatest of all human realms,
Conspicuous on all sides, the pride and honour
Of the world's lord, the right of ruling which
Rests wholly in my hands, for they are mine
And I alone confer imperial power.
Myself, I build new destinies for nations,
Having expelled the former citizens,
Nor is there any other except me
Who can enjoy such plenitude of might.
Of all this world, established by firm law,
I shall create you lord and make you king
Over all things, if you will bend the knee,
If kneeling you adore me as your god,
Here in this very spot on which we stand."
    The Tempter spoke, and smiled, and held his peace.
But Christ confuted him in grim reply:

"Cease to build up this mounting blasphemy
So often from the malice of your breast;
Have done, and flee away, for you abuse
The Most High Name. God is threefold in one.
His Person one in three. He is the Judge
Of all the universe, and He alone
Ought to be worshipped for the majesty
With which He ruled, even before He made
All things of nothing, and a thousand shapes
Of creatures for the welfare of mankind."
    Scarce had he ceased when, glorious with gold,
A Princess cast herself before his feet –
Known among idol-throngs of ancient rites
And sponsored still by ancient auspices –
Unshaken in her zeal by Christ's grim words
And not unmindful of the primal age
When men were eager for idolatry.
When Blasphemy beheld her fawning sister
Flicker her triple tongue, she reared herself
To help in wickedness, intent on prey.
With mighty foot she tramples down the grasses
Wherever in her walk she makes her way;
And everywhere she breathes, she fouls the fruit
On laden branches and defiles the fields.
Soon the base king of Orcus through the shadows
Of a far cloud-bank spies the noxious pair,
And halts, and looking backward as he flees
With lingering step, shelters beneath a tree,
And feels new joy, a mounting surge of hope
For triumph through the help that he beholds.
    But the Hero Christ, more mighty than the Thief
Of Phlegethon's dim realm, prepared to set
A limit to the fury and the sceptre
With which he governs all created things.
The Saviour therefore summons forth a throng
Of countless soldiers radiant as fire
And urges his brave ministers to arms.
    Forthwith there shone an unexpected light
Beneath the ethereal highroad of the sky
Where the ecliptic runs; the heavens blazed
As mighty legions of angelic mould

Close-mustered in their squadrons for the fray
And thronged the topmost ridges of the hill.
    But when the Enemy beheld these troops
Come flying in the clouds and saw the mountains
Hemmed in on all sides by their serried flames,
The indignant spirit forged a sudden mist
Beneath the hollow cliff, then vanished quite
Into thin air, and with a crackling sound
Scattered a hideous stench upon the air.
Meanwhile the hellish pair, fearful in flight,
Seek hiding-places in umbrageous thickets,
Hurrying downward from the mountain-top
To where among the secret cattle-tracks
A hidden path in thickest briers lurks.
Headlong forthwith they rush to luckless caves
And hope to find a refuge. Entering in,
With vain anxiety they look to doors
Barred by a Cyclopean rock that hung
Tremendous in the portals of the cave.
But two celestial spirits came, who dared
High exploits, while they lived, to God's great glory,
When they had bravely conquered enemies
Whose hostile mouths were full of blasphemy,
And all the earth in Palestinian fields
Was saturated with Assyrian gore;
For Hezekiah, kneeling at the altar
Within God's temple, trusted in Isaiah,
Who promised him deliverance, and alone,
Without the aid of implements of war,
Blasted Rabshakeh, arrogant of speech
And trusting in the weapons of a host.
These worthies, mindful of their former fight
And victory, on the foul trail made haste,
Their bosoms girt about with golden flames;
Straightway, they tore the stubborn cliff apart,
Broke down its doors, and in the shadowy cavern
Sent flashing rays. The unexpected light
Brought terror to the pale and cowering shades,
Whose mighty outcry and vociferation
Filled the whole mountain and the soaring hills,
Even to the stars. Therefore the flaming spirits,

The foes of darkness, show their prisoners
To heaven, bound with chains of adamant.
And now, brought forth amid the regiments
Of the celestial host, the monsters stand,
Nor have the vanquished any hope at all
When earth, which opened wide its granite jaws
And drew them down into its gaping throat,
Filled all the lofty welkin with their howls
And smeared the verdant fields with livid foam.
Straightway that angel who once overturned
Foundations and the reeling walls of Aphek,
Involving long ago amid the ruins
Two score and seven thousand Syrians
And two and thirty kings whose troops had joined
With bold Benhadad in his doomed campaign,
Felt ancient rage revive within his heart.
Without delay, while Furies quaked in vain,
The avenging Christ beset their impious flanks,
Raised them from out the stony deeps of earth
Through rocks and through the air above the hills
That soared on high, then hurled them headlong down
Into the valley, where he choked the breath
Out of their throats, and slew his enemies.

PR-17 (English)

EDMUND SPENSER. *The Faerie Queene*. London, 1590. Book II, Canto vii

Begins: As pilot well expert in perilous wave,
        That to a stedfast starre his course hath bent ...
  Ends: The life did flit away out of her nest,
        And all his senses were with deadly fit opprest.

The temptation of Sir Guyon, the knight of "Temperaunce," by
Mammon, "god of the world and worldlings," has long been recog-
nized as a palpable analogue of the threefold temptation of Christ
in *Paradise Regained*. Over fifty years ago, Edwin Greenlaw affirmed
in *Studies in Philology* (No. XIV, 1917, 205) that "the three days of
temptation of Guyon conclude a series of incidents that pretty certainly influenced *Paradise Regained* – Mammon's proffer of riches,

worldly power, fame; the three days without sleep or food, followed by exhaustion; the angel sent to care for Guyon after the trial is over; even the debates between Mammon and Guyon, which parallel Christ's rebukes of Satan."Spenser treats Guyon as a purely human figure, allegedly idealized as the embodiment of one of Aristotle's moral virtues in the *Nicomachean Ethics* (cf. Co-22, last paragraph), a virtue (temperance) for which Spenser's Guyon is praised by name in Milton's *Areopagitica*.

Exact parallels with Milton and the New Testament are hard to find, except in the initial setting in"wide Wastfull ground"in a"desert wildernesse."The temptation on the pinnacle of the temple is omitted and the nearest approach to the stones-to-bread temptation comes at the very end, where Mammon urges Guyon to pluck the golden apples of Proserpine and to sit down on her silver stool"to rest thy weary person in the shadow coole."The mountain-top temptation of the kingdoms of the world becomes the subterranean offer of Mammon's gold (and ultimately of his daughter) as a means of satisfying all ambitions at the price of subservience to the Tempter. The changes are rung on this enticement, first in the"gloomy glade" and then successively in the"House of Richesse,"the devils' smelter, the throne-room of Philotime, and"the Gardin of Proserpina."No opportunity is missed to elaborate the mighty series of descriptions, not least in the reminiscences of Vergil's *Ibant obscuri sola sub nocte per umbram*,[8] as Guyon and his guide walk down to the underworld by"a darksome way .../That deep descended through the hollow ground/And was with dread and horror compassed round."Spenser, like Milton, greatly expands the interchange of argument between the Tempter and the Tempted.

John M. Major[9] argues convincingly for an equal influence from Book 1 of the *Faerie Queene*. Thus he shows an identical rhetorical pattern, especially through the use of anaphora, in Spenser's description of the fall of the dragon (1, xi, 54) and Milton's description of the fall of Satan (*P.R.*, iv, 560–81). In Spenser's allegory, moreover, the Red Cross Knight (as Northrop Frye[10] has pointed out) is the conventional mediaeval symbol of Christ"as a dragon-killer,"and his victory over the dragon represents Christ's restoration of mankind to its ancient inheritance in Paradise. Christ's three temptations have

8 *Aeneid*, vi, 268
9 John M. Major,"*Paradise Regained* and Spenser's Legend of Holiness,"
   Renaissance Quarterly, xx, 4, 465–70
10 Northrop Frye, *The Return of Eden* (Toronto, 1965), pp. 119, 125

their parallels in Spenser: (i) Despair's temptation to distrust, (ii) the encounter with Lucifera, as the temptation of the kingdoms, and (iii) the attack through violence, in the case of the dragon's onslaught, and even the carrying aloft in the air of knight and horse. Other parallels pointed out by Major are the "aged man in Rural weeds" (P.R., i, 314) who resembles Archimago; the "woody maze" in which Christ has been wandering (P.R. ii, 245–6), which resembles Spenser's "wandring wood"; and the final celebration and feasting after victory.

PR-18 (English)

GILES FLETCHER, THE YOUNGER. *Christs Victorie and Triumph.* London, 1610 Part II. "Christs Victorie on Earth." Printed below in full

Begins: Thear all alone she spi'd, alas the while;
           In shadie darknes a poore Desolate ...
Ends: But now our Lord to rest doth homewards flie:
           See how the Night comes stealing from the mountains high.

This is the exuberant Early Baroque creation of a youth of twenty-two. The prosody and vocabulary, and even some of the set-pieces (Cave of Despaire, Garden of Vaine-Delight), are a close adaptation of Spenser; but, whereas the temptation of Guyon is concentrated on gold and its potential gifts, almost everything in Fletcher's version is rendered in terms of sex. Christ is a pastiche of aspects borrowed from the lover in *The Song of Solomon*: he has black hair, crisped in little curls; he has "cheekes as snowie apples, sop't in wine"; and his legs are "two white marble pillars ... vein'd euery whear with azure rivulets." Just prior to the temptation, a luscious female angel, Mercie, accompanied by "a thousand Loues," melts softly "into his brest that wearie lay." Apart from brief suggestions by an *Archimago redivivus* that a stone be turned into bread and that they rest for the night in the Cave of Despaire, the temptations are all given an erotic slant. Above the pinnacles of the temple, a temptress, Presumption, has spread her pavilion. She has a painted face, is surrounded by "a lewd throng of wanton boyes," and assures Christ that "any other shee disdeign'd to wive." But "when she saw her speech preuailed nought, Her selfe she tumbled headlong to the flore." The next scene shifts to "the bowre of Vaine-Delight," which is itself described as a fair lady "that lay as if shee slumber'd in delight." Its mistress, Panglorie, is presented as a voluptuous blend of Acrasia, Circe, and Philotime. She tries to seduce Christ with a "wooing song," whose amorous refrain is "Only bend thy knee to me,/ Thy wooeing shall thy winning be." Rejected by her intended victim, "with her Syre to hell shee tooke her flight." The victor is sent a banquet from heaven, and is supplied with dinner music by massed choirs of angels and birds.

There is no confrontation between two "mighty opposites," as in Milton and the *New Testament*. There is not even the intellectual unity of the argument between Mammon and Guyon. The young rector of Alderton seems more intent on using a succession of erotic pictures in order to secure a maximum of titillation.

Mammon's temptation of Guyon was sculptured by Spenser out of polychrome marble; Milton's *Paradise Regained* was quarried from Aberdeen granite; Fletcher's *Christs Victorie* was moulded out of Turkish delight.

Christs Victorie on Earth

1

Thear all alone she spi'd, alas the while;
In shadie darknes a poore Desolate,
That now had measur'd many a wearie mile,
Through a wast desert, whither heau'nly fate,
And his owne will him brought; he praying sate,
  And him to prey, as he to pray began,
  The Citizens of the wilde forrest ran,
And all with open throat would swallowe whole the man.

2

Soone did the Ladie to her Graces crie,
And on their wings her selfe did nimbly strowe,
After her coach a thousand Loues did flie,
So downe into the wildernesse they throwe,
Whear she, and all her trayne that with her flowe
  Thorough the ayrie waue, with sayles so gay,
  Sinking into his brest that wearie lay,
Made shipwracke of themselues, and vanish't quite away.

3

Seemed that Man had them deuoured all,
Whome to deuoure the beasts did make pretence,
But him their saluage thirst did nought appall,
Though weapons none he had for his defence:
What armes for Innocence, but Innocence?
      For when they saw their Lords bright cognizance
      Shine in his face, soone did they disadvaunce,
And some vnto him kneele, and some about him daunce.

4

Downe fell the Lordly Lions angrie mood,
And he himselfe fell downe, in congies lowe;
Bidding him welcome to his wastfull wood,
Sometime he kist the grasse whear he did goe,
And, as to wash his feete he well did knowe,
      With fauning tongue he lickt away the dust,
      And euery one would neerest to him thrust,
And euery one, with new, forgot his former lust.

5

Vnmindfull of himselfe, to minde his Lord,
The Lamb stood gazing by the Tygers side,
As though betweene them they had made accord,
And on the Lions back the goate did ride,
Forgetfull of the roughnes of the hide,
      If he stood still, their eyes vpon him bayted,
      If walk't, they all in order on him wayted,
And when he slep't, they as his watch themselues conceited.

6

Wonder doeth call me vp to see, O no,
I cannot see, and therefore sinke in woonder,
The man, that shines as bright as God, not so,
For God he is himselfe, that close lies vnder
That man, so close, that no time can dissunder
      That band, yet not so close, but from him breake
      Such beames, as mortall eyes are all too weake
Such sight to see, or it, if they should see, to speake.

7

Vpon a grassie hillock he was laid,
With woodie primroses befreckeled,
Ouer his head the wanton shadowes plaid
Of a wilde oliue, that her bowgh's so spread,
As with her leav's she seem'd to crowne his head,
    And her greene armes to'embrace the Prince of peace,
    The Sunne so neere, needs must the winter cease,
The Sunne so neere, another Spring seem'd to increase.

8

His haire was blacke, and in small curls did twine,
As though it wear the shadowe of some light,
And vnderneath his face, as day, did shine,
But sure the day shined not halfe so bright,
Nor the Sunnes shadowe made so darke a night.
    Vnder his louely locks, her head to shroude,
    Did make Humilitie her selfe growe proude,
Hither, to light their lamps, did all the Graces croude.

9

One of ten thousand soules I am, and more,
That of his eyes, and their sweete wounds complaine,
Sweete are the wounds of loue, neuer so sore,
Ah moght he often slaie mee so againe.
He neuer liues, that thus is neuer slaine.
    What boots it watch? those eyes, for all my art,
    Mine owne eyes looking on, haue stole my heart,
In them Loue bends his bowe, and dips his burning dart.

10

As when the Sunne, caught in an aduerse clowde,
Flies cross the world, and thear a new begets,
The watry picture of his beautie proude,
Throwes all abroad his sparkling spangelets,
And the whole world in dire amazement sets,
    To see two dayes abroad at once, and all
    Doubt whither nowe he rise, or nowe will fall:
So flam'd the Godly flesh, proude of his heau'nly thrall.

11

His cheekes as snowie apples, sop't in wine,
Had their red roses quencht with lillies white,
And like to garden strawberries did shine,
Wash't in a bowle of milke, or rose-buds bright
Vnbosoming their brests against the light:
    Here loue-sicke soules did eat, thear dranke, and made
    Sweete-smelling posies, that could neuer fade,
But worldly eyes him thought more like some liuing shade.

12

For laughter neuer look't vpon his browe,
Though in his face all smiling ioyes did bide,
No silken banners did about him flowe,
Fooles make their fetters ensignes of their pride:
He was best cloath'd when naked was his side,
    A Lambe he was, and wollen fleece he bore,
    Woue with one thread, his feete lowe sandalls wore,
But bared were his legges, so went the time of yore.

13

As two white marble pillars that vphold
Gods holy place whear he in glorie sets,
And rise with goodly grace and courage bold,
To beare his Temple on their ample ietts,
Vein'd euery whear with azure rivulets,
    Whom all the people on some holy morne,
    With boughs and flowrie garlands doe adorne,
Of such, though fairer farre, this Temple was vpborne.

14

Twice had Diana bent her golden bowe,
And shot from heau'n her siluer shafts, to rouse
The sluggish saluages, that den belowe,
And all the day in lazie couert drouze,
Since him the silent wildernesse did house,
    The heau'n his roofe, and arbour harbour was,
    The ground his bed, and his moist pillowe grasse.
But fruit thear none did growe, nor riuers none did passe.

15

At length an aged Syre farre off he sawe
Come slowely footing, euerie step he guest
One of his feete he from the graue did drawe,
Three legges he had, the woodden was the best,
And all the waie he went, he euer blest
    With benedicities, and prayers store,
    But the bad ground was blessed ne'r the more,
And all his head with snowe of Age was waxen hore.

16

A good old Hermit he might seeme to be,
That for deuotion had the world forsaken,
And now was trauailing some Saint to see,
Since to his beads he had himselfe betaken,
Whear all his former sinnes he might awaken,
    And them might wash away with dropping brine,
    And almes, and fasts, and churches discipline,
And dead, might rest his bones vnder the holy shrine.

17

But when he neerer came, he lowted lowe
With prone obeysance, and with curt'sie kinde,
That at his feete his head he seemd to throwe;
What needs him now another Saint to finde?
Affections are the sailes, and faith the wind,
    That to this Saint a thousand soules conueigh
    Each hour': O happy Pilgrims thither strey!
What caren they for beasts, or for the wearie way?

18

Soone the old Palmer his deuotions sung,
Like pleasing anthems, moduled in time,
For well that aged Syre could tip his tongue
With golden foyle of eloquence, and lime,
And licke his rugged speech with phrases prime.
    Ay me, quoth he, how many yeares haue beene,
    Since these old eyes the Sunne of heau'n haue seene!
Certes the Sonne of heau'n they now behold I weene.

19

Ah, mote my humble cell so blessed be
As heau'n to welcome in his lowely roofe,
And be the Temple for thy deitie!
Loe how my cottage worships thee aloofe,
That vnder ground hath hid his head, in proofe
    It doth adore thee with the seeling lowe,
    Here honie, milke, and chesnuts wild doe growe,
The boughs a bed of leaues vpon thee shall bestowe.

20

But oh, he said, and therewith sigh't full deepe,
The heau'ns, alas, too enuious are growne,
Because our fields thy presence from them keepe;
For stones doe growe, where corne was lately sowne:
(So stooping downe, he gather'd vp a stone)
    But thou with corne canst make this stone to eare.
    What needen we the angrie heau'ns to feare?
Let them enuie vs still, so we enioy thee here.

21

Thus on they wandred, but those holy weeds
A monstrous Serpent, and no man did couer.
So vnder greenest hearbs the Adder feeds:
And round about that stinking corps did houer
The dismall Prince of gloomie night, and ouer
    His euer-damned head the Shadowes err'd
    Of thousand peccant ghosts, vnseene, vnheard,
And all the Tyrant feares, and all the Tyrant fear'd.

22

He was the Sonne of blackest Acheron,
Whear many frozen soules doe chattring lie,
And rul'd the burning waues of Phlegethon,
Whear many more in flaming sulphur frie,
At once compel'd to liue and forc't to die,
    Whear nothing can be heard for the loud crie
    Of oh, and ah, and out alas that I
Or once againe might liue, or once at length might die.

23
Ere long they came neere to a balefull bowre,
Much like the mouth of that infernall caue,
That gaping stood all Commers to deuoure,
Darke, dolefull, dreary, like a greedy graue,
That still for carrion carkasses doth craue.
       The ground no hearbs, but venomous did beare,
       Nor ragged trees did leaue, but euery whear
Dead bones, and skulls wear cast, and bodies hanged wear.

24
Vpon the roofe the bird of sorrowe sat
Elonging ioyfull day with her sad note,
And through the shady aire, the fluttring bat
Did waue her leather sayles, and blindely flote,
While with her wings the fatall Shreechowle smote
       Th' vnblessed house, thear, on a craggy stone,
       Celeno hung, and made his direfull mone,
And all about the murdered ghosts did shreek, and grone.

25
Like clowdie moonshine, in some shadowie groue,
Such was the light in which DESPAIRE did dwell,
But he himselfe with night for darkenesse stroue.
His blacke vncombed locks dishevell'd fell
About his face, through which, as brands of hell,
       Sunk in his skull, his staring eyes did glowe,
       That made him deadly looke, their glimpse did showe
Like Cockatrices eyes, that sparks of poyson throwe.

26
His cloaths wear ragged clouts, with thornes pind fast,
And as he musing lay, to stonie fright
A thousand wilde Chimera's would him cast:
As when a fearefull dreame, in mid'st of night,
Skips to the braine, and phansies to the sight
       Some winged furie, strait the hasty foot,
       Eger to flie, cannot plucke vp his root,
The voyce dies in the tongue, and mouth gapes without boot.

27

Now he would dreame that he from heauen fell,
And then would snatch the ayre, afraid to fall;
And now he thought he sinking was to hell,
And then would grasp the earth, and now his stall
Him seemed hell, and then he out would crawle,
   And euer, as he crept, would squint aside,
   Lest him, perhaps, some Furie had espide,
And then, alas, he should in chaines for euer bide.

28

Therefore he softly shrunke, and stole away,
Ne euer durst to drawe his breath for feare,
Till to the doore he came, and thear he lay
Panting for breath, as though he dying were,
And still he thought, he felt their craples teare
   Him by the heels backe to his ougly denne,
   Out faine he would haue leapt abroad, but then
The heau'n, as hell, he fear'd, that punish guilty men.

29

Within the gloomie hole of this pale wight
The Serpent woo'd him with his charmes to inne,
Thear he might baite the day, and rest the night,
But vnder that same baite a fearefull grin
Was readie to intangle him in sinne.
   But he vpon ambrosia daily fed,
   That grew in Eden, thus he answered,
So both away wear caught, and to the Temple fled.

30

Well knewe our Sauiour this the Serpent was,
And the old Serpent knewe our Sauiour well,
Neuer did any this in falshood passe,
Neuer did any him in truth excell:
With him we fly to heau'n, from heau'n we fell
   With him: but nowe they both together met
   Vpon the sacred pinnacles, that threat
With their aspiring tops, Astraeas starrie seat.

31
Here did PRESVMPTION her pauillion spread,
Ouer the Temple, the bright starres among,
(Ah that her foot should trample on the head
Of that most reuerend place!) and a lewd throng
Of wanton boyes sung her a pleasant song
    Of loue, long life, of mercie and of grace,
    And euery one her deerely did embrace,
And she herselfe enamour'd was of her owne face.

32
A painted face, belied with vermeyl store,
Which light Euëlpis euery day did trimme,
That in one hand a guilded anchor wore,
Not fixed on the rocke, but on the brimme
Of the wide aire she let it loosely swimme:
    Her other hand a sprinkle carried,
    And euer, when her Ladie wauered,
Court-holy water all vpon her sprinkeled.

33
Poore foole, she thought herselfe in wondrous price
With God, as if in Paradise she wear,
But wear shee not in a fooles paradise,
She might haue seene more reason to despere:
But him she, like some ghastly fiend, did feare,
    And therefore as that wretch hew'd out his cell
    Vnder the bowels, in the heart of hell,
So she aboue the Moone, amid the starres would dwell.

34
Her Tent with sunny cloudes was seel'd aloft,
And so exceeding shone with a false light,
That heau'n it selfe to her it seemed oft,
Heau'n without cloudes to her deluded sight,
But cloudes withouten heau'n it was aright,
    And as her house was built, so did her braine
    Build castles in the aire, with idle paine,
But heart she neuer had in all her body vaine.

35

Like as a ship, in which no ballance lies,
Without a Pilot, on the sleeping waues,
Fairely along with winde, and water flies,
And painted masts with silken sayles embraues,
That Neptune selfe the bragging vessell saues,
    To laugh a while at her so proud aray;
    Her wauing streamers loosely shee lets play,
And flagging colours shine as bright as smiling day:

36

But all so soone as heau'n his browes doth bend,
Shee veils her banners, and pulls in her beames,
The emptie barke the raging billows send
Vp to th' Olympique waues, and Argus seemes
Again to ride vpon our lower streames:
    Right so PRESVMPTION did her selfe behaue,
    Tossed about with euery stormie waue,
And in white lawne she went, most like an Angel braue.

37

Gently our Sauiour shee began to shrive,
Whither he wear the Sonne of God, or no:
For any other shee disdeign'd to wive:
And if he wear, shee bid him fearles throw
Himselfe to ground, and thearwithall did show
    A flight of little Angels, that did wait
    Vpon their glittering wings, to latch him strait,
And longed on their backs to feele his glorious weight.

38

But when she saw her speech preuailed nought,
Her selfe she tombled headlong to the flore:
But him the Angels on their feathers caught,
And to an ayrie mountaine nimbly bore,
Whose snowie shoulders, like some chaulkie shore,
    Restles Olympus seem'd to rest vpon
    With all his swimming globes: so both are gone,
The Dragon with the Lamb. Ah, vnmeet Paragon.

39

All suddenly the hill his snowe deuours,
In liew whereof a goodly garden grew,
As if the snow had melted into flow'rs,
Which their sweet breath in subtill vapours threw,
That all about perfumed spirits flew.
    For what so euer might aggrate the sense,
    In all the world, or please the appetence,
Heer it was powred out in lavish affluence.

40

Not louely Ida might with this compare,
Though many streames his banks besiluered,
Though Xanthus with his golden sands he bare,
Nor Hibla, though his thyme depastured,
As fast againe with honie blossomed.
    Ne Rhodope, ne Tempes flowrie playne,
    Adonis garden was to this but vayne,
Though Plato on his beds a flood of praise did rayne.

41

For in all these, some one thing most did grow,
But in this one, grey all things els beside,
For sweet varietie herselfe did throw
To euery banke, her all the ground she dide
In lillie white, there pinks eblazed wide;
    And damask't all the earth, and here shee shed
    Blew violets, and there came roses red,
And euery sight the yeelding sense, as captiue led.

42

The garden like a Ladie faire was cut,
That lay as if shee slumber'd in delight,
And to the open skies her eyes did shut;
The azure fields of heau'n wear sembled right
In a large round, set with the flowr's of light,
    The flowr's-de-luce, and the round sparks of deaw,
    That hung vpon their azure leaues, did shew
Like twinkling starrs, that sparkle in th' eau'ning blew.

43

Vpon a hillie banke her head shee cast,
On which the bowre of Vaine-Delight was built,
White, and red roses for her face wear plac't,
And for her tresses Marigolds wear spilt:
Them broadly shee displaid, like flaming guilt,
   Till in the ocean the glad day wear drown'd,
   Then vp againe her yellow locks she wound,
And with greene fillets in their prettie calls them bound.

44

What should I here depeint her lillie hand,
Her veines of violets, her ermine brest,
Which thear in orient colours liuing stand,
Or how her gowne with silken leaues is drest;
Or how her watchmen, arm'd with boughie crest,
   A wall of prim hid in his bushes bears,
   Shaking at euery winde their leauie spears,
While she supinely sleeps, ne to be waked fears?

45

Ouer the hedge depends the graping Elme,
Whose greener head, empurpuled in wine,
Seemed to wonder at his bloodie helme,
And halfe suspect the bunches of the vine,
Least they, perhaps, his wit should vndermine.
   For well he knewe such fruit he neuer bore:
   But her weake armes embraced him the more,
And with her ruby grapes laught at her paramour.

46

Vnder the shadowe of these drunken elmes
A Fountaine rose, where Pangloretta vses,
(When her some flood of fancie ouerwhelms,
And one of all her fauourites she chuses)
To bath herselfe, whom she in lust abuses,
   And from his wanton body sucks his soule,
   Which drown'd in pleasure, in that shaly bowle,
And swimming in delight, doth amarously rowle.

47

The font of siluer was, and so his showrs
In siluer fell, onely the guilded bowles
(Like to a fornace, that the min'rall powres)
Seem't to haue moul't it in their shining holes:
And on the water, like to burning coles,
    On liquid siluer, leaues of roses lay:
    But when PANGLORIE here did list to play,
Rose water then it ranne, and milke it rain'd they say.

48

The roofe thicke cloudes did paint, from which three boyes
Three gaping mermaids with their eawrs did feede,
Whose brests let fall the streame, with sleepie noise,
To Lions mouths, from whence it leapt with speede,
And in the rosie lauer seem'd to bleed.
    The naked boyes vnto the waters fall,
    Their stonie nightingales had taught to call,
When Zephyr breath'd into their watry interall.

49

And all about, embayed in soft sleepe,
A heard of charmed beasts aground wear spread,
Which the faire Witch in goulden chaines did keepe,
And them in willing bondage fettered,
Once men they liu'd, but now the men were dead,
    And turn'd to beasts, so fabled Homer old,
    That Circe, with her potion, charm'd in gold,
Vs'd manly soules in beastly bodies to immould.

50

Through this false Eden, to his Lemans bowre,
(Whome thousand soules deuoutly idolize)
Our first destroyer led our Sauiour.
Thear in the lower roome, in solemne wise,
They daunc't a round, and powr'd their sacrifice
    To plumpe Lyaeus, and among the rest,
    The iolly Priest, in yuie garlands drest,
Chaunted wild Orgialls, in honour of the feast.

51

Others within their arbours swilling sat,
(For all the roome about was arboured)
With laughing Bacchus, that was growne so fat,
That stand he could not, but was carried,
And euery euening freshly watered,
    To quench his fierie cheeks, and all about
    Small cocks broke through the wall, and sallied out
Flaggons of wine, to set on fire that spueing rout.

52

This their inhumed soules esteem'd their wealths,
To crowne the bouzing kan from day to night,
And sicke to drinke themselues with drinking healths,
Some vomiting, all drunken with delight.
Hence to a loft, carv'd all in yvorie white,
    They came, whear whiter Ladies naked went,
    Melted in pleasure, and soft languishment,
And sunke in beds of roses, amorous glaunces sent.

53

Flie, flie thou holy child that wanton roome,
And thou my chaster Muse those harlots shun,
And with him to a higher storie come,
Whear mounts of gold, and flouds of siluer run,
The while the owners, with their wealth vndone,
    Starve in their store, and in their plentie pine,
    Tumbling themselues vpon their heaps of mine,
Glutting their famish't soules with the deceitfull shine.

54

Ah, who was he such pretious perills found?
How strongly Nature did her treasures hide;
And threw vpon them mountains of thicke ground,
To darke their orie lustre; but queint Pride
Hath taught her Sonnes to wound their mothers side,
    And gage the depth, to search for flaring shells,
    In whose bright bosome spumie Bacchus swells,
That neither heau'n, nor earth henceforth in safetie dwells.

55

A sacred hunger of the greedie eye,
Whose neede hath end, but no end covetise,
Emptie in fulnes, rich in pouertie,
That hauing all things, nothing can suffice,
How thou befanciest the men most wise?
    The poore man would be rich, the rich man great,
    The great man King, the King, in Gods owne seat
Enthron'd, with mortal arme dares flames, and thunder threat.

56

Therefore aboue the rest Ambition sat:
His Court with glitterant pearle was all enwall'd,
And round about the wall in chaires of State,
And most maiestique splendor, wear enstall'd
A hundred Kings, whose temples wear impal'd
    In goulden diadems, set here, and thear
    With diamounds, and gemmed euery whear.
And of their golden virges none disceptred wear.

57

High ouer all, *Panglories* blazing throne,
In her bright turret, all of christall wrought,
Like Phoebus lampe in midst of heauen, shone:
Whose starry top, with pride infernall fraught,
Selfe-arching columns to vphold wear taught:
    In which, her Image still reflected was
    By the smooth christall, that most like her glasse,
In beautie, and in frailtie, did all others passe.

58

A Siluer wande the sorceresse did sway,
And, for a crowne of gold, her haire she wore,
Onely a garland of rosebuds did play
About her locks, and in her hand, she bore
A hollowe globe of glasse, that long before,
    She full of emptinesse had bladdered,
    And all the world therein depictured,
Whose colours, like the rainebowe, euer vanished.

59
Such watry orbicles young boyes doe blowe
Out from their sopy shells, and much admire
The swimming world, which tenderly they rowe
With easie breath, till it be waued higher,
But if they chaunce but roughly once aspire,
    The painted bubble instantly doth fall.
    Here when she came, she gan for musique call,
And sung this wooing song, to welcome him withall.

Loue is the blossome whear thear blowes
Euery thing, that liues, or growes,
Loue doth make the heau'ns to moue,
And the Sun doth burne in loue;
Loue the strong, and weake doth yoke,
And makes the yuie climbe the oke,
Vnder whose shadowes Lions wilde,
Soft'ned by Loue, growe tame and mild;
Loue no med'cine can appease,
He burnes the fishes in the seas,
Not all the skill his wounds can stench,
Not all the sea his fire can quench;
Loue did make the bloody spear
Once a leuie coat to wear,
While in his leaues thear shrouded lay
Sweete birds for loue, that sing, and play;
And of all loues ioyfull flame,
I the bud and blossome am.
    Onely bend thy knee to me,
    Thy wooing shall thy winning be.

See, see the flowers that belowe,
Now as fresh as morning blowe,
And of all, the virgin rose,
That as bright Aurora showes,
How they all vnleaued die,
Loosing their virginitie:
Like vnto a summer-shade,
But now borne, and now they fade.
Euery thing doth passe away,
Thear is danger in delay,

Come, come gather then the rose,
Gather it, or it you lose.
All the sande of Tagus shore
Into my bosome casts his ore;
All the valleys swimming corne
To my house is yearly borne;
Euery grape, of euery vine
Is gladly bruis'd to make me wine,
While ten thousand kings, as proud,
To carry vp my traine, haue bow'd,
And a world of Ladies send me
In my chambers to attend me:
All the starres in heau'n that shine,
And ten thousand more, are mine:
    Onely bend thy knee to mee,
    Thy wooing shall thy winning bee.

60

Thus sought the dire Enchauntress in his minde
Her guilefull bayt to haue embosomed,
But he her charmes dispersed into winde,
And her of insolence admonished,
And all her optique glasses shattered.
    So with her Syre to hell shee tooke her flight,
    (The starting ayre flew from the damned spright,)
Whear deeply both aggriev'd, plunged themselues in night.

61

But to their Lord, now musing in his thought,
A heauenly volie of light Angels flew,
And from his Father him a banquet brought,
Through the fine element, for well they knew,
After his lenten fast, he hungrie grew,
    And, as he fed, the holy quires combine
    To sing a hymne of the celestiall Trine;
All thought to passe, and each was past all thought divine.

62

The birds sweet notes, to sonnet out their ioyes,
Attemper'd to the layes Angelicall,
And to the birds, the winds attune their noyse,

And to the winds, the waters hoarcely call,
And Eccho back againe revoyced all,
    That the whole valley rung with victorie.
But now our Lord to rest doth homewards flie:
See how the Night comes stealing from the mountains high.

PR-19 (Cornish)

WILLIAM JORDAN. *Passio Domini Nostri Jhesu Christi*, 1611. In *The Ancient Cornish Drama*, ed. Edwin Norris, Oxford, 1859

Begins: JESUS
    thyvgh lauara ow dyskyblon
    pyseugh toythda ol keslon ...
Ends: the welas fetel sevys
    cryst mes a'n beth cler ha war.

The only remaining specimens of Cornish drama would appear to have been based on the common mediaeval cycles of mystery plays, but the precise originals (whether English, French, or Latin) have not been identified. While there are nominally only three plays in the Cornish series, namely, the Creation, the Passion, and the Resurrection, each of these is made up of several distinct dramatic episodes. Thus, the first 172 lines of the Passion-play deal with the Temptation of Christ by Satan, in the order given in St Matthew's Gospel. The twelve disciples are present throughout the whole ordeal, and we hear edifying comments by Peter, Andrew, John, and Bartholomew. When the angels come down to congratulate the victorious Christ, their spokesman is Gabriel. There is some uncertainty as to the identity of the author. Whitley Stokes thinks that the "William Jordan" who signs the 1611 manuscript may have been only its transcriber and that the dramatic poem may have originated very much earlier.

PR-20 (English)

ROBERT AYLETT. *Joseph, or Pharaoh's Favourite.* 1623

Begins: Now dwelt the holy Patriarch Israel
         At rest, in Canaan, in his father's cell ...
  Ends: Unworthy Aegypt! of this sacred Urne,
         Who such rewards for merits dost return.

A demonstration of the Book of Job as a model for the brief epic is furnished by Aylett's five-book, 2950-line poem, *Joseph*, written in heroic couplets. His central character is Jacob (Israel), who is first portrayed like Job in the days of his primal prosperity. Satan secures permission from God to test this perfect man; and there follow the apparent deaths of his favourite sons, Joseph and Benjamin, and the acute distress that he suffers from famine.

PR-21 (Latin)

A N D R E W R A M S E Y . *Poemata Sacra.* Book IV, 143–96, "The Temptation." Edinburgh, 1633. Mi: Huntington Library

Begins: Tum loca sola petet, salebrosis invia dumis,
         Vomeris ignara, et latebris horrenda ferarum ...
  Ends: Non impune ferens, praedonem voce minaci
         Ad manes abiget, lucisque carentia regna.

This very brief (54-line) summary of the Temptation adds little to the tradition except a couple of choice epithets for Satan (*Tartareus Coluber* and *umbrarum noctisque potens*). There are no speeches, in contrast with the Vergilian *Christiad* of his fellow-Scot, Alexander Ross, who had found a good deal of *oratio recta* in the old structure from which he stole his building-stones.

PR-22 (Latin)

A L E X A N D E R R O S S . *Virgilii evangelisantis Christiados libri xiii.* London, 1638. Mi: Harvard

Begins: His actis deserta petit spelaea ferarum:
         Hic inter vastas rupes atque horrida lustra ...
  Ends: At Christus Victor manet imperterritus, hostem
         Immanem virtute fugans, et mole sua stat.

In this jigsaw cento of *Thirteen Books of the Christiad of Evangelizing Vergil*, we have a life of Christ patched together in some 13,000 hexameter lines, mostly borrowed from Vergil. The Temptation occurs in Book VIII, lines 589–674. Satan assumes the disguise of a squalid old man with a long, white beard and fiery eyes, a description that Ross simply lifted from Vergil's portrayal of Charon (*Aeneid*, VI, 299–301). His synthetic epic had to be made up of quotations from Vergil, and it is to this process, rather than to any forcible originality of imagination, that this unusual conception of Satan's disguise is due.

PR-23 (English)

JOSEPH BEAUMONT. *Psyche, or Love's Mystery, in* XXIV *Cantos: Displaying the Intercourse Betwixt Christ and the Soul.* London, 1648. Mi: Yale

Begins: Enrag'd at Heav'n and Psyche, Satan laies
　　　　His projects to beguile the tender maid ...
　Ends: That She, unable to contain its Tide,
　　　　With three deep sighs cry'd out O LOVE, and dy'd.

An elegy by Joseph Beaumont was among the 32 poems that accompanied *Lycidas* in the *Obsequies to the Memorie of Mr. Edward King* (1638, see Ly-101). In his later epic, he presents Psyche (the human soul) as undergoing trials very similar to those of Job. Satan comes to a council in heaven; Christ praises the piety of Psyche; and Satan seeks permission to test her. The tribulations that then befall her include the loss of all her possessions, the death of friends, a malady resembling Job's boils, and the nagging exhortations of false "comforters." In Canto IX of *Psyche*, Satan denounces the emperor Tiberius for his evil rule and offers his place to Christ (cf. *Paradise Regained*, IV, 90–102).

PR-24 (Latin)

HENRY OXENDEN. *Jobus Triumphans.* [London], 1656. Mi: Yale

Begins: Insignem pietate virum, famulumque Jehovae

(Cujus per totum nota patientia mundum) ...
Ends: Dum rutilans Aurora diem, noctemque silentem
Roscida mobilibus lustrabit Cynthia bigis.

A prime example of "that Epick form whereof ... the book of Job [is]
a brief model" is this Latin epic (766 hexameters) by Henry Oxenden
(1609–1670), a graduate of Corpus Christi College, Oxford, in 1627,
two years before Milton took his BA at Cambridge. In it, all the
grandiloquent diction of neo-classical epic, and all its standard formulas of action and address, are carefully worked out. Job is "Phoenix
of men, model of true virtue, unvanquished King and Martyr, vera-
cious Prophet, dauntless antagonist of the Devil, Conqueror of Hell
and Victor over the [diabolic] Tyrant."

PR-25 (English)

ANDREW MARVELL. *A dialogue between the resolved soul and created
pleasure.* First available in *Miscellaneous Poems*, 1681, British Museum.
Also in George Lord's edition (Modern Library)

Begins: Courage my soul! now learn to wield
The weight of thine immortal shield ...
Ends: (CHORUS)
The rest does lie beyond the pole,
And is thine everlasting store.

While this poem by Andrew Marvell (1621–1678), Milton's younger
contemporary and close friend, was not published before his posthumous *Miscellaneous Poems*, its composition, like that of nearly
all his lyric poetry, would almost certainly come from his early years
and hence lie well within the chronological limits imposed upon the
present volume (see p. xii). Its 78 lines marshal in miniature the
series of temptations written out large in *Paradise Regained*. After
a 10-line soliloquized presentation of the knight in Christian armour
facing a seductive army "with silken banners," there follow five brief
interchanges between Pleasure and the Soul, and then a 6-line chorus
(apparently of angels), four more interchanges, and finally a second
triumphant chorus of angels. Easily recognizable are (a) the temptation of a Lucullan feast, lines 11–16, (b) the temptation of wealth,
lines 59–60, (c) the temptations of martial or civic glory, lines 63–6,

and (d) the temptation of knowledge, lines 69–72. The Soul's rebuttal usually comes in a terse rhymed couplet in iambic tetrameter. In the case of two poets so intimately associated as Milton and Marvell, the possibility of interinfluence is very real.

 APPENDIXES AND INDEXES

APPENDIX A: ON METRE

A brief note on prosody will not be irrelevant. In the pastoral elegy in Greek and Latin (classical, mediaeval, and Renaissance), the invariable metre is the dactylic hexameter, and the same is true of epic narrative, as in the *Odyssey* and the *Aeneid*. The uniformity of prosodic texture is more apparent than real. While the hexameter has a prosodic infrastructure of six feet, the last two unchanging (dactyl and spondee) and the first four varied by modulation between dactyl and spondee, the whole is overlaid by a syntactical superstructure that intermittently overruns the metrical base. The metre and the syntax are thus placed in counterpoint; and part of the living variety of Homer's verse, or of Vergil's, lies in the tension between the two.[1] In Homer's *Odyssey*, Book IX, there are 158 enjambments in the 574 lines; in Vergil's *Aeneid*, Book I, the sense runs on in 302 lines out of 755, often in bursts of three or four as the narrative tempo is speeded up. In Vergil's *Eclogue* X, however, there are only 16 run-on lines out of 76, while in the dignified and oracular *Eclogue* IV there are only 12 out of 60. In Theocritus' *Daphnis*, there are 26 out of 70 in the dialogue, but only 11 out of 82 in the *Song of Thyrsis*, where the rhythms of emotion tend towards single-moulded lines, each emphatic in its own right. The difference in Vergil between his pastorals and his epic could be due to his using Theocritus as his model for the former and Homer as his model for the latter.[2] Even the pattern of the caesura can vary as between pastoral and epic. Since enjambment makes for rapidity of flow, one can understand why Bentley, looking at the end-stopped couplets of Pope's translation, could say (for this, as well as other reasons) "you must not call it Homer."

The non-pastoral elegiac verse of Ovid, Tibullus, and Propertius uses the elegiac couplet (a hexameter plus two half-pentameters). In the Latin prose dream, *Comus*, by Puteanus, the deity Comus sings a seductive 95-line song in Anacreontics (spondee-amphibrach-spondee). As the Renaissance pastoral elegy turned to the vernaculars, we find the emergence of *terza rima* (Sannazaro, but refined by Dante two centuries earlier out of Provençal forerunners), blank verse (Alamanni, but first used in Italian drama, a few years earlier, by Trissino, and actually evolved from the

1 For similar tension between metre and syntax in *canzone*-measure, see p. 220.
2 It could also imply, as in the evolution of Shakespeare's blank verse, a measure of its change as he increased in maturity and in fluidity of style. Incidentally, M. Marjorie Crump, in *The Epyllion from the Theocritus to Ovid* (1931), pp. 265–70, shows that "Vergil's early work contains a considerably larger number of dactylic lines than do the poems of his maturity." In the *Eclogues*, dactyls exceed spondees in 25.1 per cent of the lines and in the *Aeneid* in 19.1 per cent.

iambric senarius of Greek and Latin tragedy), canzone-measure (Sanna-zaro, following its earlier non-pastoral use by Dante and Petrarch), heroic quatrains (Marot), and heroic couplets (Ronsard in elegy, but familiar for narrative purposes in Chaucer and his fourteenth-century French con-temporaries). The Old English *Christ and Satan* used the Ur-Teutonic alliterative line.

Since, as Saintsbury pointed out over sixty years ago, neither the clas-sical hexameter nor the elegiac couplet (whether based on quantity or on accent) fits naturally into English prosody, the translator into English turns most readily to various uses of the five-foot iambic line, as in blank verse (which tends to lack pattern), heroic couplets (which are often exces-sively patterned, especially in the closed type), heroic quatrains, canzone-measure, *terza rima*, *ottava rima*, Spenserians, and other stanza forms.

I have used interwoven rhymes in pentameters for the long songs in Theocritus'[3] *Daphnis* and Vergil's *Daphnis*, for Bion, Nemesian and Castiglione, and for the whole of Vergil's *Gallus*. Enjambed heroic qua-trains have been used for the Ishtar-episode in *Gilgamesh*. At a later stage, blank verse (unrhymed iambic pentameters) is used for the Latin hexameters of Strasburgus, Vida, Sannazaro's *Phyllis*, Petrarch's *Eclogue* VI, and the *Two Nuns* of Radbertus, for the mingled *endecasyllabi sciolti* and *settinari* of a speech by Dafne in Act I of Tasso's *Aminta*, and for the unrhymed Italian Alexandrines of Alamanni's *Eclogue* I. Alliterative measures (in a looser adaptation more suited to the texture and syntax of Modern English) have been employed for the Old English *Christ and Satan*; accentual elegiac couplets have been used for the same quantita-tive metre in Propertius' lament for drowned Paetus; and *terza rima* is used for the same metre in extracts from Dante's *Inferno* and *Paradiso*, as well as in Sannazaro's *Mammilia*. My version of Gager's *Daphnis* uses an approximation to canzone-measure. For the Anacreontics of Comus's song in Puteanus, I have used rhymed octosyllabics as the nearest viable English equivalent. In nearly all cases where other men's prose versions are avail-able, these have been listed for the use of scholars. In two instances only have I printed other men's *verse* translations, namely Aurelian Town-shend's version of Beaujoyeulx (Co-19) and excerpts by Hobbes, Cowper, Chapman, Pope, and Morris in the Circe-story from Homer (Co-4), and in this latter case I have extended the diversity of treatment still further by adding one extract of my own in epic hexameters.

3 In the case of the Greek bucolic poets, since the Greek originals are less
   accessible (or familiar) to the student of today, I have added my own
   literal prose to my interwoven rhymed pentameters for the *Song of
   Thyrsis* (in Theocritus' *Daphnis*) and Bion's *Lament for Adonis*, and
   have used the near prose of run-on blank verse for the dialogue in the
   Daphnis and for the whole of Theocritus' *Harvest Home* and Moschus'
   Lament for Bion.

APPENDIX B: BIBLICAL EPICS

Note: In the notes appended to individual titles below, the following bibliographical abbreviations have been used:

RAS R.A. Sayce, *The French Biblical Epic in the Seventeenth Century* (Oxford, 1955)

BKL Barbara Kiefer Lewalski, *Milton's Brief Epic* (Providence & London, 1966)

LBC Lily Bess Campbell, *Divine Poetry and Drama in Sixteenth Century England* (Berkeley, 1955)

MTM Maudy Thibaut de Maisières, *Les Poèmes Inspirés du Début de la Genèse a l'Époque de la Renaissance* (Louvain, 1931)

WKCC Watson Kirkconnell, *The Celestial Cycle* (Toronto, 1952)

WKIS Watson Kirkconnell, *That Invincible Samson* (Toronto, 1964)

All these reference works are closely indexed. In the lists below, the number of "books" into which an epic is subdivided is indicated by a Roman numeral and the approximate number of lines in the poem by an Arabic numeral.

CREATION, FALL OF ANGELS AND OF MAN
Of the 329 analogues listed in my *Celestial Cycle* there are some 81 that might be classified as biblical epics – 36 dealing with the Creation (often plus the Fall), 26 with the Fall (often plus the Atonement), 5 with the Revolt of the Angels, and 14 with a general range of action from Creation to Doomsday. The rest of the volume is taken up with prose hexamera, dramas, histories, satires, epigrams, dream-allegories, hymns, theological treatises, novels, and lyric poems. While the reader is referred to the *Celestial Cycle* itself for a complete survey, the following epics are suggested for special consideration:
Sedulius (Caelius), *Carmen Paschale* (*ca.* 430). BKL, WKCC. IV, 1769
Victor (Claudius Marius), *Alethias, sive Commentariorum in Genesin Libri* III (*ca.* 430). MTM, BKL, WKCC. III, 2020
Avitus (Alcimus Ecdicius), *Poematum de Mosaicae historiae gestis Libri* V (501). MTM, BKL, WKCC. V, 2552
Odo of Cluny, *Occupatio* (*ca.* 900). BKL. VII, 5560
Saluste (Guillaume de, seigneur du Bartas), *La Sepmaine, ou Création* (1578). MTM, LBC, RAS, BKL, WKCC. VII, 6500
Saluste (Guillaume de, seigneur du Bartas), *La Seconde Semaine* (1584). MTM, LBC, RAS, BKL, WKCC. IV, incomplete
Valvasone (Erasmo di), *L'Angeleida* (1590). MTM, RAS, BKL, WKCC. III, 3000

Tasso (Torquato), *Le sette giornate del mondo creato* (1592).   RAS, BKL,
WKCC, MTM. VII, 8500
Taubmannus (Fredericus), *Bellum Angelicum* (1604).   BKL, WKCC. III, 1225
Sylvester (Joshua), *Du Bartas His Divine Weekes and Workes* (1592–
1604).   BKL, WKCC. 23,500
Fletcher (Giles the Younger), *Christs Victorie and Triumph* (1610).
BKL, WKCC. IV, 2120
Sanguinet (Estiene de), *La Dodécade de L'Évangile* (1614).   BKL. XII,
18,150
Mellius de Sousa (Joannes), *De miseria hominis deque reparatione humana
carmen* (1615).   BKL, WKCC. VIII, 8600
Rolim de Moura (Francisco Child), *Os novissimos do homem* (1623).
WKCC. IV, 2856
D'Argent (Abel), *La Sepmaine* (1629).   BKL. VII, *ca.* 8000
Ramsey (Andrew), *Poemata sacra* (1633).   BKL, WKCC. IV, 1660
Pordage (Samuel), *Mundorum Explicatio* (1661).   WKCC. II, 13,000
Saint-Martin (Sieur de), *La Nature Naissante* (1667).   BKL. I, *ca.* 700
Perrault (Charles), *Adam, ou la création de l'homme, sa chute et sa
réparation* (1697).   RAS, WKCC. IV, 1800
Reinoso (Felix Josef), *La Innocencia Perdida* (1804).   WKCC, 808

FLOOD
Avitus (Alcimus Ecdicius), Book IV in *Poematum de Mosaicae historiae
gestis libri quinque* (507).   PL-35, MTM, BKL. V, 2552
Sabie (Francis), *The Old Worlds Tragedie* (1596)
Drayton (Michael), *Noahs Floud* (1630).   BKL. I, 1025

ABRAHAM
Desmarets de Saint-Sorlin (Jean), *Abraham, ou la vie parfaite* (1680).
RAS, p. 258

JOB
Mellius de Sousa (Joannes), *In Librum Job Paraphrasis Poetica* (1615).
BKL
Adamson (Patrick), *Jobus, sive de Constantia* (1619).   BKL
Sylvester (Joshua), *Job Triumphant in his Trial* (1621).   BKL
Quarles (Francis), *Job Militant* (1624).   BKL
Aurelius (Abraham), *Jobus, sive de Patientia* (1632).   BKL
Sandys (George), *A Paraphrase upon Job* (1638, in *A Paraphrase upon
the Divine Poems*, also in 1648).   BKL
Manley (Thomas), *Affliction and Deliverance of the Saints* (1652).   BKL
DuPort (François), *Threnothriambos, sive Liber Job* (1653).   BKL
Oxenden (Henry), *Jobus Triumphans* (1656).   PR-24, BKL
Le Cordier (Hélie), *L'Illustre Souffrant, ou Job* (1667).   RAS, BKL
Morillon (dom Gatien de), *Paraphrase sur le livre de Job* (1668).   RAS, BKL

J O S E P H (son of Jacob)

L'Estoire Joseph (French, 12th century). BKL

Jacob and Joseph (English, 13th century). BKL

Anonymous, The story of Iacoby and his twelve sons (London, Wynkyn de Worde, 1510)

Fracastoro (Girolamo), Joseph (1555). RAS, BKL. II, 1280

Dolce (Lodovico), La Vita di Giuseppe (1561). RAS, BKL. III, 1900

Forest (William), History of Joseph (1569). BKL, LBC

Hunnis (William), The Life and Death of Joseph (1595). BKL, LBC

Aylett (Robert), Joseph, or Pharaoh's Favourite (1623). PR-20, BKL. V, 2950

Saint-Peres (Jean de), La Vie de Joseph (1648). RAS, BKL

Morillon (Julien-Gatien), Joseph, ou l'esclave fidèle (1679, 1705). RAS, BKL

Saint-Amant (Marc-Antoine Gérard de), Joseph et ses Frères en Égipte (1658). BKL, RAS

M O S E S

Drayton (Michael), Moyses in a Map of his Miracles (1604). LBC, BKL. III, 2165

Millieu (Antoine), Moyses Viator (1636–9). BKL, RAS. XXVIII, 13,728

Saint-Amant (Marc-Antoine Gérard de), Moyse Sauvé (1653). RAS, BKL. XII, 6000

J O S H U A

Coras (Jacques de), Josué, ou la Conqueste de Canaan (1665). RAS, BKL. VI, 3725

S A M S O N

Chaucer (Geoffrey), Monkes Tale, Pt. III,"Sampson,"(ca. 1375). SA-10

Quarles (Francis), Historie of Samson (1631). SA-42, BKL

Coras (Jacques de), Samson, Poème Sacré (1665). RAS, BKL. V, 2470

D A V I D

Marulić (Marko), Davideis (15th century). BKL. XIV

Du Bellay (Joachim), La Monomachie de David et de Goliath (1560). BKL, RAS. I, 300

Belleau (Remy), Les Amours de David et de Bersabee (1572). BKL, RAS. I, 380

Walther (Rudolph), Monomachia Davidis et Goliae (16th century). BKL. III, 2450

Brach (Pierre de), La Monomachie de David et de Goliat (1576). RAS, BKL. I, 388

Marbecke (John), The Holie History of King David (1579). BKL, LBC

Sabie (Francis), *David and Beersheba* (1596). An epyllion.   LBC.
Corrected in STC to "Bathsheba"
Drayton (Michael), *David and Goliath* (1630).   BKL, LBC. I, 850
Fuller (Thomas), *Davids Hainous Sinne, Heartie Repentance, Heavie Punishment* (1631).   BKL. III, 1000
Alexander (William), *Jonathan: An Heroicke Poem Intended* (1637).   BKL. I, incomplete
Aylett (Robert), *David's Troubles Remembered* (1638).   BKL. VI, 3410
Cowley (Abraham), *Davideis* (1656).   WKCC, BKL. IV, incomplete
Les Fargues (Bernard), *David, Poème Héroique* (1660).   BKL, RAS. VIII, 10,200
Coras (Jacques de), *David, ou la Vertu Couronnée* (1665).   BKL, RAS. VII, 5520
Ellwood (Thomas), *Davideis* (1712).   V, 6200

ELIJAH
"Jacquelin," *Hélie, Poème Historique* (1661).   BKL, RAS. VI, 6500
Pierre de Saint-Louis (R.P.), *L'Éliade* (1827).   RAS

JONAH
Anonymous, *Patience* (14th century).   Ed., I. Gollancz, EETS (1923)
Pierius (Christianus), *Jonas Propheta* (1555).   BKL. I, 550
Lectius (Jacobus), *Jonah, seu Poetica Paraphrasis* (1614).   BKL
Quarles (Francis), *A Feast for Wormes ... The History of Jonah* (1620).   BKL
Coras (Jacques), *Jonas, ou Ninive Pénitente* (1663).   BKL, RAS. XII, 5880

SENNACHERIB
Perrin (François), *Sennacherib, Histoire Tragique* (1599).   BKL, RAS. IX, 2550

JUDITH
Judith (9th–10th cty.).   BKL. III, 350
Godran (Abbé Charles), *Judith Viduae Historia* (1569).   BKL. I, 650
Saluste (Guillaume de, Sieur du Bartas), *Judit* (1574).   BKL, RAS. VI, 2000
Petremand (Thierry), *Paraphrase de l'Admirable Histoire de la Saincte Héroyne Judith* (1578).   BKL, RAS
Coignard (Gabrielle de), *Imitation de la Victoire de Judith* (1595).   BKL, RAS. I, 2400
Lotichus (Joannes Petrus), *Holofernes* (2nd ed., 1625).   BKL
Tortoletti (Bartolommeo), *Juditha Vindex et Vindicata* (1628).   BKL, RAS
Abbondanti (Antonio), *La Giuditta* (1630).   RAS
Bianchi (Giacinto), *La Giuditta Trionfanti* (1642).   RAS
Tortoletti (Bartolommeo), *Giuditta Vittoriosa* (1648).   BKL, RAS. IV, 4725
Pech de Calages (Marìe de), *Judith, ou la Délivrance de Béthulie* (1660).   BKL, RAS. IX, 5000

ESTHER
Oriet (Didier), *L'Esther* (1584).   BKL, RAS
Cebà (Ansaldo), *La Reina Esther* (1615).   BKL, RAS. XXI, 25,000
Quarles (Francis), *Hadassa: Or the History of Queene Esther* (1621).   BKL
Desmarets de Saint-Sorlin (Jean) ("Boisval"), *Esther* (1670).   BKL, RAS.
IV, 2000. A fuller version, 1673, in 7 books

SUSANNA
Susannah, or Seemly Susan (13th century).   BKL
Oriet (Didier), *La Susane* (1581).   BKL, RAS. III, 4320
Roche (Robert), *Eustathia or the Constancie of Susanna* (1599).   LBC.
An epyllion
Montchrestien (Antoine de), *Susane, ou la Chasteté* (1601).   RAS, BKL.
IV, 1800
D'Urfé (Anne), *Hymne de Saincte Susanne* (1608).   BKL, RAS. I, 1000
Aylett (Robert), *Susanna* (1622).   BKL. IV, 1470
Sainte-Garde Bernouin, *Suzanne délivrée* (1660).   RAS

TOBIAS
Saint-Peres (Jean de), *La Vie du Saint Patriarche Tobie* (1648).   BKL, RAS

MACCABEES
Belleperche (Gautier de), *Maccabees* (13th century).   BKL

THE VIRGIN MARY
Roswitha (or, Hrosvitha), *Maria* (ca. 965).   BKL. I, 859
Gerson (Jean), *Josephina* (ca. 1400) (on the husband of Mary).   BKL
XII, 4000
Dominicus (Joannes Corellanus), *Theotocon* (15th cty.).   BKL. IV, 3800
Mantuan (Giovanni Battista Spagnuoli), *Parthenice Mariana* (1481, 1502,
etc.).   BKL. III, 1500
La Pujade (Antoine), *La Mariade* (1605).   RAS. XII
Marino (Giambattista), *La Strage degli Innocenti* (1610).   BKL, RAS, WKCC.
IV, 3230
Campeggi (Ridolfo), *Le Lagrime di Maria Vergine* (1617).   BKL, XVI,
13,000
Cornazano (Antonio), *La Vita de la Gloriosa Vergine Maria* (1518).
BKL. VIII, 935

TEMPTATION OF CHRIST
Anglo-Saxon *Christ and Satan* (ca. 800).   BKL, WKCC. I, 733
Fletcher (Giles the Younger), *Christs Victorie on Earth* (1610).   BKL,
WKCC. IV, 2120
Strasburgus (Jacobus), *Oratio Prima* (1565).   BKL, PR-16. I, 800

SAINT MARY MAGDALEN

Valvasone (Erasmo di), *Lagrime di Santa Maria Maddalena* (1587).
RAS, BKL. I, 600

I.C., *Saint Marie Magdalens Conversion* (1603). LBC. An epyllion

Nostradame (César de), *Les Perles ou les Larmes de la Saincte Magdaleine* (1606). BKL. I, 750

Remi de Beauvais, *La Magdeleine* (1617). BKL. XX, 20,000

Robinson (Thomas), *Life and Death of Mary Magdalen* (1620). LBC, BKL. II, 1630

Le Laboureur (Louis), *La Magdalaine Pénitente* (1643). BKL. V, 1300

Cotin (Abbé Charles), *La Magdeleine au Sépulchre de Jésus-Christ* (1668). BKL. I, 615

Saint-Lucy (Pierre de), *La Madeleine* (1668)

Desmarets de Saint-Sorlin (Jean), *Marie-Madeleine, ou le Triomphe de la Grâce* (1669). BKL, RAS. X, 1960

CHRIST, PASSION

Heliand (ca. 830). BKL. I, 6000

Passion (10th century French). BKL. I, 516

Passion (12th–13th-century French). BKL

Passion of Our Lord (13th century English). BKL. I, 706

Southern Passion (13th century). BKL. I, 2250

Northern Passion (14th century). BKL. I, 1972/3575

Passion (14th century French). BKL

Cornish, *Mount Calvary* (ca. 1450). I, 2072. Cf. Edwin Norris, ed., *The Ancient Cornish Drama* (1859), pp. 437–9.   MS. in Bodleian and British Museum

Valle (Jerome), *Jhesuida* (1473). BKL. I, 500

Cicerchia (Nicolo), *Passione* (1483). BKL. I, 1364

Cornazzano (Antonio), *La Vita e Passione di Christo* (1518). BKL. III, 3180

Gomez de Ciudad (Alvarez), *Thalicristia* (1522). BKL, XXV, 16,400

Bonus (Jacobus), *De Vita et Gestis Christi* (1526). BKL. XVI, 10,000

Sannazaro (Jacopo), *De Partu Virginis* (1526), original title *Christiados Libri* III. BKL, RAS. III, 1450

Vida (Marcus Hieronymus), *Christias* (1527). BKL, WKCC, also PR-13. VI, 6000

Folengo (Teofilo), *Della Humanità del Figliuolo di Dio* (1533). BKL, WKCC, PR-14. X, 5220

Godran (Abbé Charles), *Historia Crucis Dominicae* (1565). BKL. III, 400

Otfried, *Evangelienbuch* (1571). BKL. I, 840

Foucqué (Michel), *La Vie, Faictz ... de Christ* (1574). BKL. VIII, 16,400

Fraunce (Abraham), *Countesse of Pembroke's Emanuel* (1591). BKL. II, 900

Gryphius (Othon), *Virgilii Centones* (1593). BKL. I, 2750

Klockus (Joannes), *Christiados Priscae et Novae Libri* XII (1601). BKL. XII, 16,000

La Pujade (Antoine), *La Christiade* (1604).   RAS. III, incomplete
Montreulx (Nicholas de), *Jésus Christ en l'Authel et en la Croix* (1607).
BKL. I, 19,200
Hojeda (Diego de), *La Christiada* (1611). Cf. James Fitzmaurice-Kelly,
A New History of Spanish Literature (1926), p. 342. XII
Fletcher (Joseph), *Christes Bloodie Sweat* (1613).   BKL
Escorbiac (Jean d'), *La Christiade* (1613).   BKL. V, 20,000
Donadeus (Natalis), *De Bello Christi* (1614).   BKL. XII, 8085
Du Port (François), *Le Triomphe du Messie* (1617).   BKL. II, 4860
Pleurreus (Stephen), *Aeneis Sacra* (1618).   BKL. I, 3430
Laporelli (Marcantonio), *La Christiade: Poemo Heroico* (1618).   BKL,
WKCC. XXIV, 4500
Du Port (François), *De Messiae Pugna, Victoria, Triumpho* (1621).   BKL.
III, 4700
Arnauld D'Andilly (Robert), *Poème sur la Vie de Jésus-Christ* (1634).
RAS, BKL. I, 940
Frénicle (Nicolas), *Jésus Crucifié* (1636).   BKL, RAS. V, 4700
LeNoir (Philippe), *Emanuel, ou Paraphrase Évangélique* (1630, 1638,
1668).   BKL. XV, 10,000
Bouques (Charles de), *Poème sur les Merveilles de Jésus-Christ* (1642).
BKL. V, incomplete
Bigres (P.), *Jésus Mourant* (1644).   BKL. I, 1580
Ross (Alexander), *Virgilii evangelisantis Christiados Libri* XIII (1638).
BKL, WKCC. XIII, 10,850
More (Alexander), *Laus Christi Nascentis* (1655).   BKL. I, 1600
Perachon, *Naissance de Jésus-Christ* (1665).   BKL
Milton (John), *Paradise Lost* (1667, 1674).   XXII, 10,569/10,558
Clarke (Robert), *Christiad* (1670).   BKL, WKCC. XVII, 14,000
Klopstock (Gottlieb Friedrich), *Messias* (1751–73).

GOSPEL OF NICODEMUS (incl. Harrowing of Hell)
Coutances (André de), *Gospel of Nicodemus* (13th century).   BKL. I, 2040
Anonymous, *The Harrowing of Hell* (13th century).   BKL. I, 250
Anonymous, *Develis Perlament, or Parlamentum of Feendis* (ca. 1430).
BKL, WKCC. I, 504
Mutius (Macarius), *De Triumpho Christi* (1499).   BKL. I, 317
Bonus (Jacobus), *Sub Figura Herculis Christi Praeludium* (1526).   BKL.
III, 1040

APOSTLES
Arator, *De Actibus Apostolorum* (6th century).   BKL. II, 2350
Florus of Lyons, *In Natale Sanctorum Joannis et Pauli* (9th century)
Folengo (Teofilo), *L'Agiomachia* (16th century).   BKL
Tansillo da Nola (Luigi), *Le Lagrime di S. Pietro* (1560).   BKL. XIII, 9600
Godeau (Antoine), *Saint Paul* (1654).   BKL, RAS. V, 5100

DOOMSDAY
Be Domes Daege, in *E.E. Christian Poetry*, ed. Charles W. Kennedy (1952)
Ilarione da Verona, *La Crisias* (15th century).   BKL. III, 937
Alexander (William), *Doomes-Day* (1614).   BKL, WKCC, XII, 10,520

APPENDIX C: THOMAS ELLWOOD'S EPIC

Lying outside the chronological plan of the present volume, but very relevant to it on biographical grounds, is a Biblical epic, *Davideis: The Life
of David, King of Israel*, published in 1712 by an old Quaker, Thomas
Ellwood. Fifty years before, when he was a young man of 23, he had
been introduced to Milton by Dr Nathan Paget as one who would gladly
read Latin to the blind poet six afternoons a week in return for tutoring
in that language. At the time of the Great Plague, it was Ellwood who
secured for Milton and his family the cottage at Chalfont St Giles as a
temporary refuge; it was to Ellwood that Milton, apparently not long
before his death in 1674, entrusted his collection of personal letters and
letters of state and the unpublished manuscript of his *De Doctrina
Christiana*; and it is to Ellwood's posthumous autobiography, *The History
of the Life of Thomas Ellwood* (1714) that we are indebted for a number
of otherwise unrecorded details regarding Milton. Every student has read,
at least at second or third hand, his story of how Milton, at Chalfont St
Giles, had given him the completed but unpublished manuscript of *Paradise Lost* to take home and read, and how his comment on it to the poet
was:"Thou hast said much here of paradise lost, but what hast thou to
say of paradise found?"He also mentions Milton's later remark to him,
on showing him a copy of *Paradise Regained*:"This is owing to you, for
you put it into my head by the question you put to me at Chalfont, which
before I had not thought of."Most Miltonists have detected a strong
undercurrent of irony in Milton's words.

By leaving us a full-length epic of his own composition, Ellwood has
provided us with a gauge of his own capacity. His *Davideis* runs to almost
6200 lines, or three times the length of *Paradise Regained*. It was written
in five"books"and in heroic couplets. In quality it scarcely measures up
even to Milton's own verdict on the early Dryden, as delivered to his wife,
Betty:"A good rimist, but no poet."How insensitive Ellwood must have
been to the greatness of Milton's mind and art will become obvious from
actual extracts, copied from the first (and only) edition.[1] Thus the opening
appeal for divine inspiration is worlds away from the opening paragraphs
of *Paradise Lost*:

> I Sing the Life of David, Israel's King.
> Assist, thou sacred Pow'r, who didst him bring

[1] Secured in microfilm in 1970 from the British Museum Library

From the Sheepfold, and set him on the Throne;
Thee I invoke, on Thee Rely alone.
Breath on my Muse; and fill her slender Quill
With thy refreshing Dews from Hermon-Hill
That what she Sings may turn unto thy Praise,
And to thy Name may lasting Trophies raise.

In the following passage, loose enjambment is followed by more strictly closed couplets. The chief prosodic devices are assonance and alliteration.

After King *Saul* had (by the Sin he wrought
In *Amalek*) divine Displeasure brought
Upon himself, and to the Lord provok'd
(Though his *Offence* he with *Religion* cloak'd)
That God of his *Promotion* did repent,
And, in *Decree*, the Kingdom from him rent;
Whilst the good Prophet, on his mournful String
Bewail'd the *Downfal* of the late made King:
God to him did his sacred Herald call
(*Samuel*, by whom he had Anointed *Saul*,)
And said, How long for *Saul* do'st mean to mourn?
Up, quickly fill with sacring Oyl thy Horn.
To Bethlemitish *Jesse* I intend
Thee on a special Errand strait to send:
For I, among his sons, provided have
A King, who shall my People Rule and Save.

In the following extract from David's fight with Goliath, the chief embellishments are again assonance (as in lines 3 and 4) and alliteration (as in lines 7 and 8).

While, stretch'd upon the Ground, the *Gyant* lay,
Like some great *Mole* of Earth, or *Bank* of Clay;
The nimble *Stripling*, laying by his *Sling,*
Did on his massy Shoulders lightly spring:
Where standing, forth the *Gyant's* Sword he drew;
And therewith did his *Neck* assunder hew.
Then, by the *shaggy Locks*, the *Head* did take,
And lug along, until his Arms did ake.

The epic, for all its length, is little more than an annalistic paraphrase of the story of David as found in the Old Testament. It shows no awareness of complex epic structure as found in Homer, Vergil, or Milton.

INDEX OF PERSONS

INDEX OF ANALOGUES